CLINICAL SUPERVISION
IN THE HELPING PROFESSIONS:
A PRACTICAL GUIDE

CLINICAL SUPERVISION
IN THE HELPING PROFESSIONS:
A PRACTICAL GUIDE

ROBERT HAYNES
Borderline Productions

GERALD COREY
California State University, Fullerton

PATRICE MOULTON
Northwestern State University, Natchitoches, Louisiana

THOMSON

BROOKS/COLE

Australia • Canada • Mexico • Singapore • Spain • United Kingdom • United States

THOMSON

BROOKS/COLE

Executive Editor: *Lisa Gebo*
Sponsoring Editor: *Julie Martinez*
Marketing Manager: *Caroline Concilla*
Marketing Assistant: *Mary Ho*
Assistant Editor: *Shelley Gesicki*
Editorial Assistant: *Mike Taylor*
Technology Project Manager: *Barry Connolly*
Project Manager, Editorial Production:
 Kim Svetich-Will

Production Service: *The Cooper Company*
Copy Editor: *Kay Mikel*
Permissions Editor: *Connie Dowcett*
Cover Design: *Cheryl Carrington*
Cover Image: *Eyewire*
Print/Media Buyer: *Vena Dyer*
Compositor: *Buuji, Inc.*
Printing and Binding: *Transcontinental Printing,
 Inc.*

For more information about our products,
contact us at:
Thomson Learning Academic Resource Center
1-800-423-0563

For permission to use material from this text,
contact us by:
Phone: 1-800-730-2214 **Fax:** 1-800-730-2215
Web: http://www.thomsonrights.com

Library of Congress Control Number:
2002103409

ISBN 0-534-56313-9

Brooks/Cole–Thomson Learning
511 Forest Lodge Road
Pacific Grove, CA 93950
USA

Asia
Thomson Learning
5 Shenton Way #01-01
UIC Building
Singapore 068808

Australia
Nelson Thomson Learning
102 Dodds Street
South Melbourne, Victoria 3205
Australia

Canada
Nelson Thomson Learning
1120 Birchmount Road
Toronto, Ontario M1K 5G4
Canada

Europe/Middle East/Africa
Thomson Learning
High Holborn House
50/51 Bedford Row
London WC1R 4LR
United Kingdom

Latin America
Thomson Learning
Seneca, 53
Colonia Polanco
11560 Mexico D.F.
Mexico

Spain
Paraninfo Thomson Learning
Calle/Magallanes, 25
28015 Madrid, Spain

To our supervisees and trainees,

who have taught us many lessons about how to supervise

ABOUT THE AUTHORS

ROBERT HAYNES is a licensed clinical psychologist and producer of psychology video programs for Borderline Productions. Bob received his doctorate in clinical psychology from Fuller Graduate School of Psychology in Pasadena, California, and is a member of the American Psychological Association, the American Counseling Association, and the Association for Counselor Education and Supervision. He has been actively involved in professional psychology through clinical practice as well as by teaching, consulting, leading workshops, and writing on a variety of topics. He also served as a Site Visitor for the Committee on Accreditation of the American Psychological Association. Bob recently retired after 25 years as training director of the accredited clinical psychology internship program at Atascadero State Hospital in California.

Bob has provided consultation and training in such areas as clinical supervision, criminology, disaster mental health, psychotherapy methods, stress management and burnout, suicide assessment and intervention, and theoretical approaches in counseling. His expertise also extends into the areas of conflict resolution, leadership training, management supervision, and team building. In his leisure time, Bob likes to fish, bicycle, travel, and spend time with his grandchildren. He is married to Cheryl, who is a registered nurse and also a proud grandparent. They have two adult daughters, Crissa and Errin.

Recent publications by Bob Haynes with Brooks/Cole-Wadsworth Publishing Company include the following titles:

- *Student Workbook for the Art of Integrative Counseling* (2001, with Gerald Corey)
- *Student Workbook* and *Facilitator's Resource Manual for the Evolution of a Group* (2000, with Gerald Corey and Marianne Schneider Corey)
- *Student Workbook* and *Facilitator's Resource Manual for Ethics in Action* (1998, with Gerald Corey and Marianne Schneider Corey)
- *Facilitator's Resource Manual for Living and Learning* (1997, with Gerald Corey)
- *Facilitator's Resource Manual for the Art of Integrative Counseling and Psychotherapy* (1996, with Gerald Corey)

In addition, he has published the following shorter works:

- The problem of suicide in a forensic state hospital. (1999). *Journal of the California Alliance for the Mentally Ill, 10,* 85–86
- Managing multiple relationships in a forensic setting. In B. Herlihy and G. Corey, *Boundary Issues in Counseling: Multiple Roles and Responsibilities* (1997, pp. 138–141). Alexandria, VA: American Counseling Association

Bob has produced a number of training videos in recent years. Those produced for Brooks/Cole-Wadsworth Publishing Company include *Ethics in Action, Student Version CD-ROM* (2003); *The Art of Integrative Counseling* (2001); *The Evolution of a Group* (2000); *Ethics in Action, Student Version* (1998) and *Ethics in Action, Institutional Version* (1998); *Living and Learning* (1997); and *The Art of Integrative Counseling and Psychotherapy* (1996), *Part 1: Techniques in Action* and *Part 2: Challenges for the Counselor.* He also produced *Suicide in Inpatient Settings* (1997) for the California Department of Mental Health.

GERALD COREY is Professor Emeritus of Human Services at California State University at Fullerton. He received his doctorate in counseling from the University of Southern California. He is a Diplomate in Counseling Psychology, American Board of Professional Psychology; a licensed psychologist; a National Certified Counselor; a Fellow of the American Psychological Association (Counseling Psychology); and a Fellow of the Association for Specialists in Group Work. Jerry received the Outstanding Professor of the Year Award from California State University at Fullerton in 1991 and was the recipient of the Association for Specialists in Group Work's Eminent Career Award in 2001. He teaches both undergraduate and graduate courses in group counseling, as well as courses in experiential groups, the theory and practice of counseling, and ethics in counseling practice. With his colleagues he has conducted workshops in the United States, Germany, Ireland, Belgium, Scotland, Mexico, Canada, and China, with a special focus on training in group counseling. He often presents workshops for professional organizations, special intensive courses at various universities, and residential training and supervision workshops for group leaders. In his leisure time, Jerry likes to travel, hike and bicycle in the mountains, and drive his 1931 Model A Ford.

Recent publications by Jerry Corey, all with Brooks/Cole-Wadsworth Publishing Company, include:

- *Group Techniques,* Third Edition [forthcoming] (2004, with Marianne Schneider Corey, Patrick Callanan, and J. Michael Russell)
- *Theory and Practice of Group Counseling,* Sixth Edition [forthcoming] (and Manual) (2004)
- *Clinical Supervision in the Helping Professions: A Practical Guide* (2003, with Robert Haynes and Patrice Moulton)
- *Issues and Ethics in the Helping Professions,* Sixth Edition (2003, with Marianne Schneider Corey and Patrick Callanan)
- *Becoming a Helper,* Fourth Edition (2003, with Marianne Schneider Corey)
- *Groups: Process and Practice,* Sixth Edition (2002, with Marianne Schneider Corey)

- *I Never Knew I Had a Choice,* Seventh Edition (2002, with Marianne Schneider Corey)
- *Theory and Practice of Counseling and Psychotherapy,* Sixth Edition (and Manual) (2001)
- *Case Approach to Counseling and Psychotherapy,* Fifth Edition (2001)
- *The Art of Integrative Counseling* (2001)

Jerry is co-author, with his daughters Cindy Corey and Heidi Jo Corey, of an orientation-to-college book entitled *Living and Learning* (1997), published by Wadsworth. He is also co-author (with Barbara Herlihy) of *Boundary Issues in Counseling: Multiple Roles and Responsibilities* (1997) and *ACA Ethical Standards Casebook,* Fifth Edition (1996), both published by the American Counseling Association. He has made three videos on various aspects of counseling practice: *Student Video and Workbook for the Art of Integrative Counseling* (2001, with Robert Haynes); *The Evolution of a Group: Student Video and Workbook* (2000, with Marianne Schneider Corey and Robert Haynes); and *Ethics in Action CD-ROM* (2003, with Marianne Schneider Corey and Robert Haynes). All of these student videos and workbooks are available through Brooks/Cole-Wadsworth.

PATRICE MOULTON is the chair of the Department of Psychology at Northwestern State University (NSU) in Natchitoches, Louisiana, where she directs both undergraduate and graduate programs. She is a Licensed Professional Counselor (LPC), Approved LPC Supervisor, a Board Certified Substance Abuse Counselor, a National Board Certified Counselor, a Clinical Member of the American Association of Marriage and Family Therapy, and Licensed as a Psychologist in the Commonwealth of Pennsylvania. Patrice is a member of the American Counseling Association, Louisiana Counseling Association (Board Member), and American Association of Marriage and Family Therapy. She has been actively involved in clinical practice through private practice, directing clinical programs through the Department of Health and Hospitals, teaching, conducting professional workshops, and publishing.

Patrice is married to Michael, who is a faculty member at NSU, and together they are raising Bryce, their 2-year-old son. In their leisure time, they like to travel, write, and play with Bryce.

Patrice has published in numerous professional journals and has co-authored the following books:

- *Plotnik's Instructor's Resource Guide,* Sixth Edition (2001, with S. Barnett, V. Cecchini, and T. Deka). Pacific Grove, CA: Brooks/Cole-Wadsworth Publishing Company
- *Outside Looking In: Someone You Love Is in Therapy* (1999, with L. Harper). Brandon, VT: Safer Society Foundation

CONTENTS

Chapter 4

Methods of Supervision   81

Chapter 5

Models of Supervision   108

Chapter 6

Becoming a Multiculturally Competent Supervisor   132

Chapter 7

Ethical Issues and Multiple Relationships   151

Chapter 8

Legal Issues in Supervision   182

Chapter 9

Managing Crisis Situations   225

Chapter 10

Evaluation in Supervision   243

Chapter 11

Becoming an Effective Supervisor   276

References and Suggested Readings   295

Name Index   309

Subject Index   315

PREFACE

The field of supervision is a rapidly emerging specialty area in the helping professions. In the past, supervisors often learned how to supervise based on their own experiences when they were supervisees. Until recently few professional standards specifically addressed supervision practices and separate courses in supervision were rare. Today, the trend is toward including a course in supervision in graduate programs in the helping professions. If there is not a separate course, topics of supervision are frequently incorporated into one or more courses. In addition, state licensing and certification boards are increasingly requiring formal training in the area of supervision as a part of the licensing and certification process. The result of these trends is that in order to practice as a supervisor it is mandatory to complete course work or take continuing education workshops in supervision.

This book provides a practical guide to becoming a supervisor. Our main aim was to write a book that was interesting, practical, personal, and challenging. We address topics essential to becoming an effective supervisor, with emphasis on helping students to acquire the tools and skills necessary to supervise others in a variety of settings. We believe one of the best ways to learn how to supervise is for students to reflect on what they have learned from their own supervision. Readers are encouraged to conceptualize and personalize the dynamics of supervision.

The information provided and our suggestions for becoming a supervisor are based on both the supervision literature and our collective professional experience in supervision. Throughout this book we discuss the ethics and professional codes and the relevant literature, but we also often state our own position on these topics and offer commentary on how we might approach various cases. We try to balance theory with personal beliefs, attitudes, and relevant experiences regarding supervision. A feature unique to this book, titled Voices from the Field, provides a glimpse of what other practicing supervisors have to say about these subjects.

Our hope is that our readers won't take what we present as the only approach to supervisory practice. Instead, we encourage reflective practice and integrating students' own thoughts and experiences with the material they are reading. Most of all, we recommend that students continually reflect on what supervision has been like for them at the various stages of their professional development. It is important for students to have both a solid foundation of the theories and methods of supervision and an understanding of what they have learned from their own experiences as a supervisee and as a supervisor.

This book has a practical emphasis, which can be seen throughout the text in tips for practical application, case examples, sample forms, interactive questions, and activities that can be done in small groups. The book is designed for use either as a primary or a supplementary text in a variety of doctoral level and master's level courses.

Clinical Supervision in the Helping Professions: A Practical Guide is appropriate for use in disciplines including clinical psychology, counseling psychology, counselor education, marriage and family therapy, human services, social work, psychiatric nursing, and other mental health specializations. It can also be an ideal resource for practicum, fieldwork, and internship seminars in these disciplines and for advanced undergraduate courses in human services and social work programs. In addition, this book can be used as a resource for prelicensed professionals as well as practicing supervisors.

How to Get the Most from This Book

This book is different from traditional textbooks in supervision. As much as possible our expectation is that this book will provide an interactive tool that will assist you in formulating your perspective on supervisory practice. The many questions and exercises interspersed throughout the text are intended to stimulate you to become an active learner. If you take the time to think about the chapter focus questions and do the suggested activities at the end of each chapter, your learning will be more meaningful and personal. Supervision is not a topic that can be mastered by reading about theory and research. Supervision is best learned by integrating the theoretical material with your own supervision experiences. Additional material and a self-inventory for each chapter are available on the book's Web site at http://info.wadsworth.com/haynes, and we encourage you to take advantage of this resource as well.

Several terms are used throughout the book to describe supervisors, supervisees, counselors, and the counseling process. Different disciplines in the helping professions use slightly different terms to describe the various roles and processes. We use many of these terms interchangeably because we are writing to several different disciplines: for example, *supervisee* or *trainee,* *counselor* or *therapist,* and *counseling, therapy,* or *psychotherapy.* Keep in mind that you will see these terms used interchangeably throughout the book.

Supplements to This Book

Instructor's Resource Manual   An Instructor's Resource Manual is available that contains suggestions for teaching the course, chapter objectives, key terms, class activities to stimulate interest, transparency masters, and a bank of test items, discussion questions, and online test items. Included are many multiple-choice, true-false, matching, and short essay questions from which the instructor can choose.

Code of Ethics for the Helping Professions   Each of the major mental health professional organizations has its own code of ethics. The booklet *Codes of Ethics for the Helping Professions* can be purchased at a nominal cost as an accompanying supplement to this textbook. (Special bundle must be requested by the instructor.) We recommend that you familiarize yourself with the basic standards for ethical practice of the various mental health professions, especially as they apply to supervision. Many of the codes of ethics can be accessed through the Internet or through the individual professional organizations.

Web Site Link   Readers of our book have access to a Web site at http://info. wadsworth.com/haynes that provides a number of supplementary resources, a few of which include online quizzes and self-inventories for each chapter and quotations and thoughts from a number of practicing supervisors.

Acknowledgments

We would like to thank the following people who reviewed the manuscript and made valuable suggestions: Elie Axelroth, coordinator of intern training at the Health and Counseling Services, California Polytechnic State University, San Luis Obispo, California; Kathleen Bieschke, Iowa State University; Jamie Bludworth, graduate student at Arizona State University; Susan R. Boes, State University of West Georgia; Patrick Callanan, private practice in Santa Ana, California, and part-time instructor of human services at California State University at Fullerton; Marianne Schneider Corey, private practice and consulting; Katherine Dooley, Mississippi State University; Susan W. Gray, Barry University; Ellen Whiteside, McDonnell School of Social Work; Joan Gibson, SUNY Oswego; Joshua Gold, University of South Carolina; Crissa Haynes, graduate student at the University of Nevada,

Reno; Michelle Muratori, graduate student at the University of Iowa; Michelle Naden, Seattle Pacific University; J. Laurence Passmore, Indiana State University; Patricia Polanski, The University of Dayton; John Sutton, University of Maine; Stacy Thacker, psychology internship director at Atascadero State Hospital; and Tony Wallace, graduate student in counseling at California State University at Fullerton.

We received extra help and consultation on selected chapters and topics from several people: Lindsey Huffman, Northwestern State University, Natchitoches, Louisiana; Michele Licht, attorney-at-law; Cynthia Lindsey, Northwestern State University, Natchitoches, Louisiana; Don C. Locke, North Carolina State University; Brandi Mathews, Northwestern State University, Natchitoches, Louisiana; Amanda Owen, Northwestern State University, Natchitoches, Louisiana; Paul Pedersen, University of Hawaii; Tim Stalder, Senior Organizational Development Consultant, Pacific Gas and Electric Company; and William Robiner, University of Minnesota Medical School.

We are especially indebted to the students and practicing supervisors who gave generously of their time to share their thoughts and experiences with supervision. You will find their thoughts in their own words in the Voices from the Field feature throughout the book:

> Randy Alle-Corliss, M.S.W., clinical social worker in the department of psychiatry in a large health maintenance organization, and part-time instructor of human services at California State University at Fullerton. He received his master's degree in social work from the University of Southern California.

> Steve Arkowitz, Psy.D., staff psychologist at Atascadero State Hospital, California Department of Mental Health; he received his degree in clinical psychology from Wright State University in Ohio.

> Elie Axelroth, Psy.D., coordinator of intern training at the Health and Counseling Services, California Polytechnic State University, San Luis Obispo, California. She received her doctorate in clinical psychology from the University of Denver Graduate School of Professional Psychology.

> Jamie Bludworth, B.S., doctoral student in counseling psychology at Arizona State University; he completed his undergraduate work in human services at California State University at Fullerton.

> Christiana Bratiotis, M.S.W., director of Kid's/Senior's Korner, Reno, Nevada; she received her master's degree in social work from the University of Nevada, Reno.

> Marianne Schneider Corey, M.A., licensed marriage and family therapist; she received her master's degree in marriage, family, and child counseling from Chapman College.

Mary Dubrul, R.N., nurse instructor (retired); she received her nursing degree from the Borgess School of Nursing, Kalamazoo, Michigan.

Marijane Fall, Ed.D., counselor educator at the University of Southern Maine; she received her doctorate in counselor education from the University of Maine.

Crissa Haynes, M.S.W., recent graduate in social work from the University of Nevada, Reno; she received her bachelor's degree in psychology from Sonoma State University in California.

D. Richard Laws, Ph.D., forensic psychologist (retired) and consultant, South Island Consulting, Victoria, British Columbia; he received his doctorate in educational psychology from Southern Illinois University.

Tory Nersasian, Psy.D., therapist at San Luis Obispo County Mental Health Services in California; she received her doctorate in clinical psychology from the University of Denver Graduate School of Professional Psychology.

Bill Safarjan, Ph.D., staff psychologist at Atascadero State Hospital, California, Department of Mental Health, and past president of the California Psychological Association; he received his doctorate from Rutgers University.

Heriberto G. Sánchez, Ph.D., chief psychologist at the California Men's Colony Mental Health Services, California Department of Corrections; he received his degree in clinical psychology from the University of Illinois at Chicago.

David Shepard, Ph.D., assistant professor of counseling at California State University at Fullerton, and private practitioner; he received his doctorate in counseling psychology from the University of Southern California.

John Sutton Jr., Ed.D., counselor educator at the University of Southern Maine; he received his doctorate in counseling from the University of Maine.

Stacy Thacker, Ph.D., psychology internship director at Atascadero State Hospital, California, Department of Mental health; she received her doctorate in counseling psychology from Colorado State University.

Todd Thies, Ph.D., staff psychologist at Atascadero State Hospital, California, Department of Mental Health; he received his doctorate in clinical psychology from the California School of Professional Psychology, Fresno.

Judith Walters, M.S., marriage and family therapist intern at the San Luis Obispo County Drug and Alcohol Treatment Program; she received her master's in psychology from California Polytechnic State University, San Luis Obispo, California.

Muriel Yáñez, Psy.D., staff psychologist at Atascadero State Hospital, California State Department of Mental Health, and a forensic consultant; she received her doctorate in clinical psychology from the University of Denver Graduate School of Professional Psychology.

We are indebted to Cheryl Haynes for her expertise and perseverance in preparing the manuscript for publication.

The members of the Brooks/Cole-Wadsworth Publishing Company team provided support and guidance for this project. It is a pleasure to work with these dedicated professionals. These people include Julie Martinez, acquisitions editor; Shelley Gesicki, assistant editor, who coordinated the development of this book; Lisa Gebo, executive editor; and Caroline Concilla, marketing manager. We would also like to thank Cecile Joyner, production editor, The Cooper Company; and Kay Mikel, manuscript editor of this book, for her extraordinary editorial assistance. We appreciate Mimi Lawson's work in compiling the indexes.

Robert Haynes
Gerald Corey
Patrice Moulton

INTRODUCTION TO SUPERVISION

1. What are your experiences with supervision? Have you been a supervisee? Have you been a supervisor? What have you learned from those experiences?
2. How can you best learn to become a competent supervisor?
3. What obstacles do you foresee in becoming a competent supervisor, and how will you overcome them?
4. What purpose does clinical supervision serve?
5. To what degree is protection of the welfare of the client the supervisor's responsibility?
6. Is the role of the supervisor to teach supervisees or to strive to draw out insights from supervisees?
7. What role, if any, should the supervisor play in serving as a gatekeeper for the profession?
8. How can supervisors take steps that will lead to empowerment of the supervisee?
9. What is the main goal of supervision?

INTRODUCTION

Supervision is used in virtually all of the helping professions to assist counselors in training to develop clinical and professional skills. All students will be supervised over the course of their training, and the majority of those students will themselves become supervisors at some point in their career. Supervision has been part of the helping professions from the beginning, but it is only in recent years that supervision has come to be seen as a separate and distinct field with its own set of skills and tools. Most new supervisors are anxious about learning the tasks and responsibilities of supervision, and most supervisees are anxious about being supervised and evaluated. We hope to provide you with the knowledge and skills that will assist you in becoming a competent supervisor.

In this chapter we begin by defining supervision, and follow that with a discussion of the evolution and current status of clinical supervision. The goals of supervision and the objectives for the supervisee are also addressed. We share our personal experiences and struggles in becoming supervisors to give you some insight into the personal aspects of becoming a supervisor.

If you have not yet read the preface, we strongly encourage you to take time now to read it and reflect on how you can achieve your personal goals for this course and for reading this text.

SUPERVISION DEFINED

Supervision is a unique professional relationship between a supervisor, a supervisee, and the clients they serve. This relationship changes over time and with experience. As supervisees become increasingly competent in practicing the skills of their profession, they require less direction from the supervisor. Competent supervision requires a fine balance on the supervisor's part between providing professional development opportunities for supervisees and protecting clients' welfare. While assisting supervisees to learn the art and craft of therapeutic practice, supervisors also are expected to monitor the quality of care clients are receiving. A primary aim of supervision is to create a context in which the supervisee can acquire the experience needed to become an independent professional. In most cases, the supervisor–supervisee relationship is not equal; rather, it is hierarchical, having an evaluation component as the cornerstone. It seems somewhat contradictory to place the terms "relationship" and "evaluation" in the same sentence when defining supervision, but both ideas are important components. Even though the supervisor has a monitoring and evaluating function, this does not rule out establishing a productive supervisory relationship.

The supervisor serves as supporter, teacher, consultant, counselor, adviser, and mentor. Some call supervision an art, and successful supervision certainly is artful, but it is also an emerging formal arrangement with specific expectations, roles, responsibilities, and skills. The literal definition of supervise is "to oversee." It is further defined as "to watch over a particular activity or task being carried out by other people and ensure that it is carried out correctly" (*Microsoft Encarta College Dictionary*, 2001, p. 1445).

In our view, *clinical supervision* is best defined as a process whereby consistent observation and evaluation of the counseling process is provided by a trained and experienced professional who recognizes and is competent in the unique body of knowledge and skill required for professional development. It should be noted that supervision is also defined by many external forces, including governing bodies, licensing agencies, and the settings in which we work. For example, supervisors have very different roles and responsibilities when supervising students in a training program versus supervising prelicensed professionals in a mental health agency. Supervisory practice, roles, and responsibilities will vary depending on the setting and other requirements.

There are two general categories of supervision: clinical and administrative. Clinical supervision, which we have just described, focuses on the work of the supervisee in providing services to clients, whereas *administrative supervision* focuses on the issues surrounding the supervisee's role and responsibilities in the organization as an employee—personnel matters, timekeeping, record keeping, and so forth (Bradley & Kottler, 2001). The line between these kinds of supervision is not distinct, and there is a considerable amount of overlap. Although the focus of each category of supervision is different, many of the same principles and methods discussed throughout this book apply to both types of supervision.

THE EVOLUTION OF SUPERVISION

Clinical supervision, as a distinct specialty area within the helping professions, has seen vast changes in the past 10 years. Clinical supervision derived from the practice of psychotherapy, and early models were primarily psychotherapeutic in theory and practice. As a result, it was believed that if you had some clinical experience and good counseling skills you were qualified to supervise. It was also believed that using your "good" counseling skills would be sufficient for developing trainees into productive therapists. In addition, many supervisory relationships were relatively informal. The guidelines were minimal, and they focused primarily on the number of supervision hours required.

The role of the supervisor today has little relationship to that of the supervisor of the recent past, which was primarily an informal mentoring/ therapeutic relationship between supervisor and supervisee. We are not implying that effective supervision did not occur prior to the formalization of supervisor training. Based on conversations with many of our colleagues in the mental health professions, we conclude that many of them had excellent supervisors. However, little attention was given to formal documentation procedures, and most supervisors did not have the benefit of formal training in becoming a clinical supervisor (Association of State and Provincial Psychology Boards [ASPPB], 1998).

Only in recent years has supervision, as an area of specialized training, become a focus in academic training, postgraduate training, and professional development workshops. This emphasis has evolved from the growing need for supervisors to be competent to meet the challenges of the supervisory process in a professional and accountable manner, and to adhere to the regulations of various governing bodies.

Within the past decade, many governing bodies of helping disciplines have developed specific criteria for the practice of supervision. The American Association of Marriage and Family Therapy (AAMFT) was one of the first to develop standards for supervisor training and established a designation of Approved Supervisor in 1983. The American Counseling Association (ACA) adopted the Association for Counselor Education and Supervision (ACES, 1987, 1990) Standards for Counseling Supervisors in 1989. The National Association of Social Workers (NASW) followed by publishing *Guidelines for Clinical Social Work Supervision* in 1994, and the National Board for Certified Counselors (NBCC) published *Standards for the Ethical Practice of Supervision* in 1998. Surprisingly, although the American Psychological Association (APA, 1992) has specific and detailed standards regarding training programs, they have not yet addressed the specific qualifications and competencies of supervisors.

Today, supervisors carry the responsibility for maintaining a professional supervisory relationship with each supervisee and each client that the supervisee counsels. Accountability requires a more formal arrangement consisting of professional disclosure statements and contracts that outline the model to be used in supervision, the goals and objectives of supervision, and assessment and evaluation methods. Presently, there is also much controversy regarding the roles and responsibilities of professional conduct between supervisors and supervisees. These controversies include boundaries in the relationship, multicultural issues, and dual relationships. State-of-the-art supervision today requires supervisors to have a multitude of skills and procedural knowledge:

- Formalized training in supervision.
- Knowledge of formal contracts and agreements.
- The ability to initiate and maintain a positive supervisory relationship.
- The ability to assess both supervisees and all clients they will serve.
- Multiple modes of direct observation of the supervisee's work.
- Policies and procedures for practice.
- Knowledge of proper documentation methods.
- Specific feedback and evaluation plans.
- Good risk management practices.

The body of knowledge needed to practice supervision now includes, but is certainly not limited to, roles and responsibilities, relationship dynamics, counseling skills, instructional skills, legal and ethical decision-making skills, multicultural competencies, and evaluative skills.

THE GOALS OF SUPERVISION

Many authors have addressed the issue of supervision goals (Bernard & Goodyear, 1998; Bradley & Ladany, 2001; Campbell, 2000; Holloway, 1995, 1999; Kadushin, 1992; Kaiser, 1997), and there is considerable agreement regarding the goals of supervision although different authors describe them in different ways. The various professional standards do not all address the goals of supervision directly, but the goals often can be inferred from the discussion of related topics. Box 1.1 on page 6 lists the professional standards that address the purpose and goals of supervision.

The two goals most frequently mentioned in the supervision literature and by professional standards are teaching the supervisee and protecting the welfare of the client. Monitoring the supervisee's development for licensing boards and professional associations—often referred to as the gatekeeping function—is a third goal less frequently cited. In addition to these goals, we add a fourth goal, empowering the supervisee. In our view, then, the goals of supervision are fourfold: (1) promoting supervisee growth and development through teaching, (2) protecting the welfare of the client, (3) monitoring supervisee performance and gatekeeping for the profession; and (4) empowering the supervisee to self-supervise and carry out these goals as an independent professional. Let's examine each of these goals in more detail.

Promoting Supervisee Growth and Development Through Teaching Many supervisors view teaching supervisees how to effectively counsel clients as the primary purpose of the supervision task. This is an essential component of the supervision function as supervisors must ensure the welfare of both current and future clients of the supervisee. It is not enough to simply teach about the specifics of the case or situation, however. It is hoped that the

BOX 1.1 | GOALS OF SUPERVISION

Association for Counselor Education and Supervision
Ethical Guidelines for Counseling Supervisors (1993)

1.01 The primary obligation of supervisors is to train counselors so that they respect the integrity and promote the welfare of their clients.

2. Inherent and integral to the role of the supervisor are responsibilities for:
    a. monitoring client welfare;
    b. encouraging compliance with relevant legal, ethical, and professional standards for clinical practice;
    c. monitoring clinical performance and professional development of supervisees; and
    d. evaluating and certifying current performance and potential of supervisees for academic, screening, selection, placement, employment, and credentialing purposes.

3.07 Supervisors should inform supervisees of the goals, policies, theoretical orientations toward counseling, training, and supervision model or approach on which the supervision is based.

Association for Counselor Education and Supervision
Standards for Counseling Supervisors (1990)

The counseling supervisor:
7.1 recognizes that a primary goal of supervision is helping the client of the counselor.

Association of State and Provincial Psychology Boards (ASPPB)
Report of the ASPPB Task Force on Supervision Guidelines (1998)

III. D. The supervisory process addresses legal, ethical, social, and cultural dimensions that impact not only the professional practice of psychology but also the supervisory relationship. Issues of confidentiality, professional practice, and protection of the public are central.

National Association of Social Workers
Guidelines for Clinical Social Work Supervision (1994)

Purpose and Intent of Supervision
The primary purpose of supervision is to maintain and enhance the knowledge and skill of the clinical social worker to provide improved services to and clinical outcomes for the client population. Supervision includes the development of professionalism and the evaluation of function.

Supervision may occur for the purpose of aiding professional growth and development; fulfilling the requirements for licensing, credentialing, third-party reimbursement; and meeting internal administrative requirements, external regulatory or accreditation requirements and corrective or disciplinary functions.

---

supervisee will learn from supervision about issues that will translate well into independent practice in the future. The broader definition of this goal of supervision is promotion of supervisee growth and development as a competent clinician and professional. Promoting supervisee development is clearly a major goal of supervision, but it must be balanced with the focus on the welfare of the client.

Protecting the Welfare of the Client   Many authors (Bernard & Goodyear, 1998; Campbell, 2000; Kaiser, 1997) would agree that an essential function of supervision is to protect the welfare of the supervisee's clients. Yontef (1997) takes the position that supervision has the dual purposes of personal and professional development of the supervisee and growth and protection of clients. The requirements by most states for the supervision of unlicensed mental health professionals are designed to protect the consumers of those mental health services. A major function of the supervisor is to do everything necessary to ensure that both current and future clients receive competent and professional services from the supervisee and to intervene in whatever way necessary when the client is not receiving such services.

Monitoring Supervisee Performance and Gatekeeping for the Profession One of the functions of the supervisor is to serve as gatekeeper for the profession (Falvey, 2002; Lumadue & Duffey, 1999). This involves monitoring and evaluating the supervisee's competence to become licensed in a given field such as social work, marriage and family therapy, psychology, or counseling. The gatekeeping function of the supervisor will vary depending on the setting in which supervision takes place and the level of education and training of the supervisee. For example, professionals who supervise in an undergraduate human services program may have less gatekeeping responsibility than do supervisors working with postdegree, prelicensed supervisees in the process of accumulating supervised hours toward a licensure requirement. Licensing and professional standards outline the requirements for supervisors when overseeing the clinical work of supervisees. Campbell (2000) discusses the need to evaluate the supervisee's professional and therapeutic competence as well as his or her suitability for the profession. Lumadue and Duffey (1999) discuss the role of graduate programs in serving as gatekeepers. Supervision has a pivotal role in the evaluation of competence of the supervisee to practice within the profession.

Empowering the Supervisee to Self-Supervise and Carry Out Goals   A key function of the supervisory relationship is to assist the supervisee in developing the ability to take over the supervisory function and self-supervise. So, in addition to teaching the supervisee, protecting the client's welfare, and serving as gatekeeper for the profession, an essential goal is to assist the supervisee to develop the skills, awareness, and resources necessary for self-evaluation. This is accomplished by providing the opportunity for supervisees to learn problem-solving and decision-making skills and to practice self-evaluation. These practices in supervision help supervisees learn to trust their clinical judgment. Personal and professional development is certainly a basic aspect of the supervisee's empowerment. It is our conviction that if supervisees become empowered personally and professionally, and if they are competent practitioners, they will place the client's welfare first, and they will not bring harm to clients. A competent professional will be able to self-monitor performance, be aware of the limits of competence, be able to identify how personal issues impact professional practice, and know when and how to seek consultation and additional supervision as needed to function as a self-supervisor.

Which goals are most important? Which goals take priority? What happens when goals are in conflict? Although all four goals are equally important, particular situations will determine which takes priority at any given moment. If a conflict exists between teaching the supervisee and protecting the welfare of the client, professional ethics codes require that protecting the welfare of the client be first and foremost. For example, when a supervisee reports that a client has expressed suicide ideation, the goals of the supervision quickly change from teaching the supervisee to a focus on the immediate need to protect the welfare of the client. Teaching is not abandoned but is temporarily suspended until the crisis is resolved. It is essential to return to teaching the supervisee about suicide assessment and intervention once the needs of the client have been met. It might help to think of the goals of supervision as occurring simultaneously rather than hierarchically. See the ethical decision-making model described in Chapter 7 for more on how to problem solve the ethical dilemmas. Effective supervision depends on the supervisor having a clear understanding of the goals of supervision and being able to communicate those goals to the supervisee.

OBJECTIVES FOR THE SUPERVISEE

Once the overriding goals of the supervisory process are understood, the next step is to identify specific supervision objectives to work on with supervisees. The objectives listed in Box 1.2 outline the personal and professional development we would like to see our supervisees accomplish over the course of supervision. As you read each of the objectives, think about which of the four goals of supervision each objective best relates to.

It is incumbent upon supervisors to have a clear picture of the goals of supervision as well as the specific objectives they hope their supervisees will accomplish. These goals and objectives offer excellent topics to periodically introduce for discussion in supervision.

PERSPECTIVES ON SUPERVISION

As a way of introducing ourselves to you, we want to share with you our backgrounds and experiences with supervision. Each of us will describe our work setting, our philosophy of supervision, share experiences we have had as both supervisees and supervisors, describe what we have learned from those experiences, and explain what we think we have yet to learn. By reading about our experiences, you will come to understand our point of reference in writing about the supervision process. Throughout the book we often talk about our

| BOX 1.2 | SUPERVISION OBJECTIVES |

- Become knowledgeable about counseling theories, methods, and practice.
- Become competent in the application of counseling methods for working with diverse client populations.
- Have a broad understanding of diagnosis and treatment methods.
- Know the limits of personal competence and how to seek consultation and supervision.
- Develop the basic helping skills of empathy, respect, and genuineness.
- Be aware of how personal issues affect clinical work and what impact these issues may have on clients.
- Know which clients are easy to work with and which are more difficult, and why that is the case.
- Know how to recognize and work with resistance in clients.

- Know the relevant ethical codes of the profession.
- Have sound judgment and a clear decision-making model regarding clinical and ethical issues.
- Be aware of the legal aspects that affect clinical practice.
- Have an awareness of how multicultural issues affect the counseling process and how to work with multicultural differences with clients and colleagues.
- Acquire self-confidence with increased practice.
- Develop the ability to examine one's personal role as a counselor.
- Be willing to expand skills even though there is a risk of making mistakes, and talk about this in supervision.
- Strive to create a personal style of counseling.
- Develop the practice of self-evaluation.

reactions, thoughts, and experiences regarding a particular topic, and we hope you will examine your own experiences and learning in the same way.

Bob Haynes's Personal Perspective

My Work Setting   The majority of the clinical supervision I have provided occurred in my position as director of an accredited clinical psychology internship program in a forensic hospital setting. This maximum security hospital provides care and treatment for sex offenders, those found not guilty by reason of insanity, the incompetent to stand trial, and transfers from prison in need of psychiatric care. I provided individual and group supervision for both clinical and administrative purposes. I also supervised postdoctoral fellows and prelicensed psychologists. In addition, I supervised those providing clinical supervision to interns—mainly psychologists, but also social workers, psychiatrists, and marriage and family therapists. In the private practice settings where I worked part time for more than 10 years, I participated in the peer supervision of colleagues in the group practice.

Two issues stand out for me from my work with supervisors and supervisees. First, nearly all supervisors express that they initially felt ill-prepared to become supervisors and were unclear in their understanding of the nature and purpose of supervision. For most, it took some time for them to develop confidence and clarity regarding their supervisory role. Formal training in supervision did expedite their development, but experience in supervision was also a major factor. Second, nearly all supervisees are anxious about their performance and are very concerned about the evaluation component. They expend considerable time and energy trying to determine what to say and do in supervision. Oftentimes, pleasing a supervisor seems as important as learning from the training experience for which they are being supervised.

My Philosophy of Supervision   I learned about supervision solely from supervisors. Courses in supervision were not offered in my undergraduate or graduate years in psychology in the 1960s and 1970s. There was no consideration that it was a field in itself or that specific skills were involved. At that time, supervision was seen as a subset of therapy skills. Once you had mastered therapy skills, it was assumed that you were ready to supervise others.

I view supervision as a process whereby the supervisor helps the supervisee learn and grow in knowledge, clinical skills, ethics, legal concerns, professional issues, and the personal development of judgment and maturity. From my perspective, the primary purpose of supervision is the development and empowerment of the supervisee. While pursuing this goal, it is equally important that the supervisor protect the welfare of clients and act as a gatekeeper for the profession. My greatest hope is that supervisees will move from relying on me as the supervisor to feeling empowered to provide their own self-supervision where they can effectively problem solve clinical situations and know how and when to seek help, consultation, and supervision from others.

I believe that learning is a life-long process. Learning does not end with the acquisition of an advanced degree but continues throughout our professional lives. Supervision is a learning process that results in mutual growth and self-understanding for the supervisor as well as the supervisee. As a supervisor, I am open to learning both from and along with the supervisee.

Supervision is a collaborative process and is most effective in a healthy relationship of trust, honesty, and mutual respect. I believe it is the responsibility of the supervisor to foster the collaborative process by involving the supervisee in developing the supervision goals, methods, and evaluation procedures. Trust, honesty, and respect take time to develop and can be modeled and encouraged by the supervisor. Being available for the supervisee when needed, being honest about my observations and thoughts, and respecting the beliefs and training needs of the supervisee go a long way toward developing a healthy supervisory relationship. For supervision to be effective, supervisees must be open to feedback and learning. The supervisor can model for the supervisee this sense of openness and nondefensiveness.

I employ a developmental model of supervision where the supervisee is seen on a continuum of development, and supervision begins at the supervisee's current level. Consideration must also be given to the context in which supervision occurs. That includes the purpose of supervision, my own models of therapy and supervision, the developmental level of the supervisee, the setting in which the supervision occurs, and the ethical and legal obligations that apply.

My Struggles as a Supervisor   I feel comfortable in the role of supervisor, but I still struggle with the task of supervising impaired supervisees. I have encountered supervisees with personality traits that seem contrary to those necessary for becoming an effective helping professional. I work to maintain a proper balance between supervision and counseling, and between helping the supervisee and protecting the client, the profession, and myself. In recent years, supervisees have become more likely to threaten and to take legal action against supervisors for any number of reasons. We have become an increasingly more litigious society, and that trend has not escaped the practice of supervision. Supervision has increasingly become a factor in complaints to licensing boards and in issues of liability. My actions as a supervisor have been challenged with threats of legal action on behalf of a trainee. I learned firsthand the legal responsibilities and liabilities for supervisors and for training programs. This experience consumed months of my time as I responded to the legal challenge—writing letters and reports, and consulting with agency administrators, lawyers, and the trainee's doctoral program. On the positive side, this experience forced me to more clearly define the purpose of supervision, the legal and ethical responsibilities of the supervisor and the supervisee, and the importance of detailed and accurate documentation especially when working with any problem situation. Problems such as threats of legal action often lead to improvements in various aspects of program policies and procedures.

Supervising those not responsive to supervision has been another hurdle for me. I know from my own experience that competent professionals need to be open to feedback and must be aware of their personal and professional limitations and strengths. It troubles me to see a new clinician unwilling to look at his or her work and reluctant to grow and develop.

A distinction must be made between performance anxiety and nonresponsiveness to supervision. The novice clinician often lacks confidence, and performance anxiety leads to wanting to please the supervisor. This individual can become unresponsive to supervision due to fear and anxiety, but with time and a supportive supervisor the supervisee will begin to open up. I have seen many interns who begin the training year eager to impress the training staff and become defensive when they hear the first feedback that includes the need for improvement. Typically support and encouragement of these interns is very effective as is the supervisor's assurance that most new clinicians find it difficult to hear negative feedback from supervisors. It helps to remind the supervisee that he or she is in our training program to develop both personally and professionally and that we do not expect novice clinicians to know everything.

Supervising colleagues can be challenging for me because experienced clinicians are often more set in their opinions, beliefs, and practices than novice clinicians. They often know more than I do about certain topics, and I can see that either as threatening or as an opportunity for my own learning. I have to remind myself in these situations that I am not expected to know everything as a supervisor, and a supervisee may well have more expertise on any given topic. Experienced clinicians may be given more freedom than is warranted, thus creating a potential hazard for clients. In these situations, I focus more of my supervisory effort on encouraging and modeling an openness to feedback and learning as a hallmark of a competent clinician. I try to enlist the supervisee in a collaborative effort where we examine how we can learn together about a variety of clinical topics.

I am concerned about supervising those with backgrounds different from mine, with gender and ethnicity being the major areas of difference. I find myself wondering if I am understanding their world and whether I know enough about what their world is like. In the forensic setting, for example, I know that women have unique experiences and concerns when working with an all-male population. Although I may know about those experiences and concerns, I am not certain I fully understand what it must be like for them. I usually share my perspective with supervisees and encourage them to talk about their experiences and what I need to know to provide useful supervision.

What I Have Learned About Supervision

- I don't need to have all the answers for my supervisees.
- Every situation and supervisee is a new experience with new twists and turns and provides a new learning experience for me.
- It is important and essential to do those things as a supervisor that will protect my license and professional standing.
- A written supervisory contract is best developed early in supervision.
- Documention of supervisory contacts and issues is essential.
- Support, encouragement, and respect of the supervisee are important as well as honesty and the willingness to challenge the supervisee to learn.
- It is important to maintain a healthy sense of humor with supervisees.
- The use of sarcasm with supervisees is never helpful.
- Work collaboratively with the supervisee to establish ground rules regarding supervision, and use those rules to resolve conflicts in the supervisory relationship.
- Listen carefully to supervisees and communicate my understanding to them.

What I Still Need to Learn

- Developments in legal, ethical, and licensing issues, and new developments in supervision.
- The impact that I have on supervisees, both positively and negatively.
- Ways in which I can better work with impaired supervisees.
- Better ways to understand those supervisees who are different from me in personality style, theoretical orientation, gender, and culture.

Jerry Corey's Personal Perspective

My Work Setting   Since the early 1970s I have worked in a university program in which I provide group supervision for group facilitators. Almost all of my professional experience as a supervisor has been with group supervision, which I very much value. From my vantage point, one of the best ways to teach and to supervise students wanting to become group practitioners is to conduct this supervision in a group context. In addition to working with students, my colleagues and I have done a considerable amount of group supervision in agency settings and through professional workshops. Again, this supervision is aimed at helping trainees acquire knowledge about how groups function and refine group leadership by being part of a training and supervision group.

My Philosophy of Supervision   I credit both humanistic and systemic thought on influencing my current views and philosophy of supervision. I see my role as a supervisor as being a guide in a process of self-discovery. In much the same way as in counseling, I believe in the value of establishing collaborative relationships in supervision. Clients get the most from therapy when they are educated about how therapy works and when they collaboratively design personal goals for the therapeutic work. Likewise, I think supervisees profit the most from supervision when they become partners in this endeavor. I am uncomfortable with supervision that is directed largely by the supervisor, telling supervisees what they did wrong and what they should try next. Empowerment is one of the aims of personal therapy with clients, and in many ways supervisees need to feel a sense of empowerment if they are to grow personally and professionally.

When I am doing group supervision, I generally ask the trainee co-leaders to talk about their own perceptions about the efficacy of their interventions in the group. By beginning with trainees' thoughts, reactions, intuitions, and perceptions, the stage is set for learning by self-discovery as opposed to listening to the expert who observed their work. I am not diminishing the expertise of a supervisor; rather, my goal is to guide trainees in the process of learning to monitor what they are doing in a training group, to raise their own questions, and to discover the answers to some of these questions.

My Struggles as a Supervisor   I tend to have the most difficulty supervising professionals and students who are closed about themselves, who are defensive, and who are not open to learning about themselves. I can certainly appreciate a beginner's anxieties as a group counselor and the resulting lack of therapeutic responsiveness in a group. Generally, I do not have difficulty with students who are willing to admit their fears, self-doubts, and insecurities. If they are willing to explore these personal anxieties in the context of group supervision, then many opportunities open up for significant learning. However, students who are judgmental, closed, and who exude a sense of "knowing it all" do pose a challenge for me. Included in this list of supervisees whom I perceive as "difficult" are those individuals who limit most of their interactions with others to giving advice or asking questions.

In working with supervisees in groups, I do not have the expectation that they will engage in highly personal self-disclosure pertaining to their outside lives; the training and supervision group is not a therapy group. I do, however, expect them to talk about their reactions to the here-and-now of the supervision and training group as well as being willing to bring up for exploration any difficulties they are having in fully participating in the supervision process. Supervisees in a group training setting are asked to identify personal concerns or characteristics that are likely to get in the way of effectively counseling others. I must admit that I do struggle with trainees who obviously are having many reactions to being part of the supervision group yet hold back from disclosing their thoughts and feelings. For example, trainees often have difficulty feeling competent and may want to withdraw. At the very least, I would hope that they disclose this reaction so that we can explore this in the context of group supervision.

Fortunately, the vast majority of students whom I supervise in a practicum in group leadership course are a sheer delight to work with, are eager to learn, are open to exploring how they are being affected through their work as a group facilitator, and are willing to be vulnerable. They do not view their personal vulnerability as weakness. I appreciate working with trainees who keep up to date with their readings (since this is a group counseling course) and who are willing to apply the readings to the groups they are facilitating as a part of their practicum. I find that these students are best able to acquire the skills to facilitate their groups by being willing to deal with potential barriers in themselves during the group supervision meetings.

What I Have Learned About Supervision   In more than 30 years of doing group supervision with trainees in group counseling courses, it has become evident to me that the best supervision is to encourage trainees to develop a sense of educated intuition. So often my colleagues and I discover that those group workers we train and supervise have a wealth of insights and sensitive intuition, yet all too often they do not trust their knowledge, intuition, and feelings. As a supervisor, my goal is to encourage trainees to be themselves in their role as group facilitators and to follow through on some of their clinical intuitions.

Here are some of the lessons that continue to become manifest in the context of group supervision with group counselor trainees:

- It is essential to prepare supervisees both academically and emotionally for the experience of being group counselor trainees.
- Supervisees do not need to have all the right answers to every situation they might encounter in a group counseling setting.
- It is not necessary for supervisees to worry about making mistakes. There are many ways to creatively intervene in any counseling situation,

and it is limiting to operate under the assumption that there is one best way to deal with a problem.

- Supervisees learn best in a climate of support and challenge.
- Trainees can best learn how to facilitate a group from the experience of being a group member and reflecting on what they find most useful for them personally.
- It is desirable that members of a supervision group function as teachers and supervisors for one another. The source of wisdom is not exclusively with the supervisor.
- One of the best ways to teach and to supervise is by modeling. How a supervisor behaves in the group supervision context is often a more powerful source of influence to trainees than simply telling them what to do.
- Before giving trainees my thoughts on a situation, it is often more productive to ask trainees to share their perspective on that situation. More often than not, if trainees are given a chance to explore how they might function more effectively, they will come up with their own insights and suggestions.

What I Still Need to Learn   I have been in group training sessions in which the co-leaders (whom I am supervising) allowed superficial discussion to occur. I have a tendency to define things as being "productive" or "not productive," and superficial talk seems nonproductive to me. When I first began my work as a counselor, I experienced difficulty with clients whom I perceived as engaging in "nonproductive behavior" during a session. I still need to learn the value of patience as the process is often more important than the end result. Although I agree with this intellectually, I still have difficulty emotionally accepting the value of fully experiencing the process of learning.

I can also improve at giving feedback to supervisees in a manner that they are more likely to hear. At times, group leaders in my supervision groups become so anxious that their interventions are stilted and hesitantly delivered, which frequently interferes with the process of the group. On occasion, my feedback during the process commentary time has been difficult for some supervisees to accept. I am sometimes not as tuned into how very sensitive students are to feedback from supervisors. They often hear far more criticism than is intended.

In many cases, supervisees experience transference toward me, which can be explored effectively within the group training situation. Likewise, some of my own countertransference reactions are sometimes triggered, and these can be discussed as well in working with supervisees. Exploring both transference and countertransference reactions is one of the values of doing supervision in a group setting. My intention is to give honest feedback to trainees in a way that they are more likely to receive my comments, and to accomplish this it is often essential to talk about what is going on within the here-and-now context of the supervision group itself.

Patrice Moulton's Personal Perspective

My Work Setting   I presently serve as chair of a clinical psychology department. My job responsibilities include the supervision of the program overall, the supervision of faculty, and the direct supervision of graduate students during practicum and externship experiences. In addition, I am an approved supervisor for prelicensed professional counselors in the state of Louisiana, and I serve as supervisor for the substance abuse certificate program offered through the departments of psychology and social work at the university. Prior to working in an academic setting, I served as clinical director for an adolescent psychiatric hospital, practiced privately, and supervised family programming for an addiction disorder clinic.

My Philosophy of Supervision   I view supervision as a collaborative process with a developmental emphasis. I believe in mutual respect, and this includes respecting supervisees' knowledge and life experiences as they approach the therapeutic process. Supervision is the balance of providing both opportunities and challenges while maintaining a positive and safe professional relationship. This balance requires a firm foundation of appropriate boundaries and information sharing about the process of supervision. I believe trust is established when I am forthright with supervisees about the supervisory process, including my expectations and my range of responsibilities. Honest and ethical communication is the key to providing a safe environment for supervisees.

Moreover, I see managerial responsibility and crisis intervention as components of supervision but not as acceptable models for supervision to be based upon. True supervision is about much more than putting out fires, maintaining units of service (such as the number of hours counselors spend in direct service), and documentation. In my view, supervision entails personal and professional development gained through experience and the supervisory relationship. I am a strong promoter of mentoring through modeling and of empowering supervisees to learn to view cases through multiple lenses.

Supervision requires ongoing personal and professional monitoring. I do not think personal counseling is an appropriate component in supervision. However, personal exploration, as it applies to the supervisee's ability to function as a therapist, is essential. It is appropriate to discuss a supervisee's background and personal reactions in supervision and to seek insight about how these reactions may affect his or her ability to practice therapy. The issues identified in supervision can become strengths for the evolving professional. If not identified and not addressed, however, these personal issues may become barriers to effective work with clients.

There is no substitute for experience in the field, but experience alone is not sufficient to provide quality supervision. A specific set of skills and knowledge is required to provide competent supervision. Personal and professional integrity are of primary importance in maintaining a positive supervisory relationship. Additionally, a sense of humor is an asset when used appropriately in supervision.

I value the early stages of teaching and watching ideas form with my supervisees. I appreciate supervisees who are willing to question my point of view. It is meaningful when supervisees begin to come into supervision, not to seek answers and direction but to discuss alternatives and inform me of the path they will be taking with a particular client.

My Struggles as a Supervisor   I still struggle personally with the logistics of supervision and the time that must be dedicated to quality supervision. Supervision is a tremendous commitment that requires a great deal of time and many resources. It is inaccurate to view supervision with each supervisee as a one hour per week commitment. It takes much more than this to maintain responsibility to both supervisees and the clients for whom they provide therapy. My favorite part of supervision is the relationship that is built while teaching and mentoring. My least favorite part is maintaining updated documentation including contracts, progress notes, and feedback sheets. However, I value this component and would never consider supervising without it.

I find it challenging to work with supervisees coming into the supervision relationship believing they should be competent in every aspect prior to having any supervision and with only limited experience. I must admit that I also find this somewhat frightening as I wonder if they are withholding important details in supervision sessions that may put a client and me at risk.

What I Have Learned About Supervision

- To value the process of the supervisory relationship and the transitions as I share the stages of professional development with supervisees
- To seek out the differing opinions of my supervisees, and even confrontation at times
- To be willing to share vulnerabilities about not having all the answers
- To challenge supervisees by setting high expectations and then providing the support they need to reach them
- To appreciate the need to explore case conceptualization through various lenses before determining either treatment or diagnosis
- To acknowledge and rely on consultative relationships with other professionals regarding supervisory issues
- To provide the necessary structure, though difficult at times, to protect myself, my supervisees, and our clients
- To encourage appropriate risks, expect them, and use them as windows of opportunity
- To provide the opportunity to supervisees by modeling through practice, role play, and co-leading to build confidence and competence in skill

What I Still Need to Learn

- New codes and standards as they are established for supervision
- Effective methods for teaching the supervisory process to students not yet supervising

- Ways to balance and protect the supervisory relationship in light of risk management procedures
- Legal outcomes as courts begin to pay more attention to supervisory processes
- New techniques and technologies to incorporate into the supervisory process
- Techniques for operationalizing multicultural exploration in the supervisory process

We have each learned about supervision from different experiences, but the common theme is that, in our beginnings as supervisors, we had little to guide us except learning from trial and error. We hope we can assist you in learning about supervision from the theory, literature, and personal experience we present in this book.

SUMMARY

As a supervisor, it is essential that you have a clear understanding of the goals of the supervisory process and that you communicate them to your supervisees. The main goals of supervision are the supervisee's learning, protecting the welfare of clients, gatekeeping for the profession, and empowering the supervisee. It is important to clarify the goals of supervision and to understand how your perception of the main purposes of supervision affects what you will do as a supervisor. It is also essential to have a clear picture of the specific objectives you hope your supervisees will accomplish.

SUGGESTED ACTIVITIES

1. Write about or discuss in small groups in class your reactions to the thoughts and experiences of each of the authors. What stands out for you in what each of them said? What are the commonalities? What are the differences among the authors?
2. Select someone who has been your supervisor. Arrange a meeting with that person and ask the same questions that were addressed by the authors: (a) In what settings have you been a supervisor? (b) What is your philosophy of supervision? (c) What are some ways in which you struggle as a supervisor? (d) What have you learned about supervision? (e) What do you still need to learn? Try to summarize what you have learned from this discussion with your supervisor.
3. On a 1–10 scale, with 1 = little or none and 10 = all that I need, how would you rate yourself in terms of having knowledge and skills in supervision? Then, in small groups, discuss what you each think you need to learn to become an effective supervisor. How will you go about doing that?

4. In small groups discuss what you would most want to say you have learned and accomplished at the conclusion of this course. How can this text and course help you accomplish that? Discuss in groups what you hope to learn and how you can benefit most from the reading materials. What kind of class activities would facilitate your learning experience?

5. Access the Web site for this text at http://info.wadsworth.com/haynes, and complete the self-assessment inventory. Additional supervisory perspectives and other activities specific to this chapter are also available to you through this Web site.

2

ROLES AND RESPONSIBILITIES OF SUPERVISORS

1. What is the primary role of the supervisor? What are some of the other roles of the supervisor?

2. Think about those who have served as your supervisors. What roles did they serve in as supervisors? What did you learn from your experience with them about becoming a supervisor?

3. How would you handle a supervisee who is in a personal crisis? Would you attempt to do therapy with this supervisee? Are there any conditions under which providing personal counseling to a supervisee is appropriate? Why?

4. What importance do you place on the role of the supervisor as an evaluator and monitor of the supervisee's clinical work?

5. How might supervisees benefit most from your supervision of them?

6. How might your supervisees gain the maximum benefit from fieldwork or internship experiences?

INTRODUCTION

Supervision is a complex process that entails a multitude of roles and responsibilities. *Roles* are the functional relationships between supervisors and those they supervise; *responsibilities* include the clinical, ethical, and legal duties of the supervisor. In this chapter we will discuss these roles and responsibilities and offer several case study examples to clarify this process.

Supervisors must assume responsibility for being informed and knowledgeable about what their roles entail (Riemersma, 2001). The NASW *Guidelines for Clinical Social Work Supervision* (1994) provides a very complete list of the obligations of the supervisor. Consult this list as you develop your own philosophy of supervision. One important aspect of supervision is to assist supervisees in deriving the maximum benefit from their supervision experience and from their internship or field placement. We offer several suggestions for helping supervisees achieve these goals. The suggested activities at the end of the chapter will help you focus on the key learnings from this chapter.

ROLE OF THE SUPERVISOR

The role of the clinical supervisor in the helping professions is unlike any other role that we assume as clinicians. It has elements in common with other interventions such as teaching, therapy, and consultation, yet it is distinct from any of them (Bernard & Goodyear, 1998). In most clinical activities, counselors carry out one or possibly two functions at a time. Supervisors, however, may serve many different functions—often simultaneously. In a single supervisory session, a supervisor might provide teaching of a clinical approach, act as a consultant on how to intervene with the client, act as a counselor in helping the supervisee with countertransference issues, and provide evaluative feedback to the supervisee regarding his or her progress as a clinician. In addition, the supervisor serves as a recorder and documents the supervisory session.

The role of the supervisor is a composite of many roles, and these roles change as the focus of supervision changes. Competent supervisors have a clear idea of the role in which they are functioning in any given situation, why they are serving in that role, and what they hope to accomplish with the supervisee. The role the supervisor plays may vary depending on the needs of the supervisee, the setting, and the client. Case 2.1 provides a look at how the respective roles of supervisors may differ due to the setting and the supervisee. It is important to assess each supervision situation to be sure that thorough supervision is provided. Do you think the roles assumed by Ryan and Tony are appropriate for their situations? Which supervisory role would you be more comfortable with?

A number of authors have defined the major roles in which supervisors function. Bernard and Goodyear (1998) summarize the supervisory roles suggested by several authors whose work has been most influential. Bernard (1979), Carroll (1996), Ekstein (1964), Hess (1980), Holloway (1995), and Williams (1995) all identify the supervisor's role as that of teacher and counselor-therapist, and all but one include the role of consultant. Less frequently mentioned roles are evaluator and administrator. Other roles mentioned by just one individual include lecturer, case reviewer, and one who relates and models. Corey, Corey, and Callanan (2003) suggest that supervisors operate in multiple roles as teacher, evaluator, counselor, model, mentor, and adviser. Alle-Corliss and Alle-Corliss (1998) have compiled a list of typical supervisory roles based on their experience that includes teacher, model, evaluator, mentor, counselor, and adviser.

There are many commonalties among the various descriptions of the supervisor's role, and no one role is correct for all situations. Much depends on the supervisor, the supervisee, the setting, the client, and the professional and ethical standards that apply to the role of the supervisor in that setting (see Box 2.1 on page 24). Of course, the supervisor's theory of supervision is also a factor in determining appropriate roles and responsibilities. To the roles described in the literature, we have added "empowerer." We believe this role describes the essence of the purpose and goal of supervision in the long run. This concept is implicit in much of the literature, but we believe it is important to make this role explicit. Here then is our list of supervisor roles in the helping professions:

Teacher	Adviser
Mentor	Administrator
Consultant	Evaluator
Counselor	Recorder and documenter
Sounding board	Empowerer

Now let's take a closer look at what each of these roles entails.

| CASE 2.1 | RYAN AND TONY |

Ryan is a licensed psychologist who is supervising a prelicensed psychologist in a private practice setting. In their practice, they work primarily with clients with serious mental illness and with the families of those clients. In his role as a supervisor, Ryan acts as a peer, consultant and sounding board for his supervisee. The danger here is that Ryan may overestimate the abilities and judgment of his supervisee, giving her too much responsibility too soon.

Tony is a licensed social worker who is supervising a bachelor's level counseling trainee in a community college counseling center. Students come to the center for counseling on relationship difficulties, academic performance anxiety, and personal issues such as depression. In his role as a supervisor, Tony acts as a teacher, adviser, mentor, and evaluator for his trainee. In this supervisory situation, Tony is the expert, but he must provide opportunities for his supervisee to grow in knowledge and skills through hands-on training as well.

A skilled supervisor is able to sort out the supervisory needs in various situations and assist supervisees with their work in a manner consistent with client needs and agency policy.

Teacher

The supervisor instructs supervisees on assessment, diagnosis, counseling approaches, ethics, legal issues, and a host of other topics that arise in supervision. The teaching may include assigning readings, suggesting a literature search on a specific topic, offering suggestions for attending workshops, and discussing with the supervisee any number of related topics. An important function of the supervisor as teacher is to provide information to supervisees regarding how supervision works and how they can maximize their supervision experience. For example, supervisors might provide written guidelines to their supervisees on how they can assume an active role in their field placements. Later in this chapter this function is dealt with in greater detail.

Mentor

The supervisor is the trusted guide or coach for the supervisee. The mentor role includes providing direction and guidance for supervisees and assisting them with assessing their current abilities and desired goals as clinicians. Although the role of mentor may occur in any supervision situation, it is more common between the inexperienced supervisee and the experienced supervisor.

Consultant

The supervisor consults with the supervisee to resolve a problem or to help the supervisee make a decision, such as choosing the best treatment approach for a client. The issues addressed can be clinical or administrative and

| ETHICAL AND PROFESSIONAL STANDARDS
REGARDING THE ROLES AND
RESPONSIBILITIES OF THE SUPERVISOR

American Psychological Association
Ethical Principles of Psychologists and Code of Conduct (1992)
1.22 Delegation to and Supervision of Subordinates
(b) Psychologists provide proper training and supervision to their employees or supervisees and take responsible steps to see that such persons perform services responsibly, competently, and ethically.

Association for Counselor Education and Supervision
Ethical Guidelines for Counseling Supervisors (1993)
1.01 The primary obligation of supervisors is to train counselors so that they respect the integrity and promote the welfare of their clients.

2.11 Supervisors should not establish a psychotherapeutic relationship as a substitute for supervision. Personal issues should be addressed in supervision only in terms of the impact of these issues on clients and on professional functioning.

3.02 Supervisors should teach courses and/or supervise clinical work only in areas where they are fully competent and experienced.

Association for Counselor Education and Supervision
Standards for Counseling Supervisors (1990)
2. Professional counseling supervisors demonstrate personal traits and characteristics that are consistent with the role.
The counseling supervisor:
2.6 is comfortable with the authority inherent in the role of supervisor.
2.7 demonstrates commitment to the role of supervisor.

5. Professional counseling supervisors demonstrate conceptual knowledge of supervision methods and techniques, and are skilled in using this knowledge to promote counseling development.
The counseling supervisor:
5.4 can perform the supervisor's functions in the role of teacher, counselor, or consultant as appropriate;
5.6 integrates knowledge of supervision with his/her style of interpersonal relations;
5.7 clarifies his/her role in supervision.

Association of State and Provincial Psychology Boards (ASPPB)
Report of the ASPPB Task Force on Supervision Guidelines (1998)
II. Qualifications of Supervisors
B. The supervisor is ethically and legally responsible for all of the professional activities of the supervisee.
C. The supervisor, or a qualified designee who meets the requirements as a supervisor, provides twenty-four (24) hour availability to both the supervisee and the supervisee's clients. The psychologist shall have sufficient knowledge of all clients, including face-to-face contact when necessary, in order to plan effective service delivery procedures.

National Association of Social Workers
Code of Ethics (1999)
3.01 Supervision and Consultation
(a) Social workers who provide supervision or consultation should have the necessary knowledge and skill to supervise or consult appropriately and should do so only within their areas of knowledge and competence.

National Association of Social Workers
Guidelines for Clinical Social Work Supervision (1994)
Supervisor Obligations
The supervisor has the responsibility to fulfill obligations to the auspices of supervision and to the supervisee. The supervisor should:

- ensure that the scope of his or her own responsibility and authority in agency settings has been clearly and expressly delineated,
- provide documentation of the supervisory qualifications to supervisee or auspices governing the supervisory context,
- provide oversight and guidance in diagnosing, treating, and dealing with the supervisee's clients,
- evaluate the supervisee's role and conceptual understanding in the treatment process, and his or her use of a theoretical base and social work principles,
- conduct supervision as a process distinct from personal therapy or didactic instruction,
- provide supervision in the agreed-upon format,
- maintain documentation of supervision, provide periodic evaluation of the supervisee,
- provide documentation for supervisee to meet the requirements of the supervisory context (including evaluation forms, recommendation forms, counter-signature of case materials, claim forms, and so on),
- identify practices posing a danger to the health and welfare of the supervisee's clients or to the public, and
- identify supervisee's inability to practice with skill and safety due to illness; excessive use of alcohol, drugs, narcotics, chemicals or any other substance; or as a result of any mental or physical condition.

---

typically focus on the supervisor helping the supervisee to problem solve a situation. Dougherty (2000) defines consultation as "a process in which a human services professional assists a consultee with a work-related (or care-taking-related) problem with a client system, with the goal of helping both the consultee and the client system in some specified way" (p. 10). He states that the goal of all consultation is to solve problems.

Counselor

Supervisors should not establish a therapeutic relationship as a substitute for supervision (see ACES, 1993). There has been much discussion about whether it is appropriate for a supervisor to function in the role of counselor to the supervisee. Corey, Corey, and Callanan (2003) state that there seems to be basic agreement in the literature that the proper focus of the supervision process is on the supervisee's *professional* development rather than on his or her *personal* concerns. They also state, however, that there is a lack of consensus and clarity about the degree to which supervisors can work ethically with the supervisee's personal problems.

Becoming the supervisee's therapist creates a conflict of interest, but there are times when the supervisor serves the supervisee well by functioning as a counselor. The supervisor can help the supervisee deal with issues of personal strengths and weaknesses as they relate to the supervisee's practice as a clinician, explore countertransference issues, and cope with stress and burnout. In most cases, the supervisor's role as a counselor is occasional and brief, and any need for intensive psychotherapy on the part of the supervisee should be referred out to another therapist. As Herlihy and Corey (1997) point out, supervisors are ethically obligated to encourage supervisees to face and work through personal issues that could inhibit their potential as helpers. Corey, Corey, and Callanan (2003) summarize this best when they conclude, "Although we see supervision as a separate process from psychotherapy and do not attempt to make training sessions into therapy sessions, we think that the supervisory process can be therapeutic and growth producing" (p. 325).

Sounding Board

One of the most important services a supervisor can provide is that of being a sounding board for the supervisee. Supervision should provide a safe place where the supervisee can discuss ideas with the supervisor, get feedback, and seek an objective perspective. As occurs so often in therapy, talking aloud about issues in supervision allows the supervisee the opportunity to clarify his or her thinking process and make decisions about the current issue. It is also an appropriate place for the supervisee to discuss fears, hopes, and frustrations with his or her work and training.

Adviser

Although the primary approach in supervision is to empower supervisees to learn how to make their own decisions, occasions do arise in which giving advice about a situation is in order. Issues surrounding suicide, dangerousness, duty to warn, court appearances, and treating minors may require direct intervention by the supervisor with the supervisee. In these instances, there may not be time to process the issue (although this should be done at some point for the learning of the supervisee), and immediate action may be necessary to provide for the safety of the client and others.

Administrator

Administrative functions are a necessary part of the supervisory relationship. By this we mean attending to policies and procedures of the organization, licensing body, or professional association. This could include dealing with legal and ethical matters, supervising client documentation, assisting the supervisee in learning ways to cope with bureaucracies, assuring adherence of the supervisee to licensing regulations, and reviewing with the supervisee the legal requirements involved in reporting potential violence or suspected abuse.

Evaluator

Evaluation of the supervisee is a primary responsibility in supervision. Supervisors are ethically required to provide the supervisee with regular and systematic feedback and evaluation (NASW, 1999). Frequently, supervisors are requested to provide information to licensing boards, professional associations, universities and graduate programs, and prospective employers regarding the performance and personal characteristics of the supervisee. When supervisees apply to security-oriented agencies such as correctional and law enforcement agencies, extensive background checks regarding professional activities as well as character references may be required.

Recorder and Documenter

Another role of the supervisor is that of recorder of supervisory sessions. This is essential for the protection of the supervisee and the supervisor. As well, it is good practice for a supervisor to keep track of what the supervisee is bringing to supervision. The NASW (1994) guidelines state, "The supervisor should maintain documentation of supervision . . . provide documentation for supervisee to meet the requirements of the supervisory context (including evaluation forms, recommendation forms, counter-signature of case materials, claim forms, and so on." Professional practice entails maintaining records of every session, including any major issues that arise in the discussion. The confidentiality of those records should be maintained as well.

Empowerer

The best way to sum up the many roles of the supervisor is as empowerer of the supervisee. To "empower" means to give another the ability to do something. A role of the supervisor is to help the supervisee solve immediate clinical issues. Ultimately, the supervisor's function is to teach supervisees how to handle challenges and to know when to seek help through consultation. Kaiser (1997) describes how her supervisor communicated that message of belief in her and in her ability as a social worker and counselor and said it was one of the most profoundly positive influences of her life. This is the essence of empowering the supervisee.

Now that you have an understanding of the roles supervisors play, read Case 2.2 and see if you agree with Victor's advice to Jennifer.

CASE 2.2 JENNIFER

Jennifer is a newly licensed marriage and family counselor. She works at a community mental health center with children who have severe behavioral problems. She completed a semester course on clinical supervision in graduate school and has a well-developed idea of what she hopes to accomplish in sessions with her supervisees. She has been assigned two counseling students as her supervisees and is rather nervous about taking on the new role of supervisor. Her senior colleague, Victor, has worked in the agency for years and has supervised hundreds of counseling students, most of whom have benefited from supervision with him. Victor encourages Jennifer to relax and just let the supervision happen. He says that all she really needs to do is practice good listening skills and let the supervisee do the rest. According to Victor, if you are a good therapist, you will be a good supervisor.

Would you rather be supervised by Victor or Jennifer? What advice would you give to Jennifer? Our advice to Jennifer is to examine the agency and the professional standards in determining the roles and responsibilities of the supervisor. Victor's perception of the role of the supervisor and the purpose of supervision may have been acceptable in years past, but it is not today. In some respects, supervision is similar to therapy, but different. Many of the relationship and problem-solving skills used are the same, but the main goals of supervision are to protect clients while teaching, monitoring, and evaluating the supervisee. Jennifer can probably rely on Victor as a consultant but not as someone who can help her define her role as a supervisor.

We asked a group of supervisors ranging in discipline, setting, and years of experience to comment on how they view their roles in supervision. You will see that each has a different perspective on his or her role as a supervisor. Their comments are provided in the Voices from the Field feature.

Supervisors serve in many roles, often simultaneously. The role chosen should be a good fit with the purpose of the supervisory context. The key is to be aware of the role you are functioning in and why. It is similar to developing your own model of psychotherapy. As long as you practice within accepted professional and ethical standards, there is some latitude for you to use what you think works for you and the supervisee and, at the same time, serves the best interests of the client. Self-monitoring is essential as you develop your approach to supervision and throughout your life as a supervisor.

THE SCOPE OF RESPONSIBILITY IN SUPERVISION

The scope of responsibility in supervision has been described by various authors and was discussed earlier in goals of supervision in Chapter 1. Bernard and Goodyear (1998) suggest that three main purposes of supervision are training supervisees, protecting clients, and rehabilitating impaired

VOICES FROM THE FIELD

Elie Axelroth, Psy. D.

An effective supervisor is a brave soul, plunging into the role of mentor, educator, adviser, confidant, mirror, and at times, a container to hold the frustrations of clinical work. Many of us came to supervision ill-prepared for what awaited us, and there is nothing like living the supervisor–intern relationship to discover what it really entails. An effective supervisor enjoys the process of mentoring a new professional, accepting the intern complete with blemishes, frailties, and vulnerabilities.

Randy Alle-Corliss, M.S.W., L.C.S.W.

The major struggle I encountered in becoming a supervisor was understanding my role and dealing with the resultant anxieties that occurred when I was thrust into a role for which I had little formal training or education. Whenever I have been asked to assume supervisory responsibilities, the role has come with many expectations but little formal training regarding the ins and outs of being in that role. I view my primary role as a supervisor as creating a relationship with my supervisees that will enhance the learning of knowledge and skills. I place emphasis on creating a warm, supportive, open relation-ship with my supervisees, rather than just trying to impart knowledge or having them perform activities without a chance to openly discuss their feelings, thoughts, and actions.

Stacy Thacker, Ph.D.

Primarily, I see my role as a supervisor as a combination of roles. As a supervisor, I am a model, mentor, confidant, consultant, cheerleader, and instructor. As a model, I may both directly and indirectly model appropriate behavior by purposely modeling a task (directly) or by the way I conduct myself informally on the job and with the supervisee (indirectly). As a mentor and confidant, I see my role as gently guiding the supervisee along his or her professional path. In this role, it is important that the supervisee feel comfortable discussing various issues knowing that these issues will not be inappropriately divulged to others. As a cheerleader, I encourage supervisees to practice confidently in their areas of competence. I "look out" for their best interests and applaud them for jobs well done. And as an instructor, I instruct them regarding areas in which they wish to gain new skills or competencies.

---

professionals. Kadushin (1992) concludes that the scope of clinical supervision includes three overlapping functions: administrative, educational, and supportive. *Administrative supervision* is concerned with the effective implementation of agency policies and procedures. *Educational supervision* focuses on promoting supervisee knowledge, attitudes, and skills. The *supportive function* in supervision is designed to improve supervisee morale and job satisfaction. The ultimate scope of supervision is to do that which is necessary to assure that the supervisee's current and future clients receive the best services available.

The scope of legal and ethical responsibility in supervision is far-reaching. Generally speaking, the supervisor is legally and ethically responsible for all of the professional activities of the supervisee as well as his or her own actions as a supervisor (ASPPB, 1998). Practically, this means that supervisors must have some knowledge of all the clinical activities and cases of the supervisee and be available to provide supervision whenever needed. In the course of this book, we will describe how a supervisor can provide effective supervision that meets these requirements and yet can be carried out in a practical and reasonable fashion within one's normal workload.

RESPONSIBILITIES OF THE SUPERVISOR

The responsibilities of the supervisor are numerous and varied. The major responsibilities are summarized in this section, and most will be discussed in greater detail in subsequent chapters.

1. Recognize that the supervisor is ultimately responsible, both legally and ethically, for the actions of the supervisee.   The clinical practice supervisor shares responsibility for the services provided to the client (Alle-Corliss & Alle-Corliss, 1998; ASPPB, 1998; Herlihy & Corey, 1997; NASW, 1994). Liability of supervisors has been determined by the courts and includes direct liability related to negligent or inadequate supervision and vicarious liability related to negligent conduct by the supervisee (Falvey, 2002). This topic is discussed in greater detail in Chapter 8 dealing with legal issues. Kadushin (1992) also confirms that malpractice complaints and legal decisions have held that supervisors are responsible for the decisions and actions of supervisees. He says that the doctrine of *vicarious liability* means that the supervisor is responsible for the actions of the supervisee within the scope of his or her employment. As such, the supervisee is legally regarded as an extension of the supervisor, as you can see in Case 2.3.

After you have read Karen's case, give your opinion on whether she should have been held responsible for something beyond her control that she was unaware of.

Supervision is a broad and comprehensive responsibility that encompasses everything supervisees do in their professional capacity. It is the supervisor's responsibility to "monitor and control" the actions of their supervisees. When problems occur, licensing boards will look to the supervisor to see what guidance and direction have been provided to the supervisee.

2. Have knowledge of every case/client with whom supervisee is working. Supervisors must check on their supervisee's progress and be familiar with the caseloads of the supervisee. Falvey (2002) suggests that supervisors meet at least briefly with every client with whom the supervisee is working. Many supervisors consider this to be unrealistic because of time and caseload constraints, but legal liability does attach to the supervisor so oversight must be a serious concern in supervision. The important point to make is that the supervisor should have knowledge of all the supervisee's clients and document cases. This topic will be discussed in more detail in Chapter 8.

CASE 2.3 | KAREN

Karen, a licensed counselor, was supervising an unlicensed counseling assistant who, unbeknownst to Karen, began providing counseling services to clients for a fee at another office in town. These counseling services were not supervised by any licensed professional. A complaint was filed with the licensing board against the counseling assistant for practicing (out of the second office) without a license and without proper supervision.

With the assistance of legal counsel, Karen submitted in writing to the board a complete description of her understanding of these events and how they had occurred. Because the board has jurisdiction only over licensed counselors, it was Karen rather than the counseling assistant who was disciplined. The board ruled that Karen, as the supervisor, was responsible for all the professional activities of the counseling assistant and disciplined her for the unauthorized practice of the supervisee. She was placed on probation as a licensed counselor for one year, restricted from supervising counseling assistants during the probationary period, and required to attend a course on supervision. Following the successful completion of these requirements, Karen will have her license fully restored by the board.

---

3. Provide feedback and evaluation to supervisee regarding performance. Supervisors are expected to provide feedback and evaluation to supervisees on a regular basis (ACA, 1995; Alle-Corliss & Alle-Corliss, 1998; APA, 1992; ASPPB, 1998; Falvey, 2002; NASW, 1994; NBCC, 1999). Supervisors are expected to tell supervisees how they are doing, how they see their strengths and weaknesses as they relate to their clinical work, how they are proceeding in terms of their goals for supervision, and the expectations for remediating any deficits. This evaluative function enhances supervisee self-awareness and skill development (Alle-Corliss & Alle-Corliss, 1998). Feedback from supervisors ranges from verbal and informal to very structured and standardized. In our experience, the use of standardized forms and timeframes for systematic feedback helps to objectify the process and provides a framework for constructive feedback to the supervisee. Using informal verbal feedback, without scheduled evaluations, can result in feedback being more subjective and being provided only when a problem occurs.

Supervisees typically want feedback even though they may be reluctant to ask for it. Although supervisees' stated goals for supervision are quite focused, Bordin (1983) indicates that their unspoken agenda is often the wish for global feedback about their overall level of functioning. Evaluation in supervision will be discussed in detail in Chapter 10.

4. Monitor the actions and decisions of the supervisee. Monitoring the actions and decisions of supervisees is an integral part of the notion that the supervisor is ultimately responsible for the actions of their trainees. Loganbill,

Hardy, and Delworth (1982) state that monitoring client care is the paramount responsibility of the clinical supervisor. It is essential to monitor and evaluate the diagnosis and treatment decisions of the supervisee (Riemersma, 2001). Monitoring is done in supervision sessions by being vigilant of what the supervisee is reporting, how he or she is making decisions, and the self-awareness the supervisee demonstrates regarding the limits of his or her clinical competence. One of the best ways to monitor the actions and decisions of the supervisee is to observe clinical sessions or request that the supervisee bring audiotapes or videotapes of clinical sessions to supervision. This firsthand look at the actions and decisions of the supervisee is often more reliable than the supervisee's self-report. The second part of monitoring involves intervening as necessary to help the supervisee modify his or her actions and decision-making process. Interventions depend on the nature of the situation and the degree to which clients may be put at risk by the actions of the supervisee.

5. Document the supervisory sessions.   The process of record keeping has gained in importance for helping professionals of all disciplines in an increasingly litigious era (Bernard & Goodyear, 1998). Documenting supervisory sessions is essential to keep track of the issues and clients a supervisee is working with; to provide documentation for licensing boards, professional associations, and prospective employers; and in case of litigation.

6. Supervise only within the scope of your expertise and refer out for additional supervision/consultation as necessary.   Supervisors are expected to have in-depth knowledge of the specialty area in which they provide supervision (ACES, 1993). Supervisors also need to be aware of their areas of expertise and competence and provide supervision only within those areas. When issues, topics, and diagnoses arise that are outside the supervisor's areas of expertise, the supervisor will have to decide how to provide adequate supervision. This can be done in any number of ways: reading on the topic, seeking consultation from another supervisor competent in the area, referring the supervisee to another supervisor for adjunctive supervision, or addressing the issue as a collaborative effort between supervisor and supervisee.

   It is easier to determine one's area of competence in situations where the issue is clear-cut. For example, if an issue arises regarding the possibility of organic brain damage with a client and the supervisor has had no training or experience in that area, it would seem prudent to seek consultation from a supervisor with such expertise. The consultant might meet with the supervisor and the supervisee thus offering an opportunity for both to expand their knowledge of the topic. It becomes more complex in cases where the supervisor has some knowledge of the topic but perhaps little experience. The bottom line is, how much knowledge and experience is enough to render the supervisor qualified to supervise on the topic? This same question is raised when practicing clinically within one's areas of competence. It is a judgment call on the part of the clinician and the supervisor, and the decision is usually based on the "standard of care" or what other similarly trained clinicians would consider to be the necessary knowledge and experience (Falvey, 2002). The question to ask is this: "Is it considered general or normative practice for one with credentials or training similar to mine to provide this service?"

7. Provide supervisees with due process information.   Due process is a legal term often described as "notice," and a "hearing" must be provided before a right can be removed (Disney & Stephens, 1994; Hollander, 1996). In supervision, due process includes providing supervisees with clear expectations for performance, outlining the procedure for handling adverse actions and disciplinary action, and explaining supervisees' rights to appeal such actions when performance expectations are not met. The procedures vary tremendously between academic and nonacademic settings and between public and private settings, but the basic message regardless of setting is the same: Supervisees have the right to have clear expectations for performance, to be informed of the criteria for success, and to know how things will proceed when performance expectations are not met.

Supervisees have the right to timely feedback, to be informed of how the process of providing feedback to them will proceed, how they can remediate the situation, what the steps for adverse action will be, and the mechanism for appeal. It is the supervisor's responsibility to provide this information, but this responsibility and process will vary widely depending on the setting and the context of the supervision.

Supervisors can best provide this information in a written contract, which both supervisee and supervisor review and sign to show that a clear understanding of this process has been established. This is best done at the beginning of the supervisory relationship and long before any problematic situation arises.

8. Have a written contract between the supervisor and supervisee regarding the scope and expectations in supervision.   The use of a simple, clear, comprehensive contract can clarify the many facets of the supervisory relationship and provide a framework for problem resolution. Box 2.2 is one example of a supervision contract that addresses both rights of and expectations for supervisees. A written contract is the blueprint that provides the framework for a successful supervisory experience for both the supervisor and the supervisee. As such, it protects the supervisor, the supervisee, the agency, and, most important, the client.

Holloway (1999) views a contract as an essential component of the supervisory relationship. It is essential to formulate understandings and agreements between the supervisor and the supervisee on topics including supervisory expectations, assessment criteria, evaluative process, ethical and legal obligations, and trainee learning objectives. The clarity of expectations has a direct impact on the working relationship and the establishment of specific learning goals. Holloway believes a contract should provide the supervisee with an opportunity to participate in the construction of the supervisory relationship. More detailed information regarding contracts can be found in Chapter 8.

BOX 2.2 | SUPERVISEE'S BILL OF RIGHTS: SUPERVISION CONTRACT

The supervisory relationship is an experiential learning process that assists the supervisee in developing therapeutic and professional competence. This contract is designed to assist the supervisor and supervisee in establishing clear expectations about the supervisory meetings, the relationship, and the evaluation process. Complete each section that pertains to you prior to the initial meeting.

Introductions and Establishing Expectations About the Supervisory Experience

Supervisor

_____ 1. Introduce yourself; discuss your counseling experience, and your supervisory style.

_____ 2. Describe your role as a supervisor (being a role model, mentor, monitoring client welfare, teaching therapeutic skills, providing regular verbal and written feedback and evaluation, and insuring compliance with legal, ethical, and professional standards).

_____ 3. Ask the supervisee about his or her learning style and developmental needs.

Supervisee

_____ 1. Introduce yourself and describe your clinical experience and training.

_____ 2. Briefly discuss information you want to address during the supervisory meetings.

_____ 3. Describe the therapeutic skills you want to enhance and professional development opportunities you want to experience during the next three months.

List three therapeutic skills you would like to further develop.

1. _____

2. _____

3. _____

List three specific counseling or professional development experiences you would like to have during the next three months. (Attending a conference, facilitating a group, presenting a paper, . . .)

1. _____

2. _____

3. _____

Expectations of the Weekly Supervisory Meetings

The weekly supervisory meeting will take place face-to-face in a professional environment that insures confidentiality. Decide the location, day, and time.

Location	Day	Time

Supervisee

_____ 1. Discuss your expectations about the learning process and interest in reviewing audiotapes, videotapes, and case notes.

Supervisor

_____ 1. Describe the structure and content of the weekly supervisory meetings.

_____ 2. Discuss your expectations regarding supervisee preparedness for supervisory meetings (audiotapes, videotapes, case notes).

Expectations Regarding Evaluation

Supervisee

_____ 1. Discuss your interest in receiving weekly feedback in areas such as relationship building, counseling techniques, client conceptualization, and assessment.

Supervisor

_____ 1. Discuss your style of providing verbal feedback and evaluation.

_____ 2. Provide the supervisee with a copy of the formal evaluation you will use; discuss the evaluation tools and clarify specific items that need additional explanation.

_____ 3. Discuss the benefit of self-evaluation; provide a copy of self-evaluation forms and clarify specific items that need additional explanation.

Expectation of the Supervisory Relationship

Supervisor and Supervisee

_____ 1. Discuss your expectations of the supervisory relationship.

_____ 2. Discuss how you will work toward establishing a positive and productive supervisory relationship. Also, discuss how you will address and resolve conflicts.

_____ 3. The supervisory experience will increase the supervisee's awareness of feelings, thoughts, behavior, and aspects of self that are stimulated by the client. Discuss the role of the supervisor in assisting with this process.

_____ 4. Share your thoughts with one another about the influence of race, ethnicity, gender, sexual orientation, religion, and class on the counseling and the supervision process.

Supervisee

_____ 1. Describe how you would like to increase your awareness of personal cultural assumptions, constructs, and ability to work with clients from diverse cultures.

(continued)

BOX 2.2	SUPERVISEE'S BILL OF RIGHTS: SUPERVISION CONTRACT (*continued*)

Supervisor

_____ 1. When you are unavailable to provide weekly supervision, or are unable to address crisis situations, discuss an alternate supervisor who will be available.

Dual Relationships

Supervisor

_____ 1. Discuss the nature of the supervisory relationship and the importance of not being involved in a dual relationship.

Expectations of the Supervisory Process

Supervisor

_____ 1. Describe your theory of counseling and how it influences your counseling and supervision style.

_____ 2. Discuss your theory or model of supervision.

Supervisee

_____ 1. Discuss your learning style and your developmental needs.

_____ 2. Discuss your current ideas about your theoretical orientation.

Additional Information or Concerns Not Previously Discussed

_____ 1. _____

_____ 2. _____

_____ 3. _____

_____   _____
Supervisor's Signature   Date

_____   _____
Supervisee's Signature   Date

Source: M.A. Giordano, M.K. Altekruse, and C.W. Kern. Supervisee's Bill of Rights. (2000). Reprinted with permission.

9. Monitor the personal development of the supervisee as it affects the practice of counseling. A helping professional's personal life affects his or her ability to provide effective clinical services. One responsibility of the supervisor is to monitor the personal development of the supervisee and recommend action to be taken when problematic issues are identified (NASW, 1994).

Some professional codes (see NASW, 1994) identify areas to be monitored, but supervisors are called upon to rely on their own judgment in determining which issues are identified and how they are to be monitored. It is important for the supervisor to keep a watchful eye on issues that affect the supervisee's counseling practice and to recommend action as needed. Policies and procedures for intervening with impaired professionals should be established as well. These topics are addressed in detail in Chapter 7.

10. Model effective problem-solving skills for supervisees and help supervisees develop problem-solving capabilities. Modeling and assisting supervisees in developing their own problem-solving capabilities are primary roles and responsibilities of the supervisor. The goal in supervision is to assist supervisees in developing their own system of problem solving both for themselves and for assisting clients in their problem solving.

11. Promote the supervisee's ethical knowledge and behavior. Another major responsibility for the supervisor is to assist the supervisee in becoming a competent and ethical professional, and to provide services in compliance with the ethical standards of practice (Riemersma, 2001). This is supported explicitly or implicitly by the major professional standards and codes of practice (see APA, 1992, 2001). Assisting the supervisee's development of ethical knowledge and behavior requires teaching, consulting, modeling, and providing feedback about the ethical responsibilities in counseling. As well, the supervisor will assist the supervisee in understanding specific ethical standards and codes and how they apply to the supervisee's work with clients.

12. Promote the knowledge and skills required to understand and work effectively with clients' individual and cultural differences. The supervisor is both a model and a teacher for the supervisee in understanding and working with clients' individual and cultural similarities and differences. These topics can be included in the discussion of every case to help the supervisee bring into focus how these similarities and differences play a role in the counseling process and how the supervisee can best work with them. One of the major messages supervisors can communicate to supervisees is the need to learn from clients what cultures they most closely identify with and how this might affect the counseling relationship. See Chapter 6 for a more detailed discussion of multicultural issues in supervision.

13. Educate supervisee to critical ethical issues involved when working within a managed care system. Many supervisees will eventually work in some form of managed care context, which will involve a number of ethical concerns. Supervisees should understand the ethical issues unique to this work environment. Based on a review of the literature, ethical dilemmas most commonly surface in a managed care system in these four areas: informed consent, confidentiality, abandonment, and utilization review (Acuff et al., 1999; Cooper & Gottlieb, 2000; Davis & Meier, 2001).

Informed consent. Supervisees need to know that informed consent is an ongoing process. If they expect to work within a managed care setting, they need to provide full, complete, and accurate information to their clients. It is a mistake to assume that clients will have complete information regarding how the managed care system affects their treatment. Thus, the informed consent procedure must be very clear (Cooper & Gottlieb, 2000).

Confidentiality. Although confidentiality is considered an ethical and legal duty imposed on therapists to protect client disclosures, confidentiality is seriously compromised in a managed care context (Davis & Meier, 2001). Acuff and her colleagues (1999) assert that without the assurance of confidentiality many people will not seek treatment, and clients in therapy are likely to withhold information necessary for effective therapy. Because of the restrictions on confidentiality, counselors have an obligation to inform clients from the outset of the professional relationship about the relevant limits of confidentiality under their managed care policy (Acuff et al., 1999; Cooper & Gottlieb, 2000).

Abandonment. Although the codes of ethics of the various professional organizations state that mental health practitioners do not abandon clients, clients in a managed care system are likely to feel abandoned if their treatment ends abruptly, which might well happen. Under managed care programs, termination is not often a collaborative process between the counselor and the client; rather, termination is generally a matter decided by the managed care provider.

Utilization review. Managed care programs involve the monitoring of all treatment. Utilization review refers to the use of predefined criteria to evaluate treatment necessity, appropriateness of therapeutic intervention, and therapy effectiveness. Although the needs of the client should be given primary consideration, managed care focuses on ways to contain costs.

The responsibility of supervisors to inform and educate supervisees about the process of managed care is important and has implications for treatment options. More detailed information on this topic is provided in Davis and Meier (2001).

Other supervisor responsibilities identified by Riemersma (2001) include ensuring that the supervisee works within his or her scope of practice and competence, ensuring that the supervisee provides services in compliance with the law, ensuring that the work setting the supervisee is in is appropriate, and ensuring that the supervisee understands the plan in place to address emergencies.

In summary, the roles of the supervisor range from providing support to evaluating the supervisee, from teaching to monitoring. The supervisor must be knowledgeable of the various roles, of which roles apply in which situations, and how any given role will best serve the supervisee, the setting, the client, and the supervisor. A great deal of knowledge, flexibility, and judgment are necessary to carry out the roles and responsibilities of the supervisor.

Some additional comments on the responsibilities of supervisors are provided in the Voices from the Field feature on page 40.

TEACHING SUPERVISEES HOW TO USE SUPERVISION EFFECTIVELY

A critical role of supervisors is to teach supervisees how to involve themselves in the supervisory process so that they can gain the maximum benefit from supervision. Many supervisees are likely to approach supervision as a mysterious process that entails an experienced professional giving them answers in making sense of their work with clients. Unfortunately, some supervisors will only briefly mention how supervision works, what trainees can expect from them, and what roles they will play. If this is the case, more responsibility is placed on supervisees to take an active role by asking questions and expressing what they need from their supervisor.

The first session with your supervisees might include discussion of your role as a supervisor, the focus of the supervisory sessions, the focus on management of client cases, the attention paid to personal issues of supervisees, their relationships with clients, and the supervisees' responsibilities in supervision. You can encourage supervisees to assume an active stance in supervision by asking what they hope to accomplish in supervision.

It is hoped that supervisees will want to know how supervision works, including the respective responsibilities of both the supervisee and the supervisor. Here are a few questions supervisors can encourage supervisees to raise: Will I be able to bring into supervision both personal and professional concerns, or will the supervisor direct the sessions? How much opportunity will I have to discuss the supervisory relationship itself? What do I need to do to successfully complete my work as a supervisee? How and when will I be evaluated? What supervision methods will be used? Supervisees are unlikely to ask all of these questions at the first meeting, but supervisors can encourage supervisees to pose these questions throughout the supervisory relationship. Supervisees will derive the maximum benefit from their supervision experience if they reflect on what they most want and need from their supervisor, not only at the outset, but on a session-by-session basis.

Perhaps one of the best ways to assist supervisees in learning how to use supervision effectively is for supervisors to take the initiative by giving their supervisees a written statement that clarifies their rights and responsibilities

VOICES FROM THE FIELD

Bill Safarjan, Ph.D.

In my view, the primary role of the supervisor is to teach good clinical, professional, and ethical behavior. To do so, the supervisor must assist the supervisee in translating clinical knowledge into clinical practice. In this sense, the supervisor serves as a bridge between the academic and practice communities. The supervisor must also create a learning environment within the context of a work setting. To accomplish this, the supervisor must balance the needs of the supervisee with those of managers, administrators, or the supervisor him- or herself. Moreover, the supervisor must give priority to the needs of the supervisee. The role of the supervisor is extremely important. It not only personally benefits the supervisee but benefits the public as well as the profession.

Todd Thies, Ph.D.

My role as a supervisor depends on the individual I am supervising. Therefore, I think my first role as a supervisor is to assess the needs of the person I am supervising. In general, my role as a supervisor is threefold. The first part of my role is to teach the intern the necessary skills to perform as an independent practitioner. The second part of my role is to help the intern avoid the risks and pitfalls (failing to evaluate a depressed patient for suicidal ideation) he or she will encounter while working. The third, and perhaps most enjoyable, part of my role as a supervisor is to assist interns with their own individual development. Essential to the role of a supervisor is not to produce a clone of the supervisor but to help the supervisee become the professional he or she was meant to be.

as supervisees in the supervisory process. Box 2.3, Supervisee's Bill of Rights, clarifies the nature of the supervisory relationship from initial session through evaluation and addresses ethical issues in the supervisory relationship. This document also addresses a range of expectations, including the supervisory relationship, supervisory process, supervisory sessions, and the evaluation process. Once this Supervisee's Bill of Rights is given to supervisees and discussed, a supervision contract, based on the Supervisee's Bill of Rights, can be introduced (see Box 2.2).

The initial supervisory session would also be a good time to give supervisees the Supervisee's Evaluation of Supervision Experience (Box 2.4). Explain to supervisees that they will be asked to evaluate their supervision experience near the end of their work assignment. Providing this opportunity for supervisees to look over specific dimensions of their experience that they will be asked to evaluate at a later point can help supervisees to focus their attention on what they can expect from supervision. The topics of contracts and evaluation will be discussed in detail in later chapters, but we wanted to share the information included in the Supervisee's Bill of Rights materials early in the book to provide you with an overall picture of the responsibilities of both supervisees and supervisors.

BOX 2.3 | SUPERVISEE'S BILL OF RIGHTS

Introduction

The purpose of the Bill of Rights is to inform supervisees of their rights and responsibilities in the supervisory process.

Nature of the Supervisory Relationship

The supervisory relationship is an experiential learning process that assists the supervisee in developing therapeutic and professional competence. A professional counselor-supervisor who has received specific training in supervision facilitates professional growth of the supervisee through:

- monitoring client welfare
- encouraging compliance with legal, ethical, and professional standards
- teaching therapeutic skills
- providing regular feedback and evaluation
- providing professional experiences and opportunities

Expectations of Initial Supervisory Session

The supervisee has the right to be informed of the supervisor's expectations of the supervisory relationship. The supervisor shall clearly state expectations of the supervisory relationship that may include:

- supervisee identification of supervision goals for oneself
- supervisee preparedness for supervisory meetings
- supervisee determination of areas for professional growth and development
- supervisor's expectations regarding formal and informal evaluations
- supervisor's expectations of the supervisee's need to provide formal and informal self-evaluations
- supervisor's expectations regarding the structure and/or the nature of the supervisory sessions
- weekly review of case notes until supervisee demonstrates competency in case conceptualization

The supervisee shall provide input to the supervisor regarding the supervisee's expectations of the relationship.

Expectations of the Supervisory Relationship

1. A supervisor is a professional counselor with appropriate credentials. The supervisee can expect the supervisor to serve as a mentor and a positive role model who assists the supervisee in developing a professional identity.
2. The supervisee has the right to work with a supervisor who is culturally sensitive and is able to openly discuss the influence of race, ethnicity, gender, sexual orientation, religion, and class on the counseling and the supervision process. The supervisor is aware of personal cultural assumptions and constructs and is able to assist the supervisee in developing additional knowledge and skills in working with clients from diverse cultures.
3. Since a positive rapport between the supervisor and supervisee is critical for successful supervision to occur, the relationship is a priority for both the supervisor and supervisee. In the event that relationship concerns exist, the supervisor or supervisee will discuss concerns with one another and work toward resolving differences.

(continued)

BOX 2.3   SUPERVISEE'S BILL OF RIGHTS(*continued*)

4. Therapeutic interventions initiated by the supervisor or solicited by the supervisee shall be implemented only in the service of helping the supervisee increase effectiveness with clients. A proper referral for counseling shall be made if appropriate.
5. The supervisor shall inform the supervisee of an alternative supervisor who will be available in case of crisis situations or known absences.

Ethics and Issues in the Supervisory Relationship

1. **Code of Ethics and Standards of Practice**
    The supervisor will insure the supervisee understands the American Counseling Association *Code of Ethics and Standards of Practice* and legal responsibilities. The supervisor and supervisee will discuss sections applicable to the beginning counselor.
2. **Dual Relationships**
    Since a power differential exists in the supervisory relationship, supervisors shall not utilize this differential to their gain. Since dual relationships may affect the objectivity of the supervisor, the supervisee shall not be asked to engage in social interaction that would compromise the professional nature of the supervisory relationship.
3. **Due Process**
    During the initial meeting, supervisors provide the supervisee information regarding expectations, goals, and roles of the supervisory process. The supervisee has the right to regular verbal feedback and periodic formal written feedback signed by both individuals.
4. **Evaluation**
    During the initial supervisory session, the supervisor provides the supervisee a copy of the evaluation instrument used to assess the counselor's progress.
5. **Informed Consent**
    The supervisee informs the client she or he is in training, is being supervised, and receives written permission from the client to audio tape or video tape.
6. **Confidentiality**
    The counseling relationship, assessments, records, and correspondences remain confidential. Failure to keep information confidential is a violation of the ethical code and the counselor is subject to a malpractice suit. The client must sign a written consent prior to counselor's consultation.
7. **Vicarious Liability**
    The supervisor is ultimately liable for the welfare of the supervisee's clients. The supervisee is expected to discuss with the supervisor the counseling process and individual concerns of each client.
8. **Isolation**
    The supervisor consults with peers regarding supervisory concerns and issues.
9. **Termination of Supervision**
    The supervisor discusses termination of the supervisory relationship and helps the supervisee identify areas for continued growth and explore professional goals.

Expectations of the Supervisory Process

1. The supervisee shall be encouraged to determine a theoretical orientation that can be used for conceptualizing and guiding work with clients.
2. The supervisee has the right to work with a supervisor who is responsive to the supervisee's theoretical orientation, learning style, and developmental needs.

3. Since it is probable that the supervisor's theory of counseling will influence the supervision process, the supervisee needs to be informed of the supervisor's counseling theory and how the supervisor's theoretical orientation may influence the supervision process.

Expectations of Supervisory Sessions
1. The weekly supervisory session shall include a review of all cases, audiotapes, videotapes, and may include live supervision.
2. The supervisee is expected to meet with the supervisor face-to-face in a professional environment that insures confidentiality.

Expectations of the Evaluation Process
1. During the initial meeting, the supervisee shall be provided with a copy of the formal evaluation tool(s) that will be used by the supervisor.
2. The supervisee shall receive verbal feedback and/or informal evaluation during each supervisory session.
3. The supervisee shall receive written feedback or written evaluation on a regular basis during beginning phases of counselor development. Written feedback may be requested by the supervisee during intermediate and advanced phases of counselor development.
4. The supervisee should be recommended for remedial assistance in a timely manner if the supervisor becomes aware of personal or professional limitations that may impede future professional performance.
5. Beginning counselors receive written and verbal summative evaluation during the last supervisory meeting. Intermediate and advanced counselors may receive a recommendation for licensure and/or certification.

Source: M.A. Giordano, M.K. Altekruse, and C.W. Kern. Supervisee's Bill of Rights. (2000). Reprinted with permission.

Supervisees can take responsibility for deriving maximum benefits from supervision by preparing themselves for this experience. Here are some suggestions that can help you get the most from your supervision:

- Know the general purpose of supervision.
- Recognize that different supervisors will attempt to achieve the purpose of supervision in a variety of ways.
- Accept that a certain level of anxiety is to be expected in the supervision process.
- Clarify any aspects of your contract with your supervisor regarding the content of the supervision sessions.
- Ask how and when evaluation will occur.
- Strive to be as honest and open as possible during your supervision sessions, and ask your supervisor for what you need.
- Spend time preparing before meeting with your supervisor. One way to prepare is to write summaries of your cases and identify questions in advance that you would like to explore with your supervisor.
- Engage in the supervision process in a way that is meaningful to you. Be willing to ask difficult questions of your supervisor and also of yourself.
- Do your best to work within the framework of your supervisor's style.

| BOX 2.4 | SUPERVISEE'S BILL OF RIGHTS: SUPERVISEE'S EVALUATION OF SUPERVISION EXPERIENCE |

Name: _____   Date: _____

Please circle the response that describes your supervision experience most accurately.

Strongly Disagree =   1   2   3   4   5   6   7   **= Strongly Agree**

Initial Supervisory Session

I identified personal goals for supervision.	1 2 3 4 5 6 7
I was informed of necessary preparations for regular sessions.	1 2 3 4 5 6 7
I determined areas for professional growth and development.	1 2 3 4 5 6 7
I was informed of my supervisor's expectations regarding formal and informal evaluation such as live supervision, feedback, and written evaluations.	1 2 3 4 5 6 7
I was informed of the necessity of formal and informal self-evaluations.	1 2 3 4 5 6 7
I was informed about the planned structure and nature of the supervisory meetings.	1 2 3 4 5 6 7
I provided input regarding my expectations of the supervisory relationship.	1 2 3 4 5 6 7

Supervisory Relationship

My supervisor and I have a positive rapport.	1 2 3 4 5 6 7
My supervisor considered our supervisory relationship a priority.	1 2 3 4 5 6 7
My supervisor made it comfortable to communicate with him/her.	1 2 3 4 5 6 7
My supervisor is culturally sensitive.	1 2 3 4 5 6 7
My supervisor shared and negotiated.	1 2 3 4 5 6 7
My supervisor made it comfortable for me to discuss strengths and weaknesses about my counseling skills.	1 2 3 4 5 6 7
My supervisor refrained from counseling me except in areas that addressed my effectiveness with clients.	1 2 3 4 5 6 7
My supervisor would refer me for counseling when appropriate.	1 2 3 4 5 6 7
My supervisor would provide me with the name of an alternative supervisor in her or his absence.	1 2 3 4 5 6 7

Ethics and Issues

My supervisor and I reviewed the American Counseling Association *Code of Ethics and Standards of Practice.*	1 2 3 4 5 6 7
Any potential dual relationship issues were addressed directly and appropriately.	1 2 3 4 5 6 7
My supervisor did not abuse the power differential in our relationship.	1 2 3 4 5 6 7
My supervisor explained the necessity of informing my client that I am a counselor in training who is being supervised.	1 2 3 4 5 6 7

We discussed the importance of obtaining the client's written consent to audio tape or video tape.   1 2 3 4 5 6 7

The expectations, goals, and roles of the supervisory process were explained.   1 2 3 4 5 6 7

My supervisor explained the importance of confidentiality.   1 2 3 4 5 6 7

I was informed of the need to obtain the client's written consent prior to consulting with other professionals who are serving the client.   1 2 3 4 5 6 7

I was made aware that my supervisor is ultimately liable for the welfare of my clients.   1 2 3 4 5 6 7

My supervisor monitored my client's welfare.   1 2 3 4 5 6 7

Supervisory Process

I was informed of the potential impact of my supervisor's theoretical orientation on the supervisory process.   1 2 3 4 5 6 7

I was encouraged to determine a theoretical orientation.   1 2 3 4 5 6 7

My supervisor was responsive to my theoretical orientation.   1 2 3 4 5 6 7

I was taught therapeutic skills.   1 2 3 4 5 6 7

My supervisor was responsive to my learning style.   1 2 3 4 5 6 7

Supervisory Sessions

I met with my supervisor in a confidential face-to-face environment on a weekly basis.   1 2 3 4 5 6 7

My supervisor and I discussed each of my client's progress every week.   1 2 3 4 5 6 7

My supervisor and I reviewed audiotapes.   1 2 3 4 5 6 7

My supervisor and I reviewed videotapes.   1 2 3 4 5 6 7

My supervisor and I participated in live supervision.   1 2 3 4 5 6 7

My supervisor focused on the content of the counseling session.   1 2 3 4 5 6 7

My supervisor focused on the process of the counseling session.   1 2 3 4 5 6 7

My supervisor helped me develop hypotheses about client behavior.   1 2 3 4 5 6 7

My supervisor modeled specific interventions.   1 2 3 4 5 6 7

Evaluation Process

During our initial supervisory session, I was provided with a copy of the formal evaluation instrument.   1 2 3 4 5 6 7

My supervisor initiated helpful conversations about the strengths in my counseling skills.   1 2 3 4 5 6 7

My supervisor initiated helpful conversations about areas of growth needed in my counseling skills.   1 2 3 4 5 6 7

I received written feedback or evaluation on a regular basis.   1 2 3 4 5 6 7

My supervisor would refer me for remedial assistance to overcome personal or professional limitations.   1 2 3 4 5 6 7

I received verbal summative evaluation during the final supervisory session.   1 2 3 4 5 6 7

I received a written summative evaluation during the final supervisory session.   1 2 3 4 5 6 7

Source: M.A. Giordano, M.K. Altekruse, and C.W. Kern. Supervisee's Bill of Rights. (2000). Reprinted with permission.

Yontef (1997) makes the point that supervisees have the responsibility for bringing into supervision sessions any difficulties they are encountering and defining what they need from their supervisor. Likewise, supervisors have responsibilities, some of which include giving clear and honest feedback, suggestions, and evaluation. In supervision the focus is on improving the supervisee's functioning as a counselor and promoting the growth of the supervisee's clients.

ASSISTING SUPERVISEES IN TAKING AN ACTIVE ROLE IN FIELDWORK EXPERIENCES

In addition to assisting supervisees to get the most from their supervision, we encourage you, as a supervisor, to discuss with your supervisees practical strategies that will increase their chances of deriving the maximum benefit from their fieldwork and internship experiences and the supervision that is a part of these applied experiences. Here are some practical tips you can suggest to your supervisees. Many of these tips have been adapted from Corey and Corey (2003, see especially Chapter 2). Box 2.5 provides a quick look at these tips for supervisees; now let's examine each in more detail.

Seek a variety of placements with a diverse range of client populations. If you think you want a career working with the elderly, for example, consider an internship with troubled adolescents. By working with diverse populations, you can experiment with your interests and develop new ones. If you focus strictly on the population or problem area you want as a specialization, you are likely to close off many rich avenues of learning and may also limit your possibilities of finding a job. Stretch your boundaries and discover where your talents lie. Through your field placements, you may learn what you do not want to do as well as what you would like to do.

Take courses and workshops that will prepare you for the type of work you will do. In your program you will probably be able to take elective courses in a variety of specialty areas. In addition, workshops can be a useful resource for staying on the cutting edge of new developments with special populations.

Fit into the agency, rather than trying to get the agency to fit you. Be open to learning from the staff and the clients who come to the agency. You can learn a good deal about an agency by being attentive and by talking with co-workers.

Learn as much as possible about the structure of the agency prior to your fieldwork. Ask about agency policies, about the way programs are administered, and about management of the staff. At some point, you may be involved in the administrative aspects of a program.

Recognize the limits of your training, and practice only within those boundaries. Put yourself in situations where you will be able to obtain super-

BOX 2.5 | PRACTICAL TIPS FOR GETTING THE MOST FROM YOUR FIELDWORK EXPERIENCE

 1. Seek a variety of placements with a diverse range of client populations
 2. Take courses and workshops that will prepare you for the type of work you will do.
 3. Fit into the agency rather than trying to get the agency to fit you.
 4. Learn as much as possible about the structure of the agency prior to your fieldwork.
 5. Recognize the limits of your training, and practice only within those boundaries.
 6. Be flexible in applying techniques and interventions to diverse client populations.
 7. Look for opportunities to learn, even in placements you do not particularly like.
 8. Learn how to use community resources and community support systems.
 9. Keep a journal and record your observations and personal reactions to your work.
10. Be open to trying new things.
11. Look for ways to apply your academic learning to your fieldwork.
12. Be prepared to adjust your expectations.
13. Treat your field placement like a job.
14. Think and act in a self-directed way.
15. Realize that you can be of assistance to clients who are different from you.
16. Do not allow your idealism to be eroded by others' negative attitudes.
17. Recognize that learning is never finished.
18. Be aware of the emotional and physical toll your work might have on you.
19. Recognize that you may be anxious about performing well.
20. Consider the merits of seeking personal therapy to explore issues that surface in your life as you begin working with clients.

vised experience. Regardless of your educational level, there is always more to learn. It is essential to learn the delicate balance between being overly confident and being plagued by self-doubts.

Be flexible in applying techniques and interventions to diverse client populations. Avoid falling into the trap of fitting your clients into one particular theory. Use theory as a means of helping you understand the behavior of your clients. Discuss your ideas in supervision sessions and clarify your goals and rationale for interventions.

Look for opportunities to learn, even in placements you do not particularly like. Do not write off your field placement as a waste of time. At least you are learning that working in a particular agency or with a specific clientele may not be what you want for a career. Determine what is not productive about the placement and what lessons you can learn for future situations. Think of ways to make your assignment as meaningful as possible rather than just getting through the experience. Remember, there will be difficulties at any site; use this experience as an opportunity to learn how to overcome obstacles.

Learn how to use community resources and community support systems. Draw on support systems by making connections within the community. You can do this by talking to other professionals in the field, by asking fellow students about their connections in the community, and by developing a network of contacts. This kind of networking can lead to a range of job opportunities.

Keep a journal and record your observations and personal reactions to your work. Your journal is an excellent way to stay focused on yourself as well as to keep track of what you are doing with clients. Rather than focusing on writing about the problems of your clients, strive to write about how you are being personally affected by the relationships with different clients and what lessons you are learning.

Be open to trying new things. Avoid setting yourself up by thinking that if you do not succeed perfectly in a new endeavor you are a dismal failure. Give yourself room to learn by doing, at the same time gaining supervised experience.

Look for ways to apply your academic learning to your fieldwork. Academic content comes to life when you are able to put it into action. Find ways to work cooperatively with others at your placement site and to combine your talents with theirs.

Be prepared to adjust your expectations. Do not expect the staff in an agency to give you responsibility for providing services to clients before they have a chance to know you. You will probably start your fieldwork in an observing role. Later you may sit in on a counseling group, for example, and function as a co-leader.

Treat your field placement like a job. Approach fieldwork in much the same way as you would if you were employed by the agency. Demonstrate responsibility, be on time for your appointments and meetings, follow through with your commitments, and strive to do your best. Although you may be in an unpaid placement, this does not mean you can be irresponsible on the job. Often an unpaid internship can turn into a paid position. At the least, you will be looking to your supervisors at your placement for letters of recommendation for employment.

Think and act in a self-directed way. Involve yourself in a variety of activities. If you merely wait for a supervisor or other agency staff workers to take the initiative and give you meaningful assignments, you may be less than satisfied with your placement. Look for opportunities, propose your ideas, and offer your assistance.

Realize that you can be of assistance to clients who are different from you. Some supervisees believe that to help a person they must have had the same life experience. Thus, a young male counselor may doubt his capacity to effectively counsel an elderly woman who has lost her husband and is struggling to find meaning in her life. A trainee may doubt that she can work with a client of a different race. Or a trainee who has not experienced trauma may wonder about her ability to empathize with clients who have had pain in their lives. There is value in drawing on your own life experience when working with clients who differ from you in a number of respects. Although you may not have had the same problem, it is very possible that you can identify with the feelings of loneliness or rejection of your client. It is more important to be able to understand the client's world than to have had the identical problem.

Do not allow your idealism to be eroded by others' negative attitudes. If you find yourself in an environment where your supervisor, peers, and colleagues have negative attitudes, recognize that you do not have to "go along to get along." Although you may experience feelings of discouragement at times, find a safe place where you can talk about your disillusionment and look for what you *can* do rather than focusing on all that you cannot do. A practicum seminar may offer the ideal setting to discuss your concerns. Granted, it is often risky to voice your dissatisfaction with your fieldwork placement and your supervision, but if you remain silent you are really contributing to the problem. Take the risk of being willing to express your thoughts and feelings about a situation.

Recognize that learning is never finished. More important than knowing how to work with a specific population or a specific problem is having a general background of knowledge and skills and being open to acquiring more specific abilities. As part of your fieldwork or internship placement, you will usually receive on-the-job training and supervision. Learn from co-workers and supervisors and apply that learning in working with clients.

Be aware of the emotional and physical toll your work may have on you. Certain aspects of your life that you have not been willing to look at may be opened up as you get involved with clients. If you want to work with people who have a range of human problems, be ready to deal with your own life and what might surface for you.

Recognize that you may be anxious about performing well. You may be afraid of making mistakes and be concerned about how your supervisor will view your clinical abilities. As a student or intern, you are in the placement to learn and are not expected to know everything. Do not be afraid to say "I don't know." If you find that your anxiety level becomes immobilizing, seek counseling or talk with your supervisor for guidance.

Consider the merits of seeking personal therapy to explore issues that surface in your life as you begin working with clients. Not only can your experience in therapy be a source of personal growth, but you can learn much about how counseling works by being a participant in this process. In your supervision sessions, you may identify some unresolved personal issues or areas of countertransference that will not be able to be dealt with in supervision itself. Personal therapy can be an excellent supplement to your supervision. As a therapy client, you can also explore your self-doubts, perfectionistic tendencies, feelings that are triggered by working with certain clients, and anxieties pertaining to being a trainee.

There are many different ways to maximize your fieldwork experiences. Jamie Bludworth, a doctoral student in counseling psychology, shared his thoughts on how to get the most benefit from supervised fieldwork experiences. You can read about this in the Voices from the Field feature.

Jamie emphasizes the importance of taking an active role in preparing for supervision sessions. What are your reactions to his suggestions? It is clear that Jamie is an active student and an assertive supervisee. He is motivated to get the most from his internships, and he is willing to put himself forward in achieving this goal. His account illustrates the importance of taking an active and assertive role in your supervision.

SUMMARY

The roles of the supervisor are numerous and varied, and the responsibility of the supervisor focuses not only on helping the supervisee grow and learn but also on protecting clients and the profession. Supervision is unlike any other task most clinicians perform. It is a composite of playing many roles and serving several functions simultaneously. The roles and responsibilities of the supervisor vary depending on the supervisor, the supervisee, the setting, the client, and the relevant ethics and legal codes. Clinical supervisors typically function in multiple roles with their supervisees, and self-monitoring of those roles and boundaries is essential.

Supervision can be a rewarding task for a clinician if the supervisor is knowledgeable and skilled in the concepts and methods of supervision. It is important that supervisors find the balance between assuming their roles and responsibilities fully and becoming overwhelmed by the magnitude of those responsibilities.

Supervisors are legally and ethically responsible for the actions of their trainees and are expected to have some knowledge of every case with which their supervisees are working under their supervision. A key obligation of supervisors is to become knowledgeable of the variety of multicultural differences among supervisors, supervisees, and their clients and to address these differences in supervision.

This chapter has emphasized the importance of the supervisor providing supervisees with adequate information about the supervision process so that they can assume a role in establishing goals and the means to achieve these goals in supervision. Informed consent in supervision is as important as informed consent in the client–therapist relationship. Supervisees will profit more from supervision if supervisors make a concerted effort to teach them specific ways to involve themselves as active participants in the supervisory relationship.

VOICES FROM THE FIELD

Jamie Bludworth

Even though I learned a great deal through the difficulties I experienced in my first supervision group, I believe I could have been better prepared by my instructors to utilize supervision effectively. When supervision was discussed in class, it seemed to me like a mysterious process wherein an experienced practitioner would provide answers and guidance for trainees who were struggling to make sense of their clients. It was described in generalities and then only briefly.

The various roles that a supervisor might assume were never revealed to me. I think it is important for the supervisee to be aware of the many and varied roles a supervisor may be required to assume. Is my supervisor interacting with me as a teacher? A consultant? A counselor? An advocate? How will that role influence the choice of material I bring to our sessions? An awareness of the many supervisory roles is paramount to trainees taking a more collaborative stance toward their supervision, allowing them to better assist supervisors in the creation of an experience that is satisfying for all concerned.

Beyond a cursory knowledge of supervision as a concept, I have found it very helpful to ask my supervisors at our first meeting to describe the ways in which they see their role as a supervisor. What will be our focus? Will we primarily examine client issues from a clinical perspective? Or will we primarily explore the ways in which the counseling process is impacting me as a person and a professional? Do they prefer a particular theoretical perspective? I have, to date, worked with nine different supervisors, and not one has voluntarily disclosed this information. I have always had to ask. What's more, only one supervisor has asked me what I was hoping to get from our sessions together.

It has been of fundamental importance for me to continually define what I want from supervision (not only at the outset, but on a session-by-session basis). It has been crucial for me to prepare for each supervision session beforehand, coming in with examples of my work and clear questions relating to those examples. I have also found it very helpful to ask my supervisors the rationale behind the suggestions and answers that they provide.

Being prepared for supervision comprises understanding what the process might demand of both you and your supervisor. Being prepared also means being willing to engage the process in a way that is meaningful. Sometimes that means asking difficult questions of yourself as well as your supervisor.

SUGGESTED ACTIVITIES

1. Three styles of supervision are described in the following examples. After reading each case, respond to these questions:

   - What are the roles chosen by each of the supervisors?
   - What are the legal and ethical ramifications as they apply to roles and responsibilities?

- How would you respond to the different styles of supervision?
- Which style most closely fits with your own?
- What are the elements of the supervisory relationship in each situation, and how does the relationship help or hinder the supervision?

a. Dr. Snyder, a licensed clinical social worker, believes her role as supervisor is to provide a great deal of monitoring and direction for her supervisees. She believes a social work trainee should have few independent clinical responsibilities and should have direct clinical supervision at all times. She devotes a great deal of time and energy to her supervisees and has them follow her and observe her leading groups, participating in team meetings, and conducting case conferences. Her trainees benefit from seeing her at work but do not develop clinical competencies as a result of doing the work on their own. Many of the social work trainees under Dr. Snyder's supervision come away from the training experience feeling no more confident in their clinical abilities than when they began the training.

b. Ms. Lee meets weekly with her supervisees and has clearly defined goals for the supervisory relationship. She gives her supervisees her cellular phone number so they can contact her whenever needed. She gives feedback to her supervisees on a regular basis and has a reputation for being direct if not somewhat critical of her supervisees' work. Ms. Lee is a very competent clinician. She typically tells her supervisees how to work with their clients, and her supervisees usually find her advice very helpful. Some of her supervisees think Ms. Lee could show more warmth and concern for her supervisees; however, most trainees feel that they benefit greatly from clinical work with her.

c. Mr. Adams is a supervisor who sees the supervisee as a junior colleague who should be able to function rather independently. After all, the supervisee will be out functioning independently in the next year. Mr. Adams learned through the old "sink or swim" method, and he believes in this method of supervision because that model worked out quite well for him as a trainee. His method of supervision is to allow the trainee to do his or her work and to seek his consultation only when the trainee needs assistance. Most trainees under Mr. Adams's supervision like him a great deal, but many feel they would like more structure and direction in their work experience.

2. In small groups, draw a composite picture of what the competent supervisor looks like in each of the major roles. Use your imagination and don't worry about artistic ability. Have each small group share the results with the larger group and discuss how they chose which roles to describe.

3. Break into small groups and discuss these questions:

- If you had to pick the three most important roles that supervisors serve, what would they be and why?

- In what instance would it be appropriate for a supervisor to take on the role of therapist for the supervisee?
- How could a supervisor become knowledgeable of all of the supervisee's clients in a reasonable way?
- What roles would you most like to serve as a supervisor? Which roles would you least like to assume? Which would be the most challenging for you? In what ways?

4. Access the Web site for this text at http://info.wadsworth.com/haynes, and complete the self-assessment inventory. Additional contributor perspectives and other activities specific to this chapter are also available to you through this Web site.

3 CHAPTER THE SUPERVISORY RELATIONSHIP

FOCUS QUESTIONS

1. What importance do you place on the relationship between the supervisor and the supervisee? As a supervisor, how will you develop the relationship into one of mutual trust and respect?
2. How important to you is the interpersonal aspect of supervision? Is a close interpersonal relationship essential for effective supervision to occur?
3. What are some ways you may have displayed resistance as a supervisee? As a supervisor, what can you learn from this and apply to your work with reluctant supervisees?
4. Have you ever experienced a serious conflict with a supervisor? Did you do anything about that? How did your supervisor react? As a supervisor, how would you like to handle conflicts with supervisees?
5. If your supervisee experiences client failures in therapy, how will you assist your supervisee in dealing with this in supervision?

INTRODUCTION

This chapter looks at several segments of the supervisory relationship. Personal and interpersonal issues in supervision addressed include power and authority in the supervisory relationship, the role of a supervisee's values, issues of trust between trainees and their supervisors, and conflicts between the supervisor and supervisee. We also address how supervisors might teach their supervisees to effectively deal with a range of challenges, such as: dealing with doubts and fears, recognizing personal needs, recognizing countertransference, and understanding diverse value systems of clients. Challenges for supervisors are also examined, including helping supervisees deal with their anxiety and assisting supervisees in understanding the meaning of failures with their clients.

PERSONAL AND INTERPERSONAL ISSUES IN SUPERVISION

The relationship between the supervisor and supervisee is the foundation for the work that will occur in supervision. There are common denominators between the counseling process and the supervision process. One similarity is the paramount importance of the relationship in both supervision and counseling. Of course, supervision is an educative process that involves learning specific knowledge and skills on the supervisee's part. However, for this learning to occur, a working relationship between supervisor and supervisee is essential (Lambers, 2000; Yontef, 1997).

Considerable research has been conducted on the supervisory relationship and the process of supervision. From an empirical base and practical knowledge, Holloway (1999) has identified three essential components of the supervisory relationship: (1) the interpersonal structure of the relationship, including the dimensions of power and involvement; (2) the phases of the relationship; and (3) the supervisory contract, consisting of the establishment of a set of expectations for the tasks and functions of supervision.

Holloway (1995) conceptualizes the supervisory relationship by looking at it from a contextual perspective. Her model describes three phases of the supervisory relationship. During the *early phase* of the relationship, the tasks are clarifying the nature of the relationship, developing ways to work collaboratively and effectively in supervision, designing a supervision contract, selecting supportive teaching interventions, developing competencies, and designing treatment plans. At the *mature phase,* the emphasis is on increasing the individual nature of the relationship and promoting social bonding. Behavior becomes less role bound, trainees develop skills of case conceptualization and increase their level of self-confidence, and personal issues are explored as they relate to professional performance. The *termination phase* reflects a greater collaborative working structure. Trainees understand the linkage between theory and practice more fully, and there is less need for direction from the supervisor. This is the time for a summative evaluation process, including a discussion of the meaning of termination and the feelings and thoughts associated with it. Time is also allocated for discussion of future professional development and goals.

A successful supervisory relationship provides opportunities for trainees to initiate a discussion of problems they are experiencing with their clients and to acquire knowledge and sharpen therapeutic skills. In this section, we address elements of the supervisory relationship and its importance to the outcomes of the supervisory process.

Supervisor–Supervisee Relationship

Most practitioners agree that a positive and productive relationship between supervisor and supervisee is essential if supervision is to be effective (Bernard & Goodyear, 1998; Corey, Corey, & Callanan, 2003; Henderson, Cawyer, & Watkins, 1999; Kaiser, 1997; Yontef, 1997). Corey, Corey, and Callanan (2003) put it this way:

> We believe that the most important element in the supervisory process is the kind of person the supervisor is. The methods and techniques supervisors use are more likely to be helpful if an effective and collaborative working relationship with supervisees has been established. (p. 323)

Despite the importance given to the role of the relationship in supervision, the relationship has received little attention in research studies (Kaiser, 1997).

In writing about supervision from a Gestalt therapy perspective, Yontef (1997) affirms that growth in supervision, like growth in the psychotherapeutic relationship, occurs through the medium of relationship. Yontef emphasizes that it is the supervisor's responsibility to develop an atmosphere conducive to learning. This climate includes acceptance of the person of the supervisee, even at those times when it is necessary to work with flaws and weaknesses. For Yontef, a productive learning environment is one in which the supervisee experiences a sense of safety and being cared for and feels acceptance as a person and as a professional. The Gestalt therapy supervisor is present as a person, not just as an authority figure, and encourages the development of a creative professional.

Can supervision be effective in the absence of a positive and productive supervisor–supervisee relationship? Yes, but it may not be as successful. The supervisory relationship is not an all or nothing matter, but it is likely that the greater the level of trust, openness, and mutual respect, the greater the degree to which the supervision will be effective.

Essential elements of the supervisor–supervisee relationship include establishing trust, encouraging self-disclosure, identifying transference and countertransference, examining diversity issues, and establishing appropriate boundaries.

Trust   Trust is best defined as being able to rely on another with a certain sense of predictability. In everyday relationships, trust takes time to develop. People must learn that they can rely on how others will act and react. In the supervisory relationship, trust is essential because both supervisor and supervisee need to be honest with each other. Kaiser (1997) points out that respect and safety are often listed as important elements in the supervisory relationship, and certainly these are two important factors in establishing trust. Respect is a demonstration of the supervisor's esteem for the supervisee, and safety refers to the supervisee's freedom to make interventions that may fail and to take risks without fear of an excessively judgmental response from the supervisor (Kaiser 1997). The supervisory process is most productive when the supervisory relationship is characterized by an atmosphere of mutual trust. Thus, supervisors would do well to discuss with supervisees what they both can do to create a trusting supervisory relationship. Supervisors might encourage their supervisees to bring up any concerns they have about trust during the supervisory sessions. Of course, how a supervisor responds when supervisees disclose their anxieties pertaining to trust would determine their readiness to initiate such a discussion in the future.

Self-disclosure   Self-disclosure refers to the willingness of the supervisor and supervisee to be open to and discuss all issues that may arise in the supervisory relationship. For the supervisor, self-disclosure of personal issues and experiences should occur only as it provides something constructive for the supervisee regarding the topic at hand. The purpose of the supervisory session is not to provide an arena for supervisors to resolve personal issues or vent complaints about their job. The focus should be on the supervisee. Generally, the more free supervisees are to self-disclose thoughts, fears, hopes, and expectations regarding the work they are doing, the more valuable the supervisory sessions will be. This level of openness is built on a foundation of trust.

Self-disclosure by the supervisor can be beneficial if done in a timely and appropriate manner. In their study of supervisory style and its relation to the supervisory working alliance and supervisor self-disclosure, Ladany, Walker, and Melincoff (2001) conclude that supervisors' interpersonal supervisory style can affect their ability to mutually agree on goals and tasks with their supervisees. They suggest that supervisors consider incorporating self-disclosure into their supervisory style as a method for building an emotional bond and a working alliance with their supervisees. It might well be that supervisors' self-disclosure facilitates supervisees' self-disclosure.

Transference and Countertransference   Transference is a psychodynamic term defined as the client's unconscious shifting to the therapist of feelings and fantasies, both positive and negative, that are displacements from reactions to significant others from the client's past (Corey, 2001b). In the supervisory relationship, a supervisee may transfer those feelings and fantasies to the supervisor. It is not uncommon for supervisees to begin to idealize their supervisor as a result of the help and support that they receive and because of their own feelings of insecurity and incompetence. The role of the supervisor in this instance is to be aware of this transference and to assist the supervisee in developing his or her own sense of competence and problem-solving ability. It would be a mistake, in our opinion, to challenge the supervisee directly and forcefully about his or her transference issues.

A trusting climate and encouragement by the supervisor will enable supervisees to discuss any reactions they may have that affect their ability to be open during supervisory sessions. For example, a supervisee may be anxious about "doing well" for the supervisor, and this anxiety can result in the supervisee carefully monitoring and silently rehearsing what he or she says during supervision sessions. If this supervisee takes the risk of disclosing his or her need to be seen in a positive light by the supervisor, the supervisee has already taken a significant step toward becoming more authentic in the supervisor's presence. Transference is not unusual in this very complex relationship, and it may provide a valuable learning experience for the supervisee.

Countertransference refers to the reactions therapists have toward their clients that are likely to interfere with objectivity (Corey, 2001b). Unresolved personal issues, and sometimes even problem areas that you have worked through, can be triggered through interactions with certain clients, and this same process may also be triggered with supervisees. In the supervisory relationship, countertransference involves the feelings and reactions that the supervisor has regarding the supervisee.

Countertransference on the part of the supervisor is not uncommon. Lower (1972) suggests that a supervisor's countertransference might be categorized in one of four areas: (1) general personality characteristics, (2) inner conflicts reactivated by the supervision situation, (3) countertransference reactions to the individual supervisee, and (4) countertransference reactions to the supervisee's transference. Any number of countertransference feelings toward the supervisee are possible, but two common ones are an intense need to help and rescue the supervisee or a dislike of the supervisee.

It is critical for the supervisor to be self-aware, identifying any countertransference that may arise and understanding how it is affecting the supervisory relationship. If the supervisor has a need to discuss these feelings, we recommend consultation with colleagues or consultants rather than with the supervisee. Talking about the supervisor's countertransference issues may be overwhelming for the supervisee. The supervisee has plenty to deal with in learning to become a competent clinician. After discussing countertransference reactions with a colleague, however, it may be appropriate and useful for the supervisor to share and explore some aspects of his or her reactions with the supervisee.

To discover how one licensed clinical social worker who supervises undergraduate students in a human services program and interns in a community agency approaches supervision, read the Voices from the Field on page 60.

Can you be an effective supervisor when working with an individual you don't like? This is very similar to the question of whether one can counsel a client one does not like. The challenge to the supervisor is not to like the supervisee but to assist him or her in becoming a competent clinician and to protect the welfare of the clients with whom the supervisee is working. We think supervisors can work effectively with supervisees they do not like, but supervisors must be aware of those feelings and be willing to examine the reasons for their feelings. They must be aware of how their feelings affect the supervisory relationship and take action to ensure that this does not compromise their supervisory responsibilities.

Differences between a supervisor and a supervisee vary, and a discussion of these differences can be a basic part of the supervision sessions. Most codes of ethics call for supervisors to demonstrate knowledge of individual differences with respect to age, gender, race, ethnicity, culture, sexual orientation, and disability. Furthermore, supervisors need to understand how these contextual factors influence supervisory relationships.

Diversity Issues   Holloway (1999), a proponent of the contextual approach to supervision, has summarized the research that deals with the characteristics of the supervisee that are likely to influence the supervisory relationship. Holloway identifies these factors as being particularly important: the trainee's cultural experience, gender, cognitive and ego development, professional identity, experience level in counseling, theoretical orientation to counseling, and self-presentation. Each of these dimensions needs to be addressed in supervisory relationships to lay the foundation for effective learning within the supervision setting.

Perhaps the best way for supervisors to teach their supervisees a respect for the role that diversity plays in the counseling relationship is for supervisors to take the initiative in making supervision a multicultural experience. Multicultural supervision encompasses a broad definition of culture that includes race, ethnicity, socioeconomic status, sexual orientation, religion, gender, and age (Fukuyama, 1994). Because of the power dynamics inherent

VOICES FROM THE FIELD

Randy Alle-Corliss, M.S.W., L.C.S.W.

Being an effective supervisor requires that I be willing to ongoingly examine my feelings, thoughts, and actions in relation to my interns. I have found that this is not an easy process and that I can be challenged by those students who have unfinished business in their lives that can be triggered by the dynamics of the supervisor–supervisee relationship. I continue to struggle to find the most assertive ways to directly deal with students, co-workers, and interns who consciously or unconsciously find ways to interfere with the process of learning that takes place in the supervisory relationship. I have found that it is essential that I acknowledge their feelings without becoming defensive yet, at the same time, find ways to provide them with honest feedback on their behaviors.

in the supervisory relationship, Priest (1994) believes it is the supervisor's responsibility to serve as the catalyst for facilitating discussions about diversity issues. He points out that too often supervisors emphasize client similarities and minimize racial and cultural differences. If trainees do not understand the cultural context in which their clients live, Priest believes the chances are increased that trainees will not effectively work with their clients.

There is a price to be paid for ignoring racial and ethnic factors in supervision. If supervisors do not address these factors as they become relevant, this will certainly weaken the trust level on the part of supervisees. Cook (1994) calls for routinely including discussions of racial identity attitudes as part of both therapy and supervisory relationships. The supervisor's recognition of racial issues can serve as a model for supervisees in their counseling relationships. Reflecting on racial interactions in supervision offers a cognitive framework for supervisees to generalize to their counseling practices. Cook suggests that supervisors might raise questions such as "When did you notice the client's race?" "How did this affect you?" and "What did you do in response to the client's race?"

Supervisors can do a great deal to create an open climate that will foster honesty in the supervisory relationship. To do so, however, it is essential that they possess specific multicultural competencies. Regardless of the specific aspect of diversity that is characteristic of a supervisory relationship, any factor that influences the interpersonal relationship should be a topic of discussion. The matter of multicultural competencies is dealt with in considerable detail in Chapter 6.

Appropriate Boundaries   Extending the boundary beyond supervision can easily complicate the supervisory relationship. It is not uncommon to enjoy the collegiality of the supervisory relationship, to become friendly with a supervisee, and to want to extend the relationship beyond the sessions. How far can the boundary be extended while the relationship remains ethical and professional? Supervisors need to think about the ramifications whenever they consider extending the boundaries of the supervisory relationship. Supervisors must take full responsibility for determining the limits of the relationship and take action when they believe the boundaries are becoming less clear or when expanding the boundaries is adversely affecting the supervisory task. We suggest that supervisors err on the side of conservatism when considering extending those boundaries. This topic is covered in detail in Chapter 7.

Power and Authority

Power is the ability to influence or control others, whereas *authority* is the right to do so (Kadushin, 1992, p. 84). The supervisory relationship by definition has a built-in power differential—the supervisor is the authority in the relationship. Person-centered and feminist models of supervision are based on the assumption that supervisors will do what they can to minimize the power differential and to establish a collaborative relationship. Supervisors continually evaluate the work of the supervisee and provide that evaluative information to licensing boards, prospective employers, and other requestors long after the supervisory relationship has ended. Because the supervisee has relatively less power in the supervisory relationship, supervisors are responsible to clearly inform their supervisees of the evaluative structure of the relationship, the expectancies and goals for supervision, the criteria for evaluation, and the limits of confidentiality in supervision (Holloway, 1999).

Kaiser (1997) has investigated the role of power and authority in the supervisory relationship and concludes that there is disagreement about whether the hierarchical nature of the supervisory relationship should be emphasized or minimized. The subject of power sharing in the supervisory relationship is discussed further in Chapter 5 under the feminist model of supervision.

Parallel Process

Interactions between supervisor and supervisee may offer insights into the way the supervisee relates to clients. This idea, called *parallel process*, has been explored by Loganbill, Hardy, and Delworth (1982) and Stoltenberg and Delworth (1987). Because certain aspects of the relationship between the supervisee and his or her client may be paralleled in the supervisory relationship, it is useful for supervisors and supervisees to pay attention to and explore the various forms of the parallel process in supervision. In *The Teaching and Learning of Psychotherapy*, Ekstein and Wallerstein (1972) devote a chapter to the subject of parallel process in supervision. They describe parallel process as the supervisee's interaction with the supervisor that frequently parallels the client's behavior with the supervisee in the role of counselor. They emphasize the personal development aspects as being a vital component of the supervisory process. For Ekstein and Wallerstein, although supervision is not the same as psychotherapy, a proper focus of supervision is to deal with the supervisee's emotional reactions and experiences so that the supervisee will be able to be fully present in his or her therapeutic work with clients. McNeill and Worthen (1989) also believe the parallel process in psychotherapy supervision in its multiplicity of forms can be the focus for potent and impactful interventions within the supervisory relationship. They suggest that supervisors pay close attention to the process to facilitate effective supervision as well as to encourage the personal and professional growth of supervisees.

One example of how parallel process can operate relates to a trainee's fear of conflict in her personal life. As a supervisee, Adriana may make interventions with her clients to avoid or quickly resolve any conflicts that may be emerging between her clients and herself. Likewise, she might well be quick to agree with her supervisor on all matters in the hopes that she will be able to head off any potential conflicts. If either Adriana or her supervisor recognizes this pattern and brings it into the supervision sessions for exploration, Adriana will likely be able to benefit. She can use these personal insights to become a more effective counselor. Later in this chapter we address the topic of dealing with conflicts in the supervisory relationship in more detail.

It is important that the supervisor be aware of how important the supervisor–supervisee relationship is and how these processes affect what is going on in supervisory sessions: "The supervisory relationship is not just something that needs to be operating well for treatment skills to be taught; rather, it interacts in a dynamic way with the teaching of those skills" (Kaiser, 1997, p. 5).

Personhood

Earlier in this chapter we explained how paying attention to diversity issues can strengthen the supervisory relationship. We again emphasize the importance of supervisors being aware of the many personal variables that may affect the supervisory relationship. These include values, attitudes, beliefs, age, gender, ethnicity, and spirituality of both the supervisee and the supervisor. The impact of the similarities and differences between the supervisor and supervisee can be explored in supervision. For example, although supervisors have an ethical responsibility to establish an environment that will help supervisees to grow both personally and professionally, one study indicates that female supervisees were not always given the same opportunities for growth as male supervisees (Granello, Beamish, & Davis, 1997). Granello and colleagues caution about generalizing from their study, but it suggests the importance of supervisors being aware of and sensitive to the possibility of gender bias in supervisory relationships.

As supervisors, just as with counselors and therapists, values, attitudes, and beliefs affect the supervision that we provide. Even though supervisors may believe they are able to be objective and not impose their values on the supervisee, their values can and probably will come through in many subtle ways. This is illustrated in Case 3.1.

CASE 3.1 | CAROL

Carol, a marriage and family counselor, is supervising Michaela, a marriage and family counselor in training. Michaela is talking with Carol about a case in which the parents feel their 2- and 4-year-old children are out of control, yet the parents seem unable to set limits or enforce discipline in the household. Carol forcefully lectures Michaela on the need for parents to be firm disciplinarians in this era where kids are developing a sense of entitlement at an early age.

Following the supervision session, Michaela has another counseling session with the parents. Michaela emphasizes the need for the parents to regain control of their children. She begins brainstorming with them how they might go about setting clearer limits, being more consistent in following through to enforce those limits, and providing more reinforcement when the children do act appropriately. The parents are appreciative of the direction provided but still are puzzled about whether the new approach will work. Michaela was pleased that she was able to take direction from her supervisor while adapting Carol's suggestions to fit her own counseling style and the needs of the parents.

What do you think of Carol's method of providing supervision? If you believe something strongly, should you make that belief known to your supervisee? How would you respond if you were Michaela? If you were Carol and suddenly realized you were imposing your values, how would you proceed from there?

Some of the values that may affect the supervisory process come from personal beliefs about religion, abortion, marriage and divorce, affectional orientation, parenting, spirituality, the change process, suicide, and end-of-life decisions. Value-free supervision is virtually impossible. The key for supervisors is to be aware of their own values and attitudes and how they affect the supervision provided. It is not necessary for the supervisor and supervisee to have similar attitudes and beliefs for supervision to be effective. But the established supervisor–supervisee relationship can facilitate dialogue about similarities and differences as they come into play. This also becomes an opportunity for the supervisor to model the exploration of values in a way that helps supervisees learn how to do the same with their clients.

How should value conflicts between the supervisor and the supervisee be resolved? Some supervisors think they can work with any supervisee regardless of value differences that might occur. Others are too quick to discontinue supervision when differences occur and refer the supervisee to another supervisor. Ultimately, most value differences in supervision can be worked on within the supervisory relationship. To handle value conflicts with supervisees, supervisors need to be aware of their own values and know when and how they affect the supervisory relationship. Differences need to be discussed openly and frankly, identifying what the conflicts are and how they might affect the supervisory work. If it is determined that the value conflict will create an impasse in the supervisory relationship, plans should be made to seek a mediator or to refer the supervisee to another supervisor. Consideration also should be made for continuity of supervision for client welfare. We hope the idea for a referral could be initiated by either the supervisor or the supervisee.

In our experience, we have seen a range of competence among supervisors. The outstanding ones pride themselves on self-awareness, are open to feedback from colleagues and supervisees, and show a sense of humility, recognizing that there is always something to be learned from a situation. Their supervisees are active members of the problem-solving team and usually exude a sense of confidence and calmness that they have developed through supervision.

Less effective supervisors tend to be rigid, closed to feedback, act as if they have all the answers, and use supervision as a forum to display their knowledge. These less effective supervisors tend to emphasize what they have to offer rather than assisting their supervisees in learning how to deal effectively with a range of problems they may encounter with a variety of clients. This often plants the seeds for conflict between their supervisees and themselves.

A positive and productive relationship is an important part of effective supervision. Box 3.1 provides some practical tips for establishing a good working relationship. Supervision can be effective even if the supervisory relationship is not ideal, but both the supervisor and the supervisee may need to work harder to ensure that the goals of supervision are accomplished. The next section looks at some ways supervision can be enhanced or hindered.

CHARACTERISTICS THAT FACILITATE OR HINDER
THE SUPERVISION PROCESS

A variety of characteristics associated with the supervisor–supervisee relationship can influence the outcomes of the supervision process. Lowry (2001) conducted a study of the characteristics of supervisors and supervisees that both facilitate and hinder successful supervision, gathering information from practicing psychologists who are or have been supervisors regarding their own supervisory experiences (positive and negative). Lowry also questioned supervisors about trainee characteristics they believed facilitated or hindered the supervisory process. The discussion that follows summarizes these characteristics.

Supervisor Characteristics

Participants in Lowry's study perceived the following supervisor characteristics and factors as most important to foster a positive supervisory experience (in descending order): good clinical skills/knowledge, an accepting

BOX 3.1	TIPS FOR SUPERVISORS

Establishing a Healthy, Productive Relationship with Supervisees

- Treat supervisees with respect; be open and honest about what you do and do not know.
- Work at developing a spirit of mutual trust and collaboration.
- Listen diligently to what supervisees are both saying and not saying, and try to tune into their fears, struggles, and hopes.
- Have a clear understanding of the purpose and the limits of the supervisory relationship.
- Be available, especially by being fully present during the supervisory session and by making sure that this is "protected time" that is free from interruptions.
- Be willing to seek consultation when you are unfamiliar with the topic under discussion.
- Be clear on the boundaries of the relationship.

Guarding Against Imposition of Your Values

- Work on having a clear understanding of your values, beliefs, and attitudes regarding the range of typical issues that come up in supervision.
- Discuss with your supervisees their values and beliefs, and share yours as well.
- Talk openly about how values and beliefs affect the supervisory relationship and supervisees' work.
- Initiate discussions with supervisees regarding their values about marriage and divorce, homosexuality, spirituality, suicide, child-rearing, and violence. Share your ideas if it seems that it will help supervisees and the supervisory relationship.

Working with Multicultural Issues

- Help supervisees assess what they need to learn about multicultural issues.
- Have frequent discussions with supervisees about multicultural issues.
- Instill a sense of respect and acceptance of multicultural issues in counseling by modeling that respect and acceptance yourself.
- Expand your own knowledge by attending workshops and by reading.

---

supervisory climate, a desire to train/investment in supervision, matching the supervisee's level of development, providing constructive feedback, being empathetic, being flexible and available, possessing good relationship skills, and being an experienced clinician.

Conversely, some supervisor characteristics and factors were thought to have an adverse impact on the supervisory relationship (in descending order): being judgmental or overly critical, being personally or theoretically rigid, not being committed to the supervisory process, being unavailable to the supervisee, having limited clinical knowledge and skills, being unethical or demonstrating poor boundaries, and being too self-focused. Other factors mentioned included a supervisor's lack of compassion, arrogance, the inability to provide helpful feedback, lack of preparation for supervision, and lack of supervisory experience.

Supervisee Characteristics

Characteristics of supervisees or factors that were rated as helpful in promoting a positive supervisory experience included (in descending order) a desire to learn and improve, being nondefensive and open to feedback, general openness and flexibility, possessing knowledge and good clinical skills, intelligence, being responsible and prepared for supervision, and a willingness to take initiative and risks. Other factors rated as promoting effective supervision were good interpersonal and communication skills on the part of the supervisee; the ability to be empathetic, self-acceptance, insight, genuineness, the ability to ask questions, a focus on the client, and maturity.

Characteristics of supervisees or factors that were rated as impediments to successful supervision included a lack of openness and fear of evaluation, personal rigidity, defensiveness, arrogance and a perception that they are all-knowing, lack of motivation or interest in supervision or clinical work, lack of intelligence, psychopathology, and immaturity. Other supervisee factors perceived to hinder supervision included a poor knowledge and skill base, poor interpersonal skills and boundaries, being unprepared or disorganized, a lack of personal insight, and passivity or dependency.

CONFLICTS BETWEEN SUPERVISOR AND SUPERVISEE

Conflicts are a natural part of all relationships. In most cases, conflicts can be resolved with listening, understanding, and working to clarify the ground rules about the relationship. When either or both parties in a conflict act as if they are right, the other is wrong, and the only solution is for the other party to change, the relationship usually takes a turn for the worse. The supervision relationship is unequal, with the supervisor possessing both power and authority. In this situation, conflicts can easily occur. Conflict, in itself, is not necessarily problematic. If conflicts are recognized and openly discussed in a respectful manner, both supervisors and supervisees can learn a great deal. In fact, working through a conflict can enhance the quality of the supervisory relationship.

Most supervisory relationships are healthy and productive, but some are characterized by unacknowledged conflict, discontent, and strife. Case 3.2 describes a supervisee who openly expresses her discontent with her supervisor.

Conflict in supervision is not uncommon, but it can be difficult to resolve because the problem may be due to different perceptions of the supervisory interaction. It is difficult to convince either person that his or her perception may be incorrect or distorted. Nevertheless, it is the task of the supervisor to attempt to resolve the differences. The first task is to delineate a clear understanding of the specific plan of action in cases where there are sharp differences between supervisee and supervisor. The supervisor can then return to the original contract that defines the nature of the supervisory relationship, the methods of supervision to be used, and the ground rules that define how they are going to work together. If clear ground rules are in place early in the super-

CASE 3.2 | TONY

Dr. Allen has been supervising Tony, a master's level social work intern working part-time in a university counseling center. Dr. Allen is a professor in the social work program and teaches the Clinical Interventions Seminar in which Tony is a student. In today's supervision session, Tony expresses dissatisfaction with the direction of the supervision of her work in the counseling center. Tony explains that she feels as though Dr. Allen simply tells her how to work with her clients without any discussion or input from her. To Tony, it seems like a one-way street. Tony believes she learns best through discussion and collaboration with a supervisor. Dr. Allen listens attentively but views Tony's dissatisfaction as "resistance to supervision" and sees Tony as not being open to supervision. Dr. Allen decides not to change his approach with Tony.

It took courage for Tony to offer critical feedback to her supervisor. Many supervisees are not as forthcoming about conflict with a supervisor because they do not want to challenge the supervisor, and they know that a supervisor has the ability, through evaluations and recommendations, to greatly affect their career. They find themselves suffering though the supervision until it is over and they can move on. Tony feels that she may have to make this decision too, but she wants to get the most out of her internship. She decides to try to think of another way to engage Dr. Allen and benefit from her internship under his supervision.

If you were the supervisor, how might you receive and respond to Tony's expression of dissatisfaction? What would you most want to say to Tony? Can you identify with Tony's concern that everything has to be done Dr. Allen's way? As the supervisor, how would you proceed to resolve this situation? How could you do so in a manner that would be a learning experience for Tony?

---

visory relationship, the solution to their differences may be resolved by reviewing them. For example, the contract may state that the supervision methods are largely teaching and evaluation of the clinical work of the supervisee. If this is the case, then Dr. Allen's approach (see Case 3.2 above) may be quite appropriate. If the methods are not clearly defined, then it is time to work together to develop a clearer definition regarding how they are going to work together. What appear to be personality clashes or conflicts often turn out to be a lack of clarity about the nature of the working relationship. Clarification should lead to a more productive work environment.

Another task is to ask how the supervisor and supervisee can work together to make their working relationship more satisfactory. When there is a conflict in a supervisory relationship, too often the tendency is to attribute blame to the other party. Our approach would be to ask each party to describe what the relationship would "look like" if it were working satisfactorily and to identify what would be needed to move it to that point. An open dialogue may lead to a discovery that both supervisor and supervisee have similar goals for supervision, yet each has a different idea about how to accomplish these goals. It might well be that the supervisor and the supervisee have never openly discussed their hopes and expectations for supervision and how to accomplish these goals.

It is a good practice for supervisors to seek consultation and supervision for themselves when conflicts are not resolved or when they find themselves experiencing conflicts with many of their supervisees. The ability to be open and to learn is key to being a successful supervisor.

Supervisors can take steps to enhance the supervisory relationship by demonstrating an understanding of the many challenges supervisees face. If supervisors recognize, appreciate, and understand the phenomenological world of supervisees, they are in a position to encourage supervisees to explore their struggles in working with clients and in making fullest use of the supervision sessions. Openness on the supervisor's part and a willingness to engage in frank discussions about the concerns of supervisees can deepen the supervisory relationship.

CHALLENGES FOR SUPERVISEES

Supervisees face many challenges in their supervision experience with you. These issues can be explored with supervisees as ways to maximize the supervision experience. Ask yourself this question: How might I prepare supervisees to best deal with the difficulties they are likely to encounter?

In this section we present several challenges for supervisees: dealing with doubts and fears, identifying unresolved personal problems, avoiding the role of problem solver, identifying countertransference, respecting the diverse value systems of clients, and challenging yourself. We also describe some problematic behavioral patterns of supervisees. If you apply this section to your own experiences as a supervisee, you will have a better sense of how you can assist supervisees in addressing challenges they encounter.

Take a few minutes to reflect on your own experience when you first began seeing clients and began working with a supervisor. What experiences do you most remember when you initially began to counsel others? What did you learn from these experiences? What was it like for you to be in supervision? What self-doubts did you have as a trainee? How did you deal with these self-doubts or concerns? Will these experiences help you to identify with the concerns supervisees may bring to supervision sessions with you?

Dealing with Doubts and Fears

In this section, we speak directly to the supervisee, yet many of these doubts and fears fit equally well for supervisors at various levels of development. As you read this material, we suggest that you engage in self-reflection to identify the ways in which you dealt with your doubts and fears as a supervisee and how you might facilitate a discussion on this matter with your supervisees. We hope that this information will help you work more effectively with your supervisees' concerns. Box 3.2 lists some common fears trainees face in clinical practice.

| BOX 3.2 | FEARS AND SELF-DOUBTS OF SUPERVISEES |

1. I am afraid I won't know enough to help those who seek my services.
2. Maybe I will actually make matters worse for a client by my lack of experience.
3. I am quite critical of myself and tend to demand perfection. No matter how well I do, there is still a nagging voice that tells me I could have done better.
4. When I look around at others, they all seem so confident. This makes me wonder if I have what it takes to make a difference in the lives of others.
5. Too often I compare my performance with others and tell myself that I just do not measure up.
6. Sometimes I worry that a person I am counseling will not like me and will confront me in an angry way.
7. It is very difficult for me to be fully present when I am counseling an individual because I am so concerned about what I will say or do next.
8. Whenever my supervisor is in the room I get so anxious because I am sure she will discover that I am not competent.
9. I worry about not being able to understand a client's pain if I have not had a similar kind of life experience.

Rather than pretending that you do not have any self-doubts or anxieties about being effective in your fieldwork assignment, strive to identify some of the ways your fears might get in your way. Bring these fears into the supervision session and explore them. It will help to realize that many of your peers share your anxiety. By verbally expressing how you experience your anxiety, you move in the direction of diminishing the power of this anxiety. Once you have given voice to your fears surrounding your performance and others' evaluation of you, these anxieties consume less energy.

Many trainees keep good reactions, insights, and intuitions to themselves. It can be enlightening to put words to your intuitions rather than engaging in an internal monologue. In one workshop a group counselor (Karina) was quiet throughout the group session. The supervisor asked Karina what was going on. "Well, I'm very aware that you, my supervisor, are present in this session," she replied. "I feel inhibited in following my hunches, because I'm wondering what you might think of what I'm doing. I'm afraid that I might not be measuring up very well." Karina's supervisor told her that this was what would have been best for her to say aloud. It is not necessary that you express all of your thoughts, feelings, and reactions to your clients, but in your supervision meetings it is wise to verbally express the self-talk that often remains silent within you. Challenge yourself to change an internal rehearsal into verbal expressions during your supervision sessions.

Acknowledging your fears is the first major step in conquering them. Courage is not the absence of any performance anxiety; rather, courage entails identifying and challenging these fears. Have the courage to admit your perceived imperfections and avoid becoming frozen out of fear of making the less than perfect intervention. Recognize mistakes you might make, avoid punishing yourself if you do make mistakes, and talk openly with your supervisor about them. If you are not willing to acknowledge when you make a mistake, you probably will not be willing to try anything new. You will be overly conscious about what you are doing and whether you are doing it "right." It is not necessary to know everything, to avoid making mistakes, and to be the perfect counselor in all respects. Take advantage of your role as a trainee. In this role you are certainly not expected to know everything; allow yourself the freedom to be a learner. If you can free yourself from the shackles of trying to live up to the unrealistic ideal of perfection, you will be taking significant steps toward curbing your performance anxiety. You will also realize that your clients can be your teachers in some significant ways.

Trainees are often unsure, apologetic, and unwilling to credit themselves with what they know and are able to do. Most professionals have feelings of self-doubt and question their competence at certain times and in certain situations. Your supervised fieldwork or internship is a place where you can acquire specific knowledge and where you can develop the skills to translate the theory you have learned into practice. Read the Voices from the Field feature to find out more about one author's experiences dealing with self-doubts as a supervisee.

Therapeutic goals can suffer if you have a strong need for approval and focus on trying to win the acceptance and admiration of your clients. Guy (2000) reminds us of the danger of depending on our clients as the main source of meeting our needs for admiration, approval, and acceptance. To the degree to which you are unaware of your needs and personal dynamics, you become vulnerable to using your work primarily to satisfy your own unmet needs.

Identifying Unresolved Personal Problems

Although trainees may think that they have effectively dealt with their personal problems, they are often surprised when they recognize in themselves some of the struggles their clients are talking about. Trainees may see themselves in their clients, and painful memories are frequently unleashed. These issues should be explored in personal therapy. If you are unaware of these conflicts, your unresolved personal problems can interfere with the therapeutic process to the detriment of the client. This is not to say that you must resolve all your personal difficulties before you begin to counsel others. The important point is that you can and should be *aware* of your biases, your areas of denial, and the issues you find particularly difficult to deal with in your life.

To illustrate, suppose that you experience serious difficulties in a significant relationship in your life. You may be wrestling with some pivotal decisions about what you want to do about the relationship. You may be caught between fear of loneliness and a desire to be on your own, or between your fear of and need for close relationships. How might a personal problem such as this affect your ability to counsel others effectively?

VOICES FROM THE FIELD

Jerry Corey

What stands out the most for me in my own supervision was how inadequate I felt as a counselor trainee. I did not have much confidence in my ability to tune into what a client was saying and effectively know how to respond therapeutically. As I recall, my supervisors did not devote a great deal of time or attention to talking with me about my self-doubts and my unresolved personal issues that restricted my ability to be present with a client. Most of the supervision sessions were case focused, with some discussion of possible interventions to employ with different types of client problems.

During my supervised postdoctoral year, I gathered most of my hours by doing individual counseling with college students and by co-leading therapy groups. I often felt lost, and I did not know how best to proceed in sessions with individual clients. If clients did not "get well quickly," I was convinced that this was evidence of my lack of competence as a counselor. My early attempts at providing individual counseling were characterized by what seemed like the slow progress of my clients and my desire for positive feedback from them. I compared myself to my supervisors and wondered how they would likely intervene with a client.

Co-leading intensive group therapy sessions with my supervisor proved to be the most helpful of all my supervised experiences. After the therapy sessions, we spent time processing my interventions as a facilitator and what the group brought out in me

personally. The actual co-leading with this supervisor was painful for me, however, as I constantly compared myself to this person who had many years of experience. I convinced myself that I was not measuring up and that I had little to offer anyone in the group. My supervisor's insight and clinical skills intimidated me, which heightened my own sense of insecurity and inadequacy. What stands out most for me is how totally inept I felt during these early experiences with supervised work. I seemed very mechanical and rehearsed in my responses. Rather than creating my own style, I tried to figure out how my supervisor might respond and imitated that. In essence, I lost my own unique direction by striving to become like my supervisor.

The most important learning from my early experiences with my own supervision is how critical it is to be willing to take an honest look at myself. A pattern I recognized in myself was how I had an exaggerated need for approval and acceptance from both my clients and my supervisor. This need often got in my way of being present with my clients and in bringing up material to explore in sessions with my supervisor. I recognized that a parallel process was operating and that my need for being accepted inhibited my ability to express myself as fully as I might. These experiences and insights as a supervisee taught me that I cannot take clients on a journey if I have not been willing to engage in my own self-exploration.

The critical point is not *whether* you happen to be struggling with personal questions but *how* you are struggling with them. Do you recognize and try to deal with your problems, or do you invest a lot of energy in denying their existence? Are you willing to consult with a therapist, or do you tell yourself that you can handle it, even when it becomes obvious that you are not doing so? Is there consistency between your personal life and professional life? In short, are you willing to do in your own life what you expect your clients to do?

Because you may have difficulty staying with a client in an area that you are reluctant or fearful to deal with, consider what present unfinished business in your own life might affect you as a counselor. What unresolved conflicts are you aware of, and how might these conflicts influence the way you counsel others? Are you willing to bring such concerns into your supervision, not for the purpose of getting therapy but to more clearly see how your conflicts might be blocking your progress with clients?

Avoiding the Role of Problem Solver

One form of trainee resistance is focusing too quickly on solving clients' presenting problems before clients have had a chance to identify and explore these concerns. Ask yourself how patient you are in allowing clients to get to the core of their problem areas and to struggle with finding their own answers. Do you tend to delve quickly into problem solving? Or do you have a tendency to give a great deal of advice? The tendency to rely on giving advice can easily be encouraged by clients who seek immediate answers to ease their suffering. However, the opportunity to give advice places you in a superior, all-knowing position, and you may convince yourself that you do have answers for your clients. Another aspect of this pattern might be a tendency to engage in excessive self-disclosure, especially by telling your clients how you have solved a particular problem in your own life. In doing so, the focus of therapy shifts from the client's struggle to your situation. Even if a client asks you for advice, it is a good idea to reflect on whether you might be helping or hindering the person by providing it. How might you respond to that advice-seeking client?

Identifying Countertransference

Although it is not necessarily problematic to identify with your clients in some respects, it is possible to lose a sense of yourself by overidentification with clients. In a broad sense, countertransference can be viewed as any of your projections as a counselor that can potentially get in the way of helping a client. For instance, your performance anxiety, or a need to be perfect, or the need to solve a client's problems might all be manifestations of countertransference. The appropriate course of action to take when you become aware of such reactions to clients is for you to discuss what is going on with you in your supervision.

Effective counselors use their own life experiences and personal reactions to help them understand their clients and as a method of working with them. When drawing on your personal experiences, it is essential that you be able to establish clear boundaries so that you do not get lost in your client's world. The process of working therapeutically with people is bound to open up personal themes in your life. As a partner in the therapeutic journey with your client, you can be deeply affected by a client's pain. The activation of painful memories often resonates with your own life experiences. Unfinished business is stirred up, and old wounds are opened. If your countertransference issues are not recognized, such reactions can result in a great deal of pain and stress in your life.

In the supervision of group counselor trainees, understanding countertransference is especially important. Supervisees who are conducting groups are exposed to a wider range of clients than supervisees who work exclusively with individual clients, which means that group work expands the opportunities for countertransference. According to Bemak and Epp (2001), teaching and supervising group counselor trainees to become aware of countertransference is an area that has not received much attention. Bemak and Epp contend that it is essential that trainees working with groups receive systematic attention to understanding the dynamics of countertransference. They add that dealing effectively with countertransference involves systematic reflection, discussion, and practice. In this area, experiential opportunities are at least as important as having a theoretical understanding of countertransference.

Stoltenberg and Delworth (1987) and Stoltenberg, McNeill, and Delworth (1998) describe a three-stage developmental model that has useful applications for the supervision of group counselor trainees. From this model, countertransference is most apparent when supervisees are beginning their work as group counselors. During this early phase, trainees are generally uncertain about how groups function, their role as group facilitators, the interventions they think best to employ, and their relationships with the various members. As trainees acquire increased independence, they become less preoccupied with their personal issues. They can think more about the concerns of the group members and use interventions that fit what is occurring in the group. Eventually, at an advanced stage, trainees are able to pay attention to both their clients and their own reactions.

Bemak and Epp (2001) point out how essential it is for supervisors to create a sense of safety in a supervision group that will enable supervisees to explore their emotional reactions. The supervisor does well to engage in an active way in the supervision group as a way to elicit deeper emotional responses by trainees. Bemak and Epp recommend designing supervision that facilitates a critical self-analysis of countertransference by trainees. They add that the aim of group supervision is to accentuate the awareness and attention of trainees, assisting them to further explore their personal reactions, not only within the supervisory group but outside of the supervisory relationship. Bemak and Epp emphasize that countertransference has the potential to be a powerful therapeutic force. They recommend that training and supervision incorporate identifying, analyzing, and strategically using countertransference as a tool for self-understanding and as a valuable tool in therapeutic work.

Respecting Diverse Value Systems

A problematic trait of some counselors in training is the imposition of their values on clients. Even though trainees would not want to directly impose their values on clients, they may still influence clients in subtle ways to embrace their views. It is now generally recognized that the therapeutic endeavor is a value-laden process and that all therapists, to some degree, communicate their values to clients (Richards & Bergin, 1997). There is an abundance of evidence that shows that therapy is not only value laden, but that counselors and clients often share different value systems (Zinnbauer & Pargament, 2000). Some researchers have found evidence that clients tend to change in ways that are consistent with the values of their therapists, and clients often adopt the values of their counselors (Zinnbauer & Pargament, 2000).

It will be difficult to avoid communicating your values to your clients, even if you do not explicitly share them. Your nonverbal behavior and body language give clients indications of how you are being affected. If clients feel a need to have your approval, they may respond to these cues by acting in ways that they imagine will meet with your favor. Suppose, for example, that an unhappily married man believed you thought he was wasting good years of his life in the marriage and proceeded with a divorce mostly because of his perceptions of your beliefs. Although you may have decided not to coerce clients to believe and act in ways that agree with your own values, you still need to be sensitive to the subtle messages you may project that can be powerful influences on clients' behavior. For example, a school counselor may communicate her disapproval of a teacher who has frequent classroom management issues. A student who is referred to this counselor may believe that his or her version of classroom conflict is being supported by the counselor.

Yarhouse and VanOrman (1999) assert that value conflicts between clients and therapists are inevitable. The challenge you will have is to recognize when your values clash with a client's values to the extent that you are not able to function effectively. You will be expected to honestly assess whether your values are likely to interfere with the objectivity you need to be useful to your clients. To make such an assessment, you will have to be clear about your beliefs about value-laden issues. In your supervision sessions, you can explore barriers within you that prevent you from working effectively with specific clients.

Challenging Yourself

If you are willing to recognize some ways that your personal characteristics could get in your way as a counselor and a supervisee, you are in a good position to do something about the situation. The basic message we have been developing is how essential it is for you to recognize that the person you are is perhaps the most critical element of your ability to successfully reach clients. Your life experiences, attitudes, and caring are crucial factors in establishing an effective therapeutic relationship. If you are unwilling to engage in self-exploration, it is likely that your fears, resistances, and personal conflicts will interfere with your ability to be present for clients. The challenge of participating in a process of honest self-appraisal is an essential quality if you are committed to being as effective as you can be as a counselor, supervisee, and ultimately, as a supervisor.

In the Voices from the Field feature, a student shares his first encounters with supervision. As you read his account, ask yourself these questions: To what degree can you identify with this student? Are there any lessons to be learned from his account? Have you wanted to express your thoughts and reactions to your supervisor yet found yourself holding back? What are your reactions to Jamie's account of his first supervision group experience?

CHALLENGES FOR SUPERVISORS

One of the things we often hear from supervisees is how anxious and overwhelmed they feel regarding their clinical performance and their ability to help others. It is important for supervisors to understand and appreciate this anxiety and to be willing to work with supervisees in supportive and constructive ways. If you reflect on your thoughts and feelings during your early clinical training experiences, chances are you will remember you own fears regarding performance and how these fears affected your work with clients. This section addresses the supervisor's role in assisting supervisees in dealing with anxiety and with supervisees' reactions to client failures, whether perceived or real.

Supervisee Anxiety

Something that stands out for us from our work with a range of supervisees is the high number of supervisees who are anxious about the supervision experience and their ability to perform well. Some supervisees experience more anxiety than others do, but nearly all experience it whether they are in a bachelor's level social work program or a doctoral level clinical psychology program. They are worried about performing up to standard and about the whole process of being evaluated by supervisors. Most have done well in their academic programs, but the anxiety escalates when they are in a position of putting their knowledge into practice. As supervisors, we should be aware of how common, and maybe even healthy, anxiety is for supervisees to have and what can be done to manage anxiety effectively. You can see how one supervisor dealt with his supervisee's anxiety by reading Case 3.3.

When supervision is conducted in a group, it is very common for supervisees to experience anxiety regarding how they are being perceived by the supervisor and their peers. Christensen and Kline (2001) describe participation anxiety, which is related to supervisees meeting their own expectations as well as the expectations of their peers and the supervisor. Supervisees are also concerned about their relationships with the supervisor and peers who are a part

| ## VOICES FROM THE FIELD

Jamie Bludworth (Doctoral student)

I came to my first supervision group with bright-eyed idealism. Each of us was co-facilitating personal growth groups and required to attend one and one-half hours of group supervision per week. I imagined that we were going to enrich the lives of our clients while learning the finer distinctions of counseling practice from our esteemed supervisor. I envisioned us growing individually and professionally through the process of serious self-reflection and compassionate inquiry. I was quickly disillusioned.

In group supervision meetings, I found myself disagreeing with the manner in which my peers and supervisor were discussing clinical issues relating to group practice. Instead of expressing my disagreement, I grew more and more silent. I eventually recognized that my continued silence in supervision was counterproductive. Nevertheless, I also recognized that to voice my dissatisfaction with supervision could prove to be a risky endeavor. How would my supervision group respond to me? Would speaking out put more distance between us? More important, how would my supervisor take my criticism?

Certainly, I had great respect for my supervisor's clinical judgment. Yet I strongly disagreed with the atmosphere of our supervision group. My disappointment was turning to resentment. I had to voice my concern if I was to receive any benefit from super-

vision. When I finally gathered enough courage to speak out to my supervision group, my colleagues expressed strong reactions toward me. My supervisor, however, responded graciously to my concerns. It was clear that I was alone in my sentiments, but it was also clear that my supervisor was willing to hear me.

In retrospect, I see now that I made many mistakes in the use of my first supervision experience. I was much too slow in the disclosure of my personal values. I could have displayed the kind of authenticity and congruence that I secretly demanded of the supervisor. In keeping my most powerful reactions hidden, I helped to foster an environment that I found most distasteful. What's more, I missed many of the valuable insights and suggestions offered by our supervisor in my resistance to the developing norms of the supervision group.

Although this initial experience was difficult for me, I learned volumes about myself and the ways in which I can more effectively use supervision to expand my knowledge and skill sets and, most important, better serve my clients. I learned that it is contingent upon me, and me alone, to determine how satisfying my supervision experience will be. I learned to take responsibility for my perceptions of the process. Above all, I learned the value of being true to myself in supervision, allowing my voice to be heard, authentically and respectfully.

---

of the supervision group. It is quite common for supervisees to experience fear and self-doubt regarding their ability and knowledge in group supervision. Christensen and Kline (2001) indicate that supervisees generally realize that there are clear benefits to facing their anxieties and dealing with them openly in a supervision group. By confronting their participation anxiety, supervisees are more able to initiate interactions in spontaneous ways in their supervision. Indeed, recognizing and dealing with anxiety can be a pathway to growth.

CASE 3·3 | MARLA

Marla has a bachelor's degree in psychology and has begun the master's counseling psychology program. She has gone straight through school without any time off to gain work experience except for seasonal summer jobs. She started her first semester of practicum training under the supervision of Dr. Moore at Veterans' Hospital, where he works as a psychologist. Marla is bright, young, enthusiastic, and motivated to learn. She is, however, extremely anxious about doing everything correctly, and it is clear that she is eager to please her supervisor. Dr. Moore has just observed Marla in a counseling session with a client, and it is clear that her need for the client to like her is getting in the way of her counseling. She frequently asked the client how the session was going, whether he was getting anything out of their discussion, and how the client liked working with her. She concluded the session by asking if the client thought she had done a good job in counseling him.

Marla is a very typical new, young student who is eager to please and do a good job. Dr. Moore does not want to dampen her spirit, motivation, and enthusiasm, but he needs to provide her with honest, constructive feedback and supervision without her unraveling. Support and understanding are essential with a trainee like Marla. Dr. Moore approaches Marla in this way: "You seemed like you were eager to have the client like you in that you asked him in several ways how he thought you as the counselor were doing. Being anxious to do well as a counselor is something that most of us experience, especially when we are beginning. What is crucial, however, is how you cope with your anxiety about 'doing well.' It is important that your anxiety doesn't get in the way of the counseling you are doing and obstruct your perception of the client's needs and goals. I would certainly be open to exploring ways that you might manage your anxiety effectively."

If you were supervising Marla, how would you guide her in thinking through her need for approval and how it affects her counseling relationships? What challenges is Marla facing, and how do you think she will do over the course of her supervision?

Most new trainees feel some degree of performance anxiety, which should decrease over time. Sharing some of the struggles you experienced as a trainee will go a long way toward putting your supervisees at ease. Let them know that counseling is not an exact science and that we make mistakes as we work and learn. Get supervisees into activities where they can develop a sense of mastery of some tasks and skills. Supervisees have potential to grow and learn under your supervision, and you are in a position to be of tremendous benefit to them as both supervisor and mentor. One useful intervention is to treat supervisees as colleagues when appropriate and encourage them to believe in their ability to learn and function creatively as clinicians. It may be tempting to figure things out for your supervisees and provide them with answers, but as with the client in therapy, supervisees have the ultimate task of discovering their own answers.

Supervisee Reactions to Client Failures

One of the most difficult situations for a counselor to deal with is the failure of clients to benefit from therapy. This is difficult even for the seasoned clinician, and it is especially difficult for trainees and prelicensed clinicians who want to be successful in their work. The job of the supervisor is to help the supervisee do everything possible to bring about a positive outcome in therapy and counseling, and to assist the supervisee in putting it in perspective when the outcome is not so positive.

Self-talk, or the beliefs of supervisees when they encounter what they see as failures with clients, can lead to a great deal of self-doubt. Here are a few statements that supervisees often say to themselves:

- I am fully responsible for my clients' outcomes, and negative outcomes mean that I am not competent.
- I must be successful with every client.
- I should be able to help my clients with all of their problems, and quickly.
- I must be able to adequately handle any kind of client emergency situation that arises.
- If a client is in pain, it is my responsibility to take it away.
- I have the power to control my client's life.
- I must be available at all times.
- I am the most important person in my client's life.

Most of these examples of counselors' self-talk refer to feelings of inadequacy, a fear of failing as a counselor, a nagging belief that one should be more, and a chronic sense of self-doubt. When counselors assume the giant share of responsibility for their clients, they are relieving their clients of the responsibility to direct their own lives, in addition to creating stress for themselves. Supervisors must be available to help their supervisees when, as in Case 3.4, clients create situations that lead trainees to doubt their competence.

There are many opportunities for client failures in counseling, just as there are many opportunities to experience success in the therapeutic venture. Counseling is not an exact science, and it is often difficult to determine who is responsible for either the successes or the failures in counseling. Oftentimes, clients attribute success to something other than the work of the therapist. When there are failures, however, the therapist may be identified as the cause. This may come from the client or the client's spouse or family. All too often, this identification of the cause of a therapy failure comes from the therapist, and this can be very disconcerting. Seasoned clinicians learn how to assess the factors contributing to a therapy failure, but new clinicians often lack the experience and self-confidence to self-assess. They quickly turn to themselves as the reason the therapy failed.

It is important to remember that change is a complicated process. When clients are provided with the tools for change, they frequently do not implement them. Even though they have come to therapy to change something, the change may be risky or frightening. Clients often say they want to change a

CASE 3.4 | ROBERTO

Roberto has been working with a married couple in therapy at the family service center. The couple seems to love each other and wants to be together, but as soon as they begin to talk, they fight. Roberto has been working with them on communication skills, and they seem to be making some progress. Hours before their next scheduled session, Roberto gets a call from the wife indicating that they have had another fight, have decided to seek a divorce, and would like to cancel future counseling sessions with him. Roberto asks, "What happened that led to this decision so quickly? How are you doing with this? How is your husband doing with this? What led you to want to cancel the counseling sessions? Would either or both of you be willing to come in one more time to discuss your decision?" Roberto comes to the next supervision session feeling discouraged and frustrated about this case and about his future work with couples and relationship issues.

How would you respond to Roberto's thoughts, feelings, and concerns about this case? Would you help Roberto decide what further action he could take regarding counseling this couple? What do you need to teach Roberto to help him cope with these kinds of therapy failures in the future?

---

certain behavior, yet their actions indicate they are not yet ready or willing to do what is needed to bring about this change. Clients often know why they *should* change a behavior and probably spend many hours thinking about how life would be better if they were to change.

Your role as the supervisor is to help the supervisee disengage from the successes and failures of the client. Actually learning this detachment is a very difficult process because we like to see the fruits of our work. The key to long-term survival in this field is to have a delicate and healthy balance between caring and objective disengagement. Some helping professionals are successful in achieving this balance, and some are not. Supervisors would do well to help their supervisees examine their cognitive processing of what they are saying to themselves about their clinical competence and their client failures. A cognitive restructuring approach in supervision may be in order to help supervisees develop a more realistic set of expectations about their own role and the client's role in the therapeutic process.

SUMMARY

The quality of the supervisory relationship is just as important as the methods a supervisor chooses. The essential elements of the supervisor–supervisee relationship include trust, self-disclosure, understanding transference and countertransference, acknowledging diversity, and establishing appropriate boundaries. The supervisory relationship has a built-in power differential, which can be mediated by a collaborative relationship style. Parallel processes can be seen between supervisory relationships and client relationship with supervisees. It is important for supervisors to be aware of their personal values and beliefs and those of supervisees that may affect the supervisory relationship.

Because the supervisory relationship is unequal, conflicts can easily occur. Working through a conflict can enhance the quality of the supervisory relationship. Supervisees face many challenges as they begin their clinical practice. Supervisors can help supervisees deal with feelings of self-doubt and anxiety and provide a context for talking about client failures.

As a supervisor, the time and effort you devote to establishing and maintaining a collaborative relationship with your supervisees will pay dividends in terms of the quality of their learning. The relationship is the foundation upon which therapeutic knowledge and skills are acquired. Reflecting on what you valued in your own relationships with your supervisors may be a good way for you to design your approach to supervising others.

SUGGESTED ACTIVITIES

1. In small groups, discuss the elements of the supervisory relationship you believe are essential for supervision to be effective. Discuss what you have learned about this from your own experience with supervision. How might your experiences as a supervisee assist you in getting a clearer picture of what you will want to bring to your work as a supervisor? Have each group share the common themes with the larger group.

2. Reflect on your own supervision and write in your journal about some of the fears and concerns you had when you first began seeing clients. How did these fears affect your ability to counsel? How did you manage your fears and concerns? Based on your experiences in your own supervision, what have you learned that you can apply to your work as a supervisor?

3. In small groups, identify a few strategies you can use to deal with your supervisee's reactions to a client's therapy failure. How do you view failure in your clients? How might you determine the degree to which you are responsible for client failures? As a group, explore supervisory strategies for coping with both real and perceived mistakes your supervisees might make with clients.

4. Access the Web site for this text at http://info.wadsworth.com/haynes, and complete the self-assessment inventory. Additional contributor perspectives and other activities specific to this chapter are also available to you through this Web site.

METHODS
OF SUPERVISION

1. Think about the supervision methods supervisors have used with you. What have you learned about supervision methods from being a participant in supervision?
2. What supervision methods do you think you would like to use as a supervisor?
3. How would you compare the value of individual versus group supervision? What are the pros and cons of those two approaches? Which would you use as a supervisor?
4. Would you choose supervision methods based on the competence and developmental level of the supervisee, or would you use the same methods with all supervisees?

INTRODUCTION

In this chapter, we describe some of the more common supervision methods. Some methods provide a general approach to supervising, and others involve specific techniques. Some methods have been borrowed from psychotherapy techniques; others have been developed specifically for supervising. The distinction between methods and techniques is not a clear one, and we refer to both the methods and the techniques of supervision as supervision methods.

A variety of supervision methods is available for use by supervisors. Individual supervision using the case consultation model, wherein the discussion in supervision focuses on the issues surrounding the supervisee's cases, is the model most frequently employed. Historically, supervisors have applied therapy skills and methods to the supervision setting. However, there is more to supervising than merely selecting and applying supervision methods. As mentioned in Chapter 3, the personal characteristics and the style of the supervisor are just as important as the supervisor's knowledge and skill in the application of methods.

Supervision requires many of the same helping skills used in counseling (empathy, respect, active listening, and challenging) but has a different focus than therapy. Supervisors are charged with monitoring and evaluating supervisees; therapy does not usually have monitoring and evaluation components. Clinical supervision is a rapidly expanding field, and a number of supervision methods have been developed. We will describe the most commonly used methods and discuss the utility of direct and indirect supervision methods.

When choosing supervision methods, the supervisor would best take into account several factors: the developmental level of the supervisee, the theoretical orientation of the supervisee and the supervisor, the setting in which the supervision is occurring, the role of the supervisee in that setting, and the purpose of the supervision (NASW, 1994). A clearly articulated model of supervision provides the basis for the selection of supervision methods, but "in actual practice, most supervision does not appear to follow either a theory-based or developmental approach, being atheoretical or eclectic" (Patterson, 1997, p.134). Patterson contends that most supervisors do not follow a particular theoretical model but select from a range of various methods in an eclectic fashion. As you will see in Chapter 5, we stress the importance of developing a working model of supervision that is consistent with both the supervisor's theoretical orientation and personal style.

Professional standards (AAMFT, 1999; ACA, 1995; APA, 1992; ACES, 1990, 1993; NASW, 1994) address supervision methods and techniques in a number of different ways. Some are detailed and others more general in addressing the topic (see Box 4.1). A main theme found in the standards is that supervisors are urged to have a good understanding of and ability to apply supervision methods and techniques. Face-to-face supervision is recommended. Some of the methods suggested in the standards are live observation, co-therapy, live supervision, audio and video tape recordings, role play, interpersonal process recall, suggestions and advice, feedback, and demonstration of skill. The selection of methods varies depending on the specifics of the supervisory situation.

SUPERVISION FORMATS

Supervision can be effective in either an individual or a group format. Individual supervision is the most common form. The supervisor and the supervisee meet face to face to discuss cases and a variety of topics surrounding the supervisee's development as a clinician. The frequency and duration of the meetings vary depending on the situation and the supervision requirements for licensure. One or two hour-long sessions per week are typical (AAMFT, 1999).

Group supervision is the preferred method for many supervisors both because of the economy of supervising several supervisees at once and the benefits to the supervisees of group interaction and learning from one another. Group supervision, however, is often seen as a supplement to individual supervision, and the number of hours of group supervision allowed for licensure purposes is usually limited. In California, for example, the requirement for supervision for prelicensed psychologists working 40 hours per week is 4 hours of supervision per week, at least 2 hours of which must be individual supervision (California Department of Consumer Affairs, 2000). All 4 hours may be in individual supervision, but group supervision is limited. The inference is that individual supervision provides more attention to the supervisee's work with clients. In our experience, it is most effective to use a combination of group and individual supervision.

Individual Supervision

Individual supervision can be viewed as the core of personal and professional development in supervision. It involves a one-to-one meeting of the supervisor and the supervisee, and it is used in virtually all of the helping professions. Individual supervision is required by many licensing and certification

ETHICS CODES AND STANDARDS REGARDING SUPERVISION METHODS

American Association for Marriage and Family Therapy
AAMFT Approved Supervisors: Mentors and Teachers for the Next Generation of MFT's (1999)

Supervision of marital and family therapy is expected to have the following characteristics:

- Face-to-face conversation with the supervisor, usually in periods of approximately one hour each.
- Appointments are customarily scheduled once a week, three times weekly is ordinarily the maximum and once every other week the minimum.
- Supervision focuses on raw data from a supervisee's continuing clinical practice, which is available to the supervisor through a combination of direct live observation, co-therapy, written clinical notes, audio and video recordings, and live supervision.

American Counseling Association
Code of Ethics and Standards of Practice (1995)

F.1.f. Supervision Preparation. Counselors who offer clinical supervision services are adequately prepared in supervision methods and techniques. Counselors who are doctoral students serving as practicum or internship supervisors to master's level students are adequately prepared and supervised by the training program.

Association for Counselor Education and Supervision
Ethical Guidelines for Counseling Supervisors (1993)

2.06 Actual work samples via audio and/or video tape or live observation in addition to case notes should be reviewed by the supervisor as a regular part of the ongoing supervisory process.

Association for Counselor Education and Supervision
Standards for Counseling Supervisors (1990)

5. Professional counseling supervisors demonstrate conceptual knowledge of supervision methods and techniques, and are skilled in using this knowledge to promote counselor development.
The counseling supervisor:
5.1 states the purposes of supervision and explains the procedures to be used;
5.2 negotiates mutual decisions regarding the needed direction of learning experiences for the counselor;
5.3 engages in appropriate supervisory interventions, including role-play, role-reversal, live supervision, modeling, interpersonal process recall, micro-training, suggestions and advice, reviewing audio and video tapes, etc.

6. Professional counseling supervisors demonstrate conceptual knowledge of the counselor developmental process, and are skilled in applying this knowledge.
The counseling supervisor:
6.7 uses supervisory methods appropriate to the counselor's level of conceptual development, training and experience.

National Association of Social Workers
Guidelines for Clinical Social Work Supervision (1994)

Conduct of Supervision: Format and schedule.
Methods of supervision vary on the basis of factors such as practice setting, client population, available technology, supervisor's management style, and supervisee's level of competence and learning style. Face-to-face supervision is recommended, individually and/or in a group. Some states prohibit or limit group supervision for purposes of fulfilling licensing requirements. The value of the face-to-face format is that it pro-

vides the opportunity to use verbal and nonverbal communication, to model practice style, to analyz... supervisory relationship and its impact on treatment, and to offer mutual feedback. The content of face-face sessions includes presentation of material, feedback, mutual analysis, and demonstration of skill. Group supervision requires special attention to issues such as confidentiality, the feedback process, and group members' role in performance evaluation.

agencies, largely because it lends itself to detailed personal attention to the clinical work and development of the supervisee.

Most of the methods described in this chapter can be applied to individual supervision. The most common is self-report in which the supervisee describes his or her clinical activities and conceptualizing of cases to the supervisor without the use of support case notes, recorded information, or other forms of supporting data. Gould and Bradley (2001) conclude that because self-report is solely dependent on the supervisee's memory of case information, the self-report method is best used as a method of gathering information about the supervisee's perceptions of counseling. Another common method involves the use of process and progress notes that the supervisee has recorded for each counseling session.

Direct observation methods such as co-therapy, observation, and the use of videotapes are strongly recommended for use along with self-report methods to ensure that the supervisor has a clear and direct view of the supervisee's work. The advantages of individual supervision include the ability to have a detailed focus on the clinical work of the supervisee without attending to the needs of other supervisees simultaneously and the opportunity to have time for detailed discussions of all the supervisee's cases.

Many supervisees respond best to the personal attention received in individual supervision, and they may be more comfortable disclosing information regarding their professional development than they would be in a group setting. Individual supervision does not afford the learning that occurs from the interaction in a group supervision setting, nor does it offer the opportunity to view the supervisee's interaction with other supervisees as a parallel process of how the supervisee might interact with clients. Ray and Altekruse (2000) suggest that the degree of effectiveness of individual compared with group supervision may be about the same, and York (1997) suggests that individual supervision is most effective when used in conjunction with group supervision methods. Nonetheless, individual supervision has many advantages and continues to be the cornerstone of supervision in the helping professions.

Group Supervision

Campbell (2000) describes peer and team supervision as two forms of group supervision. *Peer supervision* involves a group of similarly trained clinicians who meet together on a regular basis to informally supervise one another, discussing cases and ethical issues and providing support and feedback ut their work. These groups are informal and do not include an evaluation component. Peer supervision can be done on a one-to-one basis as well. In addition to the case consultation method, peer supervision commonly uses training tapes, journal article discussions, licensing law updates, and other didactic methods. Starling and Baker (2000) found peer supervision to be an effective method of supervision in a study that was based on supervisee perception of the supervision. Peer supervision is an excellent way to continue to develop as a clinician after the licensure requirements for supervision have been accomplished. Team supervision is found primarily in agency settings where a group of mental health professionals from different disciplines meet to discuss cases and other clinical issues much like peer supervision sessions. Other forms of group supervision include grand rounds, staff meetings where clinical issues are discussed, seminars, and tutorials.

Group supervision is a popular method for many supervisors. Supervision groups bring together between two and eight supervisees for the purpose of supervision. It is lively and economical in terms of the supervisor's use of time. Many of the methods employed in individual supervision can be used with groups. Case consultation, viewing videotapes, and work with the group dynamics as a learning experience are all methods of group supervision. Group supervision leaders should have formal training and experience in both group leadership and supervision methods. Because group supervision requires specialized skills in group dynamics and methods, this topic will be addressed in considerable detail in this chapter.

DYNAMICS OF GROUP SUPERVISION

Supervisors who conduct group supervision should have skills in group supervision methods and also have training and experience in group process. Supervisors conducting group supervision will need to do more than focus on the content of cases and the issues raised by supervisees. They need to be able to create a safe and accepting atmosphere within the supervision group that will encourage trainees to meaningfully participate in the supervision process.

Regardless of the particular method used in group supervision, group dynamics will develop and the group will move through a number of stages. Corey and Corey (2002) describe four stages of group process, which can be applied to help understand a supervision group. Let's look at each of these stages as they apply to supervision groups.

Initial Stage

In the initial stage, the focus is on orientation and exploration of the group structure, ground rules, personal goals, expectations, fears, and the beginning of the development of the group as a safe place. During the early phase of supervision, it is essential to develop a supervision contract and make sure all supervisees in the group are aware of what is expected of them and that informed consent is given. This is a time to formulate goals, to discuss how group supervision works, and to prepare supervisees to actively engage themselves in forming the agenda for each session. It is essential that supervisees take active steps to create a trusting climate by sharing their thoughts and feelings pertaining to being in the group, and the supervisor can encourage this process.

Transition Stage

In the transition stage, the group may be characterized by anxiety, resistance, struggle for control, conflicts, and problem behaviors. It is helpful for group supervisors to be calm and consistent in helping the group move toward the working stage. Supervisees may wonder about others' acceptance or rejection of them, performance anxiety is often present, and supervisees may struggle with appearing competent. This is a time for supervisees to take risks by expressing their vulnerabilities pertaining to their training experience, to risk disclosing thoughts they have pertaining to issues being explored, and to risk asking for what they want from supervision in the group setting.

Working Stage

As the group begins to feel safe and resolves conflicts and resistance, the working stage occurs wherein the group is active in problem solving and learning from each other and the supervisor. This is a time of increased cohesion, and a sense of community develops. Supervisees interact with one another and with the supervisor freely and directly. If conflict emerges in the group, it is dealt with directly and effectively. Participants are willing to bring their concerns to the supervision group, to give one another feedback, and to ask for feedback regarding their cases.

Ending Stage

At the ending stage, the group begins to prepare for taking the learning of the group and putting it into practice for themselves. Issues of termination and separation must be dealt with, including discussing what the group meant to each participant. This is a time for each supervisee to identify what was learned from the field placement and from the supervision group itself. The group supervisor assists supervisees to develop a conceptual framework that will help them understand, integrate, consolidate, and remember what they have learned in the group.

Value of Group Supervision

Group supervision is not only complementary to, but may be interchangeable with, individual supervision (Ray & Altekruse, 2000). In their discussion of empirically supported treatments, Calhoun, Moras, Pilkonis, and Rehm (1998) found that group supervision using audiotapes of sessions may be more efficient than individual supervision in terms of rate of learning. Although supervisors have traditionally relied on individual supervision, this study demonstrates the effectiveness of small and large group supervision in accomplishing the same task. Crespi, Fischetti, and Butler (2001) maintain that the value of group supervision has been documented. They see group supervision, using a case model approach, as a viable way to initiate supervisory sessions with school counselors. Although group supervision will cut into other service responsibilities of school counselors, this form of supervision can lead to greater accountability, can improve outcomes, and, in the long run, is cost effective.

Group supervision lends itself to a variety of role-playing approaches that enable trainees to become aware of potential countertransference issues and to acquire alternative perspectives in working with clients they sometimes perceive as being "difficult." Supervisees can assume the role of their clients by "becoming" the client while the supervisor demonstrates other approaches for dealing with a given client. The supervisor can then switch roles and assume the client's position while the trainee experiments with another way of dealing with the client. Of course, in a group context other supervisees can assume various roles for one another, which often results in rich discussion material after a situation is enacted. Role-playing techniques tend to bring concrete situations to life. This often has a greater impact on trainees than merely talking about problems and concerns with clients.

We think the value of group supervision may be overlooked. In groups, trainees can benefit by listening to others and by discussing cases with their peers as well as with a supervisor. Our approach is to combine individual and group supervision when this is practical and possible. For a detailed look at how one author (Jerry) conducts group supervision, see the Voices from the Field feature.

METHODS USED IN SUPERVISION

Verbal exchange and direct observation are the most commonly used forms of supervision. Historically, the verbal exchange method—wherein supervisor and supervisee discuss cases, ethical and legal issues, and personal development—has been the preferred form of supervision. Direct observation supervision methods—wherein the supervisor actually observes the supervisee practicing—have become increasingly popular in recent years, however. The verbal exchange method is more easily accomplished and can be done in person or by telephone in a crisis. The downside to "talking about" treatment and other issues is that much of the effectiveness of the supervision depends on the degree to which the supervisee is straightforward and accurate in describing his or her activities. The use of any one of a variety of direct observation methods, although requiring more time and effort, provides a more accurate reflection of the skills and abilities of the supervisee.

Because verbal exchange methods rely exclusively on the supervisee's self-report, the use of this method alone is no longer acceptable, especially

VOICES FROM THE FIELD

Jerry Corey

In conducting group supervision, teaching, and training group counselors, I use an intensive workshop approach. These all-day workshops last from three to six days and involve a combination of didactic and experiential training. Trainees function in the roles of both group members and group co-facilitators. In addition to this intensive workshop, trainers must also enroll in my semester-long group leadership practicum course, which is basically a supervision session of students who are co-facilitating peer groups on campus.

During each meeting, I talk with supervisees about group process issues, show portions of a video on group process, and conduct a live demonstration to model certain group skills. As a supervisor, I believe I can teach a great deal by actually demonstrating skills as well as by imparting information. I do a fair amount of teaching ways to intervene with material that evolves in the group. Yet giving information has its limits, and demonstration is required to bring this content to life. These demonstrations provide a context for the trainees to design their own interventions for the groups they will lead as a part of the supervision group.

Trainees spend about half of each day in an experiential group, and they have several opportunities to co-facilitate their group. I find that trainees approach this experiential part of the workshop with considerable anxiety over appearing incompetent in the eyes of their peers and supervisor. Early in the workshop I admonish participants to be active: "One sure way not to learn much in this workshop is by being extremely self-conscious and critically judging most of what you want to say or do. No matter what happens, there is something to be learned. If a group session is unproductive, you can explore what specific factors contributed to that outcome."

Group members usually react to these instructions with relief and report feeling much less anxious. As their supervisor, I let them know that I understand and empathize with their difficulty in being observed by their peers and by supervisors. Trainees often find it helpful to openly share their fears, and, paradoxically, their fears appear to be lessened by this act of acknowledgment.

Trainees have about one hour to facilitate a group session while I sit in the group with them and observe the process. The next 45 minutes are devoted to processing the group. I typically begin this process time by asking the peer co-leaders to talk with each other about their perceptions and reactions to the session. They are asked to comment about how they worked together, what they thought about the unfolding of the group, what they particularly liked, what they might have wanted to change about their co-leadership, and what they were concerned about. This offers plenty of material to explore. This seems to me like a better way to supervise than giving my comments immediately. By first listening to the co-leaders' concerns and perceptions, I am in a better place to more sensitively and effectively share my perceptions of what I observed in their training group. The other members are also asked to share their observations and reactions to the session. In this way, those who co-led the group, the other members, and the supervisor are all able to state their observations and to come up with ways to more effectively use group time.

(continued)

VOICES FROM THE FIELD (*continued*)

During the processing time, I ask questions of the co-leaders that encourage self-reflection: "Did you have any persistent thoughts or reactions during the time you were co-leading this group that you did not express? Was there a time when you felt stuck or wondered what to do?" I also often ask co-leaders to focus on specific skills such as opening a group meeting, linking members with common themes, following a member's cues as a way to deepen group interaction, and closing a group session.

My emphasis is on helping group trainees become increasingly aware of what is going on in the context of here-and-now interactions within the group and assisting them in developing interventions that are based on statements members make during a session. I emphasize that it is not a matter of "right" or "wrong"; rather, interventions are often a function of the leader's interest in something that is occurring in the group he or she is facilitating.

---

with students and novice counselors. Supervisors are strongly encouraged to ensure that supervisees have adequate skills by observing their clinical work (ACES, 1993). This protects the client, the supervisee, and the supervisor. Using both methods together combines the economy of the verbal exchange method with the accuracy of the direct observation method.

As we describe a number of commonly used supervision methods, consider how comfortable you would be using them, which would be your preferred methods, and how you would apply them in both individual and group supervision settings.

Case Consultation

The case consultation method involves a discussion of the supervisee's cases and is the most common supervision method (Goodyear & Nelson, 1997). This verbal exchange method usually involves the supervisee describing to the supervisor the major issues surrounding each case. These might include the client's purpose for seeking therapy, diagnostic formulations, therapy techniques used, relationship issues, ethical, legal, and multicultural issues, and process notes regarding the case. This method is effective in individual as well as group supervision settings. The case consultation can be used in a number of ways: "to explore assessment skills and conceptualization, to examine particular theories and techniques, to process relationship issues such as parallel process and transference, and to promote self-awareness on the part of the supervisee" (Campbell, 2000, p.72). The major disadvantage in "talking about" cases is the accuracy of self-report.

Although self-report is one of the most widely used methods, Feist (1999) indicates that it may be the least useful because it is limited by the supervisee's conceptual and observational abilities. Some supervisees are able to say all the right words about the case and what they are doing, which leads the supervisor to assume that the supervisee is on the right track (see Case 4.1 for more on this issue). This is not to say that the supervisee is deliberately trying to deceive the supervisor, but the reality is that in addition to learning from the supervisor, the supervisee hopes to receive a positive evaluation from the supervisor. This is the dilemma with the use of all verbal exchange methods of supervision. We have seen many instances in which the supervisee is able to say all the right things in supervision, but when observed directly with the client, a very different picture of the supervisee's skill level is seen. The supervisee may be able to conceptualize well, but his or her performance may be another matter. In addition, the supervisee's perception of what is going on may not accurately depict the reality of the counseling situation. Case consultation remains the supervision method of choice, however, and it can be very effective when used with other methods.

Co-Therapy

The co-therapy method involves the supervisor and the supervisee working together as co-therapists with a client or a group. It is essential that the two discuss the nature of the case or the group and the respective roles that the two of them will play as they work together as co-therapists. Sometimes supervisors take over and do therapy the way they think it should be done, not allowing the supervisee to struggle and learn in the process. Also, the client may discount the supervisee in favor of the supervisor as the therapist, which can have a negative effect on the supervisee's training experience (Goodyear & Nelson, 1997).

In co-therapy, the supervisor and supervisee typically discuss their work together in formal supervision sessions. This method offers the supervisor a firsthand view of the skills of the supervisee and provides an arena for modeling and demonstration on the part of the supervisor. According to Feist (1999), this form of supervision provides the most accurate information about the supervisee's work as a therapist. Co-therapy seems to be effective and beneficial for both trainees and supervisors. It cuts through the "talking about" therapy problem and can provide an exciting in-vivo training experience.

Live Observation

In live observation, the supervisor or observing team directly observes a supervisee in action either by sitting in on a counseling session or through a one-way mirror or on a video monitor. The focus is on the supervisee's counseling session and his or her therapy skills. Live observation, also referred to as live supervision, was first used by Jay Haley and Salvadore Minuchin in the 1960s. Montalvo (1973) developed the first ground rules for practicing live supervision, and it has become a major supervisory method for family therapy training.

Written permission of the client(s) must be given for the supervisor to sit in on the session or to observe the session from outside the room. The

CASE 4.1	TOBY

Toby is a master's level psychology trainee who is able to describe and discuss therapy cases with ease and apparent competence. He appears to have a clear understanding of the diagnostic issues, treatment goals, and methods needed in counseling clients. One of Toby's clients is an African American male with a history of chronic depression. When the trainee was observed in therapy with this client through the one-way mirror, a very different picture began to emerge. Toby did have a clear picture of the diagnostic and treatment issues, but he experienced considerable difficulty using basic helping skills. He did not take time to listen to the client or to truly understand the client's perspective and what it was like to be chronically depressed. Neither did Toby understand what role cultural issues played in

his work as a white student with an African American client.

Due to direct observation of Toby, his supervisor was able to identify the need for work on basic helping skills and multicultural competence and sensitivity. It is not uncommon to find a student who has the intellectual understanding of a case but lacks the basic helping skills to "connect" with clients. Modeling, role playing, and more direct observation supervision methods helped Toby develop his basic counseling skills with clients.

What are the main supervisory issues with Toby? What are the multicultural issues here? What supervision methods would you use to help Toby develop basic helping skills?

---

supervisor may sit in occasionally or on every session, and supervisor and supervisee meet beyond the observation sessions to discuss the case and the work of the supervisee. This method has a number of variations. The supervisor could remain silent throughout the session or could actually interrupt the session occasionally to discuss the supervisee's approach, either with or without the client present. Too many interruptions, however, can be distracting for both supervisee and client. Another variation uses built-in breaks during the session for the supervisee and supervisor to discuss the supervisee's approach. Sometimes the supervisor may take over the session to demonstrate to the supervisee how to proceed with the client. It is essential that the supervisor be aware of the potential impact of his or her presence in the session both on the client and on the supervisee. Maintaining concern for the welfare of the client and the dignity of the supervisee are of paramount importance.

Another method of observing the supervisee in action with clients is to use a one-way mirror. The supervisee and client are in one room, and the supervisor is in an adjoining room and views the supervisee's work with the client through the mirror (Madanes, 1984). Neither the client nor the supervisee can see the supervisor in the observation room, but both are aware of the supervisor's presence. The therapy room is wired for audio, which is broadcast into the observation room.

This setting offers many options for providing feedback to the supervisee. The supervisor may simply observe and provide feedback following the session, but several methods of providing feedback during the session are available as well. The "bug-in-the-ear" method uses an audio receiver that the supervisee wears in the ear, and the supervisor provides feedback and direction to the supervisee via a microphone. This allows the supervisee to make adjustments in his or her work with the client during the session rather than waiting to discuss the case later. It can become a distraction, however, if the supervisor does too much talking to the supervisee. Sometimes a buzzer is used as a signal to the supervisee that the supervisor needs to discuss the clinical work of the supervisee. The supervisee can take a break to talk to the supervisor or have a telephone available to call the supervisor. If none of these devices is available, the supervisee can take two or three prearranged breaks and come to the observation room to discuss the work in the session with the supervisor.

Using a one-way mirror is an effective way for the supervisor to observe the work of the supervisee directly and to intervene as the work of the supervisee is in progress. It does, however, require the physical set-up of the two rooms, the one-way mirror, and the audio equipment discussed. It also requires the permission and the cooperation of the client(s) involved. To learn more about this technique, read the Voices from the Field on page 94.

Videotaping

When using videotaping, the supervisee arranges to videotape one or more sessions with the client or group and views them in supervisory sessions with the supervisor. Goodyear and Nelson (1997) indicate that videotaping is the technology valued most by supervisors and supervisees alike. The supervisor can directly observe the skills of the supervisee, just as in live observation, but videotaping is preferred because the tape can be stopped and replayed as necessary (Protinsky, 1997) and the supervisee can be asked to try out different approaches. Larson and colleagues (1999) found that counselors' use of videotape to model effective counseling skills was particularly useful for novice supervisees as well. It can be seen that there are many ways videotaping can be useful in supervision. Box 4.2 on page 95 provides some suggestions for the use of videotaping in supervision.

There are several reasons videotaping is preferred over live supervision. Crucial segments of the interaction can be played as many times as needed to review the interaction. Role playing of alternate methods can be conducted with the supervisee and supervisor. Taping at various stages of therapy provides a comparison of the supervisee's progress as a therapist. The major drawback to videotaping is the possibility of complications, which often occur with the technology. A poorly recorded video is very difficult to watch. Nevertheless, if you work out the technological details in advance, videotaping can be an extremely useful supervision method.

Interpersonal Process Recall (IPR) is a long-standing and widely known method for using videotaping in supervision. Norman Kagan and his colleagues (Kagan, Krathwohl, & Miller, 1963) developed IPR to assist supervisees in processing relationship dynamics with the client and to increase self-awareness. In this method, supervisees are videotaped while they

VOICES FROM THE FIELD

Robert Haynes

I participated in the observation method many times as a supervisee, and I found it to be an excellent learning experience for me. As a young and anxious supervisee, it gave me confidence in that, should I get stuck in counseling the client, a supervisor would suggest to me via the "bug-in-the-ear" what to say next.

In my work as internship director, I have found the live observation method to be effective in establishing a baseline on interviewing skills during internship training. Early in the internship program, each intern would conduct an intake interview with a client. The purpose of the observation was to determine that the intern had the basic interviewing and helping skills necessary. In every case, the client signed a consent form agreeing to the observation by training staff and interns. Clients would be invited into the observation room to see the observation arrangement and meet those observing. The other interns were invited to be a part of the observation team. They found it valuable to observe and participate in the discussion with the observers and to par-

ticipate in providing feedback to the intern being observed. Periodically, the intern being observed would take a break and come to the observation room for feedback. At the conclusion of the session, the intern and the observers would meet to discuss in detail the intern's performance, the client's response to the intern, and the plans for future treatment with the client.

Interns typically reported that although this was one of the more anxiety-producing experiences during their training, it was generally one of the most valuable learning experiences. The supervisory staff found this direct observation to be extremely useful in getting a snapshot of the intern's abilities and deficiencies and to do so early in the training program. The clients (forensic patients) usually enjoyed being in the "spotlight" and rarely objected to participating in the observation. When they did object, they were excused from participating. Overall, the staff and I found this direct observation to be a valuable and expedient method of supervision.

---

are counseling a client and then shown the tape immediately following the interaction. When the tape is reviewed right away, supervisees are able to recall thoughts and feelings they experienced during the therapy session in detail, but for various reasons, did not express.

The supervisor and supervisee view the tape, and either may stop the tape at any point for exploration and discussion. The primary task of the supervisor, or "inquirer" (Kagan's term), is to assist the supervisee in investigating his or her own internal processes, including motives, thoughts, and feelings, that were at work during the therapy session. The IPR approach can be tedious, and it may take several sessions to get through one videotaped therapy session. Nevertheless, it has proven to be an effective method. For a list of questions the supervisor might ask during an IPR session, see Box 4.3 on page 96.

IPR is a well-established supervision method with the capacity for use with many different models of supervision. This basic approach and the ques-

| BOX 4.2 | SUGGESTIONS FOR USING THE VIDEOTAPING METHOD |

1. Set up the equipment such that the camera has a clear view of the faces and full bodies of both supervisee and client in order to be able to observe the body language.
2. The audio portion of the recording often suffers due to poor reception by the camera microphone. It is very frustrating to go to all the trouble of videotaping only to find the audio portion nearly impossible to hear. The use of an external microphone placed close to the supervisee and the client is ideal. If that is not possible, move the camcorder as close as possible to the supervisee and client for better audio recording.
3. Provide full disclosure of the taping process and tape use to clients, and obtain the written consent of clients for the taping. Assure clients that they have the option to rescind their consent at any time and that the recording will be used only for the training purposes of the supervision and then erased. Also, assure the client, who may be anxious about being recorded, that the discomfort often subsides shortly after beginning the taping session.
4. Have a definite plan for how to use the tapes in accomplishing the goals of supervision. Supervisees need to prepare themselves for presenting specific aspects of the tapes and come to supervision sessions with questions.
5. One taped session may be an hour long, making it impractical to view the tape in its entirety in the supervision session. The supervisor can select segments to review and discuss with the supervisee. Supervisees can also participate in deciding which portions of a tape they would like to review.
6. At the end of viewing, ask supervisees what they have learned from viewing the tape and what they would do in future therapy sessions based on this learning.

---

tions asked of the supervisee can be modified to be consistent with most models of supervision.

Another way videotaping can be used is by providing training tapes for use in supervision sessions. Ideally, the training tapes would be of therapists with a skill level similar to that of the supervisee, but therapy training tapes at various skill levels can be used. Videotapes of different therapy sessions can be played, and the supervisee and supervisor discuss those tapes. The supervisee can learn by acting as the supervisor for the therapist on the tape, discussing what is working and what to do differently.

Audiotaping

Audiotaping provides direct and useful information about a supervisee's work (Feist, 1999). It is not as useful as videotaping, however, because it lacks the information provided by observing body language and facial expressions. Again, consent of the client is required, and the client has the option to rescind that consent at any time. The use of a good machine is important because you need to be able to record quality audio. Tapes can then be played in supervision sessions. Audiotaping has many of the same advantages and disadvantages of videotaping, and the technology involved is simpler. If live observation or videotaping is not possible, audiotaping is a viable alternative. The "Ethical Guidelines for Counseling Supervisors" (ACES, 1993) states

| BOX 4.3 | QUESTIONS OFTEN ASKED IN IPR SESSIONS |

- What were your thoughts, feelings, and reactions? Did you want to express them at any time?
- What would you like to have said at this point?
- What was it like for you in your role as a counselor?
- What thoughts were you having about the other person at that time?
- Had you any ideas about what you wanted to do with that?
- Were there any pictures, images, or memories flashing through your mind then?
- How do you imagine the client was reacting to you?
- How do you think the client was seeing you at that point?
- Did you sense that the client had any expectations of you at that point?
- What did you want to hear from the client?
- What message did you want to give to the client? What prevented you from doing so?

Source: Bernard and Goodyear (1998, p. 102).

that "actual work samples via audio and/or video or live observation in addition to case notes should be reviewed by the supervisor as a regular part of the ongoing supervisory process" (2.06). The same procedures for consent, review, and confidentiality described for videotaping apply to the use of audiotaping.

Computer-Assisted and Online Techniques

Smith, Mead, and Kinsella (1998) and Scherl and Haley (2000) describe the use of computers in supervision where the supervisor, while observing the supervisee from an observation room, types feedback on the computer for the supervisee to view on his or her own monitor during the therapy session. Janoff and Schoenholtz-Read (1999) combine the use of face-to-face and computer-mediated group supervision for use in distance learning.

Methods and ethical issues in the use of online supervision are described by Kanz (2001). Online supervision involves the use of the Internet to provide supervision to supervisees at locations at a distance. Supervisees may be anywhere, from across campus to across continents. Some of the more common online methods currently in use are email and videoconferencing, chat rooms, instant messaging, and desktop videoteleconferencing. Kanz concludes that videoconferencing may be the most useable tool for online supervision.

There is little research to date on the effectiveness of online supervision, and it is assumed that very few mental health professionals currently use this method. The ACA's *Ethical Standards for Internet On-line Counseling* (1999) may be a useful resource for those conducting supervision via the Internet. Although supervision is not addressed specifically, these standards contain related information that supervisors may find useful. Confidentiality is an obvious ethical concern because Internet security and privacy in general cannot be guaranteed. Supervisors using online methods are encouraged to carefully consider the ethical ramifications of discussing client information online. Kanz (2001) provides these recommendations for supervisors considering the use of online supervision:

- Consider the ethical ramifications of online supervision even though the codes may not specifically address this form of supervision.
- The supervisory relationship should be established face to face before online supervision is begun.
- Clients must be informed of the nature and potential hazards of the use of online supervision and give their full, written consent.
- The supervisor and supervisee should be very careful about disclosing identifying client information in online supervision sessions.
- The supervisor and supervisee are encouraged to evaluate the use of the online supervision.

Computer-assisted and online supervision are relatively new supervision methods, but with rapidly advancing technology, the use of videoconferencing, computers, and the Internet in supervision can be expected to increase dramatically.

Role Play and Role Reversal

Role playing can be a very effective supervision method when used in conjunction with other methods described in this section. Role playing involves acting out any variety of scenarios with the supervisor and the supervisee acting as the therapist and the client. Role play can also be used creatively in a group supervision setting with many possible variations. Larson and colleagues (1999) found this technique most useful once the supervisee has mastered basic helping skills such as empathy. The real value of role playing lies in the supervisor's ability to see the supervisee in the here-and-now rather than talking about situations and issues.

Role reversal is a kind of role play in which the supervisee plays the role of the client while the supervisor plays the role of the therapist. This is useful to assist the supervisee in developing empathy for the client and the client's role in therapy. Another method of role reversal is for the supervisee to play the role of the supervisor while the supervisor plays the role of the supervisee. This invites the supervisee to examine the issues discussed in supervision from a different perspective, which can aid the learning process.

Modeling and Demonstration

Modeling is teaching the supervisee through the supervisor's behavior, showing how the supervisor would go about various professional tasks from ethical decision making to formulating and applying clinical methods. Modeling occurs throughout the course of supervision; modeling conveys attitudes and beliefs and demonstrates behaviors to the supervisee. It is hoped that an attitude of empowerment is displayed by the supervisor to the supervisee—empowerment for the supervisee to be able to self-supervise. Demonstration is showing the supervisee how to perform specific tasks and skills such as conducting an intake session or different ways of managing an angry client. Demonstration can be done in a role play or in co-therapy wherein the supervisor shows the supervisee how he or she would handle the situation. The supervisor could also demonstrate to the supervisee by talking aloud about how one might go about problem solving in a particular situation. It is important for the supervisor to emphasize that there is no one "right way" to approach a problem situation. The supervisor is merely illustrating one of many ways of intervening.

Remember that as a supervisor your actions probably speak louder than your words. In addition to showing supervisees how to do something, explain your thinking process. Be sure to give supervisees a chance to demonstrate what they have learned from your demonstration, and encourage supervisees to bring their own unique style to this work.

Coaching

Coaching is a new supervision method that was originally developed in management supervision as executive coaching (Laske, 1999; Witherspoon & White, 1996). Using this method, the supervisor facilitates the supervisee's learning by helping the supervisee examine various topics. The coach functions less in an authority role and more as a personal adviser focusing on the agenda of the supervisee. In coaching, asking the right question is often more important than having the right answer. This approach has similarities with person-centered supervision in that the job of the supervisor is to actively listen to supervisees to help them discover for themselves what they need to learn. If supervisees are encouraged to examine the issue, the assumption is that they will be able to arrive at their own conclusions.

This approach can be applied with novice or experienced clinicians, but it seems to lend itself more to work with the experienced clinician and in peer supervision. Coaching is less structured and requires the supervisee to determine what is needed from his or her supervision. Coaching is built on a relationship of trust. Some essential questions for a coach to ask are "What do you want from me?" "What do you need to learn?" and "How can we best accomplish that learning?"

Coaching can be done in brief and informal sessions or in more systematic and formal supervision sessions. This approach can be collaborative and is aimed at developing supervisee autonomy and self-direction. Coaching provides a format for the supervisor and supervisee to work in a partnership to accomplish the goals of supervision.

Methods Using Written Information

Process notes are written notes outlining the supervisee's conceptualization of the counseling including diagnosis, goals, objectives, and treatment strategies. *Progress notes* are more factual notes regarding what actually took place in counseling including the client's statements, behavior, and demeanor. These methods offer more detailed reviews of the counseling session than the supervisees's self-report alone.

Written information from the supervisee may also include logs, notes, journaling, and verbatim transcriptions of sessions (Campbell, 2000). The use of process notes can aid in the case consultation method of supervision. Written methods can be useful in encouraging the supervisee to conceptualize from the notes what is going on in the session and with the client. These can be used in conjunction with any of the other methods of supervision.

Methods Based on Psychotherapy Models

A variety of supervision methods are based on psychotherapy techniques. They include psychodynamic, cognitive-behavioral, person-centered, feminist, family systems, experiential, and integrative methods. Each approach employs specific psychotherapy methods and applies them to the supervisory setting. In most cases, the supervisor uses a psychotherapy model parallel to the one he or she actually uses when doing psychotherapy. (See Chapter 5 for an in-depth look at the models briefly described here.)

Psychodynamic methods explore the relationship and the dynamics between the supervisee and his or her clients, and between the supervisee and the supervisor (Bradley & Gould, 2001). The purpose of supervision is to teach the supervisee to understand the dynamics of resolving conflict to better work with a client. The supervisor teaches the supervisee to pay attention to aspects of the supervisory process that mirror therapy. The supervisee learns what is involved in an analytic stance, which includes patience, trust in the process, interest in and respect for the client, and an appreciation of the forms of resistance.

The *person-centered* supervision approach focuses on attitudes more than techniques. Emphasis is on the supervisee (counselor) establishing the facilitating conditions for change: genuineness, empathy, understanding, and warmth. The supervisor uses these same skills in helping the supervisee work on developing these therapy skills with clients. Didactic instruction is used infrequently. A heavy reliance is made on a theory of process in the context of the supervisory relationship (Lambers, 2000).

The *cognitive-behavioral* supervisor operates on the assumption that both adaptive and maladaptive behaviors are learned and maintained through their consequences. Supervisors using this approach are more specific and systematic than supervisors with other orientations. Cognitive-behavioral methods are described by Kurpius and Morran (1988) and include mental practice, covert modeling, cognitive modeling, cognitive restructuring, cognitive self-instruction, and cognitive self-management. The methods are designed to help the supervisee improve his or her counseling skills and to reduce anxiety. *Behavioral* methods, as described by Bradley and Gould (2001), involve five main steps: (1) establishing the supervisory relationship, (2) analyzing skill and assessment, (3) setting goals for supervision,

(4) developing and implementing strategies to accomplish the goals, and (5) evaluating and generalizing learning.

Homework

Assigning homework that might include readings, texts, and viewing tapes and CD-ROMs can be an adjunct to supervision sessions. Assignments can be made on any clinical, ethical, legal, or other topic. The supervisee should come prepared for discussion at the next supervision session. For example, if the supervisee wants to learn more about suicide assessment and intervention, he or she could read selected articles and view a videotape on this topic. At the next supervision session, the supervisee will then be prepared to discuss how he or she might assess and intervene with a client with some degree of suicide risk. The homework done by the supervisee can save the time of several supervisory sessions that it would take to teach the supervisee the same information. The supervisee and the supervisor can then spend time in the session talking about how the information applies to clients.

We have described some of the more common supervision methods. Selection of a particular method depends on the many contextual factors surrounding supervision. The supervisor's model of supervision is also a factor in determining which methods are used.

With the new emphasis on supervision by licensing boards and professional associations, supervisors are encouraged to remain current with developments in the literature regarding supervision models. We asked some of our contributing supervisors about their preferred methods of supervision, and their comments are provided in the Voices from the Field feature.

WHAT SUPERVISORS SAY TO SUPERVISEES

We want to provide you with a sample of the kinds of things that supervisors say to supervisees. These statements and questions are typical of the lead statements and questions supervisors use with many of the methods described earlier. Notice that, in most cases, the focus of the statements and questions is on the thoughts, feelings, and actions of the supervisee rather than suggesting what the supervisee should do.

Some questions and statements focus on the content of supervision:

- What would you like to accomplish during the course of our supervision together?
- Let's talk about the topics and issues you must bring to supervision to discuss.
- What ground rules do we need to establish about how we will work together that will help make our supervisory sessions a safe place for you?
- How can we work together to help you become a more confident and competent clinician?
- Where can you go to seek out more information on those topics?

VOICES FROM THE FIELD

Stacey Thacker, Ph.D.

I have used a variety of supervision methods including in-vivo supervision, videotapes, audiotapes, role playing, modeling, self-reports of sessions by the supervisee, and consultation with other professionals regarding the supervisee's work.

The strength of in-vivo supervision is that the observation is live and direct and the feedback is immediate. This enables the supervisee to use the feedback immediately in the session. The limitation is that this type of supervision can be time consuming and may be distracting to the supervisee, the patient/client, or both.

The use of videotapes and audiotapes allows the supervisor to actually see (or hear) what is occurring in the session, providing more meaningful feedback regarding a variety of different factors for the supervisee. A drawback may be the time involved in viewing/listening to the tapes and the fact that some clients and/or supervisees find taping to be a hindrance/distraction.

Using the supervisee's self-report is useful in attempting to understand how a particular supervisee views a certain client or situation. It helps to clarify what issues the supervisee finds important. It also does not require a significant amount of time as do in-vivo methods of supervision. Limitations arise when supervisors rely solely on this means of supervision.

Elie Axelroth, Psy.D.

The most frequently used method of supervision is individual face-to-face in which the intern presents case material from either memory, chart notes, or perhaps process notes written after the session. While this is the most cost-efficient use of our time, we must depend on the best recollection of our interns. This is sometimes difficult given a new intern's need to be perceived in a positive light.

Live observation involves a team observing the therapy session from behind a one-way mirror. Feedback is given during a short consulting break midway through the session. Live observation allows for the opportunity to intervene at the time of the session, and therefore blurs the distinction between training and treatment.

By definition, live observation is collaborative. The team sitting behind the one-way mirror is responsible for observing, analyzing, and providing feedback that is attentive and articulate, but concise enough to be helpful during the remainder of the session. When consulting midway through the session, we have learned to provide the intern with only two or three suggestions so that he or she is not overwhelmed when returning to complete the session.

Following the session, the team members meet to discuss the session, starting with the intern's assessment and gradually broadening to include feedback from other interns and supervisors. It is crucial that supervisors are sensitive to the intern's level of training and provide only that feedback that can be integrated in a meaningful way.

- What experiences have you had in your lifetime with other cultures?
- What do you need to learn about multicultural issues in dealing with your clients? How do the gender differences in this case affect your work with the client?

- What do the legal, ethical, and professional standards say regarding this issue?
- Let's talk about how we will handle the evaluation portion of your supervision. How could it be most useful for you?
- Where are you headed with this client? What are your goals for the client? What are the client's goals? How do you feel about the work you did with this client? How did the client affect you?
- Can you give me three different approaches for addressing this issue?
- How would you like to go about resolving this? What are the options? Which option best serves the goals of the client?

Other questions and statements focus on the supervisee's self-reflection in a way that balances challenge and support.

- What can I do as your supervisor to help you be open to hearing my feedback?
- I struggled with this when I was at the beginning stage of training as a clinician, and this is what I learned.
- Can you practice the words you will use to convey your concerns?
- What was this supervision session like for you? Was it helpful? What were you thinking or feeling when we were discussing this case?
- Can you help me understand the direction you were taking at this moment with the client?
- Talk out loud about your decision in choosing that particular approach.
- If you were to have a second chance at that session, what might you have done differently?
- What did you think was going on in the counseling session? With the client? About how you thought the client was perceiving you?
- In what way does our relationship parallel your relationships with clients?
- How do you react to your clients? Which clients lead to countertransference issues for you?
- Which of your values come into play in your counseling work?

OTHER CONSIDERATIONS REGARDING SUPERVISION METHODS

Which methods do supervisors use most frequently? Goodyear and Nelson (1997) state that there have been few studies that address the frequency of use of the various methods or their efficacy. They conducted an informal survey of training directors of university counseling centers to get a sense of the frequency of methods utilized. The results indicate that individual one-to-one supervision and group supervision are the most commonly used methods and that live observation using an assortment of feedback systems is the least used. This small sample (n = 22) may not be at all indicative of supervision methods use overall, but it provides an idea of the methods used in some university counseling centers. In another study of family therapy supervision by Wetchler, Piercy, and Sprenkle (1989), trainees' verbal reports of therapy sessions were rated by family therapy supervisors as the most frequently used method—yet one of the least effective. Systematic research and surveys are needed before we can understand the effectiveness of supervision methods.

Most of the supervision methods discussed in this chapter focus on the supervisee's work with clients and therapy. However, a considerable portion of supervision revolves around nontherapy-related issues. Here is a sample of other issues supervisors must address:

- Professional goals
- Psychological assessment
- Preparation for licensing
- Coping with the bureaucracy of agencies
- Coping with burnout
- Personal development
- Working effectively with other helping professionals
- Conflicts with other trainees

The verbal exchange method is often used in addressing these issues. However, many of the methods in this chapter could be adapted to address nontherapy issues faced in supervision. For example, coaching could easily be adapted to address coping with burnout. Using a supportive and encouraging approach, the supervisor as coach could assist the supervisee in exploring what about the bureaucracy is most frustrating, how others cope both effectively and ineffectively, what coping techniques might be most effective, what barriers to effective coping exist, and then develop a plan to implement for better coping with the bureaucracy. Supervisors in the helping professions are probably most comfortable talking about therapy issues, but they should become equally adept at providing supervision for the broader range of issues that may be a focus of supervision.

According to Corey, Corey and Callanan (2003), "A supervisor's task is to strive for an optimal level of challenge and support. The hope is that the supervisor will promote autonomy without overwhelming the supervisee" (p. 324). Supervisors must be flexible in their ability to assess the skill level and learning abilities of supervisees and in applying methods that best fit that level. The task is to determine where the supervisee currently is and what training model and methods are best suited to take the supervisee to where he or she would like to be. Growth and development is often an uneven process, and the rate at which the supervisee develops will fluctuate throughout the supervisory process.

A major question asked by many supervisors is, "How do I decide which methods to use with a supervisee?" Campbell (2000) devotes an entire chapter to this question and concludes that there is no easy answer. Research on this topic offers little help. Campbell states that one important quality needed by effective supervisors is role flexibility. Supervisors move from more of an unequal power base at the beginning of supervision to one that is equal and collegial toward the end of supervision.

Novice clinicians, in most cases, require an approach that is more supportive, facilitative, and structured. Careful monitoring, observation, demonstration, and teaching are required from the supervisor. As supervisees develop, they can become more actively involved in the supervisory interaction and more confident to bring issues to supervision and explore their own thoughts, feelings, and reactions to clients and to supervision. Toward the successful conclusion of supervision, the relationship becomes more collegial, and supervisees feel empowered to provide the direction for supervisory sessions. The time each supervisee needs to develop is unique to that individual, and it is nearly impossible to provide a standard amount of time supervisees might spend in each developmental stage. The supervisor and the supervisee must work collaboratively to assess the supervisee's level of development and the best methods by which the supervisee can learn. Morey, Burton, and Roske (1998) identify four developmental phases in supervision and the accompanying key tasks. These phases are listed in Box 4.4.

Much like therapy methods with clients, supervision methods will be much more effective if used within the context of a healthy supervisory relationship. Trust and respect should characterize this relationship and this takes time to develop. The supervisor fosters this relationship early and continuously throughout the supervision, which is essential for supervisory methods to work. The use of supervision methods without the base of a healthy relationship is like psychotherapy techniques applied mechanistically without an understanding of the context of the therapist–client relationship.

The selection and use of supervision methods is not a smorgasbord of techniques from which the supervisor can choose. The supervisor must have a clear model of supervision, a rationale for the use of any particular method, and competence in training and experience with the particular method. Several professional standards (ACA, 1995; ACES, 1990, 1993; NASW, 1994) require supervisors to demonstrate that they have the knowledge and skills to apply supervision methods. Supervisors do not increase their level of competence as supervisors simply with the accumulation of clinical and supervisory experience. They learn from courses, workshops, readings, colleagues, and supervisees. Remain open to the growth and learning that occurs from each individual you supervise. Consider these questions when choosing a supervision method:

- What are the needs of the supervisee?
- What is the goal of supervision in this instance?
- Over what period will the supervision occur?
- Is the method consistent with my style and orientation?
- How can I become more skilled in the use of this approach?
- What are the limits of my areas of expertise in providing supervision?
- How will I evaluate the effectiveness of the method?

For additional help in choosing an appropriate supervision method, consult Box 4.5.

| BOX 4.4 | PHASES OF SUPERVISION AND KEY TASKS |

Initial Phase

Supervisor Assess the supervisee's strengths and weaknesses, estimate the supervisee's level of professional development in regards to the setting, and develop a supervision plan.

Supervisees Identify goals for supervision, review strengths and weaknesses, and develop a supervision plan.

Beginning Phase

Supervisor Create a safe learning environment that allows for increasing autonomy; provide a clear agreement regarding the expectations of the supervisory relationship.

Supervisees Follow the modeling and direction from the supervisor to ensure competent and safe clinical practice; cautiously explore the training environment.

Middle Phase

Supervisor Organize the supervision environment, encourage collaborative work in supervision, and help supervisees see clinical successes as a result of their own work.

Supervisees Organize the supervision environment; decide when to function autonomously and when to consult the supervisor; develop a professional identity.

Ending Phase

Supervisor Review supervisees' progress and help them consolidate the gains made with an assessment of their strengths and weaknesses; help them prepare for their ongoing work and growth as an independent professional.

Supervisees Review learning over the course of the supervision; clarify professional goals and how to proceed to accomplish those goals.

Source: From R. Morey, D. Burton, & A. Roske, "Clinical Supervision in a Forensic Setting (Four developmental phases in supervision)," 1998. Reprinted by permission of the author.

SUMMARY

A number of supervision methods are used by supervisors. Some are specifically designed for use in supervision, and others are adapted from psychotherapy-based approaches. The case consultation model, in which the supervisee discusses with the supervisor his or her clinical cases, is the most common method, and direct observation methods are highly recommended to assure that the supervisor sees the supervisee's clinical work. Group supervision is frequently used and is best done by those with special training in group dynamics and methods. Which supervision methods work best have yet to be determined, and careful study of the efficacy of the various methods is needed.

The selection of supervision methods is determined by the supervisory situation, the needs of the supervisee, the training goals, the client, and the setting in which the supervision occurs. Supervision methods are effective mainly in the context of a healthy and productive supervisory relationship characterized by trust and respect. Supervisees will most likely benefit from being exposed to a variety of supervision methods. At the present time, the selection of supervision methods is left to the judgment of the supervisor.

BOX 4.5   TIPS FOR PRACTICAL APPLICATION FOR METHODS

1. Ask open-ended questions of supervisees to facilitate discussion.
2. Include some direct observation of the supervisee in action with clients during supervision. You want to "oversee" what the supervisee is doing, not just "overhear" what the supervisee is telling you.
3. Adapt your supervision methods to fit the learning style of the supervisee.
4. A major task of supervision is to help the supervisee conceptualize what is going on with the client (or other situation) and how to proceed. This is often difficult for supervisees who may want the supervisor to simply provide answers to their questions.
5. Remember that supervision is a collaborative process; supervison methods are most effective when applied in that spirit.
6. Because of their primary training as therapists, many supervisors focus more on the therapy with clients than on the learning and development of the supervisee (Borders, 1992). Do periodic self-assessments to assure that you are in fact focusing on the supervisee's development and not solely on your fascination with the therapy process.
7. Be supportive, facilitative, and structured with inexperienced clinicians. Be sensitive to the fact that supervisees are most likely anxious about their skills and abilities and want to perform well for their supervisor.
8. Challenge supervisees to explore thoughts, feelings, and reactions to clients and to supervision. As they develop into more experienced clinicians, allow them to take the lead in supervisory sessions and provide their own self-supervision as you work toward empowering them.
9. Model responsibility by keeping to your scheduled supervision appointments and sticking to the primary tasks of the supervision. Supervisors sometimes let topics drift into less relevant, but more interesting, discussions in supervision.
10. Maintain a healthy perspective on your role as a supervisor. Learn from your supervisees and your supervisory experiences. Don't feel as though you must have all the answers for your supervisees.
11. Have fun with your supervisory experiences while maintaining proper professional boundaries.

SUGGESTED ACTIVITIES

1. Richard is a marriage and family therapist who has been in private practice for more than 20 years. He decided to further his education and training and went back to school to work toward a doctoral degree in counseling psychology. Rosa works in the counseling center at the university where Richard is a student. She received her doctorate 5 years ago and has been licensed as a psychologist for 3 years. Richard will be a student therapist in the counseling center and Rosa will be his supervisor. Their first meeting is next week.

   • If you were Rosa, how would you prepare for the first session with Richard?
   • What do you think would be your major focus in supervision with Richard?
   • What are your fears and concerns about working with him?
   • Do you feel qualified to work with Richard?

- What supervision methods would be most applicable with Richard?
- What will be the biggest challenge in supervising him? What will be the biggest reward?
- What would you guess are Richard's fears, concerns, hopes, and expectations about working in the counseling center with Rosa as his supervisor?

2. Melissa is a first-year student in a social work master's degree program. She is young, bright, eager to learn, and eager to please; she graduated from college one year ago. Laura has been a licensed social worker for 5 years and is on the staff at the county juvenile probation department. Laura has just met with Melissa in their first supervisory session. Melissa is assigned to the probation department for 9 months of internship training. Melissa expressed her eagerness to learn anything she can and is excited to begin working with the kids.

   - If you were Laura, what would your thoughts be about working with Melissa?
   - What would you include in your contract with Melissa?
   - Where is Melissa in terms of a developmental model?
   - What supervision methods would be most applicable?
   - How would you evaluate Melissa's progress in the internship?

3. Select two or three supervision methods that seem most useful and have members of your group role-play how they might be applied in working with Richard or Melissa (see activities 1 and 2). Take turns role-playing and discuss what methods seemed to be most useful. Which methods were not useful? Why?

4. What methods of supervision would be useful in the following situations? How would you go about deciding which methods to apply in each situation?
   a. Supervising a doctoral level psychology intern in a community mental health center.
   b. Supervising a social worker who is on probation with the licensing board in a private practice setting.
   c. Supervising a psychiatric aide at a state hospital.
   d. Supervising a student in the master's program in guidance and counseling at a university counseling center.
   e. Supervising a mental health counselor who has worked in the field for years in another state and is now under your supervision until she becomes licensed in your state.
   f. Supervising a bachelor's level counseling student who is leading discussion groups in a family planning clinic.
   g. Supervising a student who is doing volunteer work with the homeless as a requirement for a class you are teaching.

5. Access the Web site for this text at http://info.wadsworth.com/haynes, and complete the self-assessment inventory. Additional contributor perspectives and other activities specific to this chapter are also available to you through this Web site.

5 CHAPTER

MODELS
OF SUPERVISION

FOCUS QUESTIONS

1. Can you identify the supervision model each of your supervisors used? Which approches can help you as a supervisor?
2. Did your supervisor discuss his or her model with you? How was the model described?
3. What approach are you most inclined to follow in your supervision practice at this time? How might this approach influence your view of what you expect from supervisees?

4. What aspects from various theories might you most want to incorporate into your own integrative supervision model?
5. If your supervisees asked you about your ideas on your model of supervision, what would you be likely to say?
6. Why is having a model of supervision important? How does a model influence supervision?

INTRODUCTION

In this chapter we discuss the theoretical foundations of supervision. Developmental models, psychotherapy-based models, and integrative models of supervision are examined. This broad view of the theories of supervision provides a basis for addressing the more applied topics in later chapters. In addition, we discuss how you can best go about developing your own model, whether it is integrative or based on one particular perspective.

In reviewing the various models, it can be seen that some are based on established psychotherapy models whereas others have been developed specifically to describe the process of supervision. Many of these models are relatively new. The way they address supervision and the methods for application are relatively uneven, making it difficult to compare and contrast models.

Only a few of the professional standards address the topic of supervision models, but the ones that do, found in Box 5.1, indicate that supervisors are expected to demonstrate knowledge of their supervision model and to inform the supervisee of the model they are using. To aid you in this process, we examine each of these models in detail and discuss how they can be applied in the practice of supervision.

UNDERSTANDING MODELS OF SUPERVISION

A *model* is a description of what something is and how it works. A model of supervision is a theoretical description of what supervision is and how the supervisee's learning and professional development occur. Some models describe the process of learning and developing as a whole; others describe the specifics of what occurs in supervision to bring about learning and development. A complete model includes both how learning occurs and what supervisors and supervisees do to bring about that learning. Effective supervisors have a clearly articulated model of supervision: they know where they are going with the supervisee and what they need to do to get there.

BOX 5.1	ETHICS CODES AND STANDARDS REGARDING MODELS OF SUPERVISION

Association for Counselor Education and Supervision
Ethical Guidelines for Counseling Supervisors (1993)

3.07 Supervisors should inform supervisees of the goals, policies, theoretical orientations toward counseling, training, and supervision model or approach on which the supervision is based.

Association for Counselor Education and Supervision
Standards for Counseling Supervisors (1990)

The counseling supervisor:
1.3 demonstrates knowledge of his/her assumptions about human behavior.
6.2 demonstrates knowledge of various theoretical models of supervision.

National Board for Certified Counselors
Standards for the Ethical Practice of Clinical Supervision (1999b)

Clinical supervisors shall:
3. Inform supervisees about the process of supervision, including supervision goals, case management procedures, and the supervisor's preferred supervision model(s).

The components of an adequate model of supervision include the following elements:

- How learning and development occur in individuals. This is commonly based on the supervisor's model of therapy and how he or she views change as occurring in clients.
- The role of individual and multicultural differences in supervision. Does one approach fit all supervisees, or must the approach be tailored to the individual?
- The goals of supervision. Is the focus on helping with immediate matters, helping the supervisee develop a problem-solving approach to clinical matters, or both?
- The role of the supervisor. Is the supervisor's primary role teacher, mentor, consultant, adviser, counselor, or some combination of roles?
- Intervention strategies the supervisor will use to assist the supervisee in accomplishing the goals of supervision.
- The role of evaluation in supervision.

Munson (1993) adds that a good theory or model has four components: (1) utility, (2) verifiability, (3) comprehensiveness, and (4) simplicity. A good model explains lots of information in a concise, understandable way.

In the writings on supervision, various authors have organized the models of supervision in somewhat different ways. Understanding how the models are categorized will help us compare and contrast the conceptual differences between models. Campbell (2000) divides supervision models into two main groups: psychotherapy-based supervision models and supervision-specific models. Psychotherapy-based models rely on the assumptions, methods, and techniques of a psychotherapy theory when training supervisees. For example, a supervisor might use the techniques of behavior therapy in supervising an individual. The second category, supervision-specific models, includes developmental models, parallel process, Interpersonal Process Recall (IPR), and interactional supervision.

Bernard and Goodyear (1998) identify the same two broad categories but add two more categories to the list. Using Holloway's idea (1992) that supervision-based models are either developmental or social role models, Bernard and Goodyear (1998) suggest these four categories: psychotherapy-based models, developmental models, social role models, and eclectic and integrationist models.

Bradley and Ladany (2001) identify three categories of models: integrative, developmental, and psychotherapy. Todd and Storm (1997) take a broader view, providing five categories: psychoanalytic, transgenerational, purposive-systematic, integrative, and postmodern models of family therapy supervision. As you can see, there is little consensus at this time regarding classification systems for supervision models. A summary of these four major categorization schemes for models of supervision can be found in Box 5.2.

Stoltenberg, McNeill, and Delworth (1998) describe how models of supervision have been developed over time. They suggest that the early models of supervision relied heavily on psychotherapeutic processes. This was consistent with the notion that once a clinician is skilled in therapy approaches he or she should accordingly be skilled in supervision. As the body of information regarding supervision has developed and supervision has come to be seen as having its own set of skills and issues, models designed specifically for supervision have been developed. The models pertaining to supervision are still in the developmental stages and will very likely look much different in the future. As a student of supervision, we encourage you to become familiar with the major models of supervision and to work toward developing a clear model that will guide your supervision and the approaches you use.

Our overview does not survey all the models described in the literature, but it provides a sample of the way models are being categorized today. We have chosen a three-dimensional system, categorizing the models as developmental, psychotherapy-based, and integrative. This schema reflects our ideas regarding the most significant models of supervision. We find these categories useful but somewhat artificial and in application there is overlap among the models. For example, a model could be both integrative and developmental, and a developmental model may incorporate some psychotherapy-based concepts and techniques. The purpose of describing these models by category is to assist you in gaining a clearer understanding of the nature and process of supervision. At the end of each section, we have listed some suggested resources for further reading for each of the models. If you wish to learn more about one or more of these models, we recommend these materials for further inquiry.

BOX 5.2 | CATEGORIZING SUPERVISION MODELS

Bernard and Goodyear	Bradley and Ladany	Campbell	Todd and Storm
Psychotherapy-Based Models	*Integrative Models*	*Psychotherapy-Based Models*	*Psychoanalytic Models*
Psychodynamic	Discrimination	Behavioral	*Transgenerational Models*
Person-centered	Interpersonal Process	Cognitive	Symbiotic-experiential
Cognitive-Behavioral	Recall (IPR)	Psychodynamic	Contextual
Systemic	Systems approach to	Adlerian	
Narrative	supervision	Existential	*Purpose-Systematic Models*
	Reflective learning	Family therapy	Structural/strategic
Developmental Models	Solution-oriented	Brief therapy and	Solution-focused
Social Role Models	Schema-focused	solution-focused	
Discrimination			*Integrative Models*
	Developmental Models	*Supervision-Specific Models*	Metaframeworks
Eclectic and Integrationist Models	Integrated developmental model	Interpersonal Process Recall (IPR)	Systemic cognitive developmental
		Parallel process	Integrative problem-centered
	Psychotherapy Models	Interactional supervision	Mythological
	Psychodynamic	Developmental models	
	Behavioral		*Postmodern Models of Family Therapy Supervision*
	Cognitive		

In summary, the supervision model is the theoretical roadmap for developing supervision techniques. Understanding how you view the supervisee, the task of supervision, and the roles of the supervisor will help determine which of the many intervention strategies you will choose. As you begin to outline your theoretical model of supervision, keep in mind that it is not a one-time event. Your model will evolve as you gain experience as a supervisor and as a clinician and as you develop the wisdom that comes with life experience.

DEVELOPMENTAL MODELS

Developmental models view supervision as an evolutionary process, and each stage of development has defined characteristics and skills. The novice clinician is characterized by a lack of confidence and limited basic skills. The more advanced supervisee has developed confidence and skill with experience and supervision and is becoming a self-sufficient clinician. In developmental models, supervision methods are adjusted to fit the confidence and skill level of supervisees as they develop and grow professionally. Case 5.1 shows how one supervisor responded to two supervisees with very different levels of skill.

CASE 5.1 | AARON AND SANDRA

Aaron and Sandra are students in a master's level counseling program, and both are beginning their internship training at a community mental health center. Aaron is new to the counseling profession, whereas Sandra has considerable course work in marriage and family counseling and has worked in community mental health settings for more than five years. They have both been assigned to the family treatment unit.

Dr. Raman is supervising both students at the center, and he performs an initial assessment of each trainee. He determines that Sandra is very knowledgeable and skilled in her work with families, whereas Aaron is a novice in his clinical experience with this population. Within a matter of weeks, Dr. Raman is primarily using the case consultation method in his supervision of Sandra. Together they brainstorm various approaches and discuss the research supporting these approaches. Dr. Raman asks, "How can we learn together about the newest methods in family work?" Both he and Sandra read journal articles on a variety of topics, and supervision sessions are used to discuss what they have learned.

In supervising Aaron, Dr. Raman takes a different approach. He has Aaron observe him conducting family therapy sessions, and discusses with Aaron the methods he is using and why they are appropriate in working with the family. After some time, Dr. Raman has Aaron participate as a co-therapist with him where he can directly observe Aaron in his clinical work. Over the course of the training, he will use direct observation and videotaping as he gives Aaron more autonomy in working with families.

With Sandra, Dr. Raman's role is more of a colleague and consultant, whereas with Aaron, he is a model and a teacher of clinical methods. The supervision approach chosen by Dr. Raman was based on the competence level of each supervisee.

One of the most useful developmental models is the integrated developmental model (IDM) developed by Stoltenberg, McNeill, and Delworth (1998). This model is based on 10 years of research and describes three levels of supervisee development and the corresponding role of the supervisor for each developmental level. These authors emphasize that, as with human developmental stages, the supervisee does not pass cleanly through the three levels. A supervisee, for example, may be highly skilled in individual therapy and yet a novice when it comes to leading group therapy. Level 1 supervisees are entry-level therapists and generally lack confidence and skill. They need more structure and direction from the supervisor. Level 2 supervisees are beginning to feel the confidence to start relying on their own abilities and decision-making processes. The supervisor may occasionally provide direction but focuses more on process issues, examining how the supervisee's own personal reactions and issues affect his or her functioning as a therapist. In Level 3, the supervisee provides most of the structure in supervision.

Confidence levels are growing rapidly, and the supervision is more informal and more collegial with the supervisor acting as a consultant. Stoltenberg, McNeill, and Delworth identify eight specific domains of clinical practice in which to assess the developmental level. Those domains include intervention skills competencies, assessment techniques, interpersonal assessment, client conceptualization, individual differences, theoretical orientation, treatment plans and goals, and professional ethics.

IDM is a well-conceived developmental model of supervision. It is useful for supervisors to understand the developmental stages of the supervisee and the corresponding skills and approaches for the supervisor. The shortcomings of the IDM model are twofold: (1) it focuses largely on the development of students as supervisees; and (2) it does not go far enough in suggesting supervision methods applicable to each supervisee level. An advantage of the IDM model is that a wide range of supervision methods and techniques can be employed to help the supervisee move through the stages in becoming a competent clinician.

An expanded developmental model has been proposed by Skovholt and Ronnestad (1992). They see the developmental process of counselors as occurring over a long period of time; it is not limited to graduate school years. They interviewed clinicians from graduate students to those with years of experience and identified eight stages that characterize counselor development. Those stages are competence, transition to professional training, imitation of experts, conditional autonomy, exploration, integration, individuation, and integrity. This model is useful in helping the supervisor conceptualize the developmental process that clinicians experience. The supervisor can then adjust his or her supervision methods to fit the needs of the supervisee.

Box 5.3 can be used as a blueprint for developmental supervision. It provides examples of the types of actions that need to take place on the part of the supervisor and the supervisee at each of the developmental stages of supervision. This list was developed by supervisors with input from their supervisees following completion of their graduate externship experience. New supervisors often ask, "What specifically should I be doing with my supervisees at each of the developmental stages?" This outline answers some of those questions and provides a roadmap for navigating the developmental stages of supervisees. The first stage involves intensive monitoring and control on the part of the supervisor. Stage 2 is characterized by sharing of responsibilities. Stage 3 reflects the independent functioning of the skilled supervisee.

These developmental stages are based on the knowledge and skill of the supervisee and may vary with the type of therapy or target population served and the theoretical model being used in supervision. Also, it is important to note that as a supervisor you will always start with the assumption that every supervisee is at the beginning stage of skill. This means that each supervisee will begin at Stage 1 and move through each stage based on his or her knowledge and expertise in that given area.

BOX 5.3	A BLUEPRINT FOR DEVELOPMENTAL SUPERVISION

1. **Beginning Stage:** The goal of this stage is to develop the relationship, assess competencies, educate, and monitor early experiences.

Supervisor

Assume primary responsibility and encourage supervisee

Assess supervisee's strengths and weaknesses in areas of training, experience, and clinical competence (assessment, direct treatment, and interpersonal style)

Use supervisee assessment information to develop goals with the supervisee

Review and sign supervisory contract and other supervisory agreements

Critically review each of the supervisee's prospective clients for appropriate placement

Set supervisory goals collaboratively with supervisee

Review policies and procedures of practice (address ethics, confidentiality, and emergency procedures)

Educate supervisee in areas of need to include ethics, liability, assessment, organization of information, documentation, and therapeutic skills

Provide direct and consistent observation of therapy (live supervision, video, one-way mirror, bug-in-the-ear)

Provide structure for supervisory sessions

Limit autonomy until competence in performance is evidenced

Provide direct feedback often and combine with information and practice as needed

Be available for direct intervention in critical incidents (with supervisee and clients)

Review and approve all documentation (assist in writing if needed)

Document supervisory activities

Supervisee

Seek and accept direction

Discuss perception of strengths and weaknesses with supervisor

Provide supervisor with information requested

Review and sign contract and supervisory agreements

Set supervision goals in collaboration with supervisor

Practice safe and prudent therapy within the structure provided by supervisor

Review policies and procedures for practice and seek clarification

Be willing to take risks and practice within the boundaries of the supervisory relationship

Question and hypothesize

Provide information to supervisor regarding wants and expectations of supervision

Recognize that anxiety is normal and discuss concerns with supervisor

2. **Middle Stage:** The goal of this stage is to transition from dependency to independent practice. This stage is often characterized by a struggle in the supervisory relationship as supervisees want to move forward and supervisors want to tread carefully.

Supervisor

Role-play, provide ethical dilemmas, play devil's advocate, and design "what if" scenarios for supervisee to explore and discuss

Suggest various theoretical approaches for each given case

Facilitate discussion of various treatment alternatives

Supervisee

Practice presenting cases in a professional manner

Explore theoretical orientation with supervisor

Actively participate in identification of treatment techniques and strategies

Consult with supervisor for direction

(continued)

BOX 5.3 | A BLUEPRINT FOR DEVELOPMENTAL SUPERVISION (*continued*)

Assist supervisee in choosing a sound course of action

Provide supervisee with opportunities to discuss client and presenting problems from supervisee's perspective

Share responsibility with supervisee

Monitor by direct observation, documentation review, and self-report

Create opportunities for supervisee to struggle with decisions and consequences

Ask questions and expect supervisee to seek answers (be prepared to assist)

Serve as a resource and reference for materials, problem solving, and practice

Encourage supervisee to present cases in a collaborative manner

Collaboratively make decisions about how much time to spend on each case

Share responsibility for the supervision session structure

Reduce directive stance and encourage democratic decision making

Provide formative feedback consistently, and develop a plan of action collaboratively with supervisee for improvement

Document supervisory practice

Initiate interventions independently

Provide information to supervisor to assure client welfare

Choose approach for case conceptualization and share with supervisor

Identify relevant questions and strategies for gaining information

Draft reports and explain formulation and process to supervisor

Assume comprehensive case management duties

Share responsibility with supervisor for client care

Share responsibility for structure of supervisory sessions

Come to supervision sessions prepared to initiate topics for discussion

Provide feedback to supervisor on the supervision received and identify and voice perceptions of unmet needs

3. **Ending Stage:** The primary goal of this stage is to foster independence and prepare supervisee for work as an independent professional.

Supervisor

Review goals and progress

Listen to and encourage supervisee

Monitor primarily through self-report and documentation with occasional direct observation

Provide summative evaluation

Take responsibility for termination of formal supervisory relationship

Document supervisory process

Acknowledge continued vicarious and direct liability throughout the supervisory relationship

Be open to and seek evaluative feedback on the supervisory process, the structure of supervision, and specific supervisory skills

Supervisee

Articulate theoretical orientation, treatment alternatives explored, and course of action chosen

Provide justification for any given course of action in treatment

Recognize and identify skills for future development

Assume primary responsibility for client welfare

Review goals and progress

Review learning during supervision

Determine future goals and course of action

Think out loud while problem solving and conceptualizing client information

Increase independent decision making

Be self-supervising

Reflect on the supervisory process and provide supervisor with evaluative feedback

For a more detailed treatment of the developmental models, see Skovholt and Ronnestad (1992), Stoltenberg and McNeill (1997), and Stoltenberg, McNeill, and Delworth (1998).

PSYCHOTHERAPY-BASED MODELS

Psychotherapy-based models use the concepts developed for psychotherapy and apply them to the supervision setting. That which is useful in bringing about change with clients is likely to be useful in bringing about change with supervisees. Five psychotherapy-based supervision models are discussed. Depending on your therapy orientation, you may find that one or more of the models resonates with your own style.

Psychodynamic Model

According to Bradley and Gould (2001), supervision "is a therapeutic process focusing on the intrapersonal and interpersonal dynamics in the supervisee's relationship with clients, supervisors, colleagues, and others" (p. 148). The primary focus of supervision is on the supervisee's development of self-awareness of these dynamics and on development of the skills necessary to use a psychodynamic approach in counseling. The supervisor is concerned with the supervisee's personal issues to the extent that these issues are influencing the course of therapy.

With this model, emphasis is placed on the dynamics of supervisees, such as resistance, their way of reacting to their clients, and the client's reactions (transference) to the therapist. Because transference is common in the therapeutic process, it is important to conceptualize the meaning of a client's reactions to a counselor and for counselors to understand their own reactions to the client's transference. The psychoanalytic model offers the richest perspective for grasping the implications of both transference and countertransference. In psychodynamic approaches, transference and countertransference are viewed as central to the therapy process. With this model of supervision, a great deal of emphasis is given to understanding how client–counselor reactions influence the course of therapy.

Parallel process is often discussed in conjunction with psychodynamic approaches. Ekstein and Wallerstein (1972) describe parallel process as the supervisee's interaction with the supervisor that parallels the client's behavior with the supervisee as the therapist. It is the supervisor's task to explore these parallel relationships or processes with the supervisee as a key to learning how to become a better therapist. For example, a counselor may experience difficulty terminating with clients. Her ambivalence about ending a therapy relationship may mirror the client's resistance to talking about ending the professional relationship. The counselor may have unresolved personal conflicts pertaining to losses and ending relationships in her own life, and this may surface when concluding the supervisory relationship. The parallel process provides a lens by which to view and understand ways that therapy may get stalled due to the therapist's unresolved personal problems.

Here are some examples of questions and statements typically made by supervisors with a psychodynamic orientation:

- What similarities do you see between our supervisory work and the relationship you share with your client?
- We've talked about your wanting my approval as a supervisor. It appears to me that you are hesitant to challenge your client lest she not approve of you.
- Think out loud for a bit about what purpose your client's resistance might be serving.
- You appear to be having a very strong emotional response to your client; where and with whom else in your life might you experience this emotion?

For further information on the supervision of psychodynamic psychotherapies, see Binder and Strupp (1997), and for a psychodynamic approach to the supervisory relationship, see Frawley-O'Dea and Sarnat (2001).

Person-Centered Model

Person-centered therapy is based on the assumption that one can direct one's own life. The client has the capacity to resolve life problems effectively without interpretation and direction from a therapist. A major goal is to provide a climate of safety and trust in the therapeutic setting so that the client, using the therapeutic relationship for self-exploration, can become aware of blocks to growth. The attitudes and personal characteristics of the therapist and the quality of the client–therapist relationship are the prime determinants of the outcomes of therapy.

Applying the person-centered approach to supervision, the assumption is that the supervisee has immense resources for both personal and professional development. The supervisor is not viewed as the expert who does all the teaching; rather, the supervisee assumes an active role in this process. Learning that occurs in the supervisory process results from a collaborative venture between supervisor and supervisee. According to Lambers (2000), the "supervisor and supervisee must be clear from the outset what the supervision relationship is about and both need to take responsibility for maintaining and managing the boundaries of the relationship" (p. 199). Rather than relying on providing supervisees with directives or advice, supervisors encourage supervisees to think about how they might best proceed with their cases. Just as therapy outcomes are greatly influenced by the quality of the therapeutic relationship, in supervision the outcomes of the process hinge on the quality of the relationship between supervisor and supervisee.

In this model, development of a trusting and facilitative relationship between supervisor and supervisee—characterized by the supervisor's empathy, warmth, and genuineness—provides an atmosphere in which the supervisee can grow and develop. It is the job of the supervisor to provide this atmosphere where growth can flourish. Then supervisees are more likely to take an active role in bringing their concerns to supervision sessions. According to Patterson (1997), the focus of this approach is on conditions commonly recognized as client-centered, but these elements are common to all major theories. Patterson maintains that working within a client-centered framework has the advantage of a shared philosophy of the supervisor and the supervisee. The supervisor allows the supervisee to direct the sessions by selecting and presenting issues to be explored in the supervisory sessions.

Supervision from the person-centered perspective downplays the evaluative role of the supervisor and questions the role of the supervisor as gatekeeper of the profession. Lambers (2000) states that the person-centered supervisor "has no other concern, no other agenda than to facilitate the therapist's ability to be open to her experience so that she can become fully present and engaged in the relationship with the client. The person-centered supervisor accepts the supervisee as a person *in process* and trusts the supervisee's potential for growth" (p. 197).

Here are some examples of the kinds of statements or questions typically used by the person-centered supervisor:

- I'd like to hear you talk more about how it was for you to be with the client for that session.
- I encourage you to begin to trust more your own internal direction.
- Even though you are saying you really don't know how to proceed, if you did know, what actions might you take?
- Tell me what you found to be important about the experience you shared with your client today.
- I'd like to hear you talk more about the climate you are creating with your client.
- To what degree do you feel you understand the world of your client?
- What are your expectations for what we might do in today's session?

In her critique of the client-centered approach to supervision, Davenport (1992) contends that supervisors must not put training needs ahead of client needs. For Davenport, this implies that evaluation and directive supervision are essential. She concludes her critique of this approach in this way: "Evaluation is often uncomfortable for both professor and student, but I am convinced it must be a part of the supervisor package. Client-centered supervision, appealing as it may be, fails to meet the rigorous ethical and legal guidelines now required of counselor supervisors" (p. 231).

For further readings in the area of person-centered supervision, see Lambers (2000) and Patterson (1997).

Cognitive-Behavioral Model

This approach had its beginning with behavior therapy, which is based on classical and operant conditioning. Although still a separate school of therapy, behavior therapy has evolved into the larger area of cognitive-behavior therapy, which focuses on one's beliefs, assumptions, and thoughts and how they affect emotion and behavior. The basic assumption is that the manner in which individuals process information influences their behavior, emotions, and physiology (Liese & Beck, 1997). One of the key tasks in cognitive-behavioral supervision is teaching cognitive-behavioral techniques and correcting misconceptions about this approach with clients. These sessions are structured, focused, and educational, and both supervisor and supervisee are responsible for the structure and content of the sessions (Liese & Beck, 1997). In supervision, the focus is on how the supervisee's cognitive picture of his or her skills affects his or her ability as a therapist. By focusing on this, the supervisee also learns how to apply these cognitive-behavioral methods with clients.

Liese and Beck (1997) outline nine steps that typically occur in cognitive therapy supervision. These steps provide an example of the content of a session.

1. *Check-in:* Asking "How are you doing?" to break the ice.
2. *Agenda setting:* The supervisor teaches the supervisee to carefully prepare for the supervision session and asks, "What would you like to work on today?"
3. *Bridge from previous supervision session:* The work of the last supervisory session is reviewed by asking, "What did you learn last time?"
4. *Inquiry about previously supervised therapy cases:* Progress or particular difficulties with previously discussed cases is reviewed.
5. *Review of homework since previous supervision session:* Homework might include readings, writing regarding cases, or trying new techniques with a client.
6. *Prioritization and discussion of agenda items:* A review of the supervisee's tape-recorded therapy sessions is a major focus for the supervisory session. Teaching and role playing are common supervision methods.
7. *Assignment of new homework:* As a result of the session, new assignments are given that will help the supervisee develop knowledge and skills in cognitive-behavior therapy.
8. *Supervisor's capsule summaries:* This involves the supervisor's reflections of what has been covered in the session to help keep the session focused and to emphasize important points.
9. *Elicit feedback from supervisee:* The supervisor asks for feedback throughout the session and ends the session with questions such as, "What have you learned today?"

These steps closely parallel the steps that occur in a cognitive-behavioral therapy session with a client. In the process of supervision, the supervisee learns both from the content of the supervision and from the supervisor modeling how to conduct a cognitive-behavioral session.

For further reading on this model, see Liese and Beck (1997) and Woods and Ellis (1997).

Family Therapy Model

Family therapy typically involves work with the family as a system by examining the various relationships and dynamics. Liddle, Becker, and Diamond (1997) state that family therapy supervision is much like family therapy—it is active, directive, and collaborative. The supervision encourages supervisees to examine their own intergenerational dynamics, values, and culture to further their own awareness and growth and to learn about becoming a family therapist. The family therapy supervisor works with the supervisory relationship as a system as well as with the supervisee and his or her clients as a system.

The family therapy approach to supervision is based on the assumption that a trainee's mental health, as defined by relationships with his or her family of origin, has implications for professional training and supervision. Supervisees can benefit from exploring the dynamics of their family of origin because this significant knowledge enables them to relate more effectively to the families they will meet in their clinical practice.

Getz and Protinsky (1994) take the position that personal growth is an essential part of training and supervising counselors. They contend that knowledge and skills cannot be separated from a counselor's personal dynamics and use of self. Getz and Protinsky point to growing clinical evidence that a family-of-origin approach to supervision is a necessary dimension of training therapists who want to work with families. The reactions of therapists to their clients' stories tend to reactivate therapists' old learned patterns of behavior and unresolved problems. By studying their own families of origin, supervisees are ultimately able to improve their ability to counsel families.

If supervisees lack awareness of ways that particular members of their own family of origin may trigger strong emotional reactions in them, it is likely that they will react too quickly or inappropriately to client families. Supervisors of family therapist trainees generally assume that it is inevitable that they will encounter similar dynamics between the family members whom they are counseling and the members of their own family of origin.

If supervisees do not understand the patterns of interpersonal behavior learned in their family of origin, they are likely to project feelings they had toward their own family onto their clients. Supervision addresses how supervisees' clinical work is influenced by their experiences with their own families of origin.

The family therapy supervisor assists the supervisee in exploring his or her own family dynamics with the use of techniques such as genograms, family history, and family sculpting. The supervisee is encouraged to identify patterns such as enmeshment, detachment, and triangulation. The purpose of this exploration is to determine ways in which one's own family of origin will affect the supervisee's ability to function as a family therapist.

For further readings on the family therapy model of supervision, see Liddle, Becker, and Diamond (1997) and Gardner, Bobele, and Biever (1997).

Feminist Model

The underlying philosophy of the feminist model is being gender-fair, flexible, interactional, and life-span oriented. This approach emphasizes that gender-role expectations profoundly influence our identity from birth onward. Feminist therapy is based on five interrelated principles:

- The personal is political.
- The counseling relationship is egalitarian.
- Women's experiences are honored.
- Definitions of distress and mental illness are reformulated.
- Oppression needs to be understood and challenged.

The aims of feminist therapy include both individual change and social change. The overall aim is to replace the current patriarchy with a feminist consciousness, creating a society in which relationships are interdependent, cooperative, and mutually supportive (Corey, 2001b).

The basic concepts of feminist therapy can be applied to the process of clinical supervision. The supervision process is clearly explained to supervisees from the beginning, which increases the chances that the supervisee will become an active partner in this learning process (Corey, 2001c). The feminist model of supervision entails striving toward an equalization of the power base between the supervisor and the supervisee. Although the supervisory relationship cannot be entirely equal, the supervisor shares power in the relationship by creating a collaborative partnership with supervisees. The supervisor–supervisee relationship is based on empowerment. Supervisors do this by modeling how to identify and use power appropriately. For example, instead of the supervisor providing specific direction to the supervisee, the supervisor can help the supervisee think about his or her clients in new ways, formulate interpretations, and devise interventions.

Martinez, Davis, and Dahl (1999) suggest that feminist supervisors foster a mutually agreed-upon approach to working with a client rather than using the usual supervisor-directed approach. Supervision focuses on the trainee's philosophy and practice of counseling. A supervisee's assumptions, beliefs, and values pertaining to gender, race, culture, sexual orientation, ability, and age are often the subject of discussion during supervision sessions.

Carta-Falsa and Anderson (2001) describe a collaborative model of clinical supervision that is based on genuine dialogue between supervisor and supervisee. In this active collaborative supervision, the supervisee is resourceful. The supervisor's role is to reinforce the strengths of the supervisee. In this new paradigm, power is shared between supervisor and supervisee. Together they participate in acquiring, sharing, and reshaping knowledge. According to Carta-Falsa and Anderson, this collaborative spirit leads to an empowered relationship that is characterized by a sense of safety. This sense of trust and security forms the basis for increased risk taking, higher levels of performance, and greater individual confidence.

One of our contributors specifically mentioned the challenge supervisors face in dealing with the power differential inherent to the supervisory relationship. This clinician is supportive of the feminist value pertaining to power, and her thoughts on minimizing the power differential between supervisor and supervisee are provided in the Voices from the Field feature.

Prouty, Thomas, Johnson, and Long (2001) maintain that feminist supervisors use supervision methods to assist supervisees in acquiring therapeutic skills, gaining self-confidence, and coming to value multiple perspectives in their clinical practice. Feminist supervision methods are grounded in the value of a collaborative interaction and minimization of the hierarchy within the supervisory relationship. Collaborative methods are especially favored as supervisees gain more experience and need less authoritative direction to carry out their duties to their clients. Feminist supervisors place a great deal of emphasis on fostering competence and getting across the message that there are multiple perspectives from which to examine a problem or to conduct supervision. Hierarchical supervision methods tend to be used by feminist supervisors only when clients pose a risk of harm to self or others or when the situation is beyond the supervisee's current therapeutic abilities. Although the expertise of the supervisor and his or her role in teaching are acknowledged, clear and open communication is valued as a way to minimize hierarchy. The use of power is designed to empower the supervisee by enhancing his or her abilities and competencies.

If you are interested in further reading on feminist approaches to supervision, see Martinez, Davis, and Dahl (1999), Carta-Falsa and Anderson (2001), and Porter and Vasquez (1997).

INTEGRATIVE MODELS

Integrative models of supervision, like integrative models of counseling and psychotherapy, rely on more than one theory and technique. A variety of theoretical concepts and intervention strategies are combined in a way that uniquely fits the clinician's beliefs and values about change, the therapeutic process, and the client's needs.

Bradley, Gould, and Parr (2001) state that the integrative model is one of the most frequently used supervision models. Integrative models of supervision are generally based on the assumption that trainees function from the perspective of integrative models of counseling. A variety of integrative approaches can be designed that are based on a combination of techniques, common principles, and concepts from a number of different theories. An integrative approach based on various techniques offers more flexibility than does a single approach.

There are multiple pathways to achieving this integration, two of the most common being technical eclecticism and theoretical integration.

VOICES FROM THE FIELD

Tory Nersasian, Psy.D.

The power differential inherent to the supervisory relationship can present significant challenges for the student. Ideally, a supervisor acts as a consultant, empowering the supervisee to make his or her own clinical decisions, offering alternative solutions and guidance when necessary. At times, however, supervisors take a more authoritarian role in the relationship, imposing a clinical opinion as the "correct" solution to a particular treatment or assessment issue. When this occurs, the supervisee is left with two choices: assert a clinical opinion in opposition to the supervisor or comply with orders. When one is in the role of colleague, the former option carries much less risk; in fact, it is much more acceptable for there to be disagreements in clinical opinion among professionals. However, when one is

in the role of supervisee, asserting an opinion that runs against the clinical beliefs of the supervisor can be professional suicide.

Oftentimes, the supervisor is also the evaluator of the supervisee and has the power to turn a clinical disagreement into a black mark on the student's permanent record. Even in cases where the supervisor would never take a disagreement as an opportunity to professionally harm the student, there is always fear within the student that this could occur. No matter how strong the level of trust is within the supervisory relationship, there will always be pressure on the supervisee to comply with the clinical opinions of the supervisor. I believe it's important for the supervisor to keep this issue in mind, discuss it with the student, and take steps to minimize the power differential as much as possible.

Technical eclecticism tends to focus on differences, chooses from many approaches, and is a collection of techniques. This path calls for using techniques from different schools without necessarily subscribing to the theoretical positions that spawned them. In contrast, *theoretical integration* refers to a conceptual or theoretical creation beyond a mere blending of techniques. This path has the goal of producing a conceptual framework that synthesizes the best of two or more theoretical approaches to produce an outcome richer than that of a single theory (Norcross & Halgin, 1997; Norcross & Newman, 1992).

An integrative perspective at its best entails systematic integration of underlying principles and methods common to a range of therapeutic approaches. To develop this kind of integration, you need to be thoroughly conversant with a number of theories, be open to the idea that these theories can be unified in some way, and be willing to continually test your hypotheses to determine how well they are working. An integrative perspective is the product of a great deal of study, clinical practice, research, and theorizing (Corey, 2001a).

An integrative perspective of the supervision process is best characterized by attempts to look beyond and across the confines of single-school approaches to see what can be learned from other perspectives. Unless you have an accurate, in-depth knowledge of theories, you cannot formulate a true synthesis. Simply put, you cannot integrate what you do not know (Norcross & Newman, 1992). Constructing an integrative orientation to counseling practice is a long-term venture that is refined with experience. Ideally, an integrative approach dynamically integrates concepts and techniques that fit the uniqueness of your personality and style of supervision.

There are some drawbacks to encouraging the development of an integrative model. Some practitioners are critical of an inconsistent eclectic approach that is reduced to a random borrowing of ideas and techniques. At its worst, eclecticism can be an excuse for practice that is not well thought out—a practice that lacks a systematic rationale for what you actually do in your work. If you merely pick and choose according to whims, it is likely that what you select will be just a reflection of your biases and preconceived ideas. It is important to avoid the trap of emerging with a hodgepodge of unamalgamated theories thrown hastily together (Corey, 2001a).

The kind of integrated model of supervision we are suggesting is based on common denominators across the different models. At its best, this involves identifying core concepts that different models share or concepts that can be usefully combined. It is essential to identify your key beliefs underlying the practice of supervision. Your philosophical assumptions are important because they influence which "reality" you perceive, and they direct your attention to the variables that you are "set" to see in carrying out your functions as a supervisor.

Beware of subscribing exclusively to any one view of human nature; remain open and selectively incorporate a framework for counseling that is consistent with your own personality and your belief system. If you attempt to blend theoretical constructs from different orientations in your own integrative model, be sure that these concepts are indeed compatible (Corey, 2001a).

Some blending simply does not make much conceptual sense. For instance, a psychodynamic perspective, which focuses on unconscious factors as the source of present-day problems, generally does not blend nicely with theories that reject the unconscious, such as cognitive-behavioral therapy. Psychodynamic theories are geared around central concepts such as exploration of past traumatic events, exploration of dreams, and working through the transference relationship. Cognitive-behavioral models do not allow much room to explore these theoretical constructs.

When blending different theoretical frameworks, it is essential that these frameworks lend themselves to a fruitful merger. For example, you will find many commonalities of philosophy shared by person-centered and feminist models of supervision. These commonalities include minimizing power differentials, focusing on supervisees' attitudes and behaviors, and striving to build and maintain collaborative relationships. Both models focus on development of the supervisee as a person, but the feminist model also has a primary goal of social advocacy and change. Even though there are some clear differences between these two models, there is enough commonality that they lend themselves to integration.

Clinicians who use an integrative model of psychotherapy are inclined to use an integrative model of supervision as well. This approach could involve the complete integration of several theories or an integration of concepts from a number of theories fashioned into one's own model. One advantage of an integrative approach is that the supervisor can uniquely tailor the supervision methods used to fit the supervisee, the client, and the setting. The limitation of an integrative approach is that it requires the supervisor to have a broad understanding of the range of supervision models and techniques.

The fundamental, overarching principle of integrative supervision is that supervisors should customize supervision to the unique needs of the supervisee (Norcross & Halgin, 1997). As a way to best discover the needs of supervisees, Norcross and Halgin believe supervision should ideally begin with a needs assessment. A key question is, "What do supervisees need and want from the supervisory experience?" Although what the supervisee wants should be elicited, articulated, and considered, this will not necessarily commit the supervisor to structure the supervisory relationship exclusively by this framework.

In the following sections, we briefly describe the discrimination model and the systems approach model, both of which are integrative models of supervision. For further reading on integrative approaches to supervision, see Norcross and Halgin (1997).

Discrimination Model

The discrimination model, developed by Bernard (1979), is rooted in technical eclecticism. In this model, the supervisor focuses on three separate areas for supervision: the supervisee's intervention skills, the supervisee's conceptualization skills, and the supervisee's personalization skills or personal style in therapy. Once the current level of functioning in each of these three areas has been assessed, the supervisor chooses a role that will facilitate the supervisee's learning and growth. In the model, the three roles available are teacher, counselor, and consultant. It is called the discrimination model because the supervisor's approach is determined by the individual training needs of each trainee (Bernard & Goodyear, 1998).

Systems Approach to Supervision

The systems approach to supervision (SAS) was developed by Holloway (1995) to guide the teaching and practice of supervisors. It is a conceptual model that organizes what supervisors do without subscribing to any particular theoretical orientation. According to Holloway (1997), there are five specific goals in the SAS model: (1) the supervisee will learn a wide range of professional attitudes, knowledge and skills; (2) supervision occurs within the context of a mutual professional relationship; (3) the supervisory relationship is the primary means of involving the supervisee in accomplishing the goals of supervision; (4) both content and process are integral to the instructional approaches within the context of the relationship; and (5) the supervisee is empowered through the acquisition of knowledge and skills.

Holloway (1995) identified seven dimensions that serve as the bases of supervision. The first three dimensions consist of: (1) the supervisory relationship, (2) supervision tasks, and (3) supervision functions. The other four dimensions are described as contextual factors: (4) the supervisor, (5) the supervisee, (6) the client, and (7) the institution or agency. The supervisory relationship is the foundation for supervision, and the SAS model describes how the interaction of the seven components affects what takes place in supervision.

Holloway (1995) identifies the phases of the supervision relationship as developing, mature, and terminating, which parallel research findings in research on friendship. The developing phase is characterized by clarifying the supervisory relationship and establishing the supervision contract. The mature phase is characterized by increasing the individual nature of the supervision specifically for the supervisee, developing the skills of case conceptualization, and confronting personal issues as they relate to clinical practice. Finally, the terminating phase involves the supervisee's understanding of the connection between theory and practice and a decreasing need for direction from the supervisor. The SAS model provides a framework and a language to guide supervision teaching and practice.

Additional Integrative Models of Supervision

Bradley, Gould, and Parr (2001) briefly describe some new models of integrative supervision that reflect the current research and development in integrative supervision. Those discussed here include the reflective learning model, the solution-oriented model, and the schema-focused model.

The Reflective Learning Model   Ward and House (1998) offer a supervision model that integrates reflective learning theory with the development of both the supervisory relationship and the supervisee as a professional. Their model links the principles of reflective learning theory to the supervisory process and the phases of supervision development. Supervisees reconstruct their counseling work using understandings, images, and actions to reframe a problem counseling situation.

Solution-Oriented Model   In solution-oriented supervision, the basic assumption is that the supervisee is the expert and has the resources to problem solve clinical situations (Thomas, 1994). According to Thomas, there are two steps in solution-oriented supervision: (1) building the conceptual map, which includes a discussion of what supervisees want from supervision, the supervisory relationship, and assumptions about solution-focused supervision; and

(2) implementing solution-oriented supervision, which includes setting goals and future orientation. Operating within the framework of a solution-oriented approach, supervisors strive to design a collaborative style in working with supervisees. Supervisees are assumed to be capable and resourceful when it comes to achieving their supervision goals. The model is based on family therapy and narrative therapy and focuses on affirming and empowering the supervisee to learn and grow in supervision.

Practitioners using a solution-oriented approach use several techniques to steer clients toward solutions. One of these techniques is the *miracle question*, which can be effective with a variety of complaints and situations (DeShazer, 1991). Miracle questions can be used as an assessment technique to determine what the client would see as a satisfactory solution to a given problem. A practitioner might ask, "If a miracle happened and the problem you have was solved overnight, how would you know it was solved, *and what would be different?*" Clients are then encouraged to enact "what would be different" in spite of perceived problems. This process reflects O'Hanlon and Weiner-Davis's (1989) belief that changing the doing and viewing of the perceived problem changes the problem.

Another technique involves asking *exception questions,* which direct clients to times in their lives when the problem didn't exist. This exploration reminds clients that problems are not all-powerful and have not existed forever; it also provides a field of opportunity for evoking resources, engaging strengths, and positing possible solutions. Solution-oriented therapists focus on small, achievable changes that may lead to additional positive outcomes. Their language joins with the client's, using similar words, pacing, and tone, but also involves questions that presuppose change, posit multiple answers, and are goal directed and future oriented.

Solution-oriented therapists also use *scaling questions* when change is required in human experiences that are not easily observed, such as feelings, moods, or communication. For example, a woman reporting feelings of panic or anxiety might be asked, "On a scale of 0 to 10, with 0 being how you felt when you first came to therapy and 10 being how you feel the day after your miracle occurs and your problem is gone, how would you rate your anxiety right now?" Even if the client has only moved away from 0 to 1, she has improved. How did she do that? What does she need to do to move another number up the scale?

There are many ways to apply the solution-oriented therapy model to an optimistic model of supervision. Such an approach has a great deal of potential for empowering supervisees. For a more in-depth discussion of the solution-oriented approach to therapy, see O'Hanlon and Weiner-Davis (1989), O'Hanlon (1999), and O'Hanlon and Beadle (1999).

The Schema-Focused Model   Greenwald and Young (1998) propose a supervision model based on schema-focused therapy, which incorporates cognitive, behavioral, experiential, and interpersonal approaches. The main supervisory experiences include getting acquainted, setting agendas, case conceptualization, case strategy, case implementation, resolving technical case problems, working on relationship issues, providing support for the supervisee, and discussing conceptual and treatment issues.

DEVELOPING YOUR OWN MODEL OF SUPERVISION

In most of the single theory models, supervisors accept an underlying philosophy and incorporate key concepts and specific methods of supervision. If you adopt a primary model (such as cognitive-behavioral), you will need to adapt this theory to your particular supervisory style. If you are interested in using an integrative model of supervision, the task is more complex, for you need to draw from several different approaches and integrate these perspectives with the person you are. Even though you will be challenged to personalize your approach to supervision, we favor an integrative approach to clinical supervision and recommend it to you. This approach is the most flexible, and it can be adapted to many situations and settings.

Whatever the basis of your integrative model of supervision, you need to have a basic knowledge of various theoretical systems and counseling techniques to work effectively with a wide range of clients in various clinical settings. Sticking strictly to one theory may not provide you with the therapeutic flexibility required to deal creatively with the complexities associated with clinical and supervisory practice.

When developing your approach to supervision, a good place to begin is by reflecting on the meaning of your own experiences when you were being supervised. What was especially helpful for you? What model of supervision enabled you to develop to the fullest extent possible? What kind of different experience might you have wanted from your supervision? How would you characterize the theory each of your supervisors operated from, and what could you learn from each of them with respect to designing your own model of supervision?

After this personal reflection on your own experiences as a supervisee, it is well to put your efforts toward mastering a primary theory that will serve as a guide for what the supervisor and the supervisee does in the supervision process. Select a theory that comes closest to your beliefs about human nature and the change process. Do your best to deepen your knowledge of a particular theory to determine what aspects of it fit best for you. Look for ways to personalize the theory or theories of your choice.

Commit yourself to a reading program and attend a variety of professional workshops. Reading is a realistic and useful way to expand your knowledge base and to provide ideas on how to create, implement, and evaluate techniques. As an extension of a reading program, attend workshops dealing with different aspects of supervision. As you attend workshops, be open to ideas that seem to have particular meaning to you and that fit the context of your work. Don't simply adopt ideas without putting them through your personal filter. As you experiment with many different methods of supervision, strive to bring your unique stamp to your work. Personalize your techniques so they fit your style, and be open to feedback from your supervisees about how well your supervisory style is working for them.

When you begin your work as a supervisor, think about what theoretical framework can help you make sense of what you are doing. Certainly your theoretical orientation to supervision will not be complete at the beginning stage of being a supervisor. Engage in reflective practice and look for a conceptual framework that will assist you in making sense of your interventions with supervisees. Rather than thinking of your choice of a theoretical orientation to supervision as something that is complete, think of your approach as evolving and developing with experience.

As you practice, be open to supervision throughout your career. Talk with other supervisors and colleagues about what you are doing. Discuss some of your interventions with other professionals, and think about alternative approaches you could take with supervisees. Although it may be helpful to begin by finding a primary theoretical orientation to guide your supervisory practice, don't get locked into any one model. Remain a long-term learner, and continue to think about alternative theoretical frameworks. Be open to borrowing techniques from various theories, yet do so in a systematic way. Think about your rationale for the manner in which you carry out your supervisory role and functions with supervisees.

We encourage you not to leave your personal style out of the process of developing your integrative approach in supervision. Continue reflecting on what fits for you and what set of blueprints will be most useful in creating an emerging model for supervisory practice. No prefabricated model will fit you perfectly. Instead, your challenge is to customize a supervisory approach, tailoring it to fit you and each of your supervisees.

SUMMARY

It is essential that supervisors have a clear understanding of the goals of supervision and the theoretical model they will use. The models of supervision have seen development and refinement in recent years but need further clarification and validation. Some of the current models are uneven in the topics they cover and the methods for application in supervision. A supervision model describes what supervision is and how the supervisee's learning occurs. Although there are many different supervision models, the most common ones are developmental models, psychotherapy-based models, and integrative models. Become familiar with the various models of supervision and begin to develop your own model.

The developmental model of supervision is based on the assessment of supervisees' knowledge and skill, which change over time. Many supervisory models currently practiced are derived from psychotherapy models originally developed for use in therapy. An integrative supervision model is developed by combining some of the best features of two or more theoretical approaches. As you practice, remain open to new learning and discuss your supervision approach with colleagues. The practice of supervision can best be viewed as an evolving and developing process.

SUGGESTED ACTIVITIES

1. Interview one or two clinical supervisors and ask them about their model of supervision. Ask how they arrived at using that model, how it is applied with supervisees, and what the pros and cons of the model are.

2. Which models of supervision seem to fit best with your interpersonal style and how you view your supervisory role? Which models seem furthest from your style? Sketch out some ideas for your own model of supervision. Discuss these ideas in small groups in class, comparing your thoughts and ideas. What common themes were identified by your classmates?

3. Working in small groups, develop a hypothetical composite model that each member in the group can agree to. Include in this model the types of activity and structure that apply. What are some of the basic components of a useful model? What kind of framework will help you be most effective as a supervisor? Have each group present their model to the entire class.

4. Identify and share with a partner dynamics in your family of origin that may positively or negatively affect your ability to work with families. How do you think some of the key concepts of family therapy can be usefully applied to your work as a supervisor?

5. Access the Web site for this text http://info.wadsworth.com/haynes, and complete the self-assessment inventory. Additional contributor perspectives and other activities specific to this chapter are also available to you through this Web site.

BECOMING A MULTICULTURALLY COMPETENT SUPERVISOR

INTRODUCTION

Multiculturalism and diversity have gained increasing focus in the counseling profession over the past decade. There have been many calls for mental health professionals to take a stand and integrate multicultural components into training and practice as a primary focus. The 2000 U.S. Census indicates that 31% of the U.S. population consists of racial and ethnic minorities (Grieco & Cassidy, 2001). By the year 2010, racial and ethnic minorities could become the numerical majority. Diversity offers both challenges and opportunities, and supervisors need to address these important issues with their supervisees. For example, how do you define culture? Does culture encompass ethnographic, demographic, status, and affiliation variables? Are within-group differences as significant as between-group differences?

In his early writings, Vontress (1979) stated that helping professionals should focus on the commonality of people rather than analyzing their cultural differences. When we view others as different and with unique needs, he suggests that we play into the hands of in-group bigots who believe that out-groups are inferior in some way. In his current writings, Vontress continues to believe that although human beings are dissimilar, at the same time, they are more alike than different (Vontress, Johnson, & Epp, 1999). Pedersen (2000) responds to this viewpoint by stating that it is an error to assume that one must emphasize either similarities or differences. He suggests that this is a false dichotomy. Multicultural counselors are not required to choose either a universal perspective, irrespective of cultural differences, or to allow each cultural group to define its own rules and roles and disregard the common ground across cultures. In other words, we all share many things in common regardless of culture, *and* we all are profoundly affected by the many cultures we identify with.

Counselor training has incorporated multicultural competencies and diversity, providing specific information and skills training for counselors. However, there is little information available regarding multicultural practices in supervision (see the Voices from the Field feature for more on this.) This chapter offers a definition and framework of multicultural supervisory practice.

DEFINING MULTICULTURALISM

Multiculturalism is a generic term that indicates some relationship between two or more diverse cultural groups. A multicultural perspective provides a conceptual framework that recognizes the complex diversity of a pluralistic society while at the same time suggesting bridges of shared concern that bind culturally different individuals to one another (Pedersen, 1991). Pedersen (2000) provides a useful working definition of the broad perspective of culture that can be applied to supervision:

> By defining culture broadly, to include within-group demographic variables (e.g., age, sex, and place of residence), status variables (e.g., social, educational, and economic), and affiliations (formal and informal), as well as ethnographic variables such as nationality, ethnicity, language, and religion, the construct *multicultural* becomes generic to all counseling relationships. (p. 36)

Feminist psychologists suggest that multiculturalism, as it applies to counseling, refers to the analysis of the social structures affecting mental health, including sexism, racism, and other levels of both oppression and privilege (Martinez, Davis, & Dahl, 1999). Sue, Arredondo, and McDavis (1992) explore the controversy of inclusive versus exclusive definitions of "multicultural counseling" and recommend a "focused" approach that stresses visible ethnicity (primarily African Americans, American Indians, Asian Americans, and Hispanics and Latinos). In other words, the assumption of primary ethnicity is based on outward appearances. However, it may be difficult to determine whether a person with dark skin is African American, Haitian, or another ethnicity. It is important to seek ethnic group membership identity from each individual.

The two terms found most often in the literature describing multicultural approaches are "broad" and "universal." Defining culture broadly is *not* the same as defining culture according to universals. "Broad" means that each of us has many different simultaneous cultural identities defined by ethnographic, demographic, status, and affiliation factors, even though they might not all be salient at the same time. "Universal" means we only look at those aspects shared across many or most cultures. This is a very important distinction.

The Venn diagram in Box 6.1 on page 136 provides a visual image to help distinguish between universal and broad definitions of culture. The universal

 VOICES FROM THE FIELD

Patrice Moulton

I began practicing supervision 17 years ago. I needed specific information on ways to define multiculturalism, strategies to explore my own worldview, and specific knowledge about cultures other than my own that would help me in my practice as a supervisor. I found little information on these issues. When I first became aware of multicultural and diversity issues, I was very confused about how best to incorporate these ideas with the diverse range of individuals with whom I was working. As a professional who cared about competence and ethics, I wondered how to go about "practicing" as a culturally competent counselor and supervisor.

Some sources stated that basically we are all more alike than different, and, therefore, all clients should be treated in a similar fashion. I fundamentally agree with the concept of commonality, but I now know that this universal perspective has the potential to cause great damage if it is used as a rationale for ignoring the need to explore how culture affects therapeutic and supervisory relationships, processes, and outcomes.

Other sources implied that I should understand each ethnicity and diversity I would encounter, but specific, practical information I could apply as a counselor and as a supervisor was lacking. Some sources recommended that I simply request that the client teach me about his or her culture or orientation. Others stated that this is inappropriate, not the client's responsibility, and a misuse of therapy time. As you can see, I had reason to feel confused, and I was motivated to continue to pursue these questions.

part is that very small open area in the center, which is shared by all circles and represents the shared aspects of all cultures. The broadly defined part is the whole collection of overlapping circles in their entirety. The lines represent each individual's experience of numerous cultural identities throughout life as defined by ethnographic, demographic, status, and affiliation characteristics.

Sue, Arredondo, and McDavis (1992) note that these two approaches are not necessarily contradictory. It goes without saying that all forms of counseling are, to some extent, culture-centered. If we limit our definition to only those aspects shared across cultures (universal), we may be ignoring very important components of therapy. At the same time, there is the danger that by diluting the definition (broad) we are somehow evading very real and difficult issues. For example, historically, counseling practice and psychological research have reflected a predominantly white middle-class value system. This approach to conceptualization and practice is no longer acceptable.

The culturally diverse model, although not universally accepted, has been adopted by many in the field as a means to correct some of the inadequacies of the past (Ponterotto & Casas, 1991). This model recognizes that cultures are different, but no culture is pathological, deficient, or inferior. Individuals are seen in light of the relationship they share with their environment and social forces.

UNIVERSAL VERSUS BROAD DIMENSIONS OF CULTURE

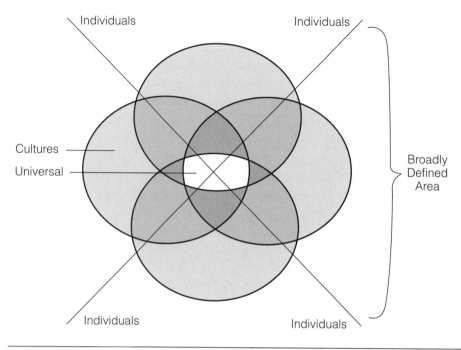

Source: Paul Pedersen (personal communication, June 2001). Reprinted by permission.

PRACTICING MULTICULTURAL SUPERVISION COMPETENCIES

According to Sue and his colleagues (1998), becoming a multiculturally competent mental health practitioner involves three dimensions. The first dimension deals with the practitioner's attitudes and beliefs about race, culture, ethnicity, gender, and sexual orientation; the need to monitor personal biases; development of a positive view toward multiculturalism; and understanding how one's values and biases may get in the way of effective helping. The second dimension recognizes that a culturally competent practitioner is knowledgeable and understanding of his or her own worldview, possesses specific knowledge of the diverse groups with whom he or she works, and has a basic understanding of sociopolitical influences. The third dimension deals with skills, intervention techniques, and strategies necessary in serving diverse client groups.

It is imperative that anyone serving in a supervisory capacity be multiculturally competent. Lopez (1997) reminds us that cultural competence is not a simple formula or a set of cultural facts but a perspective that respects the complexity of the individual within his or her cultural context. Ethics codes and standards such as ACES (1990, 1995) and APA (1992) address the requirement of multicultural competency. The codes and guidelines that apply are listed in Box 6.2.

It is impossible to give supervisees knowledge and skills that we as supervisors do not possess. Box 6.3 lists multicultural competencies supervisors can incorporate in their supervisory practice. Each of these competencies is discussed in detail in the sections that follow.

Explore Racial Dynamics in the Supervisory Relationship

Recognize the advantages and disadvantages of being of the same or different culture than your supervisee and be willing to explore these issues with supervisees. In your role as a supervisor, it is important that you understand the concerns of your supervisees. Equally important is having the ability and the willingness to communicate your understanding in a way that avoids cultural misunderstandings. Here is one example of cultural miscommunication. In Thailand, the Agency for International Development distributes food and goods with the symbol of "two hands clasped in a friendly handshake" stenciled on every bag and box to indicate the friendly intentions of the U.S. government. However, in Thailand that symbol is described as "the hand that won't let go."

It is necessary to break the taboo of speaking out loud about racial or cultural differences. Be sensitive to the fact that the appropriate way to speak out loud will be different from one culture to the next. You might be anxious about discussing cultural differences with a supervisee for fear of saying the wrong thing, sounding disrespectful, or appearing to be misinformed. Recognize your own perspective and be aware of how this may influence your supervision practices. Read the Voices from the Field feature on page 139 for one person's perspective on this.

The terms used to describe cultural differences change with frequency. The only way to overcome the initial awkwardness is to practice in safe environments, and fortunately there are many of these in our field. Safe environments can be found in training experiences, workshops, and understanding colleagues who allow us to practice and grow under their mentorship. It is the supervisor's responsibility to model appropriate and safe communication. Before initiating a discussion of culture, it is useful to "talk about talking" with the supervisee and to set some ground rules about what you can and cannot do. Seek the permission of your supervisees before asking deeply personal questions about their lives. Examples of this type of communication include asking supervisees directly about their cultural identity and how this may affect their practice of counseling (which also applies to areas of gender, sexual orientation, and spirituality), and direct discussions regarding issues of racism, privilege, sexual identity development, disability, or economic environments.

ETHICS CODES AND STANDARDS REGARDING MULTICULTURAL COUNSELING AND SUPERVISION

American Counseling Association
Code of Ethics and Standards of Practice (1995)

The ACA's nondiscrimination standard states:

1.05.c. understand the nature of social diversity and oppression with respect to race, ethnicity, national origin, color, sex, sexual orientation, age, marital status, political belief, religion and mental or physical disability.

American Psychological Association
Ethical Principles of Psychologists and Code of Conduct (1992)

The APA ethics codes indicate that part of competence implies understanding diversity:

1.08. Where differences of age, gender, race, ethnicity, national origin, religion, sexual orientation, disability, language, or socioeconomic status significantly affect psychologists' work concerning particular individuals or groups, psychologists obtain the training, experience, consultation, or supervision necessary to ensure the competence of their services, or they make appropriate referrals.

Association for Counselor Education and Supervision
Standards for Counseling Supervisors (1990)

4.1. The counseling supervisor demonstrates knowledge of individual differences with respect to gender, race, ethnicity, culture and age and understands the importance of these characteristics in supervisory relationships.

BOX 6.3 | **MULTICULTURAL SUPERVISION COMPETENCIES**

1. Explore racial dynamics in the supervisory relationship.
2. Include multicultural competencies in the supervisory agreement.
3. Assist supervisees in developing cultural self-awareness.
4. Accept your limits as a multicultural supervisor.
5. Model cultural sensitivity.
6. Accept responsibility to provide knowledge regarding cultural diversity.
7. Inform supervisees about multicultural considerations in assessment.
8. Provide the opportunity for multicultural case conceptualization.
9. Practice and promote culturally appropriate interventions.
10. Provide and model social advocacy.

During these discussions, use an open and honest communication pattern that sets the stage for open and safe dialogue. When you are unclear about what a supervisee might be saying or meaning, ask for clarification. Also, invite supervisees to ask for clarification of what you say, and ask for illustrations of their cultural experiences that may have an impact on their view of

 VOICES FROM THE FIELD

Muriel Yáñez, Psy.D.

Diversity issues come into supervision in a variety of ways. First are my own countertransference issues as a woman of color and what biases I must be aware of in my interactions with supervisees. One example is the way I may react differently to a male of color or a Latino with whom I may identify in different ways. Second, I must be open to discussing or addressing the supervisee's own experiences with diversity and values. Finally, I must also take opportunities as they arise for education regarding diversity issues without lecturing and inserting biases into the supervisee's work.

counseling. This type of communication can facilitate discussions of social constructs and how they affect case conceptualization and treatment.

Include Multicultural Competencies in the Supervisory Agreement

As a supervisor, it is your responsibility to educate your supervisees about how you will work together in the supervisory relationship. The initial sessions of supervision should allow ample opportunity to explore cultural similarities and differences between you and your supervisees. Lee (1999) suggests that an important way to minimize undesirable things happening is to clarify everyone's expectations early in the relationship.

Introduce your supervisees to the various components that are a part of being a multiculturally competent counselor (see Box 6.3). As you begin the supervisory relationship, establish an open dialogue regarding multicultural issues. Here are some questions that may help you begin a dialogue with supervisees about multicultural considerations:

- How do you describe your ethnic identity?
- What does it mean to you to identify with this group?
- If you were to think about the multiple layers of culture, what would you identify as the various cultural groups to which you belong?
- How do you think your ethnic identity might affect your role as a therapist?
- How do you think your ethnicity affected your choice of theoretical orientation? Case conceptualization and diagnosis? Treatment? What parts of your counseling approach do you most strongly identify with and why?
- Can you identify, at this time, ways in which our cultural differences or similarities may affect our supervisory relationship?
- How would you rate yourself in terms of knowledge and comfort when discussing cultural issues?

- If you find cultural discussions uncomfortable, can you identify what it is that you find awkward or threatening? Where might you have learned this fear?
- What types of academic training, professional conferences, workshops, or seminars have you completed in the area of multicultural counseling?

This is an appropriate time to set the stage for an open and safe dialogue regarding cultural issues both within the supervisory relationship and also about how client cases will be reviewed and processed. It is important to develop a relationship that is respectful and reciprocal. Encourage supervisees to bring their concerns to supervision sessions at any point in their field placement when questions arise regarding cultural perspectives.

Assist Supervisees in Developing Cultural Self-Awareness

It is important that you be aware of your feelings, attitudes, and perceptions regarding your own culture as well as that of supervisees. This kind of awareness provides congruence in the supervisory relationship. Explore your own cultural awareness as you teach supervisees to do the same.

Personal exploration provides the opportunity to examine personal agendas and prejudices so these issues may be addressed. Learning to identify your own implicit culturally learned assumptions is a significant step toward cultural competence. Brown and Landrum-Brown (1995) assert that clinical supervision is not exempt from cross-cultural dynamics and that a supervisor's worldview is likely to influence the therapeutic choices made by supervisees. It is a good practice for you as a supervisor to explore questions of bias and cultural perspectives for yourself and to provide the opportunity for your supervisees to do the same. Box 6.4 provides some guidance for this process of self-exploration.

Accept Your Limits as a Multicultural Supervisor

It is imperative that you accept your limits of expertise with regard to multicultural supervision. The majority of counselors are specialists in some area of psychological expertise, but few pronounce themselves as experts in the area of multiculturalism. Unless you have studied and practiced extensively with diverse client populations, you will find yourself lacking the detailed knowledge you need to work with certain cultures with which you have limited familiarity. However, regardless of training and experience, it will be necessary to take the time to get to know your supervisees as individuals within the context of their cultural environment. This means that you need to be careful about making generalizations about a specific individual from any given culture. You must seek information and clarification for your assumptions.

Therapists and supervisors are sometimes placed in positions requiring multicultural expertise outside their range of competence. It is not possible

| BOX 6.4 | EVALUATING YOUR CULTURAL SELF-AWARENESS |

As you grow in your role of supervisor, reflect on these questions often and recognize your deepening understanding of what it means to be a multiculturally competent supervisor.

- What lens do I view the world through?
- What is my definition of culture?
- What is my cultural heritage?
- Which cultural groups do I identify with primarily?
- What cultural values, beliefs, and attitudes do I hold, and how do these fit with the dominant culture?
- How did I learn my cultural values?
- What has been my experience with other cultures, and what has been my perception of these cultures?
- How might my beliefs affect my ability to supervise effectively?
- How do I define the relationship between culture and counseling?

to be knowledgeable in all areas, and there will be times when it will be appropriate and ethically responsible to seek consultation and possibly referral. If you find yourself in over your head and feel that you are in need of supervision regarding multicultural issues in the supervisory relationship, seek help. If you are not willing to risk making mistakes, the chances are that you are restricting your opportunities for learning. In other words, when it comes to multicultural issues in supervision, it is important to have the necessary conversations—even though it may be awkward at times and you may think you are not using the "right" words. You may tell yourself you could have asked more or better questions to explore the cultural issues. If supervisees are not accustomed to this type of discussion regarding their cultural identity, it is possible that you may unknowingly create discomfort or defensiveness for your supervisees. The task is not to do a perfect job but to learn how to recover after having said or done what you perceive to be the "wrong thing." Read the Voices from the Field feature on page 142 to see how one practitioner went about seeking help appropriately. Asking for help when it is needed is in no way a failure but the sign of a competent professional willing to accept limitations and not willing to practice outside his or her scope of competence.

Model Cultural Sensitivity

Remember that the uniqueness of the individual as well as cultural group membership needs to be respected at all times. We each belong to numerous cultures at the same time, and the salience changes quickly over time and place from one to another. This skill requires a balance of attention. If too much attention is placed on cultural group membership, it may encourage stereotyping. In this example, the supervisee's motivation was positive, but the effect was certainly not what was intended:

VOICES FROM THE FIELD

Patrice Moulton

A number of years ago, while serving as coordinator of the family therapy program for a state substance abuse facility, I was invited to begin running the first Adult Children of Alcoholics group for the Native American tribe of the Seneca Nation in Salamanca, New York. I was also to supervise a colleague running the same type of group at a reservation in Jamestown, New York. I was considered an expert in substance abuse group work and family issues, but I had limited knowledge of Native American culture and little knowledge of the Seneca Nation or the reservation. I felt very much that I was in over my head and was wondering if the rules that govern family systems applied in a similar enough way to allow for the building of rapport, trust, and respect

that is necessary to provide a positive group experience for participants.

Rather than assuming that I would be able to figure things out as I went—or expecting the group members to educate me as best they could on how their culture might affect the group dynamics, goals, and expectations—I sought help. I went to the Seneca Nation Mental Health Department and spent some time in supervision myself with one of the family counselors there. I shared with her the knowledge I had about adult children of alcoholics (ACOA) and covered the group structure and content. She helped me understand where adjustments would have to be made, and how to intertwine the cultural components into our group exercises in a way that would be meaningful to these clients.

A young man with a mobility disability came in for counseling. The counselor had just read about multicultural counseling sensitivity and saw this as an opportunity to practice these skills. After 20 minutes, the young man wheeled out shaking his head and said to his partner: "I'm never going to see him again. I had problems about money, relationships, family, grades, and lots of other things, but all he wanted to talk about was my physical disability."

On the other hand, if too much attention is placed on the individual outside the context of his or her cultural group, you may neglect the impact of the cultural environment on the individual. One is both an individual and a member of a cultural group. Giving too much attention to either identity risks denying the other identity. Read the Voices from the Field feature on page 143 for another view on balancing these two aspects of individuals.

Accept Responsibility to Provide Knowledge Regarding Cultural Diversity

Differences among psychological dimensions of culture are discussed in the model of multicultural understanding presented by Locke (1998). This model encourages exploration of the following cultural elements: acculturation, poverty and economic concerns, history of oppression, language, racism and prejudice, sociopolitical factors, child-rearing practices, family structure and

VOICES FROM THE FIELD

Todd Thies, Ph.D.

I think that many graduate schools do a disservice to clinicians when they try to teach them the characteristics of a particular culture. This can lead to not treating the client as an individual. It is certainly true that we are greatly influenced by our culture (thus, general cultural information is useful), but we are also individuals within that culture. So, the bottom line becomes one of assessing and interacting with an individual as an individual, which includes the individual's culture, diagnosis, and hopes.

---

dynamics, and cultural values and attitudes. In using Locke's approach, both the supervisor and the supervisee can evaluate their cultural practices and determine how these affect the supervisory relationship and the supervisee's practice with clients. These cultural elements can be used as an indicator of cultural knowledge regarding any given cultural group. The culturally competent supervisor will have a working knowledge of this type of information for various cultural groups and will be aware of resources to share with supervisees regarding basic information for any given cultural group. For more on the supervisor's role in providing multicultural information to trainees, see the Voices from the Field feature on page 144.

Inform Supervisees About Multicultural Considerations in Assessment

Supervisors need to be knowledgeable regarding culturally competent psychological evaluations and other types of assessment. This requires understanding how race, culture, and ethnicity may affect personality formation, vocational choices, and manifestation of psychological disorders. Locke (1998) suggests counselors ask themselves the following types of questions as part of the assessment process:

- Does something about this person's appearance make me think this person's behavior is abnormal?
- What is the basis for making these assumptions?
- What labels am I consciously or subconsciously applying to this person, and where did the labels come from?
- What other labels might be used to describe this behavior?
- To what cultural group am I assuming this person belongs, and what do I know about this group?

It is necessary to understand both the technical aspects and the limitations of traditional assessment tools. The goal for you as a supervisor is to

VOICES FROM THE FIELD

Heriberto G. Sánchez, Ph.D.

Supervisors need to provide information to their staff about multicultural issues and encourage them to participate in training programs to improve their skills in working with culturally diverse populations.

In our rapidly changing society, multiculturalism is perhaps one of the more important issues facing mental health professionals. Our ability to help our clients depends on our ability to understand them from their perspective. Cultural identity is more than just language and customs. Culture impacts cognitions, stress tolerance, and coping styles. Culture also involves history, particularly the manner in which dominant and minority groups have interacted in the past and the nature of their relationship (for example, whether it was friendly or adversarial and the current status of that relationship). Understanding the client's cultural perspective can provide a clear understanding of his or her problem and lead to solutions beneficial to the client.

The client's culture, race, sex, age, marital status, and socioeconomic status are all important factors to consider in supervision. Fortunately, many resources are now available (namely, books and journals) that mental health professionals can use to educate themselves about cultural issues. In addition, they can attend workshops and educational programs. However, it is clients who can provide the most useful information about how they view their particular situation.

The key for mental health professionals is to recognize the impact of culture. This requires having an unbiased view and taking the initiative to learn about the client's culture. Other areas to consider are the impact cultural differences could have on the therapeutic relationship and on psychological testing. Transference and coutertransference issues may arise that are related to cultural difference. Results of psychological assessment must be interpreted in the context of these cultural differences.

model and teach culturally sensitive assessment practices that allow the use of test results to benefit diverse clients.

Provide the Opportunity for Multicultural Case Conceptualization

Case conceptualization requires supervisors to gain an understanding of a client's symptoms within that client's sociocultural context. But supervisors' assumptions regarding their supervisees' abilities to incorporate these variables into multicultural case conceptualization must also be addressed. Multicultural case conceptualization will include an analysis of the impact of the client's race, class, sexual orientation, gender, age, or disability status on the client's life. McGoldrick and Giordano (1996) suggest that people differ in the following ways:

- Their experience of psychological distress
- How they describe symptoms of distress
- How they communicate about their symptoms and distress

- Their attribution of causes
- Their attitude toward helpers
- Their expectations for treatment

Work with your supervisees to help them clearly state their assumptions and how that analysis will influence their interventions with clients.

Practice and Promote Culturally Appropriate Interventions

When determining appropriate multicultural treatment strategies and interventions, remain flexible and help supervisees choose interventions that will most benefit the client. Be prepared to send and receive both verbal and nonverbal messages accurately and appropriately, and model this with supervisees in supervisory sessions. Review theoretical orientations for appropriateness or inappropriateness, and help supervisees choose treatment strategies that will validate the ethnic identity of clients. Help supervisees become aware of "cultural camouflage" (use of ethnic, racial, or religious identity as a defense against change or pain). Be realistic about the support systems available to clients, and help supervisees understand clients' value conflicts.

Provide and Model Social Advocacy

It is the supervisor's responsibility to model active social advocacy and to encourage this role in supervisees. Members of certain groups have been oppressed and discriminated against. Counselors have a responsibility to act as advocates by being willing to speak on behalf of their clients, especially those clients who have been the target of discrimination and oppression. The goal of social advocacy involves actively working to reduce, and ideally eliminate, biases, prejudices, and discriminatory practices. As a social advocate, the supervisor must attend to and work toward eliminating biases, prejudices, and discriminatory context in conducting evaluations and providing interventions, and develop sensitivity to issues of oppression, sexism, heterosexism, elitism, ageism, and racism. Take responsibility for educating your supervisees to the processes of psychological intervention, such as goals, expectations, and legal rights, and how prejudice can inhibit these processes.

Work with professional organizations and serve on committees advocating for policy changes. Encourage your supervisees to become involved in these efforts, and provide education and training for other professionals regarding multiculturalism.

ACQUIRING MULTICULTURAL COMPETENCIES IN SUPERVISION

When professionals who are not multiculturally competent take on supervisory roles and responsibilities, they will encounter professional and ethical dilemmas. The lack of cultural competence in supervision is often evidenced in one or more of the following ways:

- Failures of respect and mutuality
- Misuses of power
- Boundary violations
- Failure to take into account social forces that have an impact on supervisees' and clients' lives
- Inappropriate assumptions regarding supervisees' abilities or knowledge of multicultural case conceptualization
- Unintentional racism
- Inappropriate assumptions regarding supervisees' racial or ethnic identification
- Too much attention placed on visible ethnicity
- Not acknowledging cultural similarities and differences
- Inaccurate diagnosis and treatment

A major contribution to the counseling profession has been the development of multicultural competencies, which were initially formulated by D. W. Sue and colleagues (1982) and were later revised and expanded by Sue, Arredondo, and McDavis (1992). Arredondo and her colleagues (1996) have updated and operationalized these competencies. Sue and his colleagues (1998) have developed multicultural counseling competencies as they apply to individual and organizational development. We have taken the liberty of rethinking these multicultural counseling competencies and adapting them to apply to the supervision process. Box 6.5 outlines multicultural competencies as they apply to supervision.

For the complete description of multicultural counseling competencies, along with explanatory statements, refer to Arredondo and colleagues (1996). Sue and colleagues (1998, chap. 4) also provide a detailed list of multicultural counseling competencies.

ASSESSING MULTICULTURAL COMPETENCIES IN SUPERVISION

In 1991 D'Andrea, Daniels, and Heck wrote, "Clearly, if the multicultural counseling movement is to realize its full potential as a revolutionary force in the profession, counselor-educators must be able to distinguish those types of training models proven to be effective in terms of stimulating student development in this area" (p. 148). At the present time, there are few instruments available to assess multicultural competencies. The measures that are available are based conceptually on the multicultural counseling competence construct presented by Sue and his colleagues (1992).

Commonly used self-report measures of multicultural counseling competencies discussed by Ponterotto, Casas, Suzuki, and Alexander (2001) are the Multicultural Awareness-Knowledge-Skills Survey (MAKSS) (D'Andrea, Daniels, & Heck, 1991), the Multicultural Counseling Inventory (MCI) (Sodowsky, Taffe, Gutkins, & Wise, 1994), and the Multicultural Counseling Awareness Scale (MCAS-B) Revised (Ponterotto et al., 1996). The MCAS-B was revised recently and is now known as the Multicultural Counseling

BOX 6.5 | MULTICULTURAL COMPETENCIES IN SUPERVISION

I. Being Aware of Your Own Cultural Values and Biases
    A. With respect to *attitudes and beliefs,* culturally competent supervisors:
        1. Believe cultural self-awareness and sensitivity to one's own cultural heritage are essential.
        2. Are aware of how their own cultural background and experiences have influenced their attitudes, values, and biases about the supervisory process.
        3. Are able to recognize the limits of their expertise in multicultural supervision.
        4. Recognize their sources of discomfort with differences that exist between themselves and supervisees in terms of race, ethnicity, culture, gender, and sexual orientation.
    B. With respect to *knowledge,* culturally competent supervisors:
        1. Have specific knowledge about how their own racial and cultural heritage affects their perception of assessment, diagnosis, and treatment of the client cases that they supervise.
        2. Possess knowledge and understanding about how oppression, racism, discrimination, and stereotyping affect them and their supervisees in their work.
        3. Possess knowledge about their social advocacy responsibility as supervisors.
    C. With respect to *skills,* culturally competent supervisors:
        1. Seek out education, training, and consultation to improve their supervisory work with diverse populations.
        2. Participate in ongoing self-exploration as racial and cultural beings.
II. Understanding the Worldview of Clients and Supervisees
    A. With respect to *attitudes and beliefs,* culturally competent supervisors:
        1. Are aware of their negative and positive emotional reactions toward other racial and ethnic groups that may prove detrimental to the counseling and supervisory relationship.
        2. Are aware of stereotypes and preconceived notions that they may hold toward diverse client and supervisee populations.
    B. With respect to *knowledge,* culturally competent supervisors:
        1. Possess specific knowledge and information about the supervisees and clients for which they are responsible.
        2. Understand how race, culture, ethnicity, age, religion, gender, and sexual orientation influence the ways supervisees and clients function in the world.
        3. Understand and have knowledge about how sociopolitical factors affect the personal development of supervisees and the clients they serve.
    C. With respect to *skills,* culturally competent supervisors:
        1. Have a working knowledge and train their supervisees about mental health and mental disorders that affect various ethnic and racial groups.
        2. Interact with diverse populations professionally and in the communities they serve.
III. Developing Culturally Appropriate Intervention Strategies and Techniques
    A. With respect to *attitudes and beliefs,* culturally competent supervisors:
        1. Model respect for supervisees' and clients' religious and spiritual beliefs and values.
        2. Respect the needs of diverse populations in selecting intervention strategies that are appropriate for specific cultures.
    B. With respect to *knowledge,* culturally competent supervisors:
        1. Have a clear and explicit knowledge and understanding of the models and methods of counseling and supervision and the degree to which they fit with the values of diverse groups.
        2. Are aware of barriers that prevent diverse populations from accessing mental health care.

(continued)

| # MULTICULTURAL COMPETENCIES IN SUPERVISION (*continued*)

3. Have knowledge of the potential cultural bias in assessment, diagnosis, treatment, and evaluation.
4. Have knowledge of family and community systems of the diverse populations they serve.
5. Are aware of relevant discriminatory practices at the professional and the community level of the supervisees and clients they serve.

C. With respect to *skills*, culturally competent supervisors:
1. Use a variety of supervision methods that are congruent with the diverse backgrounds of supervisees.
2. Use relationship skills consistent with the cultural background of supervisees and their clients.
3. Are responsible to train supervisees in multicultural case conceptualization as it pertains to assessment, diagnosis, and treatment.
4. Are able to help supervisees assist their clients in determining whether a problem stems from racism or bias so that clients do not inappropriately personalize problems.
5. Are open to seek consultation for alternative treatment strategies to meet the needs of the diverse populations they serve.
6. Can teach their supervisees about potential bias and the appropriate use of traditional assessment and testing instruments when working with diverse populations.
7. Assist supervisees in reducing or eliminating biases, prejudices, and discriminatory practices as they pertain to diverse groups.
8. Take responsibility for educating their supervisees through the use of a supervision contract that includes multicultural dimensions of supervision.

Knowledge and Awareness Scale (MCKAS) (Ponterotto, Rieger, Gretchen, Utsey, & Austin, 1999). Ponterotto et al. have encouraged colleagues to use the MCKAS and the Quick Discrimination Index (QDI), a self-assessment inventory developed by Ponterotto, Potere, and Johansen (2002). The QDI specifically assesses racial attitudes toward minorities and women.

LaFromboise, Coleman, and Hernandez (1991) revised the Cross-Cultural Counseling Inventory (CCCI-R). This instrument is specifically designed for use by supervisors in evaluating counselors' multicultural counseling competencies; it also has been successfully adapted as a self-report instrument.

In a recent study, Constantine and Ladany (2000) examined the relationship between the CCCI-R, MAKSS, MCI, and MCAS-B measures, social desirability attitudes, and multicultural case conceptualization ability. Based on their findings, they suggest that there is need for further critical construct and criterion-related validity information about the instruments. In addition, they identify the need for specific personal attributes typically associated with optimal qualities for counselors to possess (such as warmth and empathy) to be explored as variables that may facilitate or impede the development of multicultural counseling competence. Finally, they encourage researchers to examine the impact of multicultural training on the development of "true multicultural counseling competence." It is important that the counseling field examine ways in which we might train the next generation of mental health professionals to meet the needs of an increasingly diverse society.

SUMMARY

Before you begin your supervisory experience, it is imperative that you gain personal insight into multicultural issues. This personal awareness serves as the cornerstone for your multicultural knowledge and skill. You have an ethical responsibility to be a competent multicultural supervisor. This means having knowledge of multicultural issues in assessment, therapy, and diagnosis and providing opportunities for your supervisees to explore and learn multicultural competencies under your supervision. This role includes teaching, modeling, mentoring, and advocating. More than anything, it requires sensitivity and openness to both the diversity and uniformity of the supervisees and clients for whom we are responsible.

All forms of counseling, to some extent, are culture-centered, and the cultural diversity model recognizes that cultures are different but not in any way deficient. It is your responsibility as the supervisor to provide a safe environment for communication with supervisees regarding cultural issues to take place.

As a supervisor, you are responsible for your own personal and professional exploration with regard to cultural differences, and you must also provide opportunities for your supervisees to explore cultural issues. You do not have to know everything about every culture to be a culturally competent supervisor, but you must acknowledge your limitations and be willing to seek assistance when necessary.

Modeling cultural sensitivity, conceptualization, and practice is probably your strongest training tool in supervision. You must be aware of cultural considerations in assessment and treatment practices to effectively supervise the training of new professionals in the field. In addition to your work with clients and supervisees, you also have a role to play as a social advocate.

SUGGESTED ACTIVITIES

1. List five common characteristics to be aware of when supervising involving the following possible sources of diversity:
    a. African Americans
    b. Native American Indians
    c. Chinese Americans
    d. Korean Americans
    e. Vietnamese in the United States
    f. Mexican Americans
    g. Puerto Rican Americans

h.   Caucasian Americans
i.   Gender
j.   Affectional orientation
k.   Age
l.   Religious or spiritual preferences
m. Socioeconomic status

2. Break into small groups and choose one of the diverse groups listed in activity 1. Discuss how the characteristics of this group may affect assessment and case conceptualization in therapy.
3. Break into small groups and have each group identify four questions they would feel comfortable asking to promote open discussion and exploration of cultural issues with supervisees.
4. Break into small groups and discuss the following questions: What values were you brought up with regarding those of different cultures? How might these values affect your ability to supervise?
5. Have each individual identify five specific ways to serve as a social advocate, and share these lists with the class.
6. In small groups, use case notes to identify different presenting problems. Ask group members to share their knowledge of various cultural characteristics and develop case conceptualizations through the lens of various cultures. Include initial diagnosis and treatment concerns.
7. Access the Web site for this text at http://info.wadsworth.com/haynes, and complete the self-assessment inventory. Additional contributor perspectives and other activities specific to this chapter are also available to you through this Web site. For example, the Web site also contains multicultural awareness assessment tools, including the Multicultural Awareness, Knowledge, and Skills Survey (MAKSS) and the Quick Discrimination Index (QDI). Although not specifically designed for use in supervision, supervisors may find these tools helpful for themselves and their supervisees.

ETHICAL ISSUES AND MULTIPLE RELATIONSHIPS

1. What do you consider to be the most critical ethical issues in supervision?
2. As a supervisor, what are your most important responsibilities toward your supervisees? The clients of your supervisees? The agency or university that employs you? The profession?
3. What kinds of training, course work, and other professional experiences are essential for competent supervision?
4. What multiple roles might you be expected to play as a supervisor? What guidelines do you have for managing multiple roles and relationships?
5. In your own experience as a supervisee, in what ways have your relationships with supervisors changed over time? What lessons can you apply from this experience when you assume a supervisory role?
6. What kinds of activities that extend beyond the formal supervisory relationship might you engage in with supervisees? How would you decide what social activities to participate in with supervisees?

INTRODUCTION

This chapter explores ethical issues frequently encountered in clinical supervision and provides guidelines for the ethical practice of supervision. Some of the topics address issues pertaining to students in training programs, yet most of the principles examined can be applied to supervisees in many different settings. A few of these topics are responsibilities of clinical supervisors, competence of supervisors, dealing with incompetent trainees, and managing multiple roles and relationships in the supervisory process.

The relationship between the clinical supervisor and the supervisee is of critical importance in the development of competent and responsible therapists. If we take into consideration the dependent position of the trainee and the similarities between the supervisory relationship and the therapeutic relationship, the need for guidelines describing the rights of supervisees and the responsibilities of supervisors becomes obvious. The Association for Counselor Education and Supervision has developed "Ethical Guidelines for Counseling Supervisors" (ACES, 1993, 1995), which addresses client welfare and rights, supervisory role, and program administration role—all major ethical issues.

ETHICAL ISSUES IN CLINICAL SUPERVISION

Some critical ethical issues in supervision are balancing the rights of clients, the rights and responsibilities of supervisees, and the responsibilities of supervisors to both supervisees and their clients. It is critical to discuss the rights of supervisees from the beginning of the supervisory relationship in much the same way as the rights of clients are addressed early in the therapy process. If this is done, the supervisee is invited to express expectations, empowered to make decisions, and becomes an active participant in the supervisory process.

The Supervisor's Roles and Responsibilities

Supervisors have a responsibility to provide training and supervised experiences that will enable supervisees to deliver ethical and effective services. It is essential for supervisors to be knowledgeable and skilled in the practice of clinical supervision. As we saw in Chapter 2, if supervisors do not have training in clinical supervision, it will be difficult for them to ensure that those they supervise are functioning effectively and ethically.

The APA (2001) has developed these standards regarding assessing supervisee performance:

> (a) In academic and supervisory relationships, psychologists establish a timely and specific process for providing feedback to students and supervisees. Information regarding the process is provided to the student at the beginning of supervision.
> (b) Psychologists evaluate students and supervisees on the basis of their actual performance on relevant and established program requirements. (7.06)

To make optimal use of supervision, supervisees need to clearly understand what their responsibilities are, what the supervisor's responsibilities are, and how they will be assessed. In one study, 9% of respondents (151 therapists in training) reported that their supervisors never explained the roles and responsibilities of the supervisee and the supervisor (Ladany, Lehrman-Waterman, Molinaro, & Wolgast, 1999). Ethical supervision involves providing periodic feedback and evaluation to supervisees so they have a basis for improving their clinical skills (ACA, 1995; ACES, 1993, 1995). In a study on the ethical practices of clinical supervisors, one-third of the participants reported that their supervisors did not provide adequate evaluations of their counseling performances, nor did they provide them with ongoing feedback (Ladany et al., 1999).

Clinical supervisors have a position of influence with their supervisees; they operate in multiple roles as teacher, evaluator, counselor, model, mentor, and adviser. It is essential that supervisors monitor their own behavior so as not to misuse the inherent power in the supervisor–supervisee relationship. Supervisors are responsible for ensuring compliance with relevant legal, ethical, and professional standards for clinical practice (ACES, 1993, 1995). The main purpose of ethical standards for clinical supervision is to provide behavioral guidelines to supervisors, protect supervisees from undue harm or neglect, and ensure quality client care (Bernard & Goodyear, 1998).

Supervisors can demonstrate these ethical standards through the behavior they model in the supervisory relationship. One of the findings of the Ladany et al. (1999) study was that 8% of the supervisees believed that their supervisors did not provide adequate modeling, nor were they responsive to ethical concerns.

The Impact of Negative Supervisory Events

In a study on negative supervisory events, Ramos-Sánchez and her colleagues (2002) attempted to determine whether negative experiences in supervision were associated with the supervisory relationship, satisfaction with supervision, or other training experiences at the training site. The negative events described by participants fell into these four categories: interpersonal relationship and style; supervision tasks and responsibilities; conceptualization and theoretical orientation; and ethical, legal, and multicultural issues. Some of their findings are particularly relevant for ethical practices in supervision:

- Respondents who reported negative experiences tended to have weaker relationships with their supervisors than those who did not report negative experiences.
- When ethical violations occurred on the supervisor's part, they may have led to a supervisee's loss of trust in the supervisor and harmed the supervisory relationship.
- Supervisees who reported negative supervisory events were found to have lower levels of satisfaction with their current supervisor than those who did not report negative experiences.
- Supervisees who reported negative supervisory events indicated that this negatively influenced their supervisory experience more than those respondents who did not report such events.

Negative supervisory events could have an impact on the confidence level of supervisees and could influence their ability to provide effective therapy to their clients.

These findings suggest that negative supervisory experience may have long-lasting effects on supervisees' self-confidence. These supervisees may question their career choice. They may engage in self-doubts about their ability to counsel effectively, and their questioning may be accompanied by feelings of disillusionment, inadequacy, and failure.

Supervisors need to pay particular attention to their role in establishing and maintaining a solid relationship with supervisees. It is especially crucial that supervisors attend to relationship issues in working with supervisees early in their training. By emphasizing the importance of a solid supervisory alliance, supervisors can do a great deal to prevent negative events from occurring. Ramos-Sánchez and her colleagues have this advice:

It is recommended that supervisors make conscious efforts to build trust, actively support and advocate for their trainees, periodically check a supervisee's feelings about the relationship, and remain open to feedback from trainees. . . . Overall, it can be inferred that development of supervisees is contingent upon a good supervisor, a strong supervisory relationship, and a swift, effective response to negative events that may occur in supervision. (p. 201)

Modeling Confidentiality

It is essential that supervisors teach and model ethical and professional behavior for their supervisees. One of the best ways for supervisors to model professional behavior for supervisees is to deal appropriately with confidentiality issues pertaining to supervisees. Supervisors must maintain the confidentiality of their supervisees. They can do this by explaining the parameters of confidentiality in the supervisory relationship. Supervisors can also model client confidentiality in supervisory sessions.

In the Ladany et al. (1999) study, 18% of the supervisees believed confidentiality issues were not handled appropriately by their supervisors. Clearly, supervisors have an evaluative role, and at times faculty members need to be apprised of students' progress. However, personal information that supervisees share during a supervision session should generally remain confidential. At the very least, supervisees have a right to be informed about what will be revealed and what will not be shared with others on the faculty. Supervisors need to put ethics in the foreground of their supervisory practices, which can best be done by treating supervisees in a respectful, professional, and ethical manner.

Supervisors have responsibilities for the clients that are being seen by their supervisees, one of which is to respect the confidentiality of client communications. Supervision involves discussion of client issues and review of client materials, and it is essential that supervisees respect their clients' privacy by not talking about clients outside of the context of supervision. By their own behavior, supervisors have a responsibility to model for supervisees appropriate ways of talking about clients and keeping information protected and used only in the context of supervision (Bernard & Goodyear, 1998). Of course, supervisors must make sure that both supervisees and their clients are fully informed about the limits of confidentiality, including those situations in which supervisors have a duty to warn, to protect, or to report. This topic is addressed in greater detail in Chapter 8.

Teaching Supervisees How to Make Ethical Decisions

A chief responsibility of supervisors is to teach their supervisees how to think about the ethical dilemmas they are bound to encounter and to help them develop a framework for making ethical decisions. To whatever degree it is possible, we suggest that supervisors teach supervisees the importance of involving their clients in the process of resolving an ethical concern. Of course, supervisees would do well to bring any ethical issues they face in dealing with their clients to their supervision sessions. As supervisees learn to be open with the ethical concerns that arise for them, they are also developing a pattern of being willing to seek consultation as they become seasoned professionals. Corey, Corey, and Callanan (2003) have suggested some procedural steps as a way to think through ethical dilemmas. Supervisors can use this model in teaching supervisees how to address ethical issues.

Identify the Problem or Dilemma   Gather as much information as possible that sheds light on the situation. Clarify whether the conflict is ethical, legal, professional, or moral—or a combination of any or all of these. The first step toward resolving an ethical dilemma is recognizing that a problem exists and identifying its specific nature. Because most ethical dilemmas are complex, it is useful to look at the problem from many perspectives and to avoid simplistic solutions. Consultation with the client and the supervisee begins at this initial stage and continues throughout the process of working through an ethical problem, as does the process of documenting decisions and actions taken.

Identify Potential Issues Involved   After the information is collected, list and describe the critical issues and discard the irrelevant ones. Evaluate the rights, responsibilities, and welfare of all those who are affected by the situation. Part of the process of making ethical decisions involves identifying competing values. Ask the supervisee for input regarding the values that must be considered. It may help to prioritize these values and principles and to think through ways in which each one can support a resolution to the dilemma.

Review Relevant Ethics Codes   Ask yourself whether the standards or principles of your professional organization offer a possible solution to the problem. Consider whether your own values and ethics are consistent with or in conflict with the relevant codes. Enlist your supervisee in research and discussions about ethics code requirements.

Know Applicable Laws and Regulations   It is essential for you to keep up to date on relevant state and federal laws that apply to ethical dilemmas. This is especially critical in matters of keeping or breaching confidentiality, reporting child or elder abuse, dealing with issues pertaining to danger to self or others, parental rights, record keeping, testing and assessment, diagnosis, licensing statutes, and the grounds for malpractice. Be sure that you discuss these issues with your supervisee as they pertain to the issue you are trying to resolve.

Obtain Consultation   At this point, it is generally helpful to consult with a colleague or colleagues to obtain a different perspective on the problem. Consider consulting with more than one professional, and do not limit the individuals with whom you will consult to those who share your orientation. If there is a legal question, seek legal counsel. It is wise to document the nature of your consultation, including the suggestions provided by those with whom you consulted. Consultation is important in court cases because consultation illustrates the attempt to adhere to community standards by finding out what your colleagues in the community would do in the same situation.

Consultation can help you think about information or circumstances that you may have overlooked. In making ethical decisions, you must justify a course of action based on sound reasoning. Include your supervisee and the client in consultation sessions when appropriate.

Consider Possible and Probable Courses of Action   Brainstorming is useful at this stage of ethical decision making. As you think about the many possibilities for action, discuss these options with your client, your supervisee, and with other professionals.

Enumerate the Consequences of Various Decisions   Ponder the implications of each course of action for the client, for others who are related to the client, for your supervisee, and for you as the supervisor. A discussion with the client about the consequences for him or her is most important, and you and your supervisee may decide to act as co-therapists when this discussion is initiated.

Decide the Best Course of Action   In making the best decision, carefully consider the information you have received from various sources. The more obvious the dilemma, the clearer is the course of action; the more subtle the dilemma, the more difficult the decision will be. Once you have made what you consider to be the best decision, do what you can to evaluate your course of action. Reflection on your assessment of the situation and the actions you took are essential if you are to learn from your experience. Follow up to determine the outcomes and see if any further action is needed. To obtain the most accurate picture, involve your supervisee and the client in this process.

These procedural steps should not be thought of as a simplified and linear way to reach a resolution on ethical matters. The aim of these steps is to stimulate self-reflection and encourage discussion with the client, your supervisee, and your colleagues. Use supervisory sessions to model this process for your trainees.

Competence of Supervisors

Supervision is a well-defined area that is rapidly becoming a specialized field in the helping professions with a developing body of research and a growing list of publications. From both an ethical and legal standpoint, it is essential that supervisors have the education and training to adequately carry out their roles. The skills used in counseling are not necessarily the same as those needed to adequately supervise trainees or to advise other helping professionals; specific training in how to supervise is needed. Ladany and colleagues (1999) assert that the supervisor has the responsibility for making appropriate disclosures to the supervisee when the supervisor or supervisee does not possess the competence to deal with a particular case or situation. These researchers report that, of the 151 therapists in training included in their study, 9% view their supervisors as lacking competence regarding the clients the supervisees were treating.

Many who function as supervisors have not had formal coursework and training in supervision theory and methods. There are many competent supervisors who lack formal training, but there are also those who are not so competent. Only in recent times has the standard for qualifying to be a clinical supervisor included formal course work and supervision of supervision. Currently, most counselor education programs offer a course in supervision at the doctoral level, and some programs provide training for supervisors at the master's level (Polanski, 2000). However, many supervisors still do not have formal training or course work in supervision. Instead, these supervisors rely on the model of supervising they experienced when they were in supervision themselves. No longer can clinical supervisors rely exclusively on this informal approach to learning how to supervise. If supervision courses were not part of their program, it is essential that supervisors acquire the specific knowledge and skills, perhaps through continuing education, that will enable them to function effectively in this role.

Becoming a competent supervisor currently involves taking course work in theories of supervision, working with difficult supervisees, working with culturally diverse supervisees, and methods of supervision. The counselor licensure laws in a number of states (Arkansas, Florida, Louisiana, Ohio, South Carolina, and Texas) now stipulate that licensed professional counselors who practice supervision are required to have relevant training experiences and course work in supervision. Licensed professional counselors in Ohio applying for status as counseling supervisors are required to have a minimum of three years of practice as a licensed counselor prior to their application (Polanski, 2000). Social workers and psychologists in California must complete formal course work in supervision to be qualified to function as clinical supervisors. In Oregon, for practitioners to qualify as supervisors, a three-credit semester course or a 30-hour continuing education course is minimal, and supervision of supervision is highly desirable (Miars, 2000). Besides course work, counselors need to be provided with training in supervision. See Box 7.1 for a list of characteristics we think are essential for competent supervision.

Polanski (2000) makes a case for teaching supervision at the master's level. Course work in supervision for counselors entering the field can teach them how to ask for what they need and influence their own supervision experiences. Trainees learn firsthand about the importance of mutuality in the supervision relationship. In short, students receiving this training become more educated consumers of supervision, and they have a better understanding of the practice of supervision when they take such a role in the future.

Supervisors not only need specialized training in methods of supervision but also need to have an in-depth knowledge of the specialty area in which they will provide supervision. It is unethical for supervisors to offer supervision in areas beyond the scope of their practice. On this matter, the NASW's (1999) ethical standard is clear: "Social workers who provide supervision or

BOX 7.1 | BASIC COMPONENTS
OF THE COMPETENT SUPERVISOR

1. Competent supervisors are *trained in supervision* and periodically *update their knowledge and skills* on supervision topics through workshops, conferences, and reading.
2. Competent supervisors must have the education, training, and experience necessary to be *competent in the area(s) of clinical expertise* in which they are providing supervision.
3. Competent supervisors must have *effective interpersonal skills* and be able to work with a variety of groups and individuals in supervision and with counselors with a range of life and clinical experience. Examples of these interpersonal skills include the ability to listen and provide constructive feedback, the ability to challenge and confront the supervisee in a helpful manner, and the ability to set professional interpersonal boundaries with the supervisee.
4. Competent supervisors must be cognizant of the fact that *supervision is a situational process* that is dependent on interaction between the supervisor, the supervisee, the setting, and the client. Skilled supervisors will be able to modify the approach to supervision as the situation dictates.
5. Competent supervisors must be flexible and *be able to assume a variety of roles and responsibilities* in supervision. The supervisory role can change rapidly depending on the needs of the situation.
6. Competent supervisors must have a *broad knowledge of laws, ethics, and professional regulations* that may apply in a variety of situations that could arise in supervision of clinical cases.
7. Competent supervisors stay focused on the fact that a primary goal of supervision is to *monitor clinical services* so that the welfare of the client is primary.
8. Competent supervisors are willing to *serve the evaluative function* with supervisees and *provide feedback* about their performance on a regular basis.
9. Competent supervisors document *supervision activities* in a timely and accurate fashion.
10. Competent supervisors *empower supervisees.* Supervisors assist supervisees at both problem-solving current situations and developing a problem solving approach that they can apply to nearly any clinical situation long after the supervision has ended. When needed, supervisors also provide teaching and consultation to assist the supervisee.

consultation should have the necessary knowledge and skill to supervise or consult appropriately and should do so only within their areas of knowledge and competence" (3.01a). The APA's (2001) position on boundaries of competence is similar: "Psychologists provide services, teach, and conduct research with populations and in areas only within the boundaries of their competence, based on their education, training, supervised experience, consultation, study, or professional experience" (2.01). If supervisees are working outside the area of competence of the supervisor, it is the responsibility of the supervisor to arrange for competent clinical supervision of those cases (Cobia & Boes, 2000).

Journey Toward Competence

Supervisors need not only specialized training in methods of supervision but also an in-depth knowledge of the specialty area in which they will provide supervision. What might you do if you find that your graduate program does not provide you with the knowledge and tools to be a competent supervisor?

Read the Voices from the Field feature to see how one counselor approached this lack.

You might well find yourself lacking in the competencies to be an effective supervisor, even if you are able to take a course in supervision as a part of your program. Today, there are many more workshops on supervision, a number of books on the topic, and opportunities to obtain some supervision by others as you begin your work as a supervisor. It may be a mistake to think that your graduate program alone will adequately prepare you with experiences in supervision or with the in-depth knowledge you will need to supervise others who are working with a wide range of client populations with special problems. Part of the answer to moving toward competence is seeking out quality continuing education programs dealing with special client populations and methods of supervision. Another factor in becoming competent as a supervisor involves becoming competent as a therapist in the areas in which you are supervising.

Incompetent or Impaired Supervisors

Although there is a growing body of literature on counselor impairment, Michelle Muratori (2001), an advanced doctoral student in counselor education, states that the topic of supervisor impairment has generally been overlooked. Muratori defines supervisor impairment as the inability to perform the functions involved in the supervisory role because of interference by something in the supervisor's behavior or environment. Some examples of supervisor impairment are engaging in exploitive or harmful dual or multiple relationships with supervisees, sexual contact with supervisees, misuse of power, substance abuse, or extreme burnout. Muratori's article "Examining Supervisor Impairment from the Counselor Trainee's Perspective," explores the implications of working with an impaired supervisor at the various levels of counselor development and discusses some of the key factors that may influence how a supervisee might deal with this problem.

According to Muratori, it is critical to be mindful of the reality that the supervisor is in an evaluative position and is expected to assess whether trainees have acquired the necessary skills and competencies to advance in the program. This fact has implications for the counselor trainee's decision of what to do in the case of having an impaired supervisor. Critical factors trainees need to consider before determining a proper course of action are the precise nature and the severity of the supervisor's impairment. Other factors that contribute to the complexity of the decision to either confront or endure working with an impaired supervisor include the power differential that is inherent in the supervisory relationship, one's level of development as a counselor trainee, and the personalities of both the supervisor and the supervisee. Muratori makes the point that trainees who have an impaired supervisor may have fewer options than a client who has an impaired counselor. Even assertive supervisees need to carefully weigh their options for action with an impaired supervisor because of the potential consequences

 | ## VOICES FROM THE FIELD

Jerry Corey

In my doctoral program during the early to mid-1960s, I had no course work in supervision; furthermore, there was no discussion in any of my courses about how to function as a clinical supervisor. Regarding my specialty area of group counseling, I had only one course (group guidance) in my doctoral studies that had anything to do with group process. To acquire knowledge and skills in the area of facilitating groups myself, I co-led a number of groups

with more experienced professionals and acquired some informal supervision in group work. Even more important, I attended many different types of group experiences as a participant of groups. I learned more about myself, others, group process, and effective group leadership from this actual participation in a myriad of groups. To learn more about basic concepts and methods of supervision, I attended some continuing education workshops and did extensive reading on the topic of supervision.

---

that could be associated with this supervisor's misuse of power. Muratori concludes that in extreme cases trainees may need to take legal action, especially if the quality of supervision is being compromised or if they believe they are being harmed by the relationship.

Incompetent or Impaired Supervisees

What is the supervisor's responsibility in cases where supervisees are clearly not competent to counsel others? What ethical issues must be addressed when supervisors encounter impaired supervisees? Supervisees may not have the fundamental knowledge or the basic helping skills required to carry out effective counseling, and to be sure, supervisees will be evaluated on their level of knowledge and skill development. But what about those instances in which supervisees are unable to function effectively because of personal problems or personality characteristics?

Trainee Impairment   Supervisors cannot ethically avoid confronting supervisees who cannot competently carry out their training role because of some personal limitation or impairment. Given the increased awareness of possible damage caused by counselors who do not possess the personal qualities of effective counselors, training faculty and supervisors are expected to address situations that involve trainee impairment (Lumadue & Duffey, 1999). After surveying the literature on evaluating the competence of trainees, Forrest, Elman, Gizara, and Vacha-Haase (1999) came to the conclusion that "we [supervisors] are struggling to understand and implement our responsibilities as gatekeepers for professional quality control" (p. 679).

A range of behaviors can adversely affect the ability of students and trainees to effectively carry out their clinical duties. Two severe problems are substance abuse and personality disorders. More subtle aspects of trainee impairment include interpersonal sensitivity, need for extreme control, and using one's position to meet personal needs at the client's expense. Bemak, Epp, and Keys (1999) note that what distinguishes impaired counselor trainees is their lack of ability to understand and resolve their own personal problems so that these issues do not interfere with their professional work with clients. These authors cite a number of dimensions of trainee impairment:

> Impaired graduate students may incorporate personal agendas into their counseling philosophy involving dogmatic religious teachings, harmful directive techniques, or antipathy towards members of a different gender, ethnicity, race, sexual orientation, or age-group. They may project their own personal issues onto their clients or interpret their clients' issues through the "distorted lenses" of their own problems. (p. 21)

Monitoring Trainee Competence   Monitoring the competence of students in training has long been viewed as an essential component in training programs. In addition to evaluating a supervisee's academic ability, knowledge, and clinical skills, it is essential to identify and evaluate a supervisee's personal characteristics, interpersonal behaviors, and professional behaviors that are likely to influence their ability to effectively deliver mental health services. There is a lack of clear, shared, and consistent language to represent the different types of problematic behaviors (Forrest et al., 1999). Sometimes trainees have personal characteristics or problems that interfere with their ability to function effectively, yet when this is pointed out to them they may deny the feedback they receive. In these cases, a program has an ethical responsibility to take action and not simply pass on a student with serious academic or personal problems. Both the ACA *Code of Ethics* (1995) and the ACES (1993) *Ethical Guidelines for Counseling Supervisors* address this issue (see Box 7.2).

Bemak, Epp, and Keys (1999) describe a five-step process model for monitoring counselor trainee development, for evaluating student progress, and for dismissing impaired students from training programs. Their model includes a consideration of both academic grades and personal and professional development as guiding criteria. See their article for a detailed discussion of this topic and their model.

Taking Action with Incompetent Supervisees   It is of the utmost importance that supervisees hear from their supervisors long before it is too late for them to take corrective measures. Due process is essential, and dismissal from a training program should be the last resort after other interventions have failed to produce any change in supervisees who exhibit deficiencies. Supervisors have an obligation to provide their supervisees with regular, specific, and ongoing feedback. If there are problems regarding supervisees' performances, they must be given opportunities to take remedial steps in correcting these problems. A few types of remediation include increased supervision, a leave of absence, personal therapy, taking a course or workshop, repeating a practicum or internship experience, or being part of a growth group.

| BOX 7.2 | ASSESSING PERSONAL AND PROFESSIONAL LIMITATIONS OF SUPERVISEES |

American Counseling Association
Code of Ethics (1995)

F.3.a. Counselors, through ongoing evaluation and appraisal, are aware of the academic and personal limitations of students and supervisees that might impede performance. Counselors assist students and supervisees in securing remedial assistance when needed, and dismiss from the training program supervisees who are unable to provide competent service due to academic or personal limitations. Counselors seek professional consultation and document their decisions to dismiss or refer students or supervisees for assistance. Counselors assure that students and supervisees have recourse to address decisions made, to require them to seek assistance, or to dismiss them.

Association for Counselor Education and Supervision
Ethical Guidelines for Counseling Supervisors (1993)

2.12 Supervisors, through ongoing supervisee assessment and evaluation, should be aware of any personal or professional limitations of supervisees which are likely to impede future professional performance. Supervisors have the responsibility of recommending remedial assistance to the supervisee and of screening from the training program, applied counseling setting, or state licensure those supervisees who are unable to provide competent professional services. These recommendations should be clearly and professionally explained in writing to the supervisees who are so evaluated.

In their review of the literature on the reasons for dismissal from a program, Forrest and her colleagues (1999) found these common categories of incompetence: poor academic performance, poor clinical performance, poor interpersonal skills, and unethical behavior. Psychological reasons for dismissal included factors such as emotional instability, personality disorder, psychopathology, and unprofessional demeanor. Forrest and her colleagues identified some general procedural guidelines for due process that should be provided to protect both the program and the trainees:

- Written description that gives reasons for termination
- Oral and written evaluations of trainees regarding their personal and interpersonal functioning
- Written action plans for remediation specifying the expected behavioral changes, a timeline, and consequences for failing to remediate
- A notification process for dismissal
- Procedures that permit trainees to appeal a decision to dismiss

Even when it becomes evident that trainees are functioning below an acceptable level of performance in academic or personal areas, there are barriers to taking the action of dismissing students from a program, some of which include difficulties in giving clear evidence to support the decision to dismiss a student, the lack of adequate procedures in place to support a dismissal decision, concern about the psychological distress for faculty and students, concern about heightened resistance and defensiveness in the trainee, the potential for receiving criticism from other faculty or supervisors who were not involved in the trainee's remediation, and lack of administrative support (Forrest et al., 1999). When there is concern about personal characteristics or problematic behavior of supervisees, both faculty and supervisors may be hesitant in taking action to prevent supervisees from continuing a program. Perhaps the major deterrent to dismissing a student is the fear of legal reprisal by that student. However, if a trainee has good grades but has serious unresolved personal conflicts or demonstrates dysfunctional interpersonal behavior, action needs to be taken. If remediation has not worked, dismissal is necessary. Yet this option should be a measure of last resort.

Challenges for Training Programs   As a pathway to ensuring competence on the part of trainees, training programs need to be designed so that students can acquire a more thorough understanding of themselves as well as acquire theoretical knowledge. Ideally, trainees will be introduced to various content areas, will acquire a range of clinical skills they can use in working with diverse clients, will learn how to apply theory to practice through supervised fieldwork experiences, and will learn a great deal about themselves personally. An ethical mandate of a good program is to do more than impart knowledge and skills. A quality program provides a supportive and challenging environment, encourages trainees to build on their life experiences and personal strengths, and provides opportunities for expanding their awareness of self and others.

MULTIPLE ROLES AND RELATIONSHIPS
IN THE SUPERVISORY PROCESS

Counseling supervisors are expected to possess the personal and professional maturity to manage multiple roles and responsibilities (ACES, 1993, 1995). A multiple relationship occurs when a supervisor is in a professional role with a supervisee and at the same time is in another role with the supervisee. Some examples of multiple relationships in supervision are a supervisor becoming the supervisee's therapist, a supervisor initiating a business venture with a supervisee, or a supervisor developing a friendship or social relationship with a supervisee. Although multiple roles and relationships are common in the context of training and supervision, it is essential for supervisors to thoroughly discuss and process issues relevant to these multiple roles with their supervisees (Ladany et al., 1999).

Ethical Standards and Multiple Roles and Relationships

Ladany and colleagues (1999) note that it is the responsibility of the supervisor to handle role-related conflicts in an appropriate and ethical manner. Ethically, supervisors need to clarify their roles and to be aware of potential problems that can develop when boundaries become blurred. Supervisors who are able to establish appropriate personal and professional boundaries are in a good position to teach supervisees how to develop appropriate boundaries.

Supervisees may be affected by the multiple roles of their supervisors, and these blended roles may influence the supervision process. As Herlihy and Corey (1997) point out, unless the nature of the supervisory relationship is clearly defined, both the supervisor and the supervisee may find themselves in a difficult situation at some point in their relationship. If the supervisor's objectivity becomes impaired, the supervisee will not be able to make maximum use of the process.

The codes of ethics of most professional organizations issue a caution regarding the potential problems involved in dual and multiple relationships (see Box 7.3). Specifically, the standards warn of the dangers involved in any relationships that are likely to impair the judgment or result in exploitation or harm to clients and supervisees.

Managing Multiple Roles and Relationships

Although multiple roles and relationships cannot always be avoided, supervisors have the responsibility to manage them in ethical and appropriate ways. The crux of the matter is to avoid multiple relationships that could reasonably be expected to impair the professional's objectivity, competence, or effectiveness in performing his or her duties. What is to be avoided are those multiple role relationships in the training and supervisory process that involve an abuse of power. Supervisees are in a vulnerable position because of the power differential and can be harmed by a supervisor who exploits them, misuses power, or crosses appropriate boundaries. Supervisors must not exploit supervisees or take unfair advantage of the power differential that exists in the context of training.

Supervisors play a critical role in helping counselor trainees understand the dynamics of balancing multiple roles and managing multiple relationships. Although students may learn about multiple relationships during their academic work, it is generally during the time they are engaged in fieldwork experiences and internships that they are required to grapple with boundary issues (Herlihy & Corey, 1997).

Burian and O'Connor Slimp (2000) point out that training staff and interns are faced with the prospect of entering into multiple role relationships with each other. These relationships may at first appear benign, and sometimes even beneficial, yet they pose some risks to interns and training staff. For example, the mentoring that occurs between faculty and students (and between supervisors and supervisees) often includes social elements, which can be beneficial to the trainee. Burian and O'Connor Slimp have designed a decision-making model pertaining to social multiple role relationships between interns and their trainers. Their model is designed to raise awareness of the issues involved in these relationships and provide a basis for evaluating their potential for harm. These authors suggest ending or postponing the social relationship if there exists more than a minimal risk of harm.

BOX 7.3 | ETHICS STANDARDS REGARDING DUAL AND MULTIPLE RELATIONSHIPS

American Association for Marriage and Family Therapy
AAMFT Code of Ethics (2001)
4.1. Marriage and family therapists are aware of their influential position with respect to clients, and they avoid exploiting the trust and dependency of such persons. Therapists, therefore, make every effort to avoid conditions and multiple relationships with clients that could impair professional judgment or increase the risk of exploitation. When the risk of impairment or exploitation exists due to conditions or multiple roles, therapists take appropriate precautions.

American Counseling Association
Code of Ethics and Standards of Practice (1995)
A.6.a. Counselors are aware of their influential positions with respect to clients, and they avoid exploiting the trust and dependency of clients. Counselors make every effort to avoid dual relationships with clients that could impair professional judgment or increase the risk of harm to clients. (Examples of such relationships include, but are not limited to, familial, social, financial, business, or close personal relationships with clients.) When a dual relationship cannot be avoided, counselors take appropriate professional precautions such as informed consent, consultation, supervision, and documentation to ensure that judgment is not impaired and no exploitation occurs.

American Psychological Association
Ethical Principles of Psychologists and Code of Conduct (1992)
1.17.a. In many communities and situations, it may not be feasible or reasonable for psychologists to avoid social or other nonprofessional contacts with persons such as patients, clients, students, supervisees, or research participants. Psychologists must always be sensitive to the potential harmful effects of other contacts on their work and on those persons with whom they deal. A psychologist refrains from entering into or promising another personal, scientific, professional, financial, or other relationship with such persons if it appears likely that such a relationship reasonably might impair the psychologist's objectivity or otherwise interfere with the psychologist's effectively performing his or her functions as a psychologist, or might harm or exploit the other party.

Association for Counselor Education and Supervision
Ethical Guidelines for Counseling Supervisors (1993)
2.11 • Supervisors who have multiple roles (e.g., teacher, clinical supervisor, administrative supervisor, etc.) with supervisees should minimize potential conflicts. Where possible, the roles should be divided among several supervisors. Where this is not possible, careful explanation should be conveyed to the supervisee as to the expectations and responsibilities associated with each supervisory role. (2.09)
• Supervisors should not participate in any form of sexual contact with supervisees. Supervisors should not engage in any form of social contact or interaction which would compromise the supervisor-supervisee relationship. Dual relationships with supervisees that might impair the supervisor's objectivity and professional judgment should be avoided and/or the supervisory relationship terminated. (2.10)
• Supervisors should not establish a psychotherapeutic relationship as a substitute for supervision. Personal issues should be addressed in supervision only in terms of the impact of these issues on clients and on professional functioning.

National Association of Social Workers
Code of Ethics (1999)
1.06.c. Social workers should not engage in dual or multiple relationships with clients or former clients in which there is a risk of exploitation or potential harm to the client. In instances when dual or multiple

relationships are unavoidable, social workers should take steps to protect clients and are responsible for setting clear, appropriate, and culturally sensitive boundaries.

We asked a number of supervisors to provide their perspective on multiple roles and relationships in the supervisory relationship. Their responses are recorded in the Voices from the Field feature. After reading these perspectives on multiple relationships in supervision, reflect on your position on the possible benefits and risks associated with dual and multiple relationships. Do you think such relationships are inevitable in supervision? If they are, what kinds of safeguards could minimize potential harm? What thoughts do you have about managing multiple roles and relationships in supervision? What have been your experiences with multiple roles as a supervisee?

Mentoring

A dynamic way to teach is through the mentoring process. Experienced supervisors are in a position to encourage their supervisees to get a vision of what they might want to accomplish professionally. This role as a mentor can include many informal activities that involve meeting outside the supervision office. Not only can mentors offer encouragement, but they can inspire supervisees to pursue their interests and can offer practical suggestions of ways trainees might accomplish their goals. In many graduate programs, supervisors often invite their supervisees and students to be co-presenters at a conference or convention. Even though different levels of responsibilities are evident here and different roles exist, this does not have to be a problem. Again, the critical point is that the person with greater power (the supervisor) initiates a discussion about this type of collaborative project. Perhaps the best way for supervisors to teach is by this kind of active process of co-presenting at professional conferences, or working together on some research project, or engaging in some kind of collaborative writing project. A potential ethical issue lies in some supervisors not giving these supervisees full credit for their participation in a project. This does not have to present a barrier and should not discourage mentoring. Instead, dialogue can address any of these potential ethical issues. The ongoing process of open discussion can provide the foundation for optimum learning. To us, this collaborative dialogue is far preferable to having a long list of prohibitions about multiple relationships.

Socializing Between Supervisors and Supervisees

One dual relationship that may need to be considered is the matter of engaging in some form of socialization. Supervisors, for example, may be invited to group functions outside of the academic or clinical setting. Faculty and

VOICES FROM THE FIELD

Stacy Thacker, Ph.D.

Multiple relationships can be very problematic for the supervisor, the supervisee, and their peers. Having multiple roles can create a great amount of confusion. For example, one person may believe that he or she is having a personal conversation while the other may view it as a professional conversation. Multiple relationships may lead to a sense of betrayal ("Why did you rate me so low, I thought we were friends?") or favoritism ("She spends time outside of work with her other supervisees, I guess she doesn't like me."). Also, the power difference between a supervisor and supervisee is inherent. Although a supervisor can argue that he or she did not use the power of his or her position as a supervisor, the power inherent in the position cannot be separated from the person, and the supervisee may feel some level of pressure to please the supervisor.

Todd Thies, Ph.D.

Multiple relationships with interns is something that I must deal with frequently. Because I am young for a psychologist, my personal interests and preferences often match those of my supervisees more closely than those of my colleagues. As a result, I commonly encounter interns I am supervising in social situations. Being in a relatively small town also compounds this issue. For me, the first step is communication. Sometimes it is not possible to avoid being placed in a social situation with someone you also supervise, so the best thing to do is keep the channels of communication open. That way, if conflicts or potential boundary violations occur, they can be addressed by the supervisor, supervisee, and colleagues. The information shared between an intern and supervisor frequently must be kept private for confidentiality reasons, but the rela-

tionship between a supervisor and supervisee should be public. To put it in one sentence: Don't do anything with a supervisee that you wouldn't feel comfortable having your colleagues see you do.

Elie Axelroth, Psy. D.

While supervision is a relationship, and at times a somewhat intimate endeavor, there are many ways in which the supervisory relationship is different from other collegial relationships. The supervisor is often called upon to evaluate the intern, to point out strengths and weaknesses, to write a letter of recommendation, and to provide critical feedback. For these reasons, it is crucial that the supervisor maintain clear professional boundaries—and it is the supervisor's responsibility to do so.

To facilitate clear boundaries, an open discussion about supervision and the limits of supervision should be an integral part of the intern orientation. A written policy should be provided to interns and discussed in detail. Interns are extremely vulnerable during their internship year, often having moved to a new geographic area, sometimes without their social support network, with the additional stress of a new job, and professional responsibilities. Supervisors must be mindful of these transitional pressures, recognizing that interns may be feeling more isolated than usual.

It is important to keep hierarchical issues in mind. While we are clear that a sexual relationship is never appropriate between an intern and supervisor, intimate relationships are also generally not appropriate between staff members and interns—even if the staff member is not a supervisor. These sorts of outside relationships can create isolation from other staff and alliances that are detrimental to the intern. Along the same lines, supervisors and interns should not engage in any outside social or financial arrangements, such as house-sitting, private practice, or consulting. Any desire on the part of the intern or supervisor to keep the activities secretive is probably indicative of crossing an inappropriate boundary. When in doubt, it is always appropriate to consult with colleagues.

Bill Safarjan, Ph.D.

I take a rather hard line on this issue and may be seen as "old school." I see the relationship between supervisor and supervisee as a special one that must not be jeopardized by forming other kinds of personal associations. One example is a supervisor who becomes a friend with a supervisee. Accepting favors or engaging in social activities weakens boundaries and undermines the objectivity and authority of the supervisor. Another example of a problematic multiple relationship involves the supervisor who becomes the supervisee's therapist. The supervisor's job is to improve the supervisee's clinical practice rather than provide therapy for the supervisee. If "therapeutic interactions" occur, they should occur in the context of the supervisee's ability to deliver psychological services or benefit from supervision. In my view, multiple relationships must be avoided because they have the potential to undermine the supervisory process and divert attention away from the primary role of the supervisor.

---

supervisors may be asked to attend a dinner or some kind of party that students are sponsoring. Although this may not be a regular event, supervisors still need to think about the potential issues that could surface and how attending a social function might either enhance or inhibit the professional relationship. More problematic is the case of a supervisee inviting a supervisor to attend a concert, go jogging, or engage in some other social event much as friends would do.

There is also the matter of supervisors and supervisees attending a professional convention. There may be many opportunities to meet at informal events at these functions, such as a party in the evening or some group tour of the city where the convention is being held. Although this kind of social contact may seem innocent, there is potential for problems. At a later time, supervisees may expect to be treated somewhat like a friend during supervision sessions, or they may be disconcerted when a supervisor gives them critical feedback during a performance evaluation review. Rigid rules are not necessarily the best answer to dealing with the fact that supervisors and supervisees may attend social functions together or have informal contacts outside of the supervision setting. Open discussions about this possibility can prevent serious problems from occurring during supervision.

In Case 7.1, Mike confronts a common dilemma involving multiple roles and relationships. Is this a clear boundary situation, or is it an "it depends" kind of situation? Is Stan crossing the line in making the invitation? What do the standards and regulations say about this? Would this situation be different if the supervisor or the supervisee had been female? Have you ever experienced multiple relationships with a professor?

| CASE 7.1 | MIKE |

Mike is a marriage and family therapist and teaches in the master's level human services program at the local university. He is currently supervising Stan, who is enrolled in the human services program and does counseling at the university's community clinic. Mike is also the instructor in one of Stan's classes, and they frequently see each other at academic and social functions sponsored by the program. Stan respects and admires Mike and sees him as a role model for himself. During a supervision session, Stan invited Mike and his wife over to his house for dinner. Mike inquires about the purpose of the din-ner and whether other students or faculty will be present. When he learns that it is purely a social invitation and that Mike and his wife are the only ones invited, Mike decides to politely decline. Stan explains how much he admires Mike and how he just wanted to invite him over to show his apprecia-tion for all the help he has received. Mike realizes that Stan is puzzled by his decline of the invitation. To help clear up Stan's confusion, Mike returns to a discussion of the parameters of the supervisory rela-tionship as outlined in the supervision contract.

Multiple relationships in the academic and clinical setting are very com-mon. Teachers and professors often serve in several roles with students and can do so effectively and ethically, but to do so requires that they be clear about what their respective roles are in various situations. Herlihy and Corey (1997) indicate that the nature of the supervisory relationship should be clearly defined. It is best if this is done in writing. When a problem occurs with the roles in the various relationships, the supervisor and super-visee can revisit their definition of who they are to each other in which situations.

It is the responsibility of the supervisor to define the relationship, to dis-cuss with the supervisee when boundaries are changing, and to protect the welfare of the supervisee (see the Voices from the Field for more on this topic). If the situation seems unmanageable with a given supervisee, the supervisor can either try to reduce the number of situations in which they are together or seek another supervisor for the supervisee.

There are so many forms of socialization that it is impossible to identify them all. Socialization can include any conversations you have or activities that you participate in with your trainees that are not directly related to their professional activities and client care. Here are a few examples of the diverse range of socializing:

- Playing golf, hiking, jogging, tennis, and the like
- Sharing meals
- Going out for coffee
- Going to the movies

VOICES FROM THE FIELD

Bob Haynes

In my earlier years as a supervisor, it was fun and enjoyable to socialize with supervisees, and I was able to maintain boundaries between the social and professional relationships. With increasing experience as a supervisor, however, I learned that these multiple relationships are not a problem until I have some difficulty with my supervisee or must give a negative evaluation of the supervisee. At that point, it becomes more difficult to be objectively critical of someone with whom I have developed a real friendship. For that reason, I have developed the position that I do not participate in social activities with supervisees unless it is unavoidable. After the supervisory relationship has concluded, I may feel freer to socialize with the individual.

- Attending professional conferences and workshops
- Carpooling
- Attending students' weddings or funerals
- Attending students' parties
- Attending parties at faculty or supervisors' homes

Each of these activities is potentially unethical or problematic. As we developed this topic, the words "it depends" came up time and again. In making decisions about these matters, there are no simple answers. What seems important to us is the supervisor's ability to define and maintain appropriate boundaries with supervisees. If a supervisor cannot establish appropriate personal boundaries, it is very likely that he or she will have difficulty developing effective professional boundaries with supervisees.

In evaluating each situation you might encounter, it is important to think through the ramifications of your actions for both you and your supervisee. It is probably best to err on the side of caution; many situations that begin innocently and with honest motivation can quickly turn into complex ethical dilemmas. Ask yourself these questions:

- How might socializing with supervisees affect my ability to carry out my roles and functions as a supervisor? What if I were to give a negative evaluation or had to terminate this supervisee?
- Can I explain and justify my decisions regarding supervisees to an ethics board?
- What advice would I give a colleague who came to me with a similar situation?
- In my setting, how appropriate is socializing and what is the level of the professional maturity of my trainees?
- How might other supervisees react or be affected by knowing I am socializing with certain trainees but not all of them?

- Am I willing for my actions to be public?
- What is the worst possible scenario that could emerge from my decision to socialize with trainees?

The supervisory relationship is a unique one, with many gray areas. Certainly, it presents problems different from those of socializing with clients. Your challenge will be to formulate your own guidelines for determining what kinds of interactions you will have (or not have) with supervisees beyond the formal professional context of supervision.

Sexual Attraction in Supervision

Ordinarily, attraction, in and of itself, is not problematic. It is what individuals do with the attraction that determines the appropriateness or inappropriateness of these reactions. It is your responsibility to provide a safe learning environment for your supervisees. It is also your job to train supervisees about sexual attraction in a way that encourages them to acknowledge their attractions and work through them in a professional manner.

Supervisor Attraction to Supervisee   There is a distinction between finding a supervisee attractive and being preoccupied with this attraction. As a supervisor, you may find yourself being physically attracted to some trainees more than others. If you find yourself sexually attracted to your supervisees, it is important that you examine your feelings. If you are attracted often and to many different trainees, you need to deal with this issue in your own therapy and supervision. If this frequently happens, consider these questions: What is going on in my own life that may be creating this intense attraction? What am I missing in my personal life? How might I be using my professional work as a way to fulfill my personal needs?

Helping Supervisees Deal with Sexual Attractions to Clients   Although transient sexual feelings are normal, intense preoccupation with clients is problematic. Housman and Stake (1999) found that 50% of the doctoral students in their study reported having experienced a sexual attraction to a client; only half of these students had chosen to discuss the attraction with a supervisor. Seeking help from a colleague or supervision or personal therapy can give counselor trainees access to guidance, education, and support in handling their feelings. Pope, Sonne, and Holroyd (1993) believe that exploration of sexual feelings about clients is best done with the help, support, and encouragement of others. They maintain that practice, internships, and peer supervision groups are ideal places to talk about this topic, which is often treated as though it were nonexistent.

Housman and Stake (1999) conducted a survey regarding sexual ethics training and student understanding of sexual ethics in clinical psychology doctoral programs. They reported that 94% of the students had received ethics training in managing sexual attractions. Programs provided an average of six hours of training. Other of their findings call attention to the importance of addressing sexual issues in therapy early in students' training. Sexual feelings for clients are common among students as well as professional practitioners. It was concluded that most students in training do not understand that sexual attractions for clients are normal. Housman and Stake's findings suggest that only half the students who are attracted will seek supervision. They note that even if students refrain from acting on their sexual feelings for clients, they may withdraw emotionally from their clients to avoid feelings they believe are unacceptable. According to Pope, Sonne, and Holroyd (1993), the tendency to treat sexual feelings as if they are taboo has made it difficult for therapists to acknowledge and accept attractions to clients. They found that the most common reactions of therapists to sexual feelings in therapy were these:

- Surprise, startle, and shock
- Guilt
- Anxiety about unresolved personal problems
- Fear of losing control
- Fear of being criticized
- Frustration at not being able to speak openly, or at not being able to make sexual contact
- Confusion about tasks
- Confusion about boundaries and roles
- Confusion about actions
- Anger at the client's sexuality

It is crucial that students acknowledge these feelings to themselves and to their supervisors and take steps to deal effectively with them.

Housman and Stake (1999) state that, in addition to supervisory consultations, clinical programs should provide all students with some form of planned experiential training for developing skills in clarifying boundaries and setting limits with clients. As a part of this experiential training, Housman and Stake recommend discussion of videotaped scenarios portraying client and therapist sexual feelings, role-playing common scenarios that could result in sexual misconduct, and opportunities to discuss personal cases. They emphasize the importance of broadening sexual ethics training to address both the emotional and cognitive aspects of attractions in the therapeutic relationship.

Wiederman and Sansone (1999) also make the case that deliberate attention to sexuality issues during training is required for the development of competent mental health professionals. Ideally, trainees will receive accurate information and firsthand experience. Hamilton and Spruill (1999) believe it is crucial to increase student awareness of sexual attraction before they begin seeing clients. They recommend the inclusion of how to deal with sexual attractions as a basic component of a preparatory clinical skills course. This training needs to create the expectation that sexual attractions will arise in therapy and to create an atmosphere of trust in which supervisees feel as free as possible to disclose these feelings and experiences in their supervision. If supervisees are not presented with normalizing information, they are likely to continue to regard sexual feelings as rare and hide rather than acknowledge them.

Sexual Intimacies Between Supervisor and Supervisee

Although multiple relationships are common in university settings, sex between students and their professors and supervisors is forbidden by ethical standards. As in the case of sexual relations between therapists and clients, sex in the supervisory relationship invariably results in an abuse of power because of the difference in status between supervisees and supervisors. Further, there is the matter of poor modeling for supervisees for their relationships with clients. Specific standards of the various professional organizations regarding sexual intimacies in the supervisory relationship are summarized in Box 7.4.

In their national survey on sexual intimacy in counselor education and supervision, Miller and Larrabee (1995) found that counseling professionals who were sexually involved with a supervisor or an educator during their training later viewed these experiences as being more coercive and more harmful to a working relationship than they did at the time the sex occurred. It seems clear that supervisors have professional power and authority long after the supervisory relationship ends.

Clear power differentials exist between supervisors and supervisees. Miller and Larrabee (1995) take the position that supervisors who engage in sexual behavior with supervisees are behaving inappropriately and unethically. Miller and Larrabee suggest that supervisors be aware of their position of power and function as professional role models. Supervisors ought to refrain from any sexual involvements with supervisees because of the detrimental impact of sexual involvements on the supervisory relationship.

Just as in instructor–student and therapist–client relationships, in supervisory relationships it is the professional who occupies the position of greater power. Thus, it is the professional's responsibility to establish and maintain appropriate boundaries and to explore with the supervisee ways to prevent potential problems. If problems do arise, the supervisor has the responsibility to take steps to resolve them in an ethical manner.

The core ethical issue is the difference in power and status between supervisor and supervisee and the exploitation of that power. When supervisees first begin counseling, they are typically naive and uninformed with respect to the complexities of therapy. They frequently regard their supervisors as experts and depend on their supervisors in a way that may make it difficult for supervisees to resist sexual advances. Supervisees may disclose personal concerns and intense emotions during supervision, much as they might in a therapeutic situation. The openness of supervisees and the trust they place in their supervisors can be exploited by supervisors who choose to satisfy their own psychological or sexual needs at the expense of their supervisees.

ETHICS STANDARDS REGARDING SEXUAL INTIMACIES IN SUPERVISION AND TRAINING

American Association of Marriage and Family Therapy
AAMFT Code of Ethics (2001)
Marriage and family therapists do not engage in sexual intimacy with students or supervisees during the evaluative or training relationship between the therapist and student or supervisee.

American Counseling Association
Code of Ethics and Standards of Practice (1995)
F.1.c Counselors do not engage in sexual relationships with students or supervisees and do not subject them to sexual harassment.

American Psychological Association
Ethical Principles of Psychologists and Code of Conduct (2001)
7.07 Psychologists do not engage in sexual relationships with students or supervisees in training who are in their department, agency, or training center or over whom the psychologist has or is likely to have evaluative authority.

Association for Counselor Education and Supervision
Ethical Guidelines for Counseling Supervisors (1993)
2.10 Supervisors should not participate in any form of sexual contact with supervisees. Supervisors should not engage in any form of social contact or interaction which would compromise the supervisor-supervisee relationship. Dual relationships with supervisees that might impair the supervisor's objectivity and professional judgment should be avoided and/or the supervisory relationship terminated.

National Association of Social Workers
Code of Ethics (1999)
3.01.c Social workers should not engage in any dual or multiple relationships with supervisees in which there is a risk of exploitation of or potential harm to the supervisee.

Sexual Intimacies Between Supervisee and Client

In addition to sexual attractions or sexual intimacies between supervisors and supervisees, there is the matter of supervisees being attracted to a client or even the possibility of a supervisee becoming sexually involved with a client. It is clear that this is a matter for supervision and that the supervisor bears both ethical and legal responsibilities for the actions of his or her supervisees. Supervisees may be reluctant to admit that they are attracted to a client, or a client to them. This dilemma highlights the importance of supervisors creating a safe climate where supervisees are more likely to bring into supervision feelings they might be having toward clients. Any form of sexual intimacy is inappropriate and unethical between supervisees and their clients. However, sexual attractions may very well occur, and being able to talk about this in supervision (see Case 7.2) is of the utmost importance.

CASE 7.2 | ELIZABETH

Elizabeth is supervising a prelicensed social worker, George, in a group practice setting. George has been seeing about 15 clients per week. One of his clients, Connie, is in therapy because she is dissatisfied with her current career and would like to obtain a master's or doctoral degree. George enjoys working with Connie as a client and can identify with her struggles. He thinks he can be a mentor in helping her decide how to proceed with her schooling. He looks forward to seeing her every week and in fact is beginning to feel sexually attracted to her. George discusses all of his cases with his supervisor, Elizabeth, including the case of Connie. He finally admits to his supervisor that he is sexually attracted to Connie.

As the supervisor, Elizabeth realizes that she is responsible for the actions of her supervisee. She knows that her first responsibility is to assure that Connie is protected from any harm that George's feelings of sexual attraction might do. Elizabeth wonders whether she should insist that George discuss his feelings of attraction with Connie. She asks George how that would help the client and/or the therapeutic relationship. George realizes that once he mentions this to Connie, the level of trust is affected and the therapeutic relationship is changed forever. If George can resolve his feelings regarding Connie in supervision, then he feels there is most likely no reason to bring it up to her. If he cannot and is faced with referring Connie to another counselor, then he may wish to discuss the reason for his wanting to make the referral.

Elizabeth has established a safe and open environment in supervisory sessions, and she helps George explore and understand how and why this attraction has occurred, why it is not acceptable, how to deal with this situation now, and how to handle similar situations in the future. With Elizabeth's help, George deals with the situation and learns from it in a way that will help him in his future professional work.

Oftentimes, feelings of attraction and infatuation overtake reason and logic. Supervisees will need to feel safe to discuss and explore their feelings, and they need to know the consequences of what will happen if they persist in their feelings and act on them.

If sex between the supervisee and the client is occurring, the supervisor has a legal and ethical obligation to do everything possible to stop it immediately. It is not sufficient to tell your supervisee that sex with clients is forbidden. In addition, you are responsible to assure that the client is not further damaged and is referred to another therapist to deal with the incident and to continue therapy. In all likelihood, you will be required to initiate further action with the supervisee. The specific actions you take are dependent on a number of variables including the ethics codes that apply, licensing and other legal regulations, and the policies of your agency or institution. As a supervisor, you are legally vulnerable if you fail to take appropriate actions (see Chapter 8 for an in-depth review of legal responsibilities).

Boundary issues and sexual attraction should be a regular topic for discussion among supervisors and their supervisees and should be covered in the supervision contract. Supervisees should be encouraged to learn as much as they can about their feelings and needs and what role they play in counseling.

COMBINING SUPERVISION AND COUNSELING

The boundaries between providing supervision and personal counseling to supervisees are not always clear. In the literature on supervision and the professional codes, there is basic agreement that the supervision process should concentrate on the supervisee's professional development rather than on personal concerns and that supervision and counseling have different purposes. There is, however, a lack of consensus and clarity about the degree to which supervisors can ethically deal with the personal issues of supervisees.

Supervisory relationships are a complex blend of professional, educational, and therapeutic relationships. This complex process can become increasingly complicated when supervisors become involved in certain multiple roles with trainees. In the supervisory relationship, it is expected that a supervisee's personal issues will be dealt with appropriately, and that referrals will be made to a therapist when a supervisee experiences a personal problem that interferes with providing adequate care to the client. Of the participants in one study, only 5% believed their supervisors failed to adhere to this ethical guideline (Ladany et al., 1999). It is the supervisor's responsibility to help trainees identify how their personal dynamics are likely to influence their work with clients, yet it is not the proper role of supervisors to serve as personal counselors for supervisees. Combining the roles of supervising and counseling often presents conflicts (Pope & Vasquez, 1998).

As personal problems or limitations of supervisees become evident, supervisors are ethically obliged to encourage and challenge supervisees to face and deal with these barriers that could inhibit their potential as therapists (Herlihy & Corey, 1997). Sometimes the personal concerns of supervisees are part of the problem presented in supervision. At these times, supervision might well involve assisting supervisees in identifying some of their concerns so that the client's therapy is not negatively affected. The purpose of discussing supervisees' personal issues—which may appear like therapy—is to facilitate supervisees' ability to work successfully with clients, not to resolve their problems. In other words, supervision can be useful in helping supervisees become aware of personal limitations or unresolved problems that intrude into their work with clients. With this awareness, supervisees are then in a position of seeking personal therapy to work through a problem rather than using supervision as a place for therapy.

There is a difference between assisting a supervisee in identifying and clarifying his or her concerns and converting supervision into sessions aimed primarily at therapy for the supervisee. If the trainee needs or wants personal therapy, the best course for supervisors to follow is to make a referral to another professional. The supervisor should not offer in-depth personal therapy to the supervisee. The ethics codes of some professional organizations caution against requiring personal therapy for trainees or converting supervision sessions into therapy sessions for supervisees. The APA (2001) standard on this matter reads: "In programs that require mandatory individual or group therapy, faculty who are or are likely to be responsible for evaluating students' academic performance do not themselves provide that therapy."

Although it is not appropriate for supervisors to function as therapists for their supervisees, good supervision is therapeutic in the sense that the supervisory process involves dealing with supervisees' personal limitations, blind spots, and impairments so that clients are not harmed. Working with difficult clients or dealing with resistance tends to affect supervisees in personal ways. Certainly, it is a challenge for both trainees and experienced therapists to recognize and deal with transference in effective therapeutic ways. Countertransference issues can work either in favor of or against the establishment of effective client–therapist relationships. A study by Sumerel and Borders (1996) indicates that supervisors who are open to discussing personal issues with supervisees in an appropriate manner do not necessarily affect the supervisor–supervisee relationship negatively.

As a part of the informed consent process in supervision, boundaries need to be discussed and clarified regarding how personal issues will be addressed in supervision. If the nature of the supervisory relationship is not clearly delineated from the beginning, both supervisor and supervisee might well find themselves in difficult positions at some later point. If supervisors overextend the boundaries of a supervisory relationship, their objectivity can become impaired, and the supervisee will then be inhibited from making full use of the supervision process.

Ramos-Sánchez and her colleagues (2002) recommend that graduate students participate in personal therapy while they are in training as a way to expand their self-awareness, foster their personal and professional development, and enhance the supervisory relationship. We also believe it is appropriate for supervisors to encourage their supervisees to consider personal therapy with another professional as a route to becoming more effective both personally and professionally. Counselors in training can greatly profit from a self-exploration experience that opens them up to insight and teaches them about vulnerability, discipline, and freedom in their professional training.

CHANGING ROLES AND RELATIONSHIPS

It is sometimes said, "Once a client, always a client." When it comes to the supervisory relationship it is not quite so clear cut, and it is difficult to assert, "Once a supervisee, always a supervisee." Indeed, many of our one-time students and supervisees are now our valued colleagues. In fact, these former students and supervisees might be working with us in the same agency or in a department on the same faculty. It is important to have open discussions to sort out any issues that might get in the way of present collegial relationships. To illustrate how roles and relationships change over time, let us take a closer look at one of the author's work history.

For almost 30 years I (Jerry) have been a professor in an undergraduate human services program. For eight of those years, I served as the program coordinator in addition to teaching counseling courses. In a number of instances, former students have later become colleagues. I can think of at least a dozen graduates from our program—students in my classes or who were part of the group counseling supervision and training program I taught—who later joined the faculty in our human services program. This could have presented problems when I was the coordinator of the program, because part of my administrative responsibility involved visiting the classes our faculty taught for purposes of evaluation of teaching performance. There was not a single incident, however, where this changing relationship (from student to colleague) became problematic. Perhaps what averted conflicts was an open discussion about potential difficulties.

Of course, former students experienced an adjustment period when assuming their new role. When some of these new faculty people began, especially when they were fresh out of graduate school, their confidence in their ability to teach waffled a bit. However, I invited these new faculty to talk to some of the seasoned faculty members or to discuss their concerns with me. Had we not had these discussions, I am quite certain a hidden agenda would have interfered with their ability to teach effectively.

To illustrate how roles change, let me cite the example of two full-time faculty members I had the responsibility of evaluating for tenure and promotion purposes. As I did with all the part-time faculty members, I visited their classes and wrote detailed letters each semester based on their teaching performance, scholarly work, contribution to the department, and professional endeavors. In both cases, these individuals eventually received tenure and, over the course of the years, progressed from assistant professor to full professor. As the program coordinator, I was required to write an evaluation letter and recommend (or not recommend) tenure status and advancement in academic rank. Fortunately, these two faculty members were of the highest caliber, which meant I could honestly write positive evaluations and could recommend tenure and promotion.

But what if their performance in the classroom had been substandard? What if they had many conflicts with their students? What if they had not produced any journal articles or done any of the research required for advancement? What if they were not contributing to the health of the department? Certainly, it would be difficult if I were in the position of having to write negative evaluations. To avoid such awkward situations, my guiding principle is to initiate open and ongoing discussions about any problem areas early on. Waiting until a decision time has arrived to inform faculty of their deficiencies is, in my opinion, unethical.

After many years, one of these professors became the coordinator of the program, and our formal relationship was reversed. A few years later, she became the dean of our school and my direct administrative supervisor. Changing roles and relationships cannot always be avoided, for in reality, roles and relationships do evolve over time. What is absolutely necessary is that trust has been established so that everyone can play with open cards and that all concerned feel free to express their desires, frustrations, concerns, wants, and complaints. From my perspective, there is no simple formula that can solve all potential multiple role and relationship concerns. We need to learn how to identify potential problems and then collaboratively we must formulate guidelines that will result in adjusting to any changes in roles and relationships.

SUMMARY

Effective supervision needs to be considered within the context of ethical practice. Although there are ethics codes and guidelines for ethical practices in clinical supervision, both supervisors and supervisees will be challenged to interpret these guidelines and apply them to specific situations. In this chapter, we have looked at the rights and responsibilities of supervisees, the roles and responsibilities of supervisors, the importance of informed consent in the supervisory relationship, becoming competent as a supervisor, and handling supervisees who function below an acceptable standard in academic and personal areas. We also addressed managing multiple roles and relationships in the supervision process. Here a few challenges include establishing clear and appropriate boundaries, avoiding sexual intimacies between supervisors and supervisees, distinguishing between supervision and counseling, learning how to make supervision personal without converting supervisory sessions into therapy sessions, and understanding the changing roles and relationships from being a supervisee to becoming a colleague.

A supervisor is required to play many different roles—consultant, teacher, evaluator, mentor, model, counselor, and adviser. From both an ethical and legal standpoint, supervisors must have the education and training to carry out their roles. Continuing education in supervision is often required to fill in the gaps in one's graduate training.

Supervisors are responsible for informing their supervisees of the relevant legal, ethical, and professional standards for clinical practice. Informed consent is a crucial part of supervision, and this process is best achieved by written documents and ongoing discussions between supervisors and supervisees. The challenge of multiple role relationships in the supervisory process is to avoid the potential for abuse of power and to learn how to manage multiple roles and relationships.

SUGGESTED ACTIVITIES

1. Role-play a situation that involves a supervisor realizing that he or she does not have the competence required to help supervisees with cer-

tain client populations. Discuss how the supervisor might deal with the situation.

2. Set up another role-playing situation. In this case, the supervisor does not provide any information about how supervision works, how the evaluation process will be handled, or what the expectations are for adequate performance. Critique what is being enacted and discuss some appropriate alternatives.

3. Investigate some of the community agencies in your area to learn what supervision they offer to interns and to newly hired practitioners.

4. Interview at least one clinical supervisor to determine what he or she considers to be the most pressing ethical issue in the supervisory relationship. Ask questions to determine what process this supervisor uses to make decisions about ethical issues in his or her practice.

5. In small groups, formulate guidelines for handling incompetent or impaired supervisees. What kinds of remedial measures can your group suggest? If attempts at remediation fail to bring about change in problematic supervisees, what other steps can your group devise?

6. In small groups, explore the challenges involved in learning how to manage multiple roles and relationships in the supervisory relationship. Have each group pick one of the following areas and develop guidelines for practice:

    a. Socialization between supervisors and supervisee: What kind of socialization, if any, might be beneficial and appropriate in the context of supervision?

    b. Combining supervision and counseling: How can personal problems be addressed in supervision without changing supervisory sessions into therapy sessions?

    c. Helping supervisees deal with sexual attractions: What are some ways that a supervisor can offer help to supervisees who report experiencing a sexual attraction to a client? How can supervision be made safe in a manner that will allow for an open discussion of sexual attractions?

7. Access the Web site for this text at http://info.wadsworth.com/haynes, and complete the self-assessment inventory. Additional contributor perspectives and other activities specific to this chapter are also available to you through this Web site.

8 LEGAL ISSUES IN SUPERVISION

CHAPTER

1. What are the supervisor's responsibilities with regard to legal issues?
2. Why is it important for a supervisor to have a working knowledge of the ethics codes and the law?
3. What are the major legal issues concerning clinical supervision?

4. How do ethical and legal issues differ?
5. Why is informed consent a critical aspect of clinical supervision?
6. If you were to draft an informed consent document for your supervisees, what elements would you include?

INTRODUCTION

Many professionals view ethical and legal aspects of clinical practice and supervision as virtually synonymous. Ethical guidelines serve as the basis for the standard of care in supervision, and unethical practice often implies illegal conduct. However, this is not always the case: numerous actions that would be considered unethical, if exploited, are not illegal. For example, bartering and accepting gifts from clients may pose ethical problems but are not necessarily illegal. It is important for supervisors to separate the legal aspects of supervision from ethical considerations.

The purpose of this chapter is to provide a brief legal primer for supervisors and a risk management model to address the many liabilities involved in supervisory practice. Bradley and Ladany (2001) suggest that supervisors be aware of the risks involved in practice and protect themselves by identifying the legal implications of providing supervision.

LEGAL PRIMER

Legal aspects of supervision may seem overwhelming at first. Most helping professionals are not versed in legal theory and practice, have little course work in this area, and find the concept of liability quite frightening. Many mental health professionals perceive liability primarily in light of the prospect of losing their license to practice. This is a narrow view and one that leaves supervisors open to legal risks. Supervisors must have a working knowledge of the basic legal principles that affect supervisory practice. Let's start by defining some basic terms that are fundamental to understanding legal issues in supervision. Box 8.1 lists some concepts you should become familiar with. In the next sections, we will examine these concepts in some detail.

It is imperative that supervisors be aware of all factors involved in the practice of supervision. It is necessary to have a working knowledge of ethics codes and state licensing laws. Ignorance of the law is not an acceptable

LEGAL PRINCIPLES THAT AFFECT SUPERVISORY PRACTICE

Standard of care	The normative or expected practice performed in a given situation by a given group of professionals.
Statutory liability	Specific written standard with penalties imposed, written directly into the law.
Negligence	When one fails to observe the proper standard of care.
Negligent liability	When one fails to provide an established standard of care.
Vicarious liability	Being responsible for the actions of others based on a position of authority and control.
Direct liability	Being responsible for your own actions of authority and control over others.
Privileged communication	The privilege allowed an individual to have confidential communications with a professional. It prevents the courts from requiring revelation of confidential communication.
Duty to warn	The obligation of a therapist whose client presents a serious danger of violence to another person to warn and protect the third party.
Duty to protect	The obligation of a therapist to take the necessary steps to protect a client with suicidal intent.
Duty to report	The obligation of a therapist to report abuse or suspected abuse of children or the elderly in a timely manner.

excuse and certainly no defense against liability. In addition, it is important to stay abreast of the case law and theories upon which liability may attach. This type of ongoing professional development along with supervisors' clinical expertise is needed to provide a sound and complete risk management plan to protect clients, trainees, and supervisors.

Standard of Care

At this time, courts are defining the standard of care in supervision primarily by reviewing the licensing statutes and case law because there is neither a consensus nor an explicit statement of the standard of care in psychotherapy supervision by mental health professionals. The many different codes of ethics and practice make it difficult for the courts to establish liability due to the lack of clear guidelines. Even within the counseling field, which shares the ACA *Code of Ethics* (1995), there may be distinctly different standards of care or normative practices for given situations determined by setting or type of counselor.

Recently, while attending a state conference, a scenario was provided to a group of counselors regarding the possible liability of the actions of a school counselor intervening with a 13-year-old student who eventually committed suicide. There was a remarkable difference in the response to the counselor's intervention in the scenario based on the type of counselor responding. Clearly there was a vast difference between the perceptions of the school counselors and mental health counselors, with different expectations regarding actions to be taken based primarily on the setting of the incident. This is but one example of the many differences we might find in standard of care in the helping professions.

Five underlying principles must be considered when establishing standard of care for supervisory practice (Corey, Corey, & Callanan 2003; Kitchener, 1984):

- *Autonomy:* promote self-determination, or the freedom of clients to choose their own direction
- *Nonmaleficence:* avoid doing harm, which includes refraining from actions that risk hurting clients, either intentionally or unintentionally
- *Beneficence:* promote good for others
- *Justice:* foster fairness or a means of providing equal treatment to all people
- *Fidelity:* make honest promises and honor commitments to those served

These principles can serve as a foundation for developing a standard of care in practice.

The ACES (1993) and APA (1992) codes of ethics emphasize competence, confidentiality, informed consent, monitoring, and evaluation and feedback in the supervisory process. Beyond these themes, the professional codes have little to say specifically about legal issues. Saccuzzo (1997) reports that five major ethical principles were found repeatedly in statutes, case law, ethical codes, and the professional literature: (1) competence, (2) confidentiality, (3) avoidance of dual relationships, (4) welfare of the consumer, and (5) informed consent. Standard of care in mental health supervision is based on these concepts. Examples of standards of care that can be extracted through review of licensing statutes, case law, and clinical practice include supervising only within your areas of competence based on training and experience, providing a supervisory contract, providing appropriate feedback and evaluation, consistently monitoring and controlling supervisees' activities, accurately documenting supervisory activities, and providing consistent and timely supervisory sessions.

Statutory Liability

State licensing laws provide the basis for statutory liability. This type of liability is relatively clear; the standards are explicit, as are the penalties imposed should the law be broken. This area of liability is rather difficult to discuss in depth due to the fact that there are differences in statutes state by state. It is important for supervisors to have a clear understanding of the specific statutes they must abide by within the state in which they practice and supervise. For example, state laws vary on how supervisors are to monitor the performance of supervisees, whether supervisees may pay their supervisors for supervision or office space, restrictions on advertising by supervisees, and documentation required in the supervisory relationship.

Negligence

Negligence may be found when one has failed to observe the proper standards of care in supervision. Corey, Corey, and Callanan (2003) suggest that to succeed in a malpractice claim the following four elements of malpractice need to be present: (1) a professional relationship with the supervisee and/or supervisor must have existed; (2) the supervisee or supervisor must have acted in a negligent or improper manner or have deviated from the "standard of care"; (3) the supervisee or client must have suffered harm or injury, which must be demonstrated; and (4) a causal relationship between the negligence or breach of duty and the damage or injury claimed by the client or supervisee must be established. The burden of proof that harm actually took place is the client's or the supervisee's, and the plaintiff must demonstrate that all four elements applied in his or her situation. Here is a brief discussion of each of the four elements as described in *Black's Law Dictionary* (Garner, 1999).

1. *Duty.* There are two aspects of establishing a legal duty: one is the existence of a special relationship, and the other is the nature of that special relationship. A duty exists when a therapist (or supervisor) implicitly or explicitly agrees to provide professional services.
2. *Breach of duty.* Once the plaintiff proves that a professional relationship did exist, he or she must show that the duty was breached. Therapists (or supervisors) have specific responsibilities that involve using ordinary and reasonable care and diligence, applying knowledge and skill to a case, and exercising good judgment. If the therapist (or supervisor) failed to provide the appropriate standard of care, the duty was breached. In supervision, this breach of duty may involve either actions taken by the supervisee or supervisor or a failure to take certain precautions.
3. *Injury.* Plaintiffs must prove that they were harmed in some way—physically, relationally, psychologically—and that actual injuries were sustained. In supervision, injuries can occur to either the supervisees or the clients they serve. An example of such an injury is lack of due process when terminating a supervisee from a training program.
4. *Causation.* Plaintiffs must demonstrate that the therapist's (or supervisor's) breach of duty was the proximate cause of the injury suffered. The test in this case lies in proving that the harm would not have occurred if it were not for the therapist's (or supervisor's) actions or omissions.

One example of negligence in the standard of care is illustrated in Case 8.1.

Negligent Liability

Negligent liability is not as clear cut as statutory liability and is seen by many as a greater danger to supervisors. There is a process to becoming negligently liable for client care and supervisory practices. The construct of liability is based on two components. The first step in the process of negligence is estab-

CASE 8.1 | KATHLEEN

Kathleen is a trainee providing direct services to children in an inpatient setting under the supervision of Dr. Snow. Kathleen is seeing a young boy, Jamie, with very serious acting out behaviors and a disturbing family history. Jamie has been living with his aunt while his mom has been in a drug rehabilitation facility. Kathleen makes the decision to share family information that Jamie has given to his aunt to "help" with Jamie's transition at discharge. Dr. Snow is not aware of this disclosure, which is a breach of confidentiality, as Jamie's aunt is not his legal guardian. Jamie's aunt uses this information in a custody hearing to help Jamie's father gain primary custody of the boy. Jamie's mom files suit against Kathleen and the inpatient clinic for breach of confidentiality. In this instance, Dr. Snow was found guilty of both ethical and legal violations.

lishing a standard of care. In mental health law, standard of care is derived primarily from licensing statutes, case law, and ethics codes of conduct. In fact, many state laws include specific ethics codes as part of the statute. The second step is determining negligence. One cannot be found liable without first being found negligent. Only when there is an established standard of care and one has failed to observe proper standards of care, and therefore has been negligent, can there be a charge of liability. You will need to have a working knowledge of these components when providing supervision.

There are two main types of negligent liability: vicarious liability, in which the supervisor is held liable for the actions of the supervisee regardless of any fault on the part of the supervisor, and direct liability, in which the supervisor is held directly liable for his or her own negligent supervisory practice. Both negligent and vicarious liability are outlined in Box 8.2.

Vicarious Liability

A supervisor may be held vicariously liable under one of three separate doctrines: respondent superior, the borrowed servant rule, or enterprise liability. Let's examine each of these doctrines.

Respondent Superior   One who occupies a position of authority or control over another may be held legally liable for damages caused by the subordinate. In terms of supervision, this means that supervisors can be held liable for the actions of supervisees. This liability pertains whether or not the supervisor breaches a duty. It appears that the doctrine of respondent superior is inherent to the practice of supervision. Case 8.2 illustrates this doctrine and points out that the supervisor is liable even when he or she lacks specific knowledge about the supervisee's client.

BOX 8.2

ETHICS CODES AND STANDARDS
REGARDING LEGAL ISSUES

American Psychological Association
Ethical Principles of Psychologist and Code of Conduct (1992)

Relationship of Ethics and Law
1.02 If psychologists' ethical responsibilities conflict with law, psychologists make known their commitment to the Ethics Code and take steps to resolve the conflict in a responsible manner.

National Association of Social Workers
Guidelines for Clinical Social Work Supervision (1994)

Legal Issues
The clinical practice supervisor shares responsibility for the services provided to the client. Liability of supervisors has been determined by the courts and includes direct liability related to negligent or inadequate supervision and vicarious liability related to negligent conduct by the supervisee.

Clinical social work supervisors in agency or institutional settings should be familiar with the scope of their own responsibility and authority. This scope should be specified in writing either as part of the agencies' policies, supervisor's position description, or in a written contract. Many factors related to the degree to which the supervisor has responsibility and authority for both the clinical and administrative practices of the supervisee affect the supervisor's liability. For example, does the supervisor determine the size and nature of assigned caseloads? Does the supervisor have direct access to outside consultation or is another level of clearance or consultation required? Who has authority to respond to requests for access to client records?

The requirements and expectations of the supervisor's position also may affect liability. For example, supervisors who have too many supervisees, too many cases, or other competing demands on their time may not be able to provide adequate supervisory responsibilities. This situation would likely have clinical and ethical implications and could have legal consequences as well.

Direct Liability
Direct liability may be charged whenever harm is caused by erroneous action or omissions by the supervisor, such as inappropriate advice or direction that is carried out to the client's detriment. Direct liability can also be charged when a supervisor assigns duties for which the supervisee is inadequately prepared.

Sexual violations represent the largest number of claims against social workers, and supervisory negligence may be charged in these situations. It is imperative that the supervisor address boundary issues and provide special assistance in dealing with feelings, including sexual feelings toward a client, and all of the feelings, including sexual feelings, the client may have toward the supervisee.

Vicarious Liability
Vicarious liability may be charged against the supervisor for erroneous acts or omissions. Supervisees can be held to the same standard of care and skill as their supervisors, and they are also expected to abide by the duty to warn or protect as first enunciated in *Tarasoff v. Regents of the University of California* (551 P.2d 334, 131 Cal. Rpter. 141976) and now embodied in statutes and court decisions in most states.

For purposes of risk management, the supervisor should:

• ensure that the services provided to clients by the supervisee are above minimal standards.
• maintain documentation of supervision.
• ensure that the client is informed of who the supervisor or administrative authority is and how to contact him or her.
• monitor the supervisee's professional functioning.
• identify practices that might pose a danger to the health and welfare of the supervisee's clients or to the public and take appropriate remedial measures, and

- identify the supervisee's inability to practice social work with reasonable skill and safety due to illness; excessive use of drugs, narcotics, chemicals, or any other substance; or any mental illness, serious personal problem, physical condition, or environmental stress.

To guard against conflict of interest, the supervisor should not supervise his or her own parents, spouse, former spouses, siblings, children, anyone sharing the same household, or anyone with whom there is a romantic, domestic, or familial relationship.

CASE 8.2 | MIKE

Mike is a supervisee providing therapy to a young woman in her early twenties who has met the criteria for an eating disorder diagnosis. In addition, she reports symptoms of major depression. Mike is comfortable with his knowledge and ability to treat the depressive symptoms, so this is what he has focused on in treatment. The young woman's physical health is deteriorating. There is need to consult a specialist, but Mike's supervisor does not realize this. Using the self-report method during supervisory sessions, Mike has reported only the facts of the case pertaining to the diagnosis and treatment of depression. The client is presenting symptomology outside the scope of competence for the supervisee to provide quality care. She deteriorates further and becomes suicidal. The client's family seeks legal action against the supervisor, and the supervisor is found liable.

Borrowed Servant Rule This rule is used to determine who had control of the supervisee at the time of the negligent act. In determining if a person is the servant of another, the essential test is whether a person is subject to another's control or right of control with regard not only to the work to be conducted but also to the manner of performing that work (Saccuzzo, 1997). The criterion regards the power to control the supervisee at the time of the negligent act. For example, in university training programs students are often placed in hospitals or community mental health facilities to provide services. The student may then be under the supervision of the university supervisor as well as the licensed staff at the placement facility. Under these circumstances, supervisory liability may be determined under the borrowed servant rule. The critical factor in determining liability is in determining who had control of the supervisee at the time of a negligent act.

There is debate in the field regarding the amount of control that supervisors can have regarding this type of liability. Remley and Herlihy (2001) raise the question as to whether there are distinctions in types of supervising based on applied practice. For instance, it has been suggested that someone providing secondary supervision—some use the term indirect or clinical supervision—may not be as likely to be held vicariously liable due to the fact that this person is not the primary or administrative supervisor. The distinction is that the administrative supervisor has the direct responsibility of hiring, firing, and monitoring, whereas the clinical supervisor serves more as a consultant to the supervisee and defers to the guidance of the administrative supervisor for direct service performance. This type of distinction is important for those who may choose to supervise prelicensed professionals in that they can set up contracts that implicitly state the limits of services provided. Administrative supervisors are vicariously responsible generally for all actions of their supervisees. Case 8.3 provides an example of the use of the borrowed servant rule.

Enterprise Liability   In this doctrine, the costs of compensating for injuries are balanced against the benefits derived by the supervisee or supervisor; damages are viewed as a part of the cost of conducting business. This theory focuses on the foreseeability of the supervisee's actions in view of the nature of the duties to be performed. If the supervisor stands to make a profit from the work conducted by a supervisee (billing for services and profiting after salary and overhead), the supervisor should be willing to bear the risk of damages to clients.

Direct Liability

Supervisors are held responsible for negligent supervisory practices, which may include any of the following:

- Allowing a supervisee to practice outside your and/or his or her scope of practice
- Not providing consistent time for supervision sessions
- Lack of emergency coverage and procedures
- Not providing a supervisory contract
- Lack of appropriate assessment of the supervisee and the clients he or she serves
- Lack of sufficient monitoring of supervisee's practice and/or documentation
- Lack of consistent feedback prior to evaluation
- Violation of professional boundaries in the supervisory relationship

To establish direct liability for negligent supervision, a clear link must be provided between the actions of the supervisor and the damages incurred. Attempts by the supervisor to negate responsibility due to not directly performing the therapy that was negligent in some manner and caused damages to the client are unlikely to succeed. The court places emphasis on proper monitoring and determining that the supervisee's competence is appropriate to the therapeutic duties assigned. Supervisors are expected to monitor and control the actions of their supervisees. The court has confronted two major issues when direct liability has been charged due to negligent supervisory practices. First, did the supervisor have a direct duty of care arising from the

CASE 8.3 | CHERIE

Cherie has agreed to supervise Jon for his required hours toward supervision. Jon is working for Miguel, his administrative supervisor, at the local mental health clinic. Cherie agrees to meet with Jon once a week to consult with him on his practice and to assist in his professional development. Although Cherie will have to document the supervisory hours she spends with Jon and complete an evaluation for the licensing board stating that she views Jon to be competent to practice independently as a counselor,

she does not sign off on Jon's case documentation, and she is not on emergency call. She defers to the guidance that Miguel provides and in no way interferes with his work setting.

Should negligence occur, Miguel would be held to stricter standards of vicarious liability than Cherie based on the roles they carry out in supervision. Cherie has placed herself one step away, and although not exempt, she is less likely to be held liable under the borrowed servant doctrine.

---

supervisor–supervisee relationship? Second, did the supervision meet the standard of care for applicable service?

In addition to the possibility of clients filing suit against the supervisor for direct liability, the supervisor must also be prepared for the possibility of direct liability suits filed by supervisees. The primary reason cited for these suits is based on the legal concept of due process. In this context, due process involves fairness on the part of the supervisor toward the supervisee. With regard to supervision, this means that supervisors are acting negligently if they give negative evaluations without supplying adequate feedback, remediation guidelines and the opportunity for improvement. Here is an example of the need for due process in a university training program:

> A student trainee is dismissed from a graduate training program based on unsatisfactory performance in a practicum experience. There is minimal documentation of supervision, no documentation of direct observation, no procedure for formal feedback or remediation, and no due process prior to termination. The graduate student seeks legal action. The university settles out of court.

Privileged Communication

This brief legal primer would not be complete without a review of the legal concept of privileged communication as it relates to supervision. An evidentiary privilege is a law that prevents the court from requiring revelation of confidential communications. Remley and Herlihy (2001) state that "privileged communication means that a judge cannot order information that has been recognized by law as privileged to be revealed in court" (p. 85). Privilege statutes are primarily granted only to professionals who are licensed or certified.

The privilege belongs to the client and, therefore, may be waived by the client, in which case the witness (supervisor, supervisee) is obligated to testify fully. Any communication made to the supervisor by the supervisee or the client is considered privileged. However, although all privileged communications are confidential, not all confidential communications are privileged. Courts generally require a statutory or legal basis for finding a communication privileged. It is also important to remember that many states define exceptions to otherwise privileged communication.

Supervisors must be fully aware of the implications of privilege and be able to determine the duty to testify. Failure to do so may lead to breach of confidentiality when testimony is not legally mandated or to civil liability and/or criminal sanctions due to refusing to testify when testimony is mandated (Disney & Stephens, 1994). Supervisors are responsible for securing appropriate legal consultation when confidential information is demanded.

Duties to Warn, Protect, and Report

The specific definitions and requirements of the duties to warn, protect, and report vary across states. Although the definition may vary, the supervisor's responsibilities are relatively clear. Supervisors are responsible to be knowledgeable regarding their duties to warn, protect, and report and must ensure that supervisees have a clear understanding of their duties to warn, protect, and report. Supervisors must educate supervisees about agency policies and procedures, review legal statutes pertaining to duties to warn, protect, and report, and establish an emergency plan that includes the supervisee notifying the supervisor immediately. Supervisors are responsible for training supervisees in appropriate assessment of violence potential, suicidality, and abuse. Bernard and Goodyear (1998) state that "in the eyes of the law it is more important that reasonable evaluation be made than that the prediction be accurate" (p. 179). Supervisors are ultimately responsible for the actions carried out by their supervisees.

RISK MANAGEMENT

As you read, you may be having some reservations about taking on supervisory responsibility. Even though the responsibilities are numerous and at times the path is somewhat treacherous, there truly are safeguards in supervision that are reasonable to pursue. This section on risk management outlines the multiple tasks you are responsible for as a supervisor and suggests an organized approach to managing these multiple tasks in the supervisory process. To help you get started, we have provided an orientation checklist to assist you in your first session with a new supervisee (Box 8.3). The checklist will ensure that you have reviewed the primary components included in risk management as part of supervisee orientation.

| BOX 8.3 | SUPERVISION FIRST SESSION CHECKLIST |

Because of the extent of detail and number of items to be addressed in order to structure the supervisory relationship, it is recommended that the duration of the first session be a minimum of two hours.

___ Build rapport

___ Review supervision contract

___ Inform supervisee of factors regarding supervisor that might influence supervisee's decision to work with him/her

___ Address cultural differences/similarities and how they might affect the supervisory relationship

___ Review the ethical issues relevant to supervision

___ Review the process of supervision

___ Review policies and procedures

___ Review all forms

___ Discuss crisis management strategies

___ Structure supervision (day, time, length)

___ Assess supervisee's competence

___ Establish goals and objectives

Source: Adapted from Northwestern State University, Natchitoches, LA, Department of Psychology, and designed by Cynthia Lindsey and Patrice Moulton, June 2001. Reprinted with permission.

It is important to keep supervision in perspective. Liability is simply a consistent component of our field due to the nature of the work we do, whether practicing directly or supervising practice. Sound and accountable actions can minimize the risk to supervisors from the liabilities inherent to supervision. Each of the items listed in Box 8.4 is discussed individually in the sections that follow.

Don't Supervise Beyond Your Competence

Competence in supervision requires appropriate training and experience both in areas of clinical expertise and in supervision itself. Getz (1999) provides a structure for assessing supervisor competence in seven core areas:

- Models of supervision
- Counselor development
- Supervision methods and techniques
- Supervisory relationships
- Legal, ethical, and professional regulation
- Evaluation
- Administrative skills

| BOX 8.4 | SUPERVISORS' ACTIONS THAT MINIMIZE LIABILITY RISKS |

- Don't supervise beyond your competence.
- Evaluate and monitor supervisee's competence.
- Be available for supervision consistently.
- Formulate a sound supervision contract.
- Maintain written policies.
- Document all supervisory activities.
- Consult with appropriate professionals.
- Maintain working knowledge of ethics codes, legal statutes, and licensing regulations.
- Use multiple methods of supervision.
- Practice a feedback and evaluation plan.
- Purchase and verify professional liability insurance coverage.
- Evaluate and screen all clients under supervisee's care.
- Establish a policy for ensuring confidentiality.
- Incorporate informed consent in practice.

Training in supervision is essential in making sound judgments about your supervisory practices. This includes choosing an appropriate supervisory model from which to work given the setting, the level of training of supervisees, and the target population that will be served. Supervisors should not supervise cases that they would not feel competent to counsel independently. If a client of the supervisee has a presenting problem that is outside the supervisor's scope of training, make alternative arrangements for supervision of that client's case, or make an appropriate referral for the client. This type of responsible practice requires careful screening and monitoring not only of supervisees but of each of the clients they serve.

Evaluate and Monitor Supervisees' Competence

Supervisors are also responsible for making sure supervisees practice within their scope of competence. It is necessary to assess the level of knowledge and skill of each supervisee to appropriately assign clients and duties. ACES (1993) specifies that such assessment is critical to the supervisor's ability to restrict supervisees' activities to "those that are commensurate with their current level of skills and experiences." Components of assessment may include education, licensure or certification, goals and interests, clinical practicum experience and treatment settings, supervision received, cultural diversity of experience, past criminal history and disciplinary actions, experience with assessment, diagnosis, treatment, and documentation, and ability to interface with other professionals. Remember that evaluating competence is not only a preliminary activity in supervision but an ongoing process that requires careful monitoring through observation, work samples, feedback, and formal evaluation.

Remind yourself that you have a choice about whether to begin or continue supervision with a supervisee that you believe to be incompetent for the tasks that would be assigned in your setting. Discuss the competencies required and the results of the assessment with the potential supervisee. A referral to a different setting may be the reasonable choice. If you determine incompetence after beginning the supervisory relationship, it is important to decide if the area of incompetence is one that you can teach, coach, and/or mentor. If not, provide alternatives for both you and your supervisee. These alternatives may include actions such as referral, shared supervision, consultation, or remediation.

Be Available for Supervision Consistently

Being available on a consistent basis to supervisees is a common struggle for supervisors who are active professionals. Competent supervision requires much more than the understood hour per week face-to-face meeting with a supervisee. The concept of being available includes being available to monitor, to review documentation, and to assist if a crisis arises. This also requires having adequate and competent supervisory coverage when you are, in fact, unavailable and having an emergency plan in place so that supervisees are never left without appropriate backup should they need help. If you, as the supervisor, are off-call for a specified period of time, provide not only emergency numbers but arrange consistent, on-site coverage for supervision of your supervisees. Many situations need to be addressed as they happen; these problems can turn into serious liability issues without timely intervention. Having an emergency plan in place provides a model for supervisees to follow, under close supervision, to learn the steps for primary emergencies. For instance, there should be a policy in place about the specific steps to take when a client reports immediate danger to self (suicidality). Every setting has a slightly different process based on type of population served and resources available. However, you should have in place a list of actions to be taken that includes primary contacts (police, emergency rooms, coroner, and physicians who assist in involuntary admits) and phone numbers. Specify when you expect to be contacted if you are not present at the time of an emergency.

Formulate a Sound Supervision Contract

The use of a contract in supervision is essential to protect the client, the agency, your supervisee, and yourself as the supervisor. Falvey (2002) suggests that a well-formulated contract provides a clear blueprint for what is to occur in supervision and serves as a reference if problems should occur in the supervisory relationship. The majority of governing boards either strongly recommend or require a written agreement or contract for supervision (Box 8.5

| BOX 8.5 | SUPERVISION CONTRACT |

I, _____ (print name), as the supervisor, offer this agreement to you, _____ (print name), as the supervisee, and consent to the following conditions set forth for this supervisory relationship. Please read the agreement and sign your name if you fully understand and consent to the conditions.

Professional disclosure of supervisor:

_____

_____

_____

_____

Supervision model of supervisor:

Example: I follow the developmental model of supervision in which I provide fairly intense supervision early in the relationship, including direct observation of therapy sessions, frequent homework assignments and role playing, providing more guidance, etc. Then as you progress in skills, knowledge, and competency, you will be given more responsibility and the supervision will be less intense. This is not to imply you will ever work independently as we will always share 100% of the responsibility. It simply means that as you develop professionally, I will encourage you to exercise more judgment and confidence in your skills and decision-making abilities.

As the supervisor, I agree to the following:

- I will provide one hour of individual supervision weekly for the patients you are providing services to as part of the requirements of the university practicum.
- I will adhere to APA's *Ethical Principles of Psychologists and Code of Conduct* and help you with the awareness of and application of the ethical principles and standards. As part of my ethical responsibilities, I will disclose any factors that might influence your consent to participate in a supervisory relationship with me.
- During supervisory sessions, I will focus on two primary areas: your personal development as a professional and the development of your clinical skills. As part of this concentration, I will help you with developing skills in the areas of case conceptualization, selecting and applying empirically supported techniques, and identifying processes, types of clients, or skills with which you may have difficulty.
- I will not allow you to accept a case that is outside the limits of my competency or too complicated for your level of skill. Therefore, I will observe your intake session of each prospective client and you and I will discuss each case to determine if it is appropriate for your level of skill and my areas of competency.
- In addition to weekly informal feedback, I will evaluate your performance and provide you with written, formal feedback three times during the semester. The areas of the evaluation will include your professional development, clinical skills, and performance/behavior in supervision and with your peers in practicum. The semester will be divided quarterly and the evaluation will occur at the end of each quarter. At that time, I will review the evaluation with you and ask that you sign it to indicate your receipt of the evaluation. You will receive a copy. Please be aware that the original evaluation will be entered

into your student file and will be discussed with other members of the graduate faculty who participate in your training. Such practice is usual and customary for training programs in clinical psychology.

Also be aware that if you receive a negative evaluation from me, it can serve as full or partial basis for your retention in or dismissal from the program. If such a situation should occur and depending on the reason(s) for the evaluation, then you may have the remainder of the semester to make improvements, you may have to repeat the practicum, or you may be dismissed from the program. If you disagree with the evaluation that you receive, then you may follow the appeals process described in the Student Review & Retention Policy located in your student handbook.

From you, the supervisee, I expect the following:

- You are to have knowledge of and adhere to the APA's *Ethical Principles of Psychologists and Code of Conduct.*
- You are to act in accord with the practicum policies and procedures.
- You are to be prompt and prepared for each of the supervisory sessions. Being prepared means you are to bring the case files with completed progress notes and forms for review and my signature and the videotape(s) for that week's session(s). It also means you are to have identified on the videotape any areas during the therapy session that are of particular concern to you and that you want to discuss.
- At the outset of treatment with each prospective client, you are to present him/her with the informed consent form, read it aloud, and explain each of the components verbally, specifically including the limits of confidentiality. This explanation is to include your status as a student-in-training and that you are being supervised by me. You are also to explain that as your supervisor I will often be observing the sessions behind the one-way mirror and/or on the videotapes. This explanation should also include any other individuals who might observe your work, such as other graduate students or faculty members who will be observing your work as part of peer-observation and group supervision. Please provide the client with my name and university phone number. I want your videotape of this session and I want your progress notes to indicate what you told the potential client regarding the elements of informed consent, limits of confidentiality, and your status as a student-in-training. The notes should also reflect the response of the client that indicated his or her understanding.
- You are expected to maintain healthy boundaries with your clients. Sexual contact with your clients is **ABSOLUTELY FORBIDDEN.** However, it is not uncommon for clients or therapists to experience feelings of sexual attraction for one another; therefore, I must be informed of any sexual attraction between you and your client so that we may discuss the experience and the best manner with which to handle the situation if deemed necessary.
- Since you and I share 100% of the responsibility for your client's welfare, I expect you to **immediately** inform me or the on-call supervisor of any problems. Such problems include but are not limited to suspected child, elder, or dependent abuse; domestic violence; if your client may be a danger to self or others; or if you use any nontraditional treatment methods.

Signature of Supervisee   Date

Signature of Supervisor   Date

Source: Adapted from Northwestern State University, Natchitoches, LA, Department of Psychology, and designed by Cynthia Lindsey and Patrice Moulton, June 2001. Reprinted with permission.

provides one example of a supervision contract). Todd and Storm (1997) remind us that it is important for contracts to be "real." Contracts need to be operational, and supervisors must be prepared to behaviorally support them. For example, if you require supervisees to videotape sessions, make certain that you view them and cue them for effective use in supervision. Contracts should be in writing with signatures and dates required of both supervisee and supervisor. Complete contracts as early in the supervisory relationship as is practical.

Suggested items for inclusion in the contract are listed here, but you can customize the contract by selecting the relevant items for your situation:

- Purpose and goals of supervision
- Logistics of supervision including frequency, duration, and structure of meetings
- Roles and responsibilities of supervisor and supervisee
- Brief description of supervisor's background, experience, and areas of expertise
- The model and methods of supervision to be used
- Documentation responsibilities of supervisor and supervisee
- Evaluation methods to be used including schedule, structure, format, and use
- Feedback and evaluation plan including due process
- Supervisee's commitment to follow all applicable agencies' policies, professional licensing statutes, and ethical standards
- Supervisee's agreement to maintain healthy boundaries with clients
- Supervisee's agreement to function within the boundaries of his or her competence
- Supervisee's commitment to provide informed consent to clients
- Reporting procedures for legal, ethical, and emergency situations
- Confidentiality policy
- A statement of responsibility regarding multicultural issues

It is important to clarify the distinction between a supervision contract and informed consent documents. The supervision contract is the larger document. It may, in fact, contain the informed consent between supervisors and supervisees as well as forms and guidelines needed for informed consent between supervisees and clients. We often speak of the supervisors'–supervisees' informed consent and the supervision contract synonymously because there is much overlap of information. This informed consent primarily outlines duties, training philosophy, expectations, and evaluation of the supervisee. The supervisee–client informed consent document outlines the boundaries of the counselor–client relationship, training status of the supervisee, and confidentiality (see Box 8.6 for a sample document). These forms and guidelines are often contained within the supervision agreement along with additional materials for assessment and agreement.

BOX 8.6	SUPERVISEE/CLIENT INFORMED CONSENT

1. You are volunteering to participate in treatment and shall have the right to refuse treatment. If you choose to terminate before the end of the five sessions, you can do so without penalty and your teacher will be informed of the number of sessions attended so you may receive your extra credit points.

2. You are volunteering for five sessions *only*. If at the termination of those five sessions you feel you need additional assistance, you will receive a referral to the University Counseling Center.

3. If the issues you present are deemed to be outside the scope of training, you will be referred to the appropriate services.

4. This will be a joint effort in which you and your therapist work together as a team. You will be actively involved in decision making. If at any time you are confused, uncomfortable, or do not agree with the therapist, then please speak up and let your therapist know.

5. You have the right to be treated in a manner that preserves and enhances your self-respect and individuality.

6. You have the right to obtain current information concerning the evaluation, treatment, and prognosis in understandable terms. If you do not understand, please ask your therapist to explain.

7. You have the right to receive information necessary to give informed consent before the start of any procedure or treatment.

8. There are no guarantees with therapy. In other words, although change is possible, results cannot be guaranteed.

9. The therapists are graduate students in training and are therefore being supervised and observed to ensure the quality of care you are receiving and to assist the therapists with their training. Individuals who will have access to your information will be the supervisors and his or her peers in training. However, everyone involved will be expected to abide by the rules of confidentiality.

10. The personal information you provide and records about you shall be kept strictly confidential within the training setting, except under special legal circumstances. Such circumstances include, but are not limited to, the following:

    a. When the therapist suspects abuse or neglect of a child, an elderly person, or a disabled or incompetent person.

    b. If the client poses a danger to self or others.

       If you report any of the above circumstances in either a or b, your therapist is ethically and legally required to breach confidentiality in order for you to receive additional support from the appropriate services.

    c. If a court orders the records to be made available.

11. As part of the training, your therapist is required to videotape all sessions, again, to ensure the quality of care you are receiving and for feedback to the therapist regarding his or her skills and professional development. The videotape may be viewed by the therapist's supervisor(s) and peers in training. The videotape will be kept secure so that your confidentiality will be protected and then erased at the end of the practicum.

12. As part of protecting your confidentiality, your therapist cannot approach you if you see one another in public or leave messages regarding your appointments without your consent. Therefore, please let your therapist know how you would like this to be handled.

13. For you volunteering to participate in therapy, you will receive 20 extra credit points for all five sessions. Your instructor will only be informed of whether or not you attended.

14. Please give at least 24 hours notice if you need to cancel an appointment.

(continued)

SUPERVISEE/CLIENT INFORMED CONSENT (*continued*)

Complaint Procedure
Clients who have a complaint or question are encouraged to first address the issue with their therapist. The client may then call the therapist's faculty supervisor. If the foregoing does not provide satisfaction to your complaint, please address it to Patrice Moulton, Ph.D., Chair of the Department of Psychology (318) 357-6594, or Anthony Scheffler, Dean of Graduate Studies and Research (318) 357-5851. In addition, you may make a complaint to the Louisiana State Board of Examiners of Psychologists, 11924 Justice Avenue, Suite A, Baton Rouge, LA 70816, (504) 293-2238.

Source: Adapted from Northwestern State University, Natchitoches, LA, Department of Psychology, and designed by Cynthia Lindsey and Patrice Moulton, June 2001. Reprinted with permission.

Maintain Written Policies

Many of the policies supervisors need to provide for supervisees already exist (professional standards and guidelines). It is a supervisor's responsibility to review these documents with supervisees. The types of written documents needed may include but certainly are not limited to the following: state legal statutes, codes of ethics, informed consents, emergency procedures, supervisee–client rights, and agency policies and procedures.

Document All Supervisory Activities

Supervisors are responsible for keeping records regarding all of their supervisory activities and contacts. In addition, supervisors are responsible for reviewing and co-signing all client documentation written by supervisees. This signature is intended to ensure that supervisors have reviewed the information. It serves as protection for the supervisees, supervisors, and agencies. Some examples of supervisee documentation include client information sheets, intake reports, psychological evaluations, treatment plans, progress notes, and termination summaries.

Supervisory documentation consists of three primary components: (1) supervisory agreements and contracts, (2) supervision notes, and (3) feedback and evaluation materials. We have already discussed the supervisory contract and agreements (see section titled Formulate a Sound Supervision Contract). Now let's examine the remaining two components. Supervision notes for each supervisory session need to minimally include a summary of cases reviewed, concerns, recommendations made, actions taken, and justification for decisions regarding high-risk situations. In addition, if supervisees fail to follow the supervisor's directions, this should be noted. Box 8.7 illustrates a sample supervision note form, which includes the items listed as well as a review of the activities provided for the development of the supervisee and feedback.

BOX 8.7 | SUPERVISION NOTES

Date of supervisory session: _____

Supervisee: _____

Case Review
Follow-up regarding previous recommendations for clients:

_____

_____

_____

Clients reviewed:

_____

_____

_____

Specific concerns:

_____

_____

_____

Recommendations:

_____

_____

_____

Development of Therapist
Follow-up regarding previous recommendations for therapist's development:

_____

_____

_____

Education/remediation/practice:

_____

_____

_____

(continued)

BOX 8.7 | SUPERVISION NOTES (*continued*)

Recommendations:

_____

_____

_____

Evaluation
Therapist's Progress:

_____

_____

_____

_____   _____

Supervisor's Signature   Date

Source: Adapted from Northwestern State University, Natchitoches, LA, Department of Psychology, and designed by Cynthia Lindsey and Patrice Moulton, June 2001. Reprinted with permission.

The third component of supervisory documentation consists of forms completed by the supervisee in clinical practice. These documents can be used in supervisory sessions to provide feedback and evaluation for supervisees.

Sample forms used in a graduate training program in clinical psychology are provided at the end of this chapter. These forms include a client information sheet, an intake worksheet used by supervisees at the time of intake, a model intake report that provides direction to students and an expected format, an intake summary, a treatment plan, and a progress note. These forms are not intended to be used without adaptation but are offered with the hope that they may provide a starting place for new supervisors struggling with the documentation requirements.

Moline, Williams, and Austin (1998) state that "supervisors often forget the importance of examining their supervisee's records on a routine basis. They need to treat these records as if they were their own. If they find that a supervisee is writing inadequate records, it is worth their time to teach the supervisee how to execute adequate record keeping" (p. 67). It is important to refer to state requirements to determine the timeframe for retaining clinical records, which include supervisory documentation.

Consult with Appropriate Professionals

Maintaining consultative relationships with other professionals such as other supervisors, attorneys, and physicians is an imperative step toward risk management. These relationships provide a forum for discussion of roles, responsibilities, and concerns regarding supervision. It is an appropriate place to ask for feedback about issues such as vicarious liability, confidentiality, dual relationships, and power differential situations. It is essential for the supervisor to share concerns and limitations along with knowledge and success to get the most from consultation. A certain level of trust and vulnerability are required for maximum benefit.

Maintain Working Knowledge of Ethics Codes, Legal Statutes, and Licensing Regulations

It is essential for both the supervisor's and the supervisee's protection, as well as the client's welfare, to have a working knowledge of ethics codes and legal statutes and an awareness of current trends in the field. For example, an area of increasing concern in the counseling field is that of appropriately handling acts of threats and violence. These situations are a challenge for both supervisors and supervisees, and the frequency of these acts seems to be increasing. Case 8.4 illustrates the need to be aware of ethical and legal statutes regarding reporting and intervening in acts of violence.

What are your thoughts about the degree of risk of violence in this case? As Katie's supervisor, what additional assessment would you suggest? What are your responsibilities as a supervisor? Would your actions be any different if you were handling the case yourself?

The supervisor must be familiar with the relevant legal and ethical requirements pertaining to reporting and intervening with threats and acts of violence and abuse. The supervisor should assure that the supervisee is aware of those requirements as well and that the supervisee will bring these topics to supervision for discussion as outlined in the supervision contract. The supervisor can help the supervisee assess the situation, determine if there is an imminent risk, decide whether reporting to the authorities is required legally or is necessary for the protection of those involved even if there is no requirement for reporting, and devise a plan for how to proceed.

There are many ramifications of reporting (or taking action) and not reporting (or not taking action). Taking action may aggravate a domestic abuse situation, and the client may not return for counseling. On the other hand, taking no action could result in the threats of violence being carried out. The possible outcomes should be discussed with the supervisee in a way that will enable the supervisee to be able to problem solve these kinds of situations after supervision has concluded. It is important to note that supervisors are responsible for the actions of their supervisees and this situation is no exception. The supervision you provide and the suggested direction you give to your supervisee is your responsibility legally and ethically.

Use Multiple Methods of Supervision

Relying on self-report as the sole method of supervision is no longer acceptable. Supervision standards regarding monitoring supervisees' work state that "reasonable steps" should be taken to ensure appropriate client care.

| CASE 8.4 | KATIE |

Katie is a student in a marriage and family counseling program and is doing her internship at the local community mental health center. She is seeing a client, Dena, who is married, has two children, and wants to return to school to get a degree in secondary education. Dena reports that her husband has slapped her on the face on two occasions. Dena hasn't expressed major concerns about her safety or that of her children, but she has reported recently that he seems to be getting increasingly more upset as she talks of returning to school. Katie is at a loss about determining what degree of threat to the safety of Dena and her children is present and what to do about it.

Katie takes her dilemma to her supervisor, and together they talk about what is in the best interest of Dena (and her children). They also consider what has the highest probability of a positive outcome. The supervisor suggests that Katie obtain more specific information from Dena regarding her husband's agitation. When does it occur? How does he act? What does he say? How is it resolved? In addition, the supervisor suggests that Katie ask Dena to have her husband accompany her to counseling for further assessment and to enlist his support for Dena. Katie may be able to head off potential violence through counseling with Dena and her husband.

However, these standards do not specify what constitutes "reasonableness," and often this is not debated until after damage has occurred. Monitoring supervisees' practice based on level of education, training, and experience is strongly recommended. This is a developmental perspective of monitoring where supervision for beginning supervisees consists of direct supervision, videotaping, close review of all documentation, and ongoing assessment. As experience and skill are gained, supervision may transition into less direct observation, audiotaping, use of self-report, and selected therapy notes. During the later phases of training, supervision may transition once again to primarily, but not only, self-report and documentation review.

Practice a Feedback and Evaluation Plan

It is the supervisor's duty to assess and evaluate supervisees' performance. Supervisors are typically expected to evaluate supervisees' progress over a specified period of time and render judgment regarding supervisees' competence to practice independently. The key to success in this area is to have an evaluation process that is followed consistently and to inform all supervisees of this process as they begin supervision. It is important to remember that there is a direct relationship between the constructs of competence, fairness, and due process. In other words, the use of a professional disclosure statement is strongly encouraged to inform supervisees of (1) how they will be evaluated, (2) what standard evaluation will take place, (3) how and when feedback will be provided, and (4) how information will be shared. Feedback should be provided in both written and oral form throughout supervision. It is essential that supervisees have the opportunity to implement feedback from the supervisor. Providing information about specific areas and skills that need improvement and providing appropriate time and attention for remediation prior to a negative summative evaluation is the essence of due process. Cobia and Boes (2000) suggest comprehensive evaluation of supervisees' skills in these areas: appraisal and assessment, case conceptualization, and ability to plan, deliver, and evaluate counseling services.

Purchase and Verify Professional Liability Insurance Coverage

Professional liability insurance is a must for both supervisors and supervisees. Check with the company that holds the malpractice policy, prior to purchase, to confirm coverage for damages incurred outside of direct service or due to negligent supervision. In addition, confirm that coverage applies to supervisees' level of education or training.

Evaluate and Screen All Clients Under Supervisee's Care

Supervisors have a responsibility to evaluate both the client and the supervisee. It is essential that supervisors carefully assess each client that receives services from the supervisee. This assessment is for the dual purpose of making certain that the case is within the supervisor's area of competence and that the case is referred to the appropriate supervisee based on training, skill, and experience. It is the supervisor's responsibility to continue assessing each client under the care of the supervisee. From a legal perspective, it is expected that supervisors will have adequate knowledge of each of their supervisee's clients. Falvey (2002) defines this requirement as meaning that supervisors meet with every one of their supervisee's clients. It is important that you have sufficient knowledge of each of your supervisee's clients and that you consider the legal ramifications should you not have that information.

Establish a Policy for Ensuring Confidentiality

Establish a process to ensure confidentiality. Have a written agreement with supervisees that includes the right of the supervisor to have consultative discussions with appropriate colleagues regarding the supervisory relationship and duties. Have supervisees use appropriate disclosure statements for clients describing the supervision process, clearly identifying the supervisee "in training," and the limits of confidentiality and privilege. Review the ethics codes regarding confidentiality as part of the orientation to supervision and discuss for clarification.

Never take for granted that a supervisee is prepared to handle difficult situations where confidentiality is concerned. Check this out first by providing situations and requesting a course of action by the supervisee to determine his or her working knowledge of confidentiality. As a supervisor, model appropriate confidential behavior regarding discussion of both your supervisees and the clients they serve. Make expectations regarding confidentiality very clear. For example, if clients are only to be discussed within the confines of a therapy room or your office, state this clearly. If you expect your supervisee to communicate his or her status in training before the first formal counseling session, state this expectation clearly. Explain the consequences of breaches of confidentiality.

Provide the message to supervisees that supervisors are not expected to have all the answers regarding confidentiality. You may wish to share instances where you have needed guidance in this area. Make it clear that supervisees are expected to raise questions and seek guidance whenever there is a concern. Acknowledge that self-report is not sufficient to monitor most instances where confidentiality is breached. Observation is often required to assess and prevent these situations. Breaches of confidentiality are also less likely to be reported in supervision due to the supervisee's lack of awareness. These breaches often occur with good intent, but they are breaches none the less. Audio, video, or other methods of direct observation are encouraged to monitor these issues.

Establish a procedure that can be shared with clients regarding the process of supervision of cases. This process should include who the case information will be shared with, and how the information will be managed following either ending of supervision or termination of treatment.

Incorporate Informed Consent in Practice

Proper informed consent serves to provide information to and to protect both supervisees and the clients they serve. In much the same way that therapists provide their clients with a professional disclosure statement, it is wise for supervisors to inform supervisees about the relevant aspects of the supervision process. Cobia and Boes (2000) suggest that supervisors make use of professional disclosure statements for supervision so that supervisees are informed of the potential benefits, risks, and expectations of entering into the supervisory relationship. For the supervisor–supervisee relationship, informed consent outlines the duties, training philosophy, expectations, and evaluation procedures of the supervisor. These elements are often found within the supervisory contract (see Box 8.5). For the supervisee–client relationship, informed consent should specify boundaries of the relationship, training status of the supervisee, and confidentiality (see Box 8.6).

SUMMARY

As the role of the supervisor becomes more defined, legal responsibility and accountability are strongly shaping that definition. The legal issues of negligence and liability, specifically vicarious liability, can be somewhat daunting, and it is important to remember that there are clear guidelines for risk management. This chapter has provided a brief legal primer for understanding what liability actually is in the practice of supervision. We have also provided you with guidelines for risk management that, if practiced, can minimize the risk of liability for you and your supervisees.

Know your own limits and scope of practice, and practice within your limits. Remember that you have a choice about whom you supervise and which cases you directly supervise.

Provide supervisees with a thorough supervisory contract and sound orientation. Document all supervisory activities, and provide supervisees with clear emergency policies. Never assume that supervisees have an adequate working knowledge of ethics. Give honest feedback and evaluations and document them. Identify appropriate professionals for consultative relationships, and carry liability insurance.

SUGGESTED ACTIVITIES

1. Form small groups and have each group develop a detailed case scenario (from problem presentation through sanctions, if any) of liable supervisory practice. Then have groups exchange scenarios and answer the following questions:
    a. Was the supervisor competent to supervise in this situation?
    b. Was the supervisee competent to treat this patient given the level of supervision?
    c. How was the supervisee monitored?
    d. How was this monitoring process documented?
    e. Did the supervisor follow accepted ethical principles, such as providing timely and periodic evaluations of the supervisee?
    f. Was there a dual relationship of any kind?
    g. Was the client fully informed as to the training status of the supervisee, the role of the supervisor, the limits of confidentiality, and other relevant factors pertinent to the relationship?

    The ability to answer these questions in a positive light at any given time during supervisory practice has become essential.

2. Read this case example and discuss it in small groups. Then reconvene into a large group and share your answers.

    A supervisee has been working with a teenage girl in a private family clinic. The girl reports having taken some drugs in the past. The counselor gets a call late one night from the girl who is at home, and she says she just needs to talk. It comes out in the conversation that the girl has taken some drugs, and she is not feeling well. The supervisee insists that she put her mom on the telephone, and the supervisee tells the mom what has happened and that the girl should be taken to the hospital. The girl survives, but her parents threaten a malpractice case against the supervisee for not having told the parents of the girl's past drug use. If they had known about the previous situation, they believe they could have prevented the current one from happening. The supervisee calls his supervisor first thing the next morning to report what has transpired. This call is the first knowledge that the supervisor has of the details of the case.

    a. What are the ethical, legal, and clinical issues in this case?

    b. What kinds of questions would you raise with your supervisee regarding this situation?

    c. What would you most want to say to your supervisee?

    d. How would you guide your supervisee in thinking through this situation including the ethical, legal, and clinical issues?

    e. How would you help your supervisee formulate a plan of action and think through the consequences of the various courses of action?

    f. If a malpractice suit is filed, is the supervisor alone responsible or is the supervisee also responsible?

3. As you read each of the examples that follows, answer these questions: Is this an example of vicarious or direct liability? What risk management steps could have been taken to prevent the situation?

    a. The supervisor or agency provides an intake form to be used by the trainee, but it omits relevant questions (homicidal tendencies, suicidal tendencies, previous therapy). The client receives improper treatment and injures himself or others.

    b. The trainee takes relevant notes during therapy; however, the supervisor does not study these notes and does not realize that the notes describe a therapy method not usually used in counseling.

    c. Even with the supervisor's help, the trainee is incapable of offering proper therapy. There is a need to refer to a more competent professional.

    d. A medical problem, which would have been discovered by a person with more training, is not discovered by the trainee. A physician is not consulted and treatment continues even though the psychological problem is caused by a hearing loss, a vitamin deficiency, or other physical imbalance.

    e. Psychological tests are conducted and a diagnosis and treatment plan are based on the test results. The diagnosis is improper due to inappropriate norms of the test and lack of supervision regarding test selection and multicultural case conceptualization.

    f. The diagnosis is improper, the prognosis is faulty, or the treatment plan ineffective. The supervisor does not discover the error in any of the three areas or the interrelationship of one to the other, and therapy continues inappropriately.

    g. Written progress notes are inadequate or do not support the treatment plan.

    h. The trainee and patient (or trainee and supervisor) have a conflict of personalities, yet the treatment continues.

    i. The trainee becomes socially involved with the client, but cleverly hides the involvement from the supervisor. The supervisor should have known by more complete supervisory sessions.

    j. The trainee goes on vacation, and there is no adequately prepared relief therapist.

    k. The trainee breaches confidentiality and shares a particularly intriguing story with a co-trainee or friend, and word gets back to the client. The supervisor had not warned the trainee of the importance and mean

    l. The client consents to treatment but does not know it will be provided by a trainee. He assumes it will be provided by a qualified professional.

    m. The trainee is subpoenaed to testify in court and is improperly prepared by training or experience for courtroom testimony.

    n. A student trainee is released from a graduate training program based on unsatisfactory performance in a practicum experience. There is minimal documentation of supervision, no documentation of direct observation, no procedure for formal feedback, and no due process prior to termination.

4. Access the Web site for this text at http://info.wadsworth.com/haynes, and complete the self-assessment inventory. Additional contributor perspectives and other activities specific to this chapter are also available to you through this Web site.

Sample Forms Used by Students in Clinical Psychology Practicums

BOX 8.8   CLIENT INFORMATION SHEET

Client Name: _____   Client No.: _____

Age: _____   DOB: _____/_____/_____

Sex: M F   Race: _____

Classification: Freshman Sophomore Junior Senior

Major: _____

Address (local): _____

    Street Address   Apt. #

    _____
    City   State   Zip Code

Telephone: (____)_____

Is it okay to call? Yes No   Is it okay to leave a message? Yes No

Where do you live?   ❏ Dorm   ❏ Apartment (alone)
    ❏ Apartment (w/roommate)   ❏ Apartment (w/significant other)
    ❏ With Parents   ❏ With Spouse

Emergency contact:

    _____
    Name   Address   Phone

Instructor (for extra credit): _____

Therapist: _____   Telephone No.: _____

Supervisor: _____   Telephone No.: _____

Peer Observer: _____

Dates of sessions: 1st session: _____

2nd session: _____

3rd session: _____

4th session: _____

5th session: _____

Source: Adapted from Northwestern State University, Natchitoches, LA, Department of Psychology, and designed by Cynthia Lindsey and Patrice Moulton, June 2001. Reprinted with permission.

BOX 8.9 | INTAKE WORKSHEET

Client Name: _____   Date of Intake: _____/_____/_____

Age: _____   DOB: _____/_____/_____

Sex: M F   Race: _____

Classification: Freshman Sophomore Junior Senior

Major: _____

Address (local): _____
        Street Address   Apt. #

        _____
        City   State   Zip Code

Telephone: (_____)_____

PRESENTING ISSUE(S)

What issues/problems are you experiencing? (This should include details of specific behavior.)

When did they begin? How frequent? How severe?

Relevant history (past episodes/incidents/examples):

What solutions to your problem have been most helpful?

BACKGROUND HISTORY
Family History

How many brothers and sisters do you have?

What are their ages?

Where are you in the birth order?

(continued)

BOX 8.9 | INTAKE WORKSHEET (*continued*)

Please describe your relationships with your siblings:

Father: alive or deceased? How old is he now/how old was he at the time of his death?

If deceased, what was the cause of his death? How old were you when he died? What was that experience like for you?

Describe your father. What is your relationship like with your father?

Mother: alive or deceased? How old is she now/how old was she at the time of her death?

If deceased, what was the cause of her death? How old were you when she died? What was that experience like for you?

Describe your mother. What is your relationship like with your mother?

Who raised you?

What was it like growing up in your house?

How would you describe your culture? What does it mean to you? How does your culture contribute to who you are?

Have you ever been physically, sexually, or emotionally abused? Please describe.

Did you witness any domestic violence in your home while growing up? Explain.

What is your marital status?

If married: How long did you and your spouse date before you married? How long have you been married?

What is your spouse's name? age? occupation?

Describe your marriage:

Does you marriage present any special problems? Explain.

How many times have you been married?

Reasons for divorce:

If in a committed relationship: What is your partner's name? age? occupation?

Describe your relationship:

Does you relationship present any special problems?

How many children do you have? What are their names, ages, and sexes?

Are you experiencing any problems with your children?

Dating/Sexual History

Describe your dating history (how many relationships, typical length of relationships, typical problems experienced):

(continued)

BOX 8.9	INTAKE WORKSHEET *(continued)*

At what age did you first learn about sex? How?

At what age were you when you first became sexual?

How many partners have you had?

Overall, how well have you known each of them before becoming sexually involved?

Have you ever experienced any anxiety or guilt feelings as a result of sex or masturbation?

Is your present sex life satisfactory? If not, please explain.

Educational History

Where did you graduate from high school?

What were you like as a high school student? (academically and socially)

Academic strengths and weaknesses

How are you doing in college? (academically)

What are your strengths? weaknesses?

Have you experienced any difficulties adjusting to college?

What are your educational goals?

Work History

Are you currently employed? If so, where?

What sort of jobs have you held in the past?

Have you ever been terminated from a job? If so, why?

What type of work has satisfied you?

What are your professional/vocational goals?

Medical History

Any medical problems, allergies, serious illnesses, surgeries, injuries, hospitalizations, and number of pregnancies:

What nonpsychiatric medications are you currently taking?

Mental Health History

Have you ever been in inpatient or outpatient therapy? For what (diagnosis)? With whom? When? How long? Outcome?

What psychiatric medication are you currently taking? (state name, dosage, how long taken, who prescribed, and any effects)

What psychiatric medication have you taken in the past?

Have you or are you suffering from depression, anxiety, relationship problems, or any other type of problem?

(continued)

BOX 8.9 | INTAKE WORKSHEET (*continued*)

Check all that have been experienced (indicate if present or past and indicate when in the past):

	Present	Past	(When?)
Thoughts of hurting self? ☐ others? ☐	_____	_____	
Thoughts of committing suicide? ☐	_____	_____	
Making plans to commit suicide? ☐ harm others? ☐	_____	_____	
Attempted to commit suicide? ☐	_____	_____	
Stated threats to commit suicide? ☐ harm others? ☐	_____	_____	

Explain:

Check all substances you have used, past and present, how often, and how much:

	Present	Past	How Often?	Amt?		Present	Past	How Often?	Amt?
Nicotine	____	____	____	____	Amphetamine	____	____	____	____
Caffeine	____	____	____	____	Hallucinogens	____	____	____	____
Alcohol	____	____	____	____	P.C.P.	____	____	____	____
Marijuana	____	____	____	____	Designer drugs	____	____	____	____
Crack/Cocaine	____	____	____	____	Sedative/Hypnotic	____	____	____	____
Heroin	____	____	____	____	Opiates/Synthetic	____	____	____	____
Barbiturate	____	____	____	____	Inhalant	____	____	____	____

What age did you start using _____? drinking _____?

When did you last use _____? drink _____?

Does any member of your family suffer from depression, anxiety, alcoholism, or anything else that might be considered a "mental disorder"? Please explain.

Has any relative attempted or committed suicide? Explain.

Has any relative had serious problems with the law? Explain.

Have you ever had serious problems with the law? Explain.

Social History

Do you make friends easily? Explain.

Do you keep friends? Explain.

Describe any experiences in which you were bullied or severely teased.

What type of organizations were you in as a child?

What organizations/activities were you in during high school?

What type of organizations are you involved in now?

Current Support System: ❏ excellent   ❏ good   ❏ fair   ❏ poor

Explain:

_____   _____
Practicum Student   Date

_____   _____
Supervisor   Date

Source: Adapted from Northwestern State University, Natchitoches, LA, Department of Psychology, and designed by Cynthia Lindsey and Patrice Moulton, June 2001. Reprinted with permission.

BOX 8.10 | MODEL INTAKE REPORT

Client Name: _____   Case No.: _____

Therapist: _____   Supervisor: _____

Date of Intake: _____/_____/_____

Identifying Information

Brief description of client
Living situation
Vocational/educational status

Presenting Issue

Client's description of the issue, its duration, frequency, severity, and any relevant history

Background History

Family History, including cultural issues, history of abuse, and domestic violence
Educational History
Work History
Medical History
Mental Health History, including homicidal/suicidal ideation and substance use/abuse
Legal History
Social History

Behavioral Observations

Physical description of client
Mental status
Client's behavior during interview

Case Conceptualization

Description of issues/problems and contributing factors

Diagnostic Impression

All five axes

Treatment Goals/Recommendations

Goals identified by client
Tentative plan of action

_____   _____
Practicum Student   Date

_____   _____
Supervisor   Date

_____

Source: Adapted from Northwestern State University, Natchitoches, LA, Department of Psychology, and designed by Cynthia Lindsey and Patrice Moulton, June 2001. Reprinted with permission.

BOX 8.11 | INTAKE SUMMARY

Client Name: _____   Client No. _____

Date of Intake: _____/_____/_____

Age: _____   DOB: _____/_____/_____

Sex: M F   Race: _____

Classification: Freshman   Sophomore   Junior   Senior

Major: _____

Address (local): _____

       Street Address   Apt. #

_____

    City   State   Zip Code

Telephone: (_____) _____

Relationship status: _____   No. and ages of children _____

Where do you live?
- ❏ Dorm
- ❏ Apartment (w/roommate)
- ❏ With parents
- ❏ Apartment (alone)
- ❏ Apartment (w/significant other)
- ❏ With spouse

Emergency contact: _____

    Name   Address   Phone

Presenting Issues:

1. _____

2. _____

3. _____

Relevant History:

1. _____

2. _____

3. _____

Has client reported a history of or current experiences of any of the following?

	Yes	No
Suicidality	❏	❏
Homicidality	❏	❏
Abuse/Neglect	❏	❏
Substance use/abuse	❏	❏
Physical Illness	❏	❏
Mental health history	❏	❏

(continued)

BOX 8.11 | INTAKE SUMMARY (*continued*)

Previous experience(s) in therapy: With whom? For what (diagnosis)? When? How long? Outcome?

List allergies, serious illnesses, surgeries, injuries, hospitalizations, and number of pregnancies:

_____

_____

_____

Current support system: ❑ excellent   ❑ good   ❑ fair   ❑ poor
Explain:

_____

_____

Diagnostic Impression (DSM-IV)
Axis I

_____

Axis II

_____

Axis III

_____

Axis IV

_____

Axis V

_____

Issues to be addressed:

1. _____

2. _____

3. _____

Treatment goals:

1. _____

2. _____

3. _____

Prognosis: ❑ excellent   ❑ good   ❑ fair   ❑ poor

Recommended referrals/aftercare:

1. _____

2. _____

3. _____

_____
Supervisee's Signature/Degree   Title/Position   Date

_____
Supervisor's Signature/Degree   Title/Position   Date

Source: Adapted from Northwestern State University, Natchitoches, LA, Department of Psychology, and designed by Cynthia Lindsey and Patrice Moulton, June 2001. Reprinted with permission.

BOX 8.12	TREATMENT PLAN

Client Name: _____   Client ID No. _____

Date: _____/_____/_____

Presenting Issues:

1. _____

2. _____

3. _____

Goals

Please use the following key to indicate how the objectives will be measured:

SR = self-report   OR = others' report   DO = direct observation (by therapist)

Goal 1

Objectives	Addressed (✔)	Measured by	Date assessed	Accomplished (✔)
1.				
2.				
3.				

Goal 2

Objectives	Addressed (✔)	Measured by	Date assessed	Accomplished (✔)
1.				
2.				
3.				

Goal 3

Objectives	Addressed (✔)	Measured by	Date assessed	Accomplished (✔)
1.				
2.				
3.				

Prognosis   ❑ excellent   ❑ good   ❑ fair   ❑ poor
Explain:

_____

_____

Referrals

_____

_____

_____

_____

Signatures

_____   _____
Client   Date

_____   _____
Practicum Student   Date

_____   _____
Supervisor   Date

Source: Adapted from Northwestern State University, Natchitoches, LA, Department of Psychology, and designed by Cynthia Lindsey and Patrice Moulton, June 2001. Reprinted with permission.

BOX 8.13 | PROGRESS NOTE

Client Name: _____   Case No.: _____

Date of Session: _____/_____/_____   Length of Session: _____

Therapist: _____   Peer Observer: _____

Objective:

_____

_____

_____

Objective:

_____

_____

_____

Action Taken:

_____

_____

_____

Plan:

_____

_____

_____

_____

Therapist's Signature/degree   Title/Position   Date

_____

Supervisor's Signature/degree   Title/Position   Date

Source: Adapted from Northwestern State University, Natchitoches, LA, Department of Psychology, and designed by Cynthia Lindsey and Patrice Moulton, June 2001. Reprinted with permission.

MANAGING CRISIS SITUATIONS

1. Have you ever experienced the loss of someone you know who committed suicide? What was it like for you? For the victim's family members? How to you think you would react to a client's suicide?
2. How do you think you could be of most help to a supervisee whose client has attempted or committed suicide?
3. Should you intervene with a supervisee to help him or her through a personal crisis? Under what conditions? How would you assist the supervisee? When would you refer the supervisee for personal counseling?
4. What reactions might you have to witnessing a violent act in a school? How would you help a supervisee cope with an incident of school violence?
5. How can supervisors best help their supervisees cope with a crisis situation? What do you think supervisees need most from supervisors in these situations?
6. Have you experienced a natural disaster or been the victim of a crime? What was it like for you? What was helpful to you in recovering from the incident? How would you help a supervisee handle a critical incident (for example, a shooting or a threat of violence) that occurs in the clinical setting?

INTRODUCTION

In this chapter, we discuss some of the crisis situations that occur in supervision and provide a framework for how you as the supervisor can work with these situations. These crises could involve situations supervisees encounter in or apart from their clinical work that affect supervisees in such a way that it becomes a focus for supervision. Many supervisees are inexperienced and feel poorly equipped to deal effectively with crisis situations. Other supervisees may see themselves as being better equipped to handle these situations on their own, without being aware of the limits of their competence and consequences of the decisions they make. In either case, it is the job of the supervisor to help supervisees examine the situation, act in the best interest of the client, do what is legally and ethically appropriate, and learn from the situation so that supervisees are able to problem solve independently in the future.

For the purposes of this chapter, a *crisis situation* is defined as any unusual event involving the supervisee that might have an adverse impact on the supervisee's ability to function in the role for which he or she is being supervised. These situations might include client suicides or suicide attempts; witnessing violent events including incidents of school violence; and personal crises such as death, divorce, or illness. In this chapter, we will address many of these situations and discuss how to work with them effectively as a supervisor. Each situation is illustrated by a case example followed by commentary regarding ways in which the supervisor might handle the situation. The situations described are not all inclusive but represent the more common ones found in supervision. This approach to problem solving can be applied to the variety of situations that may arise in supervision.

A FRAMEWORK FOR MANAGING
CRISIS SITUATIONS IN SUPERVISION

In our work as supervisors, we have experienced many crisis situations in supervision, and each of these situations posed a new challenge. In crisis situations, it helps to have a basic idea of what to expect from supervisees and a framework for how to approach these problems. For example, it is clear that being threatened by a client or witnessing a violent act can be very disturbing to supervisees. In these circumstances, it is essential to first allow supervisees to talk about the incident and express their reactions and concerns prior moving to problem solving. Supervisees often overreact to these crisis situations and want to proceed without thoroughly examining the situation and the ramifications of their actions. From our perspective, we would not want to curb our supervisees' inclination to initiate action. However, we see it as our obligation to help supervisees proceed using sound, objective assessment and problem solving of the clinical situation.

New supervisors may have a tendency to act too quickly to solve the problem, instructing the supervisee on how to proceed. These special situations offer fertile ground for the supervisee's learning, but great patience and reserve are required by the supervisor to allow the supervisee to process the information, examine courses of action, and proceed with the best intervention for the situation. As a supervisor, there are times when quick action is necessary to save a life or protect a victim. In those situations, you are obligated to intervene as quickly as possible. However, in most crisis situations there is time to help the supervisee do the major portion of the problem solving and subsequent intervention. These learning experiences will foster long-term growth for the supervisee.

New supervisors may also experience their own anxiety when providing supervision in a crisis situation. This might be due to limited experience as a supervisor or lack of training and experience with the crisis at hand, or both. It is essential for supervisors to be aware of their anxiety or misgivings about working with a particular crisis situation and know when to seek outside consultation or supervision. It is effective modeling, as well as ethical practice, for a supervisor to share with the supervisee the limits of the supervisor's knowledge and competence and to work with the supervisee in devising a plan for obtaining the needed assistance.

As a clinical supervisor, you will need to have a variety of ways to work with a supervisee who encounters a crisis situation. Although there is no cookbook approach to addressing these crisis situations, we have provided a framework for crisis management in Box 9.1. You should develop your own plan well in advance of entering into a supervisory relationship.

The "Ethical Guidelines for Counseling Supervisors" (ACES, 1993) make it clear that client welfare is the first priority. Federal and state laws that address this should be the first point of reference. Where laws and standards are not clear, the good judgment of the supervisor should be guided by

| BOX 9.1 | A FRAMEWORK FOR CRISIS MANAGEMENT |

1. Be prepared for crisis situations that occur in supervision and address this in the supervision contract.
2. Have emergency procedures in place and communicate those to the supervisee (Falvey, 2002; Neufelt, 1999).
3. Assess the situation and identify the various components including the clinical, legal, ethical, personal, and client safety issues involved.
4. Assure that the rights, welfare, and safety of the client are protected.
5. Use consultation and referrals where appropriate.
6. Use critical incident debriefing interventions (described later in this chapter) when needed.
7. Have a plan in mind for re-entry of the supervisee into the work setting following a crisis situation.
8. Consider the effect that crisis situations might have on other supervisees and staff as well as clients.
9. Consider the clinical, legal, and ethical ramifications for you as a supervisor for any action that you suggest.
10. Rely on supervision contracts and ground rules already established with your supervisee.

relevant legal and ethical standards, client welfare, supervisee welfare, supervisor welfare, and program or agency needs. This is a sound framework for decision making for any of the helping professions. To further refine your plan for crisis management, address the principles of risk management presented in Chapter 8. Some specific problem-solving steps you might take with a supervisee are provided in Box 9.2.

Few professional standards specifically address crisis situations in supervision, yet most of the standards address topics related to handling these situations. Box 9.3 provides standards that specifically address crises. In addition, the system for the supervisee contacting the supervisor when a crisis situation occurs should be in place and communicated to the supervisee (ACES, 1993).

UNDERSTANDING SPECIFIC CRISIS SITUATIONS

Suicide and Suicide Attempts

One in five psychologists involved in direct client care will lose a client to suicide (Bongar, 1991, 2002). In addition, one in six psychology graduate students experience a client's suicide during training. Suicide and suicide attempts on the part of a client can be devastating for a helping professional, and especially for a supervisee (Foster & McAdams, 1999; Kleespies, Smith, & Becker, 1990). A client suicide usually results in feeling shock, grief, loss, guilt, depression, and responsibility. This event and the feelings it evokes may shake the confidence of a novice clinician. DeAngelis (2001) cites an unpub-

CRISIS INTERVENTION PROBLEM-SOLVING STEPS

1. Gather as much information as you can from the supervisee about the situation. Ask questions and listen carefully to what the supervisee has to say.
2. Review any clinical records available regarding the situation.
3. Review the legal, ethical, and professional standards that might apply.
4. Assess whether an immediate danger might necessitate a quick intervention.
5. Ask the supervisee to review all the possible courses of action and their potential consequences.
6. Discuss what other information is needed in deciding how to proceed, including consultation.
7. Choose the course of action that best fits the situation.
8. Evaluate the outcome of the intervention.
9. Discuss with the supervisee the decision-making process, learning that occured, better interventions for handling similar situations, and ways to use the problem-solving process to resolve similar situations in the future.

ETHICS CODES AND STANDARDS REGARDING MANAGING CRISIS SITUATIONS IN SUPERVISION

Association for Counselor Education and Supervision
Ethical Guidelines for Counseling Supervisors (1993)
2.05 Procedures for contacting the supervisor, or an alternative supervisor, to assist in handling crisis situations should be established and communicated to supervisees.

3.20 Supervisors should use the following prioritized sequence in resolving conflicts among the needs of the client, the needs of the supervisee, and the needs of the program or agency. Insofar as the client must be protected, it should be understood that client welfare is usually subsumed in federal and state laws such that these statutes should be the first point of reference. Where laws and ethical standards are not present or are unclear, the good judgment of the supervisor should be guided by the following list.
a. Relevant legal and ethical standards (e.g., duty to warn, state child abuse laws, etc.);
b. Client welfare;
c. Supervisee welfare;
d. Supervisor welfare; and
e. Program and/or agency service and administrative needs.

National Board for Certified Counselors
Standards for the Ethical Practice of Clinical Supervision (1999)
In addition to following the NBCC Code of Ethics pertaining to the practice of professional counseling, clinical supervisors shall:
6. Establish procedures with their supervisees for handling crisis situations.

lished survey of 91 therapists conducted by the American Association of Suicidology that found that therapists commonly cited sadness, depression, hopelessness, guilt, and anger as reactions to a client's suicide. Bongar (1991) concludes that trainees look to their supervisors for emotional support and assistance in understanding the suicide. Yet DeAngelis (2001) states that mental health professionals who have lost a patient to suicide say they received little or no support from colleagues, supervisors, or administrators. Although supervisees may be trained to work with a range of disorders and emotions in clients, they are rarely prepared for the personal and professional toll suicide can take. Consider the case of George as he experiences the suicide of a client.

The Case of George George is a prelicensed counseling psychologist working at a university counseling center. He has a doctorate in counseling psychology, was recently hired as a counselor at the counseling center, and is under the supervision of a licensed counseling psychologist at the center. George has been seeing Aaron for five sessions to help him work on improving his relationship skills. Aaron was in the midst of a rocky relationship with his girlfriend when he came in for counseling and wanted help on what he could do to make things better. He would keep his feelings to himself and did not communicate well with his girlfriend. George thought they were making good progress on these issues in the counseling sessions. At their last counseling session, Aaron reported that his girlfriend wanted to break up with him. He was upset and confused, and George worked with him to sort things out and develop a plan for how he would deal with the imminent breakup. It seemed that Aaron was feeling better by the end of the session. A day before their next scheduled session, George got word from the campus police that Aaron had been found dead in his garage: the car was running and the garage door was closed; he had asphyxiated himself. George was shocked and dismayed; he immediately went to his supervisor to tell him what had happened.

QUESTIONS FOR REFLECTION

- What kinds of questions would you raise with George regarding this situation?
- What would you most want to say to George about this situation?
- How would you guide George in thinking through this situation including the ethical, legal, and clinical issues?
- How would you expect the agency administrators to react to this situation?
- How would you help George decide how to proceed from here?
- How might you work with George if he told you that he kept telling himself that he missed something and that he was partially responsible for Aaron's suicide? Did he miss something? Is he directly or indirectly responsible?
- How should supervision have addressed the possible concern of suicide potential?

Commentary   As a supervisor, your responsibility is to help George manage his reactions and take care of his agency responsibilities regarding the situation. Let George know that it is common for helping professionals to assume an inordinate degree of responsibility when something like this occurs. The most common reaction of helping professionals to an event like this is to believe that had they done something different, said something different, not overlooked signs and symptoms from the individual, then the suicide would not have occurred. Aaron appears to have given little indication of suicide risk prior to the suicide event. Perhaps the point at which Aaron was seen as upset and confused should have alerted George to do a more careful assessment of depression and/or suicide ideation. In most cases of suicide, there are warning signs, but in this case, it seems that few indications were present.

It is important to be cognizant of suicide potential and warning signs, but it is not always possible to predict what individuals will do or how they will react to their situation. We must do everything we can to help individuals, but we have to be able to identify when we cannot—and put it behind us. It is the task of the supervisor to try to help George adopt a balanced attitude between caring and maintaining an objective perspective. Here are some ways George's supervisor might initiate a discussion with George:

- "Let's talk about the course of events leading up to the suicide and your interventions and see what we can learn from this."
- "George, I can see this is very upsetting for you. Talk with me more about how this is affecting you."
- "This is always a painful event for counselors. Although I am quite sure you feel a sense of responsibility for Aaron, there is no way we can control the actions of others. At best, we can give them the tools, and it is up to them to use them for change."
- "I really hope you see that if individuals choose to take their own lives you cannot stop them. You did your best for Aaron, and now we need to discuss how this situation is affecting you both personally and professionally."

It is important that supervisors not be too quick to "fix," provide solutions, or excuse the supervisee from responsibility. Supervisees need an opportunity to fully express their thoughts and feelings surrounding a problematic situation. Once supervisees have had a chance to express themselves, supervisors have a basis for deciding which responses are most appropriate.

While George is dealing with his own feelings of grief, loss, and responsibility, the supervisor must assess what other immediate actions are necessary. This might include carefully documenting the events of the last few sessions and conducting a psychological case review to see what can be learned from the case. Agency regulations often require an immediate review of the incident, and administrators may seek accountability and want answers about how this could have happened while a client is under the care of a counselor. The supervisor would be liable, however, only if it was determined that the supervisee's treatment of the client was substandard and that this treatment was a factor in the client's death. DeAngelis (2001) concludes that the supervisor's conflicting roles—supporting trainees and being responsible for trainees' actions—illustrate how supervisors may feel caught in the middle in an agency setting. It is essential that supervisors attend to the personal feelings and reactions of the supervisee as well as the regulatory needs of the agency.

George may never be quite the same as a result of a client suicide, and he will need to examine how this incident may affect his clinical attitude and work. He may have a tendency to become overly cautious and to detect suicide potential in many clients he will see in the future. It may be beneficial to increase the frequency of supervision depending on George's reaction to the suicide. In addition, the supervisor should review the topic of suicide assessment and intervention with George so that he is fully prepared if this situation occurs in the future. There are many variables in assessing suicide risk, and some of the more common indicators are presented in Box 9.4.

This case illustrates the role of the supervisor in suicide risk management. Whenever suicide risk is suspected by the supervisee, this topic should be explored in supervision sessions. The supervisor needs to have a working knowledge of all the supervisee's clients so that risk assessment is not left solely with the supervisee. The supervisor is also responsible to ensure that both he or she and the supervisee are well trained in the topic of suicide assessment and intervention before assigning a supervisee to work with a client with known suicidal risk (Bongar, Lomax, & Marmatz, 1992; Peruzzi & Bongar, 1999).

As discussed previously, supervisors are responsible for all the clinical work their supervisees perform under supervision. For further information on suicide, see "Training and Supervisory Issues in the Assessment and Management of the Suicidal Patient" (Bongar et al., 1992), "Surviving a Patient's Suicide" (DeAngelis, 2001), and "Risk Factor Model for Suicide Assessment and Intervention" (Sánchez, 2001).

Personal Threats by Clients

Threats of violence or actual assaults by clients are rare, but they do occur. The supervisor should be prepared for any situation that might arise with the supervisee and have a plan in place for how to proceed. Threats of violence or actual assaults can affect a supervisee both physically and emotionally and may shake the very core of his or her confidence as a helping professional. Concern for the safety of both supervisee and client is paramount. The supervisor can work with the supervisee to find ways to continue to work with the client while managing these heightened emotional reactions. Let's examine the case of Kendra as an example of a supervisee's personal reaction to a client.

The Case of Kendra   Kendra has worked as a group counselor in a prison setting for 15 years. She is well trained and experienced in working with

| BOX 9.4 | INDICATORS OF SUICIDE RISK |

- Depression
- Talk of suicide or preoccupation with death
- Suicide notes
- Feelings of hopelessness
- Chronic or terminal physical illness
- Changes in appetite or sleep patterns
- Giving away possessions and getting things in order (will, life insurance)
- Loss of spouse, relationship, or job
- Sudden and unexplained euphoria
- History of suicide attempts or a history of suicide in the family
- Presence of a specific plan and availability of the lethal means to commit suicide
- Chronic psychiatric disorder

Any one of these signs by itself may not be an indication of increased suicide risk, but several of them taken together along with other indications may be cause for a more careful assessment of suicide risk.

---

inmates. Several of her colleagues meet weekly in a peer supervision group for support and to problem solve clinical cases. Yesterday an inmate who has participated in her group wrote a note to Kendra threatening her life if she did not give him a positive evaluation to assist with his release. Kendra met with the peer supervision group today and talked about the fact that this has affected her dramatically. She is truly frightened and is considering resigning from her position at the prison.

QUESTIONS FOR REFLECTION

- What are the ethical, legal, and clinical issues in this case?
- What kinds of questions would you raise as a peer supervisor regarding this situation?
- What would you most want to say to Kendra about this situation?
- Do you think Kendra should resign from her position? If not, how would you help her proceed?
- Have you ever been threatened? What was it like for you? What did you learn that you could use in working with Kendra?
- Is there any obligation to warn and inform the authorities about this threat?
- Do you think the peer supervision group can handle this, or should someone else in authority in the prison address it?

Commentary This situation should be reported to Kendra's superiors so the institution can handle it appropriately. It is important to do whatever is necessary to ensure the safety of the individual and any other staff involved. The peer group members can help Kendra sort through what has happened, what brought it about, and what it is about this particular threat (she has probably experienced others in her 15 years there) that has been so upsetting. Support and understanding may be more important than providing answers. The peer supervision group could discuss what action is necessary in notifying the prison authorities and prison police. Kendra might consider a legal consult if there is any uncertainty about how to proceed. The peer supervision group can also help Kendra develop a plan for how to deal with this situation and how she will handle these kinds of events in the future. Kendra might benefit from some time off from the job. Her documentation of this event is essential.

Once Kendra has recovered from the fear and shock of the threat, the supervision group could help her review the case and options that she has for talking with this individual in the future. The use of role play could assist Kendra in exploring ways for her to talk with the inmate. Members of the group might take turns playing the inmate and the therapist to try out different ways of responding. Then Kendra might role-play talking with the inmate.

The interventions discussed here would be equally applicable had Kendra been a supervisee rather than a member of the peer supervision group. The supervisor, however, would have greater responsibility and liability than does the peer group. For further reading on violence see *Violence and Mental Disorder* (Monahan & Steadman, 1994).

School Violence

School counselors and their supervisors are increasingly having to deal with school violence, which presents both legal and ethical issues. When counselors are called to the scene of a violent act, their work affects them personally and they frequently require debriefing and personal counseling. Those who supervise school counselors who deal with the aftermath of a violent incident will need the skills to effectively work with their supervisees' personal reactions. Furthermore, both supervisees and their supervisors have some responsibility to take action before such incidents happen if they become aware of a potential problem in the making. Trainees, counselors, and supervisors need to be vigilant in monitoring and reporting students who have threatened to commit violent acts or who have been part of previous violent activity. They may also need to act on student reports of their peers who intend violence. The basic standard of care for school counselors and their supervisors is clear. Courts have uniformly held that school personnel have a duty to protect students from foreseeable harm (Hermann & Remley, 2000).

The Case of Jake   Jake is a high school student who has been seeing Myra, a school psychology intern. Jake was referred by a teacher because he has been disruptive in class and his academic performance is rapidly declining.

After the first counseling session, Myra sees that Jake is depressed, anxious, and currently quite agitated. He is upset at the teacher for referring him to counseling, and Jake says that he has "ways to take care of teachers like that." After some further discussion, Myra excuses herself for a moment from the counseling session and immediately calls her supervisor to discuss what has transpired and seek direction about how to proceed.

QUESTIONS FOR REFLECTION

- What are the ethical, legal, and clinical issues in this situation?
- As Myra's supervisor, what additional information would you like to hear from her?
- What would you instruct Myra to do in regard to the immediate situation?
- What are the immediate issues to address with Myra? What will you want to discuss in her next supervision session?

Commentary   The first task is to find out more from Myra about Jake's statement that he has ways to take care of teachers like this. Did she ask Jake exactly what he meant? If not, she should discuss that with Jake to obtain more detailed information. Other questions might focus on Jake's history of other incidents, problems at home, whether he is having problems only in one class or in others as well, his access to weapons, and his use of drugs or alcohol. Because Myra is an intern and this situation could rapidly become a crisis, her supervisor may want to assist Myra as a co-therapist with Jake. This can be a major learning experience for Myra as she participates in the co-therapy with her supervisor and in discussion of the situation in supervisory sessions.

Costa and Altekruse (1994) recommend that school counselors make an assessment of dangerousness according to the student's plans for implementing the violent act and the student's ability to carry out the act. Mulvey and Cauffman (2001) suggest that preventing violence in schools rests more on developing a positive and supportive organizational environment in school than on developing more sophisticated assessment tools. They found that in many cases of school violence other students were aware of the planned activities of high-risk students. A supportive environment that encourages students to talk openly with teachers and counselors is often the best deterrent of violent actions.

Given the violent climate of today's schools, school counselors and their supervisors would do well to take every threat of violence seriously (Hermann & Remley, 2000). School personnel may be held accountable if a student's writing assignments contain evidence of premeditated violence. Preventing students from harming other students seems to be implicit in the duty of school personnel. However, whether warning students of other students' threats of violence against them can be considered to be a part of this duty has yet to be determined (Hermann & Remley, 2000). Both counselors and their supervisors might find themselves legally responsible for preventing students from bringing about harm to others by acting on any evidence indicating that a student may be violent and warning others of threats of violence made against them.

For further reading on the topic of school violence, see Sandhu and Aspy (2000) and Capuzzi and Gross (2000). For more on supervising school counseling trainees, see Nelson and Johnson (1999).

Witnessing Disasters and Violent Events

Those of us who have experienced some kind of disaster—fire, flood, hurricane, accident, war—know the strong emotional impact such events have on each of us. Although the helping professions have recognized these emotional effects for years, only in the last two decades has a response been developed and organized to systematically help victims of a disaster cope with their emotional reactions and head off the posttraumatic stress response.

More recently, the terrorist attacks of September 11, 2001, have radically changed life in the United States. This has had a dramatic impact on the emotional status of our citizens and the counselors who work with them. Michelle Muratori (personal communication, October 21, 2001) stated, "Our lives have all been profoundly affected by the terrorist attacks. Who ever imagined we would have to be so concerned about this type of terror? Since this is expected to be a 'long-term' war against terrorism, how will this impact the counseling field and the way we work with clients?" This is something that all in the helping professions are affected by and must deal with.

These events have had an impact on every facet of our society—the economy, personal safety and security, air travel, the postal service, media, schools, to name just a few. We are seeing violence and its emotional toll on a grand scale, and counselors and supervisors must be trained and prepared to work with clients, communities, and supervisees. Supervisors need to be able to deal with their own as well as their family members' existential anxiety about the uncertainty of our times, about not knowing from moment to moment what will happen. Supervisors need to be trained and ready to assist their supervisees and their supervisees' clients in dealing with the anxiety and fear that result from terrorist violence.

Those in the helping professions provide disaster mental health services, but these professionals are also subject to disasters and subsequent emotional reactions. It is within the scope of supervision to identify when supervisees need help to cope with their own reactions as well as those of their clients. Consider Devin's experience.

The Case of Devin   Devin is a prelicensed psychologist completing his post-doctoral training in a community mental health setting. He has three years of clinical experience in a variety of settings and has been at the community mental health setting for six months. Yesterday a client came in with a gun and threatened to shoot one of the mental health workers. Devin did not see it happen but heard the commotion and ran into the hallway to see the gunman pointing the gun at the worker. As the gunman turned his sights on Devin, some of the agency staff wrestled the gunman to the floor and subdued him. Devin will be meeting with his supervisor this morning in an unscheduled meeting to talk about what transpired the day before.

QUESTIONS FOR REFLECTION

- If you were Devin, what would you most need from your supervisor?
- What are the ethical, legal, and clinical issues in this case?
- What kinds of questions would you raise with Devin regarding this situation?
- How would you guide Devin in thinking through this situation?
- How would you help Devin decide what to do now?
- What kind of reactions would you expect from Devin?
- How might it affect the supervisory relationship?
- What kind of interventions will Devin need to help cope with this situation?

Before we discuss the case of Devin, let's consider another case involving a natural disaster.

The Case of Jody   A southeastern state in the continental United States has just suffered one of the worst hurricanes of the decade. Ten people were killed, and thousands of homes were destroyed. Jody is a marriage and family counselor intern at a community mental health center, and she was also a victim of the hurricane. Her apartment was badly damaged, and she lost all her belongings to the resulting flood. Her supervisor is a licensed clinical social worker who has worked at this mental health center for 12 years. The center will be providing counseling for the next several weeks to victims of the hurricane.

QUESTIONS FOR REFLECTION

- What are the ethical, legal, and clinical issues in this case?
- What kinds of questions would you raise with Jody regarding this situation?
- How would you guide Jody in thinking through this situation where she is both a victim of the disaster and the potential provider of services to other victims?
- What is your role as the supervisor in this case?
- What help would you like to give to Jody?
- Would you consider serving as Jody's counselor for a brief time, since her own situation is affecting her ability to provide effective counseling?
- Do you think Jody should be counseling other victims of the hurricane? Why or why not?
- What interventions are you likely to use with Jody?

Commentary   The two events described are both disasters: the attempted shooting is a human-caused disaster, and the hurricane is a disaster created by nature. Any kind of a disaster can take its toll on the victims and on those caring for them. Helping professionals are typically called upon to provide services following a disaster, and they must be properly prepared to work with victims and with supervisees. It is essential that helping professionals who will provide services and supervision in disaster mental health receive formal training on this topic. This has become a specialized field in recent years, with research available on assessment and intervention strategies. Supervisees who will be providing disaster mental health services must receive formal training as well.

When disasters occur, people react in a variety of ways. Some are affected little and others are traumatized. Some common reactions are disbelief, shock, anger, depression, frustration, hopelessness, and grief. The message we want to give to these victims is twofold: they should expect some kind of emotional reaction, and they can expect to recover (normalize) in time. The amount of time recovery takes varies among individuals.

One common intervention for victims of disaster is Critical Incident Stress Debriefing (CISD) (Mitchell & Everly, 1994; Weaver, 1995). CISD is typically held 24 to 72 hours after the critical incident or disaster and is designed to help victims deal with their emotional reactions to the event. By providing victims with an opportunity to talk about the event and their reactions, victims can conceptualize what is happening to them, know what to expect over the next hours, days, and weeks, and learn ways to better cope with their reactions. Debriefings are attended by those who were directly involved, those who witnessed the event, and/or those most severely affected by the event.

Debriefings are led by mental health professionals who have had specialized training and experience in the debriefing process. CISD is not a therapy session although the effect can be very therapeutic. It provides for ventilation by the participants, support from the group and leaders, and information and education about what individuals can expect to experience and how to best manage their reactions to the stressful event. There is tremendous value in having the group hear from one another how each of them experienced the event and how they are doing. CISD helps to prevent the development of posttraumatic stress reactions, which occur more frequently when the emotional reactions of victims go unattended.

A supervisor could provide CISD individually or in a group setting with supervisees; however, the group format seems to lend itself more readily to the debriefing process. The debriefing process is typically a one-time session in which the group facilitators lead the discussion with these kinds of questions:

- What was the individual's role in the incident? Where were they when it happened, or how did they first hear about it?
- What was their personal reaction to the incident? What was it like for them? What were their first thoughts?
- How did it affect them? What was the worst part of it for them?
- How are they doing now? What kinds of reactions are occurring?

- What coping strategies are working for them? How have they been able to cope?
- How can the recovery process be facilitated?

Debriefing leaders provide education and information about the emotional reactions following an incident, what to expect, how to take care of oneself, and resources to use if individuals are not recovering as quickly as expected.

Both Devin and Jody will need special attention and monitoring. Individuals who are victims of or witnesses to a human-caused disaster such as the attempted shooting may have stronger reactions than those that are not human caused (flood, hurricanes, earthquakes). As Devin's supervisor, it might be best to conduct a mini-debriefing with him during the session scheduled the morning after the incident. Find out what he saw and what it was like for him, what his thoughts have been in the last 24 hours, and how he is coping with the situation currently. Provide support and reassurance that his reactions are normal, and talk with him about possible reactions he can expect over the next days and weeks to come.

Devin should be encouraged to attend a formal debriefing session scheduled for agency staff involved in the incident and possibly follow-up counseling. He could resume counseling clients, but his supervisor will need to carefully monitor the kinds of cases he is working with and refer cases to others that might pose particular difficulty for him. This can be an excellent opportunity for Devin to learn from his own experience, his subsequent reaction, and from the debriefing process. He can learn what happens to an individual following a critical incident and how to help manage the reaction in a way that will lead to normalization.

Jody presents a particular difficulty in that she is herself a victim of the hurricane yet may be called upon to counsel other victims. As with Devin, the supervisor might meet with Jody to talk about the incident and how she is doing and refer her to one of the CISD sessions if appropriate. Jody should be involved with agency staff in providing debriefing sessions to victims of the hurricane only if she has had formal training in disaster mental health and in co-leading CISD sessions. In addition, she would provide CISD services only after she has attended her own debriefing and had the opportunity to discuss with her supervisor her current level of adjustment as a victim of the disaster.

The first obligation is to protect the welfare of clients. If Jody has strong reactions to the event, she should not work with victims at this time. If she is handling the reaction in a positive way and is making a good adjustment, her participation in debriefing and counseling victims could be very productive. She knows what it was like for them and what they are experiencing. In any case, debriefing work should be done as a co-leader. Jody should probably not do any grief counseling with those who have lost family and friends in the hurricane. The intensity of that process may be more than she is ready to handle. Nonetheless, with sound supervision Jody can recover from the disaster personally, provide helpful counseling and assistance to other victims, and learn from this entire experience in a way that increases her sense of empowerment to self-supervise in the future.

For further reading on the topic of disaster mental health, see Weaver (1995).

Coping with Personal Crises

Personal crises such as divorce, relationship problems, family difficulties, death, or financial problems can have a profound effect on the work and training of mental health professionals. Supervisees who are experiencing such crises are often ill equipped to continue to work and train effectively. Supervisors must decide how to help supervisees deal with a personal crisis while they continue to provide clinical services. What is your role as a supervisor to assist the supervisee in dealing with the crisis? To what extent, if at all, do you offer limited counseling to your supervisee? Let's look at the following case illustration.

The Case of Trevor   Trevor is a student in a master's level social work program. Before enrolling in the program, he had been a probation officer for five years. He is enthusiastic about his training program and demonstrates strong clinical knowledge and skills. At the last supervisory session, Trevor reluctantly talked about the fact that he and his wife recently separated and he is experiencing a great deal of difficulty dealing with the situation. He is depressed and having trouble concentrating on his schoolwork and on his clients in the counseling center.

QUESTIONS FOR REFLECTION

* What are the ethical, legal, and clinical issues in this case?
* What kinds of questions would you raise with Trevor regarding this situation?
* What would you most want to say to Trevor about this situation?
* How would you help Trevor decide how to proceed from here?
* Do you think a supervisor should address personal issues such as divorce, family, or financial problems in the supervisory relationship? How might that be relevant to supervision?
* Would you allow yourself to do counseling with Trevor under any conditions?
* What restrictions on Trevor's counseling work might be appropriate?

Commentary   First, the supervisor would best listen, support, and try to understand what is occurring with Trevor and how he thinks the crisis might be affecting his work. The power of allowing Trevor to talk through the situation and explore how it is affecting him cannot be underestimated. As a supervisor, you can counsel the supervisee to the extent that the situation has an impact on his work and training. The focus of your discussion should be on how the personal situation affects the work with his clients and not on simply helping him resolve his marital difficulties. Avoid the temptation to become the supervisee's therapist—and it is a temptation because you may feel that you could be of considerable help. Be cautious about how far to go, and be aware that the boundaries can become unclear very quickly. Talk with Trevor about seeking out a therapist to focus on his feelings about the separation. If you believe Trevor is impaired in his work with clients, you have an obligation to take action and have him refer his clients to other clinicians while he is dealing with the situation. At the very least, it would be best if Trevor does not work with clients who are going through a divorce or having other relationship problems, at least until his personal situation is having less of an impact on him.

As supervisors, we have to constantly assess how we can be helpful and therapeutic for our supervisees without becoming their personal therapists. It is essential to learn when to refer the supervisee to someone who can provide support and counseling who is removed from the supervisory relationship.

SUMMARY

Any number of crises can and will occur in supervision. It is essential that the supervisor have a general plan for approaching these situations, be current on the professional and legal standards that apply, and have a variety of supervision methods to use depending on the nature of the situation. Develop written emergency procedures for the variety of crisis situations that can occur, and address those procedures in the supervision contract. Review the emergency procedures in discussion with the supervisee.

Be sure the supervisee knows which situations must be brought to the attention of the supervisor and in what time frame. For example, suicide threats should be reported immediately to the supervisor. The supervisee should have phone numbers for the supervisor and the alternate supervisor if the supervisor is not reachable. Become familiar with all of your supervisees' clients, and receive regular updates on cases that involve some level of risk.

Train your supervisees in handling crisis situations. Discuss these in supervision, and refer supervisees to readings and workshops if you feel they need more training. Take courses and workshops regarding the various kinds of crises that can arise in supervision. You need to stay current on assessment and intervention in these situations and the related ethical and legal issues.

Take time to listen to what your supervisees have to say about a situation. Ask open-ended questions that will give you a more complete understanding of the situation. Supervisees often present only the information they think you want to hear. Exercise care in assigning to supervisees clients who appear to have a high degree of risk unless there is assurance that your supervisee has the clinical competence and judgment necessary.

In every case, strive to make the crisis situation a learning experience for supervisees. If the situation permits, help them think through the facts, issues, possible courses of action, and their consequences. The goal for supervisees is to handle situations like these on their own. If an immediate intervention is required, discuss the situation in detail after the intervention has been made. Let supervisees know how you thought through the situation and how you arrived at your chosen course of action.

SUGGESTED ACTIVITIES

1. Interview at least two supervisors and ask them what crisis situations they have encountered as supervisors. Find out what it was like for them and how they intervened in the situation.

2. In small groups, identify a crisis situation in supervision and role-play the scenario. Have different members in the group take turns role-playing interventions with the supervisee. Then discuss what seemed to work best with this situation.

3. Brainstorm a list of all the possible crisis situations that might occur in supervision. Identify the ones that would be the most difficult to handle and brainstorm possible interventions for those.

4. Invite an experienced supervisor to come to class and discuss his or her experience handling crisis situations in supervision. Ask what he or she has learned from those experiences.

5. In small groups, have each member discuss which crisis situations would be most difficult and which would be easiest to handle. See where there are commonalities, and have a spokesperson from each small group share those themes with the class.

6. Access the Web site for this text at http://info.wadsworth.com/haynes, and complete the self-assessment inventory. Additional contributor perspectives and other activities specific to this chapter are also available to you at this Web site.

EVALUATION IN SUPERVISION

1. What do you think of when you hear the term *evaluation* as it relates to supervision? What is the value of evaluation? Must it always be a part of supervision? Explain.

2. What were some of your experiences when you were evaluated by a supervisor? Generally, was the evaluation experience helpful or not? What did you learn from those experiences that will influence your role as an evaluator in supervision?

3. What methods of evaluation did your supervisor use? Did you find them useful? Could you see yourself using similar methods?

4. What do you think you could do to decrease the anxiety many supervisees experience surrounding the evaluation process?

5. What value do you place on objective versus subjective evaluation methods in supervision?

INTRODUCTION

Evaluating supervisees is challenging for most supervisors. Professional standards exist regarding evaluation, but few standards address issues such as the specific tools, procedures, and frequency of the evaluation process. Although the professions of psychology, social work, and counseling are based on a foundation of research and objectivity, the evaluation of supervisees has little standardization. The purpose of this chapter is to define the process and methods of evaluation so that supervisors can approach the task of evaluation with a clearly defined plan.

Much of this chapter is based on my (Bob Haynes's) 28 years of experience as a training director and clinical supervisor with doctoral level psychology interns and prelicensed psychologists. The ideas in this chapter reflect what I have learned about the evaluation process from experimentation and by paying attention to feedback from interns, students, and colleagues. As a part of my work, I had the opportunity to serve as an accreditation team member reviewing internship programs throughout the country. The programs I visited had developed a variety of evaluation methods and procedures, which broadened my perspective on the methods that clinical programs and training sites rely on to evaluate their supervisees. What I found most useful about these experiences was that they served as the catalyst for self-reflection on what evaluation is and how best to accomplish it.

Evaluation is an essential component of accomplishing the four defined goals of supervision.

1. In promoting development and teaching the supervisee, evaluation measures the degree to which learning is taking place.

2. In protecting the welfare of the client, evaluation ensures that the supervisee is measuring up to established standards of clinical and ethical competence.

3. In serving the gatekeeping function for the profession, monitoring supervisee performance is a cornerstone in providing information about the

supervisee's professional and clinical competence as well as his or her suitability for the profession.

4. In fostering the empowerment of the supervisee to be able to work as an independent professional, the evaluation process serves as a model for the supervisee to learn how to self-evaluate and continue to learn and grow throughout his or her career as a helping professional.

Evaluation can be defined as the objective appraisal of the supervisee's performance based on clearly defined criteria that are realistic and attainable (Kadushin, 1992). Evaluation results should be communicated to supervisees in a regular, periodic, and systematic manner that fosters continued learning and development as a helping professional.

Evaluation of supervisees is required by most of the professional and licensing standards. Box 10.1 lists some of the professional standards relevant to evaluation in supervision. Although these standards may vary in detail in addressing evaluation, there is consistency across the professions regarding the need for regular feedback and evaluation as an expected part of supervision. Supervisors, then, are obligated ethically and legally to provide feedback and evaluation to the supervisee regarding his or her clinical work. Evaluations have a legal aspect in that some degree of liability goes with both the responsibility of evaluating the supervisee's performance and evaluating the performance accurately for the supervisee, professional associations, licensing boards, and employers. An evaluation that is inaccurate can have serious implications for the supervisee as well as the supervisor. The Voices from the Field feature supports Robiner's (1998a) opinion that there is a widespread leniency bias within psychology's quality assurance mechanisms.

This chapter focuses on guidelines for conducting evaluations, methods of evaluation, and concerns of both supervisors and supervisees regarding the evaluation process. In addition, we discuss how to write letters of recommendation and the importance of empowering supervisees to conduct self-evaluations as part of their career-long professional development.

We provide samples of various evaluation tools in this chapter, but it is not enough to simply use some objective measure to evaluate performance. The competent supervisor should examine the various issues in the evaluation process and develop a personal position on the standards, objectives, and methods of supervision. It is essential for supervisors to demonstrate a willingness to continue to learn about how they can best use evaluation as a communication tool with supervisees to help them learn, grow, and develop confidence as professionals.

ESSENTIAL FEATURES OF EVALUATION

Objective Versus Subjective Evaluation

In our experience, most evaluation by supervisors has been largely subjective rather than objective. Very few standardized methods of evaluating supervisees have existed, and supervisors have had to develop their own systems to

| # ETHICS CODES AND STANDARDS REGARDING EVALUATION IN SUPERVISION

American Counseling Association
Code of Ethics and Standards of Practice (1995)
F.2.c. Evaluation. Counselors clearly state to students and supervisees, in advance of training, the levels of competency expected, appraisal methods, and timing of evaluations for both didactic and experiential components. Counselors provide students and supervisees with periodic performance appraisal and evaluation feedback throughout the training program.

American Psychological Association
Ethical Principles of Psychologists and Code of Conduct (1992)
6.05 Assessing Student and Supervisee Performance
(a) In academic and supervisory relationships, psychologists establish an appropriate process for providing feedback to students and supervisees.
(b) Psychologists evaluate students and supervisees on the basis of their actual performance on relevant and established program requirements.

Association for Counselor Education and Supervision
Ethical Guidelines for Counseling Supervisors (1993)
2. Supervisory role
Inherent and integral to the role of the supervisor are responsibilities for:
c. monitoring clinical performance and professional development of supervisees; and
d. evaluating and certifying current performance and potential of supervisees for academic, screening, selection, placement, employment, and credentialing purposes.

2.12 Supervisors, through ongoing supervisee assessment and evaluation, should be aware of any personal or professional limitations of supervisees which are likely to impede future professional performance. Supervisors have the responsibility of recommending remedial assistance to the supervisee and of screening from the training program, applied counseling setting, or state licensure those supervisees who are unable to provide competent professional services. These recommendations should be clearly and professionally explained in writing to the supervisees who are so evaluated.

3.16 Evaluations of supervisee performance in universities and in applied counseling settings should be available to supervisee in ways consistent with the Family Rights and Privacy Act and the Buckley Amendment.

Association for Counselor Education and Supervision
Standards for Counseling Supervisors (1990)
10. Professional counseling supervisors demonstrate knowledge and competency in the evaluation of counseling performance.
The counseling supervisor:
10.1 can interact with the counselor from the perspective of evaluator;
10.2 can identify the counselor's professional and personal strengths, as well as weaknesses;
10.3 provides specific feedback about such performance as conceptualization, use of methods and techniques, relationship skills, and assessment;
10.4 determines the extent to which the counselor has developed and applied his/her own personal theory of counseling;
10.5 develops evaluation procedures and instruments to determine program and counselor goal attainment;
10.6 assists the counselor in the description and measurement of his/her progress and achievement; and

10.7 can develop counseling skills for purposes of grade assignment, completion of internship requirements, professional advancement, and so on.

Association of State and Provincial Psychology Boards
Report of the ASPPB: Task Force on Supervision Guidelines (1998)
Evaluation of Doctoral Candidates for Licensure
I.V. Written and Oral Evaluation
A. Evaluations provide objective assessment and direct feedback about the supervisee's competence in order to facilitate skill acquisition and professional growth. They are necessary to ensure that supervisees achieve identified objectives. At the outset of the supervisory period each supervisor together with the supervisee shall establish a written contract that specifies: a) the competencies to be evaluated and the goals to be attained; b) the standards for measuring performance; c) the time frame for goal attainment. Direct feedback should be ongoing with written evaluations provided at least quarterly. Written evaluation of the supervisor by the supervisee should be provided at the end of the training program.

National Association of Social Workers
Code of Ethics (1999)
3.01 Supervision and Consultation
(d) Social workers who provide supervision should evaluate supervisees' performance in a manner that is fair and respectful.

3.03 Performance and Evaluation
Social workers who have responsibility for evaluating the performance of others should fulfill such responsibility in a fair and considerate manner and on the basis of clearly stated criteria.

National Association of Social Workers
Guidelines for Clinical Social Work Supervision (1994)
Supervisor Obligations
The supervisor has the responsibility to fulfill obligations to the auspices of supervision and to the supervisee. The supervisor should:
- Evaluate the supervisee's role and conceptual understanding in the treatment process, and his or her use of a theoretical base and social work principles,
- Provide periodic evaluation of the supervisee.

National Board for Certified Counselors
Standards for the Ethical Practice of Clinical Supervision (1999)
In addition to following the NBCC Code of Ethics pertaining to the practice of professional counseling, clinical supervisors shall:
7. Provide supervisees with adequate and timely feedback as part of an established evaluation plan.

---

evaluate performance and professional behavior. Individual training programs have developed their own assessment and evaluation procedures, which have lacked specificity and empirical foundation (Robiner, 1998b). In a survey of psychology internship programs, Robiner, Fuhrman, Ristved, Bobbitt, and Schirvar (1994) found that evaluation practices lacked validation, were fairly general, and varied in scope, scaling, and content. In recent

VOICES FROM THE FIELD

Bob Haynes

A doctoral psychology student came to our internship training program for a year of intensive clinical training. When she began to show deficiencies in basic clinical tasks in assessment and therapy early in the training year, I went back to the application to review what faculty and clinical supervisors had said about her abilities. The letters of recommendation were consistently positive about her abilities, without a single reference to any deficiencies. When I contacted the training director at the doctoral program, I received a somewhat different picture of the intern. Deficiencies had been suspected and noted by some faculty and supervisors—but not consistently enough to result in any of the referees mentioning

this in their letters of recommendation. This situation was difficult for our training staff as well as for the intern. No one had counseled her previously about these deficiencies, and she thought her clinical performance was adequate. This failure to provide accurate evaluative information both to the student and to our program resulted in considerable time and energy being expended with this student. In addition, the student struggled throughout the year trying to determine whether the problem was with her clinical skills or with our evaluation process. It was a difficult situation for all of us, and one that could have been avoided had accurate and objective feedback been provided to the student from the beginning.

years, more objective and standardized evaluation tools have been developed, but this area is in its infancy. Standardization of evaluation procedures and the development of tools based on research are fertile fields for further study.

Robiner, Fuhrman, and Ristvedt (1993) suggest that evaluation falls into two major categories: formative and summative. *Formative evaluation* involves providing ongoing evaluation, typically in the form of feedback throughout the supervisory process, to facilitate the supervisee's long-term professional growth and development. *Summative evaluation* refers to evaluation episodes wherein a supervisor provides specific evaluation of how a supervisee is performing. Supervisors seem to be more comfortable with formative evaluation as a normal part of their role and function and less comfortable with summative evaluation.

Standardization of Methods

Supervisors are more likely to participate in the evaluation process when standardized procedures and evaluation forms are in place. Many agencies, schools, and field training sites have developed rating forms and other tools by which to provide evaluation of supervisees and supervisors. Many of these forms are thorough and objective, though few have undertaken the rigors of reliability and validity testing that should be conducted on these measures. Progress with the standardization of evaluation tools is demonstrated by the University of Minnesota *Quality Assessment and Improvement Systems*™ (Robiner, 1998b). The main instrument is the Minnesota Supervisory Inventory (MSI), which is used to evaluate supervisees using an anchored scale of items reflecting a range of areas of professional functioning. This instrument will be described in detail later in the chapter under the topic of Objective Evaluation Tools. For a look at how one professional views the evaluation process, read the Voices from the Field feature.

Criteria for Evaluation

It is extremely helpful when supervisors have specific and clear criteria for evaluation and these are included in the supervision contract. Having established criteria gives the supervisor standards by which to measure the performance and conduct of the supervisee. The difficulty is that standards of competence in the helping professions are not clear-cut. However, professional associations and licensing bodies, as well as doctoral programs and training sites, have attempted to determine the criteria for measuring competence. The MSI provides one way to delineate criteria (Robiner, 1998b). The criteria domains found in this evaluation instrument include assessment competence, psychotherapy and intervention competence, consultation competence, professional conduct, ethical and legal conduct, responsiveness to supervision, professional presentations/case conferences, and research.

Supervisors must distinguish between performance and personality. In the helping professions, the personal characteristics of supervisees play a major role in their clinical abilities. It is possible for supervisees to perform adequately yet receive a negative evaluation from their supervisors based largely on personality factors. The difficulty, then, is in learning to separate out and measure those personal characteristics that are essential to clinical competence. Frame and Stevens-Smith (1995) have operationalized those personal characteristics for the purpose of evaluation. They identified nine supervisee characteristics often cited in the literature related to counselor success: openness, flexibility, positive attitude, cooperative, willingness to accept and use feedback, awareness of one's impact on others, ability to deal with conflict, accepts personal responsibility, and expresses feelings appropriately.

In summary, there is still much to be learned about the criteria for measuring competence in the helping professional. Nonetheless, supervisors can use criteria and measures that have been developed rather than relying on subjective or poorly defined criteria and measures of clinical competence. The competent supervisor is one who is looking for better ways to accomplish the goals of supervision using criteria for evaluation.

VOICES FROM THE FIELD

Heriberto G. Sánchez, Ph.D.

In my view the supervision process involves assessing, correcting or improving, and monitoring. The supervisor and supervisee must assess the strengths and weaknesses of the supervisee, develop a plan to correct or improve weaknesses, and monitor the effectiveness of the supervision plan. There must be a clear baseline and identifiable goals. Rating scales that identify key areas of work performance are good evaluation tools. Rating scales provide standardization and easy comparison with other supervisees. However, evaluation tools must be able to address the specific needs of the supervisee. In most situations, the supervisor will also need to individu-

alize some portion of the supervision plan and develop a method to assess those individualized areas. Obviously, the supervisor and supervisee must meet on a regular basis to exchange information and review their progress toward the identified goals. This is the most critical part of the evaluation process. The supervisor must be able to provide feedback in a constructive and nonthreatening manner. It is also important that the supervisor use these sessions to congratulate supervisees for their good work. Feedback should be provided on an ongoing basis so supervisees can incorporate this information in their work.

Organization of Evaluation

The evaluation process is most effective when it is planned and organized and discussed with the supervisee at the beginning of the supervisory relationship. It is essential that evaluation procedures, methods, and time frames be clearly spelled out in the supervision contract. This encourages the supervisor to have a well-developed plan about the role and methods of evaluation rather than having to develop something at the eleventh hour before the evaluation is scheduled to occur. The American Counseling Association *Code of Ethics and Standards of Practice* (1995) states this idea clearly:

> Counselors clearly state to students and supervisees, in advance of training, the levels of competency expected, appraisal methods, and timing of evaluations for both didactic and experiential components. Counselors provide students and supervisees with periodic performance appraisal and evaluation feedback throughout the training program. (F.2.c.)

It is essential that evaluation occur throughout the course of supervision on a regular and systematic basis. Supervisees have a right to know when to expect evaluations as well as to be familiar with the forms, methods, and processes used for evaluation. It is crucial that evaluation be conducted early enough in the clinical experience of the supervisee so that he or she has adequate time to correct any deficits identified by the supervisor. The supervision contract should include due process information regarding how the process will proceed when deficiencies are identified and what recourse the supervisee has to challenge and/or remediate the deficiencies.

Due Process

Due process, as defined in the chapter on legal issues, is a means of providing to supervisees clear expectations for performance and a procedure for handling adverse actions when those performance expectations are not met. The supervisor is obligated ethically to provide due process regarding evaluation of supervisees. Supervisees have a right to be informed in writing of the procedures for evaluation, which include how and when it will occur, what the consequences of a serious negative evaluation might be, what recourse they will have to correct any deficiencies identified, what they can do if they would like to challenge the evaluation results, and what the course of appeal is in the case of a seriously negative evaluation with which they do not agree.

Long-Term Consequences of Evaluations

Evaluation of supervisees often has significant long-term effects on the careers of helping professionals. Once evaluations are completed, they become a permanent part of the supervisee's record and become the basis for making recommendations for employment, licensing, and professional association membership. As an internship director, I (Bob) received many requests each year to verify supervisees' performance during internship, in some cases going back more than 25 years. Evaluation results become a part of the supervisee's record for many, many years. It would be helpful for both supervisors and supervisees to consider these far-reaching effects when participating in the evaluation process. Supervisees do not have to agree with the results of an evaluation just to be compliant. If they disagree with the evaluation, they can take steps to contest the evaluation before it becomes a part of their permanent record. Supervisors are obligated ethically and legally to ensure that the evaluation is objective and fair and provides due process for the supervisee.

Empowering the Supervisee to Conduct Self-Evaluation

The ultimate goal for supervision is to empower the supervisee to be able to self-supervise throughout his or her professional career. A major part of this self-supervision includes the ability to self-evaluate. This ability to assess one's owns strengths and deficits, to know the limits of one's competence, to seek supervision and consultation when necessary, and to continue to learn through reading and continuing education is the hallmark of a competent helping professional.

Supervisors can foster the development of self-evaluation in their supervisees by modeling this same behavior and demonstrating openness to learn and grow, to be open to feedback about their own performance as a supervisor, and to provide the tools and skills necessary for self-supervision.

Todd (1997) indicates that one way to do this is to discuss with the supervisee that a major goal of supervision is to develop the supervisee's ability to self-supervise and self-evaluate. By bringing this goal of supervision into focus, the supervisory relationship changes and supervisees become more equal in the supervisory process. In Todd's model, supervisees learn about the process of self-supervision as the supervisor openly participates in a process of self-examination regarding feedback on how the supervisory process is going. He likes to reserve 5 minutes at the end of each supervisory session for a discussion of what was helpful for the supervisee in the session and why. This process of self-evaluation on behalf of the supervisor serves as an excellent model in helping the supervisee learn to self-supervise.

EVALUATION OF THE SUPERVISOR

Supervision is very often a one-way street in which the supervisor evaluates the performance of the supervisee. However, a comprehensive evaluation process includes an assessment of the performance of the supervisor by the supervisee and by the agency, department, or the supervisor's supervisor where appropriate. Some supervisors are simply not open to this idea, but those that are can use this feedback as an opportunity for their growth and learning. The supervisor and supervisee could review and discuss the feedback from the supervisee and discuss what actions can be taken to improve the supervisory process. This requires a supervisor who is well grounded, confident, and open to improvement. Here are some of the topics on which supervisors can be evaluated:

- Availability
- Communication skills
- Cultural competence
- Ethical and legal knowledge
- Clinical and professional knowledge
- Professionalism
- Provision of useful feedback and evaluation
- Punctuality
- Responsiveness to supervisee's needs and ideas
- Resolution of issues/conflicts promptly and professionally
- Role model for the supervisee
- Supervision of psychotherapy
- Supportiveness
- Use of supervision interventions

It is helpful to learn what feedback supervisees have regarding your performance as a supervisor. Supervisees are more likely to be forthcoming with both positive and negative feedback when the evaluation is in writing and is conducted at the conclusion of the supervisory relationship. This is not to say that you should not have ongoing evaluation and discussion of how the supervision is going for the supervisee, but most often the true feelings of a supervisee are more likely to come out after the supervision has concluded. Even so, supervisees know that you will be asked to write letters of recommendation for many years to come, and they may be reluctant to provide feedback that is too critical or negative. The candor in providing honest feedback to the supervisor directly relates to the level of mutual trust and respect that developed in the course of the supervisory relationship.

Box 10.2 illustrates one type of supervisor evaluation form, which was developed as part of the University of Minnesota program on *Quality Assessment and Improvement Systems*™ (Robiner, 1998b). This is an excellent example of a comprehensive tool for use by supervisees in evaluating supervisors. The abbreviated form presented here contains a representative sample of the actual items.

ETHICAL AND LEGAL RAMIFICATIONS OF CONDUCTING EVALUATIONS

Supervisors are ethically bound to provide accurate evaluations of the supervisee's progress (ACA, 1995; ACES, 1990, 1993; APA, 1992; ASPPB, 1998; NASW, 1994, 1999; NBCC, 1999). The report of the Association of State and Provincial Psychology Boards (1998) captures the requirements for evaluation in supervision best:

> Evaluations provide objective assessment and direct feedback about the supervisee's competence in order to facilitate skill acquisition and professional growth. They are necessary to ensure that supervisees achieve identified objectives. At the outset of the supervisory period each supervisor together with the supervisee shall establish a written contract that specifies: a) the competencies to be evaluated and the goals to be attained; b) the standards for measuring performance; c) the time frame for goal attainment. Direct feedback should be ongoing with written evaluations provided at least quarterly. Written evaluation of the supervisor by the supervisee should be provided at the end of the training program. (I.V.A.)

This standard addresses the evaluation of doctoral candidates for licensure, but it is readily applicable to most supervision situations.

Written evaluations and letters of recommendation that are inaccurately positive or negative can have serious consequences. Supervisors should avoid the tendency to minimize or omit any negative information or to give inaccurately positive evaluations. On the other hand, a supervisee could sue a supervisor who provides an inaccurately negative evaluation that hampers the supervisee's ability to seek employment, licensure, and professional association membership. The burden is on supervisors to provide accurate and fair evaluations based on objective information that supports their findings.

BOX 10.2 | MINNESOTA SUPERVISOR EVALUATION:
SUMMARY BY SUPERVISEE
(abbreviated sample document)

Supervisee:_____   **Supervisor:**_____
Date: _____to_____   **Rotation:**_____

Instructions: This form enables a supervisee to provide constructive feedback about their experiences with their supervisor. The ratings range from "Excellent" to "Attention Desired" and are based on comparisons with training experiences with other supervisors. Rate only those items that pertain to your training experience this past training period. For areas in which contact with this supervisor was too limited to make a valid determination, please indicate "does not apply."

A. **General Characteristics of Supervision** THE SUPERVISOR:	Attention Desired	Meets Needs	Excellent	Does Not Apply
1. Was accessible for discussion, questions, etc.	1	2	3	N A
2. Allotted sufficient time for supervision and scheduled supervision meetings appropriately.	1	2	3	NA
3. Kept sufficiently informed of case(s).	1	2	3	NA
17 items deleted from sample document				
Other/comments:				

B. **Development of Clinical Skills** THE SUPERVISOR:	Attention Desired	Meets Needs	Excellent	Does Not Apply
1. Assisted in coherent conceptualization of clinical work.	1	2	3	NA
2. Assisted in translation of conceptualization into techniques and procedures.	1	2	3	NA
3. Was effective in providing training in assessment, evaluation, and diagnosis.	1	2	3	NA
5 items deleted from sample document				
Other/comments:				

C. **The Rotation Experience**	Attention Desired	Meets Needs	Excellent	Does Not Apply
1. The supervisee's role as a professional on the rotation:	1	2	3	NA
2. The supervisee's development of assessment skills (i.e., interviewing, observation, psychometric, diagnosis, and report preparation):	1	2	3	NA
3. The supervisee's development of intervention skills (i.e., therapy competence and proficiencies):	1	2	3	NA
6 items deleted from sample document				
Other/comments:				

D. **Summary**	Attention Desired	Meets Needs	Excellent	Does Not Apply
1. Overall rating of supervision with this supervisor.	1	2	3	NA
2. Overall rating of rotation experience with this supervisor.	1	2	3	NA
3. Describe how the supervisor and the rotation contributed to your learning:				
4. Describe how supervision and/or the rotation could be enhanced:				

_____   _____   _____   _____
Supervisee's Signature   Date Reviewed   Supervisor's Signature   Date Reviewed

GUIDELINES FOR CONDUCTING EVALUATIONS

From our experience, the evaluation of supervisees can be a positive and valuable experience for both the supervisee and the supervisor. Those positive experiences occur when evaluation is taken seriously as an important part of supervision and when careful planning and development have gone into the evaluation process. Let's look at some of the guidelines for developing the evaluation process and conducting evaluation sessions. It is essential that supervisors have a clear picture of the evaluation objectives, criteria, and process, and make sure the supervisee is informed of these early in the supervisory relationship and in the supervision contract.

Evaluation seems most effective as a continuous process. It is best that evaluation formally occur several times over the course of supervision, and also on a regular informal basis. Present a balanced evaluation of both the supervisee's strengths and deficiencies. Some supervisors tend to focus more heavily on the deficiencies.

When the supervisee is not open to feedback and evaluation, help the supervisee become aware of and explore that aspect of his or her learning. That could be done by helping the supervisee look at the feedback provided from various sources and how he or she has processed that information. Conduct evaluations frequently enough to keep the supervisee apprised of his or her progress and need for improvement, and give the supervisee ample time to remedy any deficiencies. The frequency of evaluations depends on the needs of the situation and the length of time over which the supervision will occur.

Be clear on the administrative structure for the evaluation and who else needs to be involved. How does this evaluation process fit into the agency evaluation process, and is it compatible with employment practices? Does this evaluation process satisfy the needs of the graduate training program or licensing board?

Try to involve in the evaluation process those who have significant contact or supervision with the supervisee. If they cannot attend the evaluation meeting, call them or send them a form to complete to give input into the progress of the supervisee.

Involve the supervisee in the evaluation process. If feedback is given routinely, there will be no surprises for the supervisee when the formal evaluation session occurs. Encourage supervisees to evaluate their own progress and discuss how their evaluation may vary from yours.

In conducting the evaluation conference, be sure the supervisee knows when and where it will occur and what to expect in the session. Try to meet in a room or office that is private and free of interruptions from the phone or drop-ins. Be as clear as possible in stating your evaluation of the supervisee's performance. Use specific examples of his or her performance to illustrate. Ask supervisees to evaluate their training, including the value of the supervision and what could be improved about the supervisory relationship.

Be clear on what needs to be accomplished from here; that is, explain the remediation necessary to correct any problems and include time frames, behavioral expectations, how progress will be assessed, and who will conduct the assessment. Document the session. It is essential to have accurate records of the supervisee's performance and conduct. Ongoing documentation of the supervisory sessions and critical incidents will provide a basis for the periodic formal evaluations and serve as a record for providing information regarding the supervisee's performance under your supervision to employers, licensing boards, and professional associations.

The issue of openness to supervision should be a major topic of any evaluation—this is key in the supervisee's ability to grow and learn. As a supervisor, model openness to feedback. Try to evaluate performance and behavior and not personality styles. On the other hand, personal issues that affect the supervisee's clinical work should be addressed as a part of the evaluation process.

Be sure to address the supervisee's awareness and abilities with multicultural issues. Box 10.3 provides a list of areas to include in the evaluation of the supervisee.

Concerns of Supervisors

For some supervisors, being trained as a counselor may not translate well to being an evaluator. The training in many counseling, marriage and family therapy, social work, and psychology programs emphasizes that a good counselor is one who does not form judgments about clients. Counselors work hard not to judge and evaluate the client. The tendency is to foster that same approach in the supervisory relationship, which many supervisors liken to the counseling relationship.

Some supervisors do not want to provide what they consider to be negative feedback, especially when they have formed a collegial relationship with the supervisee (Welfel, 2002). Ladany and Melincoff (1999) found in their study that the most frequently cited nondisclosure by supervisors is that of negative reactions to supervisees' counseling and professional performance.

Many supervisors simply do not have evaluation tools available to them and have to rely on their own devices to develop the tools and the procedures for evaluation. Supervisors may struggle with the problem of whether they are evaluating the performance or the personality characteristics of the supervisee and what role each plays in clinical competence.

Sometimes a supervisor does not enjoy working with a particular supervisee. In those instances, the evaluation of the supervisee may become more difficult as the supervisor tries to sort out his or her feelings about the supervisee versus his or her objective evaluation of the supervisee's performance.

The supervisor may determine that the supervisee can do the basic clinical work but that he or she does not seem well suited for the profession. This may be due to the personal characteristics of the supervisee, idiosyncrasies of the supervisor, personality differences between the supervisee and supervisor, or some other reason. In any case, if the supervisor truly believes the supervisee is not appropriate for the profession, the task is how to determine that objectively and how to present specific feedback to a supervisee in a timely way that allows for the possibility of remediation. It is essential that due

AREAS TO ASSESS
IN EVALUATING SUPERVISEES

- Intervention knowledge and skills
- Assessment knowledge and skills
- Relationships with staff and clients
- Responsiveness to supervision
- Awareness of limitations and knowing when to seek outside help
- Communication skills
- Ethical and legal practice
- Multicultural competence
- Judgment and maturity
- Openness to personal development
- Compliance with agency policies and procedures

process be provided to the supervisee. Supervisors must realize that one letter to a licensing board stating that the supervisee is unfit for the profession could be sufficient to ruin a career.

Supervisors are being held increasingly accountable and ethically and legally liable for evaluations by professional associations, licensing boards, employers, and supervisees themselves (Falvey, 2002). For that reason, many supervisors do not like to put their observations and evaluative statements on paper. Many issues that supervisors have with evaluation lead to a desire to avoid the evaluation process altogether, but supervisors must be able to substantiate their observations and their evaluation of the supervisee. By developing a system of evaluation using established criteria and measures, supervisors can find their role as evaluators tolerable and productive for both the supervisor and the supervisee.

Concerns of Supervisees

Supervisees have many concerns about the evaluation of their performance and conduct as well. They have a lot on the line, including years of schooling, success in their new career, future income, and the simple concern of wanting to perform well as a new counselor with acceptance into the profession.

Most trainees and professionals experience anxiety about being evaluated. Concerns about performing well, being liked, and having the basic skills are common to all professionals and certainly those in the helping professions. It is reassuring to hear from a respected supervisor and professional in one's field that one is progressing, performing well, and has what it takes to contribute as a helping professional. Anxiety associated with being evaluated by a supervisor is very common among supervisees.

Dealing with the hypercritical supervisor is difficult for a supervisee, and there are some supervisors who delight in being the all-knowing teacher and in telling the supervisee what he or she is doing wrong. Some supervisors see this as their primary task as a supervisor and are unwilling to temper the negative feedback with feedback about a supervisee's strengths. A supervisee in this situation is facing a dilemma about how to respond to the hypercritical supervisor: "Do I challenge the supervisor? Do I keep quiet and try to get through the experience? Do I seek out another supervisor? What will be the consequences of these actions? Will I make the supervisor feel bad if I challenge him or her?"

Because most supervisees would like to receive a positive evaluation, the tendency for them is to present an overly positive description of their clinical work when self-reporting to their supervisors. This is a major problem for supervisees and supervisors because supervisees will not receive accurate feedback from their supervisors unless they are honest in providing information about their clinical work. Supervisors will not get an accurate reading of the skills and abilities of their supervisees if they are not forthcoming. Supervisors need to develop a supportive and trusting atmosphere to foster supervisees' forthrightness. Direct observation of supervisees' work is necessary to ensure an accurate picture of supervisees' clinical abilities.

Supervisees suffer from not knowing what to expect from the supervision, from the clinical experience, and from the evaluation process. It is imperative that supervisors clarify all of this in the supervision contract and the informed consent agreement early in the supervisory relationship. If not, supervisees will expend a considerable amount of their training energy trying to determine what is expected of them and how they will be evaluated.

Supervisees are not always told who has access to information from the supervisory sessions. Is the information that is shared between supervisor and supervisee confidential? Can the supervisor share it with others? With whom? Can the supervisee share it with others? With whom? Can information from evaluations jeopardize a supervisee's career? The supervisor has the responsibility to inform trainees of the parameters of confidentiality regarding the supervisory relationship.

What recourse does a supervisee have if he or she disagrees with the evaluation? Supervisees are often at a loss as to what recourse is available if they receive an evaluation with which they disagree. Can they challenge it? Should they? How do they proceed if they want to challenge? Supervisees have the right to challenge an evaluation and should be informed of the process for doing so early in supervision.

METHODS OF EVALUATION

One type of evaluation is the initial assessment of a new supervisee. This first task in supervision is to make an assessment of the needs and goals of the supervision, the setting, the client, and your own areas of expertise as a supervisor. This means taking time before the first supervision session to jot down ideas regarding assessment and also to provide an agenda for discussion in the first supervision session.

Here are some areas to consider as you formulate a supervision plan:

- What are the goals of supervision for this group or individual?
- What are the main supervisory roles that I will serve for the supervisee(s)?
- What are the licensing and/or agency policies pertinent to this supervision?
- Will group or individual supervision provide the most effective and economical approach?
- Which supervision methods will serve the goals of this supervision best?
- What methods of evaluation will I use and will there be requirements for documentation or reporting on the supervisee's performance?
- Where and when will we meet?
- Can I anticipate any legal or ethical concerns that might arise?
- What are the particular issues about the individual or group that I will be supervising? Are there multicultural considerations?

Considering these issues prior to the first session should assist you in developing a clear plan for supervision.

Individual and Group Evaluation

Supervisors provide evaluation in a variety of ways. The most common is providing evaluative feedback one-on-one with the supervisee. This can be done at any time in supervision as well as at predetermined sessions for formal evaluation. Another form of evaluation commonly used is for a group of professionals who have worked with the supervisee to arrange a meeting with the supervisee to provide evaluative feedback. The advantage of the group method is that it provides for identification of common themes that those working with the supervisee have seen. It also gives a chance for the group to discuss the training objectives of the supervisee for the next period. Read the Voices from the Field feature to see how one program handles ongoing evaluation.

Written Evaluation

In some instances, the supervisor completes a written evaluation form and discusses the results with the supervisee. This can serve as the basis for the individual or group evaluation session and can provide some structure for that meeting. Some forms have a place for the supervisee to sign to indicate that he or she has read it and to indicate whether the supervisee agrees with the ratings on the evaluation.

Evaluation of Direct Observation

Evaluation can be done following the direct observation of the supervisee's clinical work. Supervision methods discussed in Chapter 4 describe this process. Evaluation following a direct observation can be very effective because it is based on current observation of performance.

VOICES FROM THE FIELD

Bob Haynes

In the internship program which I directed, intern performance is evaluated in several ways. Early in the training year, interns, with input from their major supervisor, develop a list of goals they would like to accomplish for the training year and a list of the activities they hope to participate in to accomplish those goals. That list of goals and activities serves as one basis for reviewing whether interns accomplish what they set out to over the year. Supervisors are asked to complete a written evaluation regarding each intern on the established rating form every quarter. The supervisor then discusses his or her evaluation of the intern's performance, and the intern signs the evaluation form indicating whether the evaluation was discussed with the trainee and whether he or she agreed with the ratings.

At six months and at the end of the training year, a group evaluation session is scheduled, which is attended by the intern and all of his or her supervisors and seminar leaders. Each supervisor shares verbally how he or she thought the intern performed and what areas need further work in the next quarter. The intern is included in a discussion of the findings from the supervisors. In addition, the intern gives feedback on the performance of the supervisors and the strengths and deficiencies of the training program. Interns also complete written evaluations of the program and their supervisors at six months and at the end of the year.

Objective Evaluation Tools

Most formal academic and clinical training sites use written evaluation forms. More often than not, the program or site has developed its own evaluation form. Few standardized evaluation tools have been available, and each program or site has its own specific evaluation needs. Three sample forms are provided here, but none may suit your particular needs entirely. Nevertheless, you can begin to see what topics are addressed by examining these evaluation tools.

An abbreviated version of the MSI form can be found in Box 10.4. The abbreviated MSI provides the format and sample items found in each of the competency areas. The MSI has been empirically derived and uses an anchored scale for supervisors to evaluate the clinical work of supervisees in eight domains. The University of Minnesota *Quality Assessment and Improvement Systems*™ (Robiner, 1998) serves as a model for a comprehensive supervisory system that provides standardized materials addressing numerous aspects of supervisor and supervisee functioning and providing tools and procedures for dealing with a range of administrative and supervisory functions. This program evaluation system comprehensively appraises trainee performance, supervisor performance, and multiple program elements. The tools described in the *Quality Assessment and Improvement Systems*™, including the MSI, may be adapted to fit the evaluation needs of various programs and sites.

BOX 10.4	MINNESOTA SUPERVISORY INVENTORY *(abbreviated sample document)*

Supervisee: _____   Supervisor: _____

Training Site: _____   [   ]Primary Supervisor   [   ]Secondary Supervisor

Population: _____   School: _____

Date _____

Primary Psychotherapeutic Orientation(s) of Supervisee _____

Introduction and Directions: The Minnesota Supervisory Inventory (MSI) is designed to provide constructive feedback to psychology supervisees regarding their professional development in multiple areas. The inventory samples a broad range of professional endeavors in order to enhance content validity and offer the most specific feedback possible. Supervisors are asked to use the 3-point scale below to rate skills, competencies and conduct observed during the experience. The <u>NA</u> response should be used <u>as often as necessary</u> to designate skills or behaviors that were either not applicable or not observed sufficiently so that the MSI documents areas only in which supervisees had supervised training experiences. Therefore, no supervisee will receive numeric ratings on all items. In addition to the ratings, supervisors are encouraged to provide narrative comments about supervisees' professional development. Additional narrative comments can be appended to this form. The MSI also includes ratings of skill levels at the beginning of supervised experiences in order to reflect initial preparedness and subsequent progress. Previous experience and competence should be ascertained through discussion with supervisees. It is recommended that supervisees receive copies of the MSI during their orientation to provide a clear model of the expectations and standards of supervisors and sites. It may also be useful to have supervisees complete the MSI about themselves at the beginning of supervised experiences and review it with supervisors or training directors to elucidate areas in which they believe they have the strongest skills and areas in which they need the greatest development.

Ratings for each competency area (e.g., assessment, etc.) are summarized on the final page. The manner in which ratings affect administrative actions (i.e., pass, probationary pass, fail) is determined by each site. A weighted average of item ratings and/or summary ratings may be helpful in making administrative decisions, though critical incidents, specific items and the constellation of ratings also need to be considered. Transcribing summary scores from each section to the summary section on page 6 facilitates the feedback process.

1   Development Required: Further training and supervision is required to meet expectations.
2   Meets Expectations: Functions adequately to above average for level of training.
3   Exceeds Expectations: Functions exceptionally for level of training.
NA Not Applicable: Not Applicable/Not Observed/Cannot Say.

Summary of Previous (A) and Current (B) Training and Professional Experiences

A. 1. Previous competence in assessment: Limited 1 2 3 4 5 High CS (cannot say)
    2. Previous experience in assessment: Limited 1 2 3 4 5 High CS (cannot say)
    3. Previous competence in intervention: Limited 1 2 3 4 5 High CS (cannot say)
    4. Previous experience in intervention: Limited 1 2 3 4 5 High CS (cannot say)

B. Total number of individual therapy hours: _____ Total number of individual therapy patients:_____
    Total number of group therapy hours:_____ Total number of group therapy patients:_____
    Total number of patient assessments:_____ Mean number of patient assessments weekly:_____
    Description of Current Training: _____

(continued)

BOX 10.4 | MINNESOTA SUPERVISORY INVENTORY *(continued)*

1 = Development Required 2 = Meets Expectations 3 = Exceeds Expectations NA = Not Applicable

1. **ASSESSMENT COMPETENCE**
   1. Judgment in selecting assessment approaches — 1...2...3...NA
   2. Rapport with clients of diverse clinical, age, gender, and cultural groups — 1...2...3...NA
   3. Diagnostic interviewing — 1...2...3...NA
      18 items deleted from sample document
      Overall Competence In Assessment — **1...2...3...NA**
      Progress and Comments about Assessment: _____
      _____

2. **PSYCHOTHERAPY AND INTERVENTION COMPETENCE**
   1. Skill and effectiveness as a therapist — 1...2...3...NA
   2. Rapport with clients — 1...2...3...NA
   3. Empathy, warmth, and genuineness with clients — 1...2...3...NA
      16 items deleted from sample document
      Treatment Modalities
      1. Behavior therapy — 1...2...3...NA
      2. Biofeedback — 1...2...3...NA
      3. Brief or Time-limited therapy — 1...2...3...NA
      17 items deleted from sample document
      Overall Competence In Psychotherapy and Intervention — **1...2...3...NA**
   Progress and Comments about Psychotherapy and Intervention: _____
   _____

3. **CONSULTATION COMPETENCE**
   1. Understanding and handling of consultation role — 1...2...3...NA
   2. Understanding of institutional and systems' dynamics and functions — 1...2...3...NA
   3. Effectiveness as a consultant — 1...2...3...NA
      6 items deleted from sample document
      Overall Competence In Consultation — 1...2...3...NA
   Progress and Comments about Consultation:

4. **ETHICAL, LEGAL, AND PROFESSIONAL CONDUCT**
   1. Awareness of/adherence to APA Ethical Principles,
      Code of Conduct, and other Professional Standards — 1...2...3...NA
   2. Awareness of/adherence to legal (e.g., mandatory reporting, commitment,
      testimony) and regulatory (e.g., Board of Psychology) standards — 1...2...3...NA
   3. Maintains and understands when to suspend confidentiality — 1...2...3...NA
      13 items deleted from sample document
      Overall Ethical, Legal, and Professional Conduct — **1...2...3...NA**
   Progress and Comments about Professional, Ethical, and Legal Conduct: _____
   _____

   Critical Incidents (specify): _____
   _____

5. **SUPERVISION**
   1. Openness and responsiveness to supervision — 1...2...3...NA
   2. Cooperation with supervisor — 1...2...3...NA
   3. Communication with supervisor — 1...2...3...NA
      5 items deleted from sample document
      Overall Response to Supervision — **1...2...3...NA**
   Progress and Comments about Supervision: _____
   _____

1 = Development Required 2 = Meets Expectations 3 = Exceeds Expectations NA = Not Applicable

6. **PROFESSIONAL PRESENTATION(S)/CASE CONFERENCE(S)**
    1. Preparation for presentation(s)   1...2...3...NA
    2. Organization and quality of presentation(s)   1...2...3...NA
    3. Appropriate level of presentation(s)   1...2...3...NA
            3 items deleted from sample document
            Overall Professional Presentation(s)/Case Conference(s) 1...2...3...NA
    Progress and Comments about Presentations: _____

7. **SITE-SPECIFIC- COMPETENCE, SKILLS, AND CONDUCT**
    1. Specify: _____   1...2...3...NA
    2. Specify: _____   1...2...3...NA
            4 items abbreviated from example
            Overall Site-Specific   1...2...3...NA
    Progress and Comments: _____

8. **EVALUATION AND ADMINISTRATION**
    1. Evaluation (e.g., program evaluation)   1...2...3...NA
    2. Program development   1...2...3...NA
            1 item deleted from sample document
            Overall Evaluation and Administration   1...2...3...NA
    Progress and Comments about Evaluation/Administration: _____

9. **RESEARCH**
    1. Conducts research professionally and ethically   1...2...3...NA
    2. Formulation, design, and organization of research   1...2...3...NA
    3. Preparation of literature review (e.g., comprehensive computer searches) 1...2...3...NA
            6 items deleted from sample document
            Overall Research   1...2...3...NA
    Progress and Comments about Research: _____

10. **SUMMARY**
    1. **Assessment** (from p. 2)   1...2...3...NA
    2. **Psychotherapy and Intervention** (from p. 3)   1...2...3...NA
    3. **Consultation** (from p. 4)   1...2...3...NA
    4. **Ethical, Legal, and Professional Conduct** (from p. 4)   1...2...3...NA
    5. **Supervision** (from p. 5)   1...2...3...NA
    6. **Professional Presentation(s)/Case Conference(s)** (from p. 5) 1...2...3...NA
    7. **Site-Specific** (from p. 5)   1...2...3...NA
    8. **Evaluation and Administration** (from p. 5)   1...2...3...NA
    9. **Research** (from p. 6)   1...2...3...NA

Administrative Action: _____Pass_____Probationary Pass_____Fail_____Other:_____

Recommendations For Further Training/Supervision: _____

Supervisor's Signature	**Date**	**Supervisee's Signature**	**Date Reviewed**

The practicum evaluation (Box 10.5) and supervisee performance evaluation (Box 10.6) tools have not been empirically derived but provide samples of evaluation tools being used in university and internship training settings. See Campbell (2000), Falvey, Caldwell, and Cohen (2002), and Storm and Todd (1997) for other samples of evaluation forms.

WRITING LETTERS OF RECOMMENDATION

A natural result of evaluation in supervision is the subsequent letter of recommendation that supervisees request be sent to prospective employers, licensing boards, and professional associations. These letters are commonly based on information resulting from the evaluation of the supervisee. Several studies (Grote, Robiner, & Haut, 2001; Miller & Van Rybroek, 1988; Robiner, Saltzman, Hoberman, Semrud-Clikeman, & Schirvar, 1997) have reviewed the process of writing letters of recommendation for psychology internship applications. They found that these letters were typically exaggerated and inflated in their claims regarding the abilities of the applicant and hence were of questionable value to internship programs in the selection process. As a result of their survey of both writers and readers of letters of recommendation, Grote, Robiner, and Haust (2001) conclude that one cannot presume that letters fully disclose applicants' limitations and problems. Writing letters that are accurate and useful can be both a time-consuming and troubling process for the supervisor who tries to determine how to depict an accurate and objective picture of the supervisee.

When supervisees seek letters of recommendation, keep in mind that most individuals will choose those whom they think will provide the most positive description of their abilities. One supervisor who has worked for many years in the field was quoted as saying, "I've never seen a negative letter of recommendation—and most of them use flowery and complimentary phrases. I just don't put much credence in these letters." This is the case for several reasons. It is counter to our culture to make negative comments about others. When there is negative information, referees are often reluctant to write it down. It may be that they do not want to have to justify their observations, or they may worry about liability issues. Robiner and colleagues (1997) found that many supervisors in their survey indicated that guilt or fear about damaging a supervisee's career was a major factor in being lenient in their letter writing. A referee will sometimes be more candid about an evaluation in a phone conversation, which is off the record.

Some supervisors have ulterior motives for writing the letter. If there is a problem employee or student who has applied for a position elsewhere, the referee may want to write a positive letter to assure that the individual moves on to another department or agency. The letter may not be inaccurate but may fail to describe some of the negatives regarding the individual. Most letters are accurate in what is said, but many do not give a realistic picture of all the strengths and weaknesses of the individual.

BOX 10.5 | PRACTICUM EVALUATION FORM

Northwestern State University
Department of Psychology
Evaluation of Practicum Student

Graduate Student: _____ Date: _____

Faculty Supervisor: _____ Date: _____

Circle one: First Quarter Evaluation   Second Quarter Evaluation   Final Evaluation

Instructions: Please use the following scale to evaluate the student.

N/A = Case did not indicate a need for the behavior and therefore was not observed.

POOR = Behavior is rarely or not evident.

AVERAGE = Behavior sometimes evident.

EXCELLENT = Behavior always evident.

		N/A	Poor	Below Average	Average	Above Average	Excellent
I.	**Initial Sessions**						
A.	Establishes Rapport Responds to client's initial discomfort; uses small talk appropriately to help relax client	0	1	2	3	4	5
B.	Presents Self Professionally Prepared; presents self as a competent professional; prompt	0	1	2	3	4	5
C.	Structures Therapeutic Relationship Verbalizes role and function of therapist and client; explains the therapist's status and supervisory relationship; explains limits of confidentiality; explains & obtains informed consent	0	1	2	3	4	5
D.	Performs Initial Structuring Tasks Use of forms/materials; scheduling information; answers client's questions; permission to audio/videotape	0	1	2	3	4	5
II.	**Facilitative Conditions**						
A.	Conveys Empathic Understanding Reflects client's affect; reflects client's content; responds beyond client's words	0	1	2	3	4	5
B.	Conveys Genuineness Interacts with spontaneity; responds to client's emotions; expresses congruent words/feelings; uses self-disclosure appropriately	0	1	2	3	4	5
C.	Conveys Unconditional Positive Regard Facial expression/words are not judgmental; normalizes clients concerns appropriately	0	1	2	3	4	5

(continued)

BOX 10.5 | PRACTICUM EVALUATION FORM (*continued*)

		N/A	Poor	Below Average	Average	Above Average	Excellent
				2	3	4	5
D.	Conveys Effective Listening Appears attentive; appropriate posture and eye contact; makes physical contact appropriately	0	1	2	3	4	5
E.	Therapist Use of Confrontation Identifies client discrepancies/distortions in content/affect and between verbal and nonverbal behavior; confronts with purpose and in a supportive manner; directs client to deal with confronted content/affect; follows confrontation with active listening/empathy/here and now	0	1	2	3	4	5
F.	Focuses on Therapeutic Relationship Deals with here/now and relationship issues as necessary; responds to client's expressed concerns with the therapy process	0	1	2	3	4	5
III.	**Appropriate Movement through Stages of Therapy Process**						
A.	Stage 1: Clarification of the Problem Obtains present behaviors, feelings, symptoms associated with the present problem; obtains relevant background information	0	1	2	3	4	5
B.	Stage 2: Understanding and Goal Setting Identifies client themes by tying prior events to present; restructures client themes when needed; shares impressions with client; uses interpretation appropriately; offers useful/objective perspectives; provides information; identifies/clarifies specific goals	0	1	2	3	4	5
C.	Stage 3: Facilitating Action Utilizes techniques/theory; develops action strategies; facilitates action; evaluates outcomes; offers feedback; models desired behaviors	0	1	2	3	4	5
IV.	**Structures Closing of Session** Alerts client to closing state; uses summary statements at end of session; asks client to clarify/summarize session content; reviews "homework" assignment; ascertains client affective state at closing	0	1	2	3	4	5

		N/A	Poor	Below Average	Average	Above Average	Excellent
		0	1	2	3	4	5
V.	**Termination of Therapeutic Relationship** Appropriately alerts client of termination throughout the relationship; encourages independence; summarizes goals and outcomes; plans for future; addresses closure of therapeutic relationship; describes nature of appropriate future contacts	0	1	2	3	4	5
VI.	**Other Skills/Activities**						
A.	Time management Begins sessions promptly; maintains time limitations	0	1	2	3	4	5
B.	Comfort with/appropriate use of silence	0	1	2	3	4	5
C.	Ability to conceptualize case	0	1	2	3	4	5
D.	Class participation	0	1	2	3	4	5
E.	Promotes positive work climate	0	1	2	3	4	5
F.	Interacts effectively with colleagues	0	1	2	3	4	5
G.	Interacts effectively with supervisors	0	1	2	3	4	5
H.	Demonstrates writing skills	0	1	2	3	4	5
I.	Demonstrates file management	0	1	2	3	4	5
J.	Demonstrates professional behavior	0	1	2	3	4	5
K.	Demonstrates ethical behavior	0	1	2	3	4	5
L.	Is multiculturally sensitive	0	1	2	3	4	5
M.	Demonstrates use of good judgment and counseling skills	0	1	2	3	4	5
N.	Provides appropriate referrals	0	1	2	3	4	5
O.	Accepts and learns from feedback	0	1	2	3	4	5

Summary: Please provide a narrative of your evaluation of the student's performance and indicate what actions you are recommending to help the student with remediation/improvement of those areas of concern.

Overall skills

Overall process

Actions taken

_____   _____
Therapist   Date

_____   _____
Faculty Supervisor   Date

Source: Based on Carkhuff, R. (2000). *The art of helping* (8th ed.). Amherst, MA: Human Resource Development Press; Campbell, J. M. (2000). *Becoming an effective supervisor.* Philadelphia, PA: Accelerated Development. Designed by Cynthia Lindsey and Patrice Moulton (2001). Reprinted with permission.

BOX 10.6	SUPERVISEE PERFORMANCE EVALUATION

Supervisee: _____

Period Rated: _____

Supervisor: _____

Please rate the supervisee's performance for the period indicated. Rate the supervisee in comparison with the average supervisee at the same level of training. Include comments at the bottom when assigning Below or Well Below standard ratings. Review this evaluation with the supervisee and have the supervisee sign at bottom.

Circle one:
1 = Well below standard   2 = Below standard   3 = Standard   4 = Above standard
5 = Well above standard   NA = Not applicable

Professional Practice

a.	Attendance/punctuality	1	2	3	4	5	NA
b.	Responsiveness to supervision	1	2	3	4	5	NA
c.	Relations with staff	1	2	3	4	5	NA
d.	Relationships with clients	1	2	3	4	5	NA
e.	Ethical practice	1	2	3	4	5	NA
f.	Verbal communication	1	2	3	4	5	NA
g.	Written communication	1	2	3	4	5	NA
h.	Treatment team participation	1	2	3	4	5	NA
i.	Understanding of multicultural issues/individual differences	1	2	3	4	5	NA
j.	Seeks supervision when needed	1	2	3	4	5	NA
k	Seeks consultation when needed	1	2	3	4	5	NA
l.	Initiative/independence	1	2	3	4	5	NA
m.	Judgment/maturity	1	2	3	4	5	NA
n.	Open to personal development	1	2	3	4	5	NA

Assessment Skills

a.	Knowledge of instruments and methods	1	2	3	4	5	NA
b.	Formulation of referral questions	1	2	3	4	5	NA
c.	Test administration:						
	Intellectual	1	2	3	4	5	NA
	Neuropsychology	1	2	3	4	5	NA
	Personality	1	2	3	4	5	NA
	Projectives	1	2	3	4	5	NA
d.	Test interpretation:						
	Intellectual	1	2	3	4	5	NA

Neuropsychology	1	2	3	4	5	NA
Personality	1	2	3	4	5	NA
Projectives	1	2	3	4	5	NA
e. Rapport with clients	1	2	3	4	5	NA
f. Report writing	1	2	3	4	5	NA
g. Provides feedback to client	1	2	3	4	5	NA

Intervention Skills

a. Individual therapy skills	1	2	3	4	5	NA
b. Group therapy skills	1	2	3	4	5	NA
c. Rapport/empathy in therapy	1	2	3	4	5	NA
d. Developing a clear treatment plan	1	2	3	4	5	NA
e. Intervention based on theory/research	1	2	3	4	5	NA
f. Intervention based upon client needs	1	2	3	4	5	NA
g. Evaluates progress regularly	1	2	3	4	5	NA
h. Addresses termination issues	1	2	3	4	5	NA

Other

a. _____	1	2	3	4	5	NA
b. _____	1	2	3	4	5	NA
c. _____	1	2	3	4	5	NA

Overall Performance	1	2	3	4	5	NA

COMMENTS:

_____   _____
Supervisor Signature   Date

This evaluation has been reviewed with me. I agree_____ disagree_____ with the evaluation.

_____   _____
Supervisee Signature   Date

Source: Adapted from Northwestern State University, Natchitoches, LA, Department of Psychology, and designed by Cynthia Lindsay and Patrice Moulton, June 2001. Reprinted with permission.

Grote and colleagues (2001) found that letter writers are more likely to include information regarding marginal test administration skills and therapeutic treatment skills and less likely to include information regarding chemical abuse, anxiety or depressive disorders, or unethical behavior. Of those surveyed, 56.4% would refuse to write a letter for a supervisee who has demonstrated unethical behavior, and 46.5% would refuse to write a letter for a supervisee who has problems with chemical abuse. Grote and colleagues indicate that it may be naïve to expect changes in the behavior of letter writers unless there is a culture change and broad efforts within the professions to change this pattern within the quality assurance process. They conclude, "Until supervisors perceive that the other letter writers are expected, and likely, to be accurate and honest, they may well continue to be unwilling to mention any relative weaknesses in their letters for fear of singling out a student" (p. 660). Nonetheless, those authors encourage letter writers to acknowledge in the letters they write that no supervisee is perfect and that the writer will describe some areas of personal and professional growth that the supervisee should work toward accomplishing.

Be aware of the implications and consequences of what you say about the supervisee. Because the majority of letters are so positive, when one writes a letter with both positives and negatives, it is difficult to decipher whether the referee is trying to present an objective picture or send up a subtle red flag. Miller and Van Rybroek (1988) indicate that letters that contain a balanced picture of strengths and deficiencies can appear negative when compared with those that discuss only the positive aspects of the applicant. The letters that stand out are personable and talk about the referee's experience of the supervisee and whether he or she would hire this individual. These letters often include examples of those things the trainee did well or out of the ordinary. To ensure that letters are descriptive and accurate, follow these tips for writing letters of recommendation:

- Develop a plan for addressing strengths and deficiencies. To overstate or understate strengths and deficiencies could be an ethical and a liability issue.
- Keep in mind that many readers look for summary paragraphs and may only read the first and last paragraphs. Give a good, clear summary of how you have experienced the individual in one or both of those paragraphs.
- Letters of recommendation are typically requested at a time when the supervisee is applying for a job, a license, or a professional association membership. Complete the letter in a timely fashion, usually a few weeks. It is best to ask the individual when it is due.
- Keep a copy for your file, and send a copy to the supervisee if appropriate.
- Check to be sure you have the name and address of the person to whom you are sending the letter (misspellings of names can irritate the reader and have a negative impact on how that person views the letter). Also, try to learn something about the setting to which you are writing so you can emphasize topics that would be of most interest to them.

- Be brief and to the point—longer is not better.
- Be sure you are familiar enough with the supervisee's work to write an accurate letter. If you do not know the individual well and you are obligated to write the letter, rely on the evaluations from others and cite or quote their comments regarding the individual.
- When writing a letter that includes a description of serious deficiencies, inform the supervisee, if possible, of the information you plan to include in the letter.
- Do you need a release of information to write a letter? Usually, yes. When you receive requests for letters, you should also receive a release from the individual. Do not write a letter (or for that matter talk to an employer or professional association) about the supervisee unless you have written or verbal (note the date) consent to release the information.
- Be very careful about how you describe deficits. Make sure you use objective, behavioral terms and include examples to illustrate your point. Rather than saying, "He is not a very good clinician," you might say, "His knowledge of cognitive-behavioral interventions is sound, but he tries to use techniques without first building a relationship based on empathy, trust and respect." Describe what the supervisee has done to remediate the deficiencies and how open to feedback and supervision the supervisee was. Keep in mind that since there are so few negatives in these letters the reader will read this very carefully and may attempt to "read between the lines" in determining what you are really trying to say.

By their nature, most letters of recommendation are in fact letters. An alternative is to develop and use a standardized form when asked to write a letter of recommendation. The rating form could conclude with a narrative summary evaluation of the individual. Another option that supervisors who have written many letters of recommendation have chosen is to develop several templates for letters. A template could be developed for each of the several types of letters that supervisors write: employment, licensing applications, postdoctoral fellowships, professional association memberships, and so forth. It is then a matter of filling in the blanks with the names and key evaluative information for the particular individual. When working from a template, you can be sure you are including all of the necessary information.

Ask your supervisees to help you write the best and most accurate letter you can write. You may want to ask that supervisees provide you with the following information in writing: name and address of person receiving the letter, purpose of the letter, and two to three highlights or facts that they would like to have included. The purpose of this information is not to have the supervisee write for you but to have the supervisee actively participate in providing pertinent information. If possible, provide supervisees with the opportunity to review letters of recommendation prior to mailing. Use the checklist in Box 10.7 to be sure you have included all relevant information.

BOX 10.7 | LETTER OF RECOMMENDATION CHECKLIST

When you write a letter of recommendation for a trainee, check this list to be sure you have included these relevant items.

✓ Your position now and when you supervised the supervisee, and how familiar you are with the supervisee's work
✓ How long you have been in your position
✓ Position and function of the supervisee
✓ Dates the supervisee was under your supervision
✓ The supervisee's duties and responsibilities, and how he or she performed
✓ Give examples of particular things the supervisee did that illustrate your observations: for example, "She took the initiative to seek out additional training experiences on her own by working as a co-leader in the stress management group and the parenting education group, and sat as an observer on the ethics committee for the entire year."
✓ Level of clinical knowledge and skills
✓ Was supervisee open to supervision, growing, and learning?
✓ Did supervisee work well with individuals and groups? Is supervises a team player? (Many employers look very carefully at this item because so many positions involve working with a team.)
✓ Does supervisee have good common sense?
✓ Does supervisee demonstrate good judgment?
✓ Does supervisee demonstrate an awareness of and an ability to work with multicultural issues?
✓ Was supervisee enjoyable to work with?
✓ Was supervisee familiar with legal and ethical standards? Did supervisee demonstrate in practice that he or she can manage these well?
✓ How have you experienced the supervisee, and is this someone you would hire?

TEST YOUR EVALUATION SKILLS

In the three case examples that follow, read the case description and answer the questions before you read our commentary on the case.

The Case of Susan

Susan is a bright, energetic and motivated student in a school counseling program. Maggie is her supervisor and has worked with hundreds of trainees. Maggie likes Susan and is optimistic about her future as a school counselor but observes that Susan has little experience or working knowledge of clinical issues. The first formal evaluation session with Maggie and Susan is rapidly approaching, and Maggie is unsure about what to say to Susan. She does not want to hurt her feelings or dampen her enthusiasm or motivation, but she wants to be candid about what she has observed.

- What do you think this would be like for Maggie? For Susan?
- Can you identify with the ambivalence Maggie feels about being candid with Susan?

- What advice would you give to Maggie?
- How would you handle the feedback session with Susan?

Commentary   This is a common scenario for supervisors when working with students. Most are enthusiastic and motivated and at the same time inexperienced and sometimes naïve about the work. The goal should be to assist Susan to acquire the experience and knowledge she needs to succeed in the profession. To do otherwise would be a disservice to Susan. It all begins with a clear contract about what is expected and a supervisory relationship built on trust and respect. If Maggie has been honest with Susan continuously, then the information she will present at the evaluation session should not come as a surprise. Maggie might assume the role of mentor and teacher with Susan, use live observation and co-therapy with her, and insist that Susan spend a fair amount of time shadowing Maggie so Susan can observe what is involved in the role of the school counselor and how Maggie carries out that role. If Maggie thinks of the evaluation process as beginning in the first supervisory contact and continuing throughout, then the formal evaluation sessions should provide a summary of feedback that Susan has already heard.

The Case of Luther

Luther has been your supervisee for the last year. As a counseling student, he has barely adequate counseling skills. He is knowledgeable of the various therapeutic approaches and how to apply them, but he is somewhat insensitive to the feelings of others and you can see this in his work with clients. He is abrasive and has a sarcastic side that can really put people off. His clinical skills are barely adequate, and his people skills leave a lot to be desired. He has some awareness of how he comes across to people but has not shown much progress in changing this.

- How would you supervise Luther?
- What interventions would you use?
- Do you think there is hope for Luther to alter his behavior and improve his people skills?
- How do you think Luther will respond to the evaluative feedback?
- What would be your plan for providing regular and systematic evaluation for Luther?
- If you were asked by a licensing board whether Luther is qualified for licensure, what would you say?

Commentary   With structure and direction, it is likely that Luther can increase his awareness of how he affects others and can develop those basic helping skills of empathy, respect, and active listening. Using a developmental model, Luther is a novice in using basic counseling skills. As his supervisor, you might best provide structure and direction with lots of constructive feedback. Your role would be more of a teacher. Live observation and role playing would be a good way to give direct feedback regarding the development of those helping skills. At his current level of functioning, it would be difficult to give a favorable recommendation to the licensing board. However, with support, feedback, and his desire for growth and learning, Luther will most likely show considerable improvement. It would be essential to report your observations of his performance to the licensing board regarding the manner in which he accepted the feedback and progressed while under supervision. Focus on behavioral observations, and try to stay away from making value judgments about his work.

The Case of Tyrone

Tyrone is the most capable student you have worked with as a supervisor. In addition to his current work in the doctoral counseling program, he has worked in the field as a mental health counselor for more than 20 years. He has experience, knowledge, clinical skills, good judgment, and the personal characteristics that make him a true pleasure to work with. You find yourself wondering if you are providing any supervisory help to Tyrone. Your supervisory sessions seem more like consultations than supervision, and you feel you learn more from Tyrone than he does from you.

- Do you believe you can supervise Tyrone?
- How do you work with someone who has more knowledge than you do? What can he learn from you?
- What are the potential problems in working with a supervisee like Tyrone? What are the benefits?
- Would you feel defensive if Tyrone challenged something you said?
- What evaluation methods would be most appropriate?
- How would you expect the evaluation process to go with him?

Commentary   With supervisees like Tyrone, who have years of experience and are enjoyable to work with, the tendency of supervisors is to not supervise very carefully. It would be best to supervise very carefully in the beginning, using live observation and assessing his clinical abilities. Develop the supervision contract and implement the usual evaluation procedures as with any supervisee. As the supervisor, you are ultimately responsible for Tyrone's work, and you need to be sure that all the bases are covered. Having years of experience in the field and being an enjoyable person to work with are no assurance that Tyrone has the knowledge, skills, and judgment necessary to function independently.

SUMMARY

Evaluation is an essential function of supervision that should be described in the supervision contract. It helps us assess what progress the supervisee has made in developing the necessary clinical skills as well as ethical and multicultural competence to function independently. It is of the utmost importance that evaluation be planned, organized, systematic and objective. Supervisees are typically anxious about being evaluated, and a supportive and trusting atmosphere can go a long way toward reducing that anxiety. Evaluation needs to be scheduled regularly throughout supervision, and the criteria for evaluation need to be clearly specified. The effective supervisor will find that this evaluation process is a communication tool that helps the supervisee get honest, fair feedback toward becoming an independent professional capable of conducting self-evaluation.

SUGGESTED ACTIVITIES

1. Role-play an evaluation of a supervisee using these different scenarios:
   - When the supervisee is performing quite well
   - When serious deficiencies have been identified
   - When the supervisor informs the supervisee that he or she must be terminated from the clinical experience

2. Interview at least two practicing supervisors to learn how they view the evaluation of supervisees and what methods of evaluation they employ. Ask how often they conduct formal evaluations of supervisees, how the feedback is communicated to the supervisees, whether they use any formal mechanism for obtaining feedback from their supervisees, and how they have changed their supervision practices as a result of that feedback from supervisees.

3. Break into small groups and work together to write a hypothetical letter of recommendation that the group thinks is complete, objective, and balanced. Invent different scenarios. For example, one group could write a letter regarding a supervisee who has marginal skills and will require considerable improvement before successfully completing the supervised experience. Share these letters with the whole class.

4. In small groups, have class members discuss their own experiences with being evaluated as supervisees and brainstorm on how they might improve the evaluation process as supervisors. Discuss how the evaluation process can be most beneficial to the supervisee, and how the evaluative feedback can be communicated in the most constructive manner.

5. In small groups, discuss the optimal frequency of feedback and evaluation to supervisees. Think about formal and informal evaluation procedures and how often each should occur. What obstacles might get in the way of maintaining the optimal frequency of evaluation? How could a supervisor overcome those obstacles?

6. Access the Web site for this text at http://info.wadsworth.com/haynes, and complete the self-assessment inventory. Additional contributor perspectives and other activities specific to this chapter are also available to you through this Web site.

CHAPTER 11

BECOMING AN EFFECTIVE SUPERVISOR

1. Think about the people who have supervised you. Which of them would you describe as effective supervisors? What are the key characteristics of those individuals?
2. What additional characteristics do you think the effective supervisor should have?
3. What is the relative importance of a supervisor's knowledge and skill versus his or her relationship abilities?

4. To what degree do you think you will have many of the characteristics of an effective supervisor when you first become a supervisor?
5. What struggles do you anticipate when you first start to supervise? How can you effectively deal with these challenges? What would be most helpful for you?

INTRODUCTION

Chances are that you now have a clearer understanding of what supervision is about and how it works. Perhaps you have a picture of the approach you would take in fulfilling the many responsibilities of supervision. What steps will you need to take to move in this direction? Be patient with yourself. Becoming a competent and confident supervisor takes time, experience, and practice. We are convinced that this process can be a dynamic, professionally stimulating, and meaningful experience.

In this chapter we describe the characteristics of effective supervisors. We also asked our contributors to share their perspectives on this topic and to describe the "ideal" supervisor. We adapted that information into the characteristics of the "effective" supervisor. The *ideal* is something that we strive for, whereas the *effective* is something we can actually accomplish. In addition, we describe some of the struggles of new supervisors. The chapter concludes with some thoughts on finding your own style as a supervisor, and developing a plan for how to proceed beyond this book in becoming an effective supervisor.

QUALITIES OF THE IDEAL SUPERVISOR

Carifio and Hess (1987) found that the ideal supervisor seems to embody many of the same personal characteristics as the ideal psychotherapist. In their survey of theory and research pertaining to supervision, Carifio and Hess addressed the question, "Who is the ideal supervisor?" They found that high-functioning supervisors perform with high levels of empathy, respect, genuineness, flexibility, concern, and openness. Furthermore, effective supervisors are able to perform a number of tasks during their interactions with supervisees. This involves experience and knowledge about psychotherapy supervision. Good supervisors are concrete in their interactions with supervisees, use appropriate teaching and goal-setting techniques in their supervisory interactions, and make use of effective feedback strategies. Competent supervisors tend to be supportive and noncritical individuals who have a great deal of respect for their supervisees. Good supervisors appreciate keeping appropriate boundaries, and they do not attempt to convert a supervisory relationship into a psychotherapy venture.

Although Carifio and Hess (1987) conducted this survey more than 15 years ago, the degree of consistency between their description and relatively recent findings about what constitutes an effective supervisor is striking (see Martino, 2001; Ramos-Sánchez et al., 2002). Notice also the close relationship between the portrait of the ideal supervisor just described and the composite perspectives of the various supervisors who addressed this question in this chapter.

Ramos-Sánchez and colleagues (2002) investigated the relationship between supervisee developmental level, working alliance, attachment, and negative experiences in supervision. They conducted a national survey of randomly selected psychology internship directors and psychology doctoral program training directors. Ramos-Sánchez and colleagues affirm that the supervisory relationship is central in effective supervision. It is within the supervisory relationship that the supervisor trains and guides the supervisee's development in becoming a skilled therapist. They conclude that effective supervision cannot occur without a solid supervisory relationship.

As the supervisee develops in clinical skills and case conceptualization, the supervisee and the supervisor are more likely to agree on the tasks and goals of supervision, and the supervisory relationship becomes less didactic and more collegial. Supervisees at more advanced stages of development reported having a better working relationship with their supervisor and a higher level of trust, leading to a greater opportunity for development of the supervisor–supervisee relationship. The Ramos-Sánchez and colleagues (2002) survey resulted in several recommendations for effective supervision:

- Harsh criticism and judgmental attitudes on the part of supervisors can result in serious consequences for supervisee development.
- Supervisors are encouraged to build trust, to support and advocate for supervisees, and to be open to feedback from supervisees.
- Supervisor evaluation by the supervisee should be implemented to improve the supervisor's performance.
- Supervisors are encouraged to explore the supervisee's goals for supervision and to be clear about their own expectations for the supervisee's performance.

In another study of effective supervision, Martino (2001) describes the information obtained from graduate students regarding their experiences with both effective and ineffective supervision. This study rated the top 10 factors contributing to "best" supervisor (descending order):

- Clinical knowledge and expertise
- Flexibility and openness to new ideas and approaches to cases

- Warm and supportive
- Provides useful feedback and constructive criticism
- Dedicated to student's training
- Possesses good clinical insight
- Empathic
- Looks at countertransference
- Adheres to ethical practices
- Challenging

The top 10 factors contributing to "worst" supervisor were also rated (descending order):

- Lack of interest in student's training and professional development
- Unavailable
- Inflexible to new ideas and approaches to cases
- Limited clinical knowledge and experience
- Unreliable
- Unhelpful, inconsistent feedback
- Punitive/critical
- Not empathic
- Lack of structure
- Lack of ethics

Magnuson, Wilcoxon, and Norem (1999) identified some similar themes in the description of ineffective supervisors: unbalanced focus of supervision, intolerant of differences, poor model of professional and personal attributes, untrained as a supervisor, and professionally apathetic.

As you read the contributors' descriptions of the ideal supervisor, we suggest that you compare them with Martino's findings. We encourage you to think about the ways the contributors' ideas affect your thoughts about becoming a competent supervisor. We hope you take the time to reflect on the questions and activities provided throughout the chapter. Think about each individual's description of the ideal supervisor and try to identify those attributes that fit with your picture of the ideal supervisor.

Graduate Student Perspectives

Crissa Haynes   A graduate student in social work at the University of Nevada, Reno, Crissa had this to say about the ideal supervisor: "I believe ideal supervisors should be as skilled in human relations as they are in the job itself. To have a supervisor who knows and understands people is essential in creating a healthy work environment. They should have a good sense of humor and the ability to remain flexible, calm, and understanding. They should welcome feedback and input from their supervisees.

"It is important that supervisors remain calm and in control, while helping supervisees to do the same. Supervisors can accomplish this by being supportive, direct, providing guidance, and by letting supervisees know they are approachable. By allowing supervisees to ask questions or make suggestions, supervisors help supervisees develop self-confidence. This in turn increases one's productivity in the workplace."

- As a supervisor, what are some actions you would take to develop a positive work environment for your supervisees?
- How will you let your supervisees know that you are approachable?

Judith Walters, M.S. A marriage and family therapist intern, Judith expressed her views on the ideal supervisor thusly: "For me, there is but one quality that must be present in order for any other qualities to be of benefit. Simply stated, it is the ability of the supervisor to intuitively join with and enter the world of the intern in such a way that the intern can develop his or her own artistry as a therapist . . . because I have come to believe that therapy is in fact an 'art.' The professional therapist must possess skills far beyond the intellectual knowledge of theories, interventions, and counseling techniques. The intuitive supervisor can be that element which nurtures the intern into the often uncharted territory of self-exploration, which must be reckoned with as a prerequisite to effective relationships with clients.

"Specifically, what does the 'intuitive supervisor' do to accomplish this important task? I have identified the following qualities, which I have benefited from most in my own development as a therapist: the ability to sense when interns are ready for deeper and more difficult experiences and to push them forward; the ability to encourage the intern in such a way that questions are ultimately answered by the intern based on self-insight; and the ability to share experience, wisdom, and skills by modeling the very type of relationship I hope to establish with clients—one in which clients are able to 'do their work' without being judged. The skilled supervisor will teach, encourage, nurture, confront, be deliberate, role model, challenge, and provide information and constructive feedback, all the while 'keeping themselves out of the way.' I believe it is within this environment that interns will learn to depend upon their own self-artistry and will arrive at their destination with clarity and confidence."

- What does "entering the world of the supervisee" mean to you, and how might you accomplish that as a supervisor?
- If you were a supervisor, what obstacles might you need to overcome to "keep out of the way" and allow your supervisees to develop?

Supervisor Perspectives

Here is what some postdegree clinicians with a variety of backgrounds and years of clinical experience had to say with regard to what constitutes an ideal supervisor.

Elie Axelroth, Psy.D. Elie describes the ideal supervisor in an internship setting: "It is impossible to describe the ideal supervisor without characterizing the ideal trainee, the training environment, the client, and the relationship between all of them. At the outset, the ideal supervisor understands that new interns arrive at their setting in a vulnerable state, in need of reassurance, direction, and compassion. This vulnerability must drive much of the initial work of orientation and relationship-building. Interns come to the setting filled with hopes for engaging in challenging life's work, a set of skills, and enormous anxiety about their capacity to perform. The ideal supervisor assesses new interns' training needs, is tuned in to the developmental stages of the interns, and is willing to adjust the training program to their skills and needs.

"In the first weeks of internship, the ideal supervisor spends time orienting new interns by touring the setting and introducing them to staff and referral sources; reviewing crisis procedures, basic issues of confidentiality, and reporting guidelines; walking them through the paperwork and note-taking guidelines; and reviewing risk management issues such as assessment of violence and lethality. This orientation to the setting not only provides the groundwork for solid clinical work but also helps to allay interns' anxiety by establishing clear expectations. Interns need to be oriented to the informal norms of the setting as well as to the more formal policies. It is often the informal norms that create the most anxiety and uncertainty.

"While we are all pulled by the realities of clinical work, the demands on our time, the pressures of service delivery, and the challenge of balancing the numerous hats we wear, ideal supervisors leave their door open when they are available and make themselves accessible and interested, particularly in those early stages of adjustment.

"The ideal supervisor is also knowledgeable, well versed in ethics and the law, and is able to articulate a framework for making those difficult ethical decisions. Ideal supervisors can communicate a theoretical framework in terms that are accessible to the intern. They listen to the intern, are not too quick to make assessments about the client, and respect the intern's right to disagree.

"Supervision is a dialogue, and the ideal supervisor recognizes that good supervision opens the supervisor as well as the intern to new insights, new learning, and excitement about the work. Like good teachers or mentors who are tuned into their students, we learn something new from teaching others. Supervision at its best is a mutual collaborative relationship, and one in which curiosity, excitement, and new insights are opened up to both supervisor and intern.

"A talented clinician, one with a flair for the work, is not necessarily the ideal supervisor. The ideal supervisor is willing to highlight the strengths of the intern and not his or her own glowing achievements. This person is a seasoned clinician as well as an experienced supervisor and is able to tailor a variety of interventions to meet the needs of the intern and, at the same time, the therapeutic goals of the client. There are times when didactic instruction is needed to help interns move beyond their knowledge set. As the intern matures and builds in confidence and skill, the ideal supervisor helps the intern to develop more abstract interventions through interpretation and insight. The supervisor, like any skilled clinician, carries a bag of strategies that can be used intentionally, like any therapeutic intervention."

- What messages might you give your supervisees to reassure them as they begin their role as therapists?
- What do you think are the necessary components involved in orienting new supervisees to the supervisory process?
- Identify boundaries that would be important to you to maintain in the supervisory relationship.
- What are your thoughts and reactions when you imagine evaluating your supervisees?

Todd Thies, Ph.D.   Todd has this to say about the characteristics of the ideal supervisor: "The ideal supervisor is one who can maintain an appropriate balance between providing direction to the supervisee and allowing the supervisee to develop independently. A good supervisor recognizes that the goal of supervision is not to make duplicates of him- or herself but to assist the supervisee to develop into the professional he or she was meant to be. To achieve this goal, the supervisor must be able to clearly identify those things that must be done in a specific way (for example, when to report child abuse) and those that can be left to the personality and individual strengths of the supervisee. An ideal supervisor would also serve as a role model that the supervisee can emulate. However, the parts of the supervisor the supervisee wishes to emulate must be left up to the supervisee."

- Identify parts of your personality or practice that you might be tempted to want your supervisees to emulate.
- How could you balance your responsibilities between providing direction and encouraging your supervisees to find their own direction?
- What kind of role model would you hope to be for your supervisees?

Steve Arkowitz, Psy.D.   Steve talks about the importance of honoring supervisory sessions: "I believe an effective supervisor is very aware of the value of 'protected' supervision time. That is, the supervisor devotes the supervision hour to the supervisee. A protected supervision hour includes structuring the supervision time with clear start and end times and scheduling the hour at the same time every week. I think this provided me with a sense of continuity and even reassurance when I was in the earlier stages of my training. I also appreciated it when supervisors did not allow phone calls or other interruptions during the supervision hour. For me, this conveyed that the supervisor valued the supervision relationship.

"Moreover, I believe the supervision hour should be structured so that the trainee is given an opportunity and expected to discuss issues from the prior week before the supervisor brings up issues that he or she wants to address. Knowing I was expected to come to supervision prepared to discuss a topic forced me to examine my cases more closely. Ideally, the supervision hour should be structured enough so as to provide the supervisee with a sense of security but be flexible enough that the training needs of the supervisee can be met.

"A less practical but perhaps more fundamental element of supervision involves the subject of autonomy. In my experience, effective supervisors have been those who recognized the need to match the level of clinical autonomy with the supervisee's level of experience. This may seem like a basic concept, but I have been surprised how often supervisors have not taken it into account. I have learned the most and been the most effective as a clinician when my supervisors permitted me a level of independence commensurate with my experience and training."

- How might you create "protected supervision time" for your supervisees?
- How would you expect your supervisees to prepare for the supervision hour?

Marianne Schneider Corey, M.S., M.F.T. Marianne reminds us of the importance of developing our own style and being encouraged to so do: "In my training I had three different supervisors. Although they each had a somewhat distinct style of supervision, they were all warm and personable individuals, and they provided a good balance of demonstrating caring and being willing to challenge me. They encouraged me to stretch my limits rather than to surrender to my fears. They seemed to believe in my potential to become an effective counselor at a time when I wondered if I should stay in the field. When I thought I couldn't meet a challenge, they provided me with a sense that I could do more than I was giving myself credit for being able to do. They provided a safety net by being available for help.

"A key lesson they all taught was to understand how vital the role of the counselor as a person is to the outcomes of counseling. When I was discouraged, they provided encouragement. I recall wondering if I could continue my work as a counselor because I felt triggered by so much of the pain my clients expressed. One supervisor let me know that he would be worried if I didn't have concerns in this area, yet he also helped me see the value in identifying and exploring my own personal issues. When I was concerned that I would make a mistake and thus ruin a client, one supervisor reminded me that I did not have this much power, nor would my clients be likely to give me that kind of power. All of these supervisors had good boundaries and were able to blend therapeutic work with supervision, yet they did not take over as my therapist. They kept the focus on how my own pain might influence my interventions with clients.

"Although all of my supervisors stressed the importance of honing my skills and expanding my knowledge, they stressed that I not lose that part of me that I already had before I pursued my education as a counselor. When I began counseling clients, I was tempted to pattern my therapeutic style after my supervisors. All of them encouraged me to learn from what they had to offer but stressed the importance of finding my own way as a counseling practitioner rather than becoming a carbon copy of them."

- How could you encourage your supervisees to "stretch their limits rather than surrender to their fears"?
- To what degree are you affected by the pain your clients express? How might you help your supervisees cope with the pain their clients will express?
- What might you say to a supervisee who tells you, "I am afraid I will make a mistake and that it will ruin my client forever"?

Tory Nersasian, Psy.D.   Tory found modeling and demonstrations most useful during her supervision: "The ideal supervisor possesses basic qualities such as likeability, respect for students, and a sense of humor. In addition, achieving the ideal supervision style frequently depends on the personal preferences of the student. For example, one student may desire a relaxed approach, another may prefer more structure. I have found it very beneficial to have an initial supervision meeting during which the student's preferences and expectations of supervision are discussed.

"I have tremendous respect for the supervisor who not only tells the supervisee what works in treatment or assessment but also demonstrates the approach with a real client. Allowing students to watch your therapy sessions, read your evaluations, co-lead your treatment groups, and watch you present a lecture or testify in court carries much more power than discussing these experiences after they have occurred."

- How comfortable would you feel in teaching supervisees through demonstration? What might get in your way of using demonstration methods?
- How might you use your sense of humor appropriately to enhance the supervisory process? Have you experienced situations where a sense of humor has gotten in your way?

Bill Safarjan, Ph.D.   Bill provides a succinct list of ideal supervisor traits: "An ideal supervisor would be enthusiastic about his or her work, clinically competent, tolerant of diverse viewpoints, objective, responsible, open to new ways of thinking, versatile in her or his teaching strategies, and courageous in confronting the tough issues that could negatively impact the future of the supervisee. An ideal supervisor would also have broad interests; clear, well-defined boundaries; high ethical standards; and a love of teaching and of the profession."

- Which of these traits would you most want supervisees to use to describe you as a supervisor?
- Which of these characteristics would be the most challenging for you to acquire?
- Are there any additional characteristics that you think are essential?

David Shepard, Ph.D.   David believes supervisors must have a passion for the field and communicate their passion to supervisees: "When students begin working in a mental health setting, they will meet counselors who are experiencing burnout. Students may not realize that they are witnessing burnout and may assume that such feelings are an inevitable part of the profession. The 'passionate' supervisor counters these negative messages by modeling the exhilaration this field can *continually* generate provided that counselors practice self-monitoring and self-care.

"Is the ideal counselor a wise expert and brilliant counselor, comfortable with a variety of theoretical approaches and familiar with 'best-possible treatments' for every diagnosis in the DSM-IV? I would argue that supervisors need not be so-called master therapists but rather counselors who envision themselves as participating in a lifelong journey of growth as a helper and as a person. They share the discoveries they are making along this journey. They model as supervisors what it means to be a self-reflective practitioner. Ultimately, the ideal supervisor is someone who, like the ideal teacher, inspires. Their supervisees leave the supervisory experience with a passion for their work, with the expectation that failure and uncertainty are necessary experiences on their journey of growth, with respect for the limits of their knowledge, and with a joyous anticipation of continued learning."

- What plan might you put in place that would maintain your passion for your work and decrease your chances of burnout?
- Have you been inspired by any of your supervisors? What might you do to inspire your supervisees?

We can use the descriptions of the ideal supervisor to formulate a composite picture of the supervisor we would each like to be. Take a few minutes now to write down your own decription of an ideal supervisor. Doing this will help you to understand how you view the process of supervision. The contributors did a thorough job of describing the attributes of the ideal supervisor, and we have summarized some of the common themes in Box 11.1. Review this list often as you grow into your supervisory role and responsibilities.

STRUGGLES AS SUPERVISORS

In addition to asking supervisors to describe the characteristics of the ideal supervisor, we invited them to share with us some of the difficulties and challenges they experienced when they began their role as supervisors. The following excerpts provide some sense of the pathway toward becoming an effective supervisor.

Marianne Schneider Corey, M.S., M.F.T.   "My experience as a supervisor has been in the area of training and supervising group workers as they facilitate groups. I believe the best training can be provided in an experiential group where the trainees function as co-leaders with my supervision. An early challenge for me was to set clear boundaries regarding the purpose and context of group training and to communicate that to the supervisees.

CHARACTERISTICS OF AN EFFECTIVE SUPERVISOR

- Aware of clinical, legal, and ethical issues
- Possesses good clinical skills
- Demonstrates empathy, respect, genuineness, listening
- Establishes an accepting supervisory climate
- Creates a supervisory relationship characterized by trust and respect
- Determines the developmental level of the supervisee and provides supervision methods that will best serve the training needs of the supervisee
- Has a sense of humor
- Develops clear boundaries
- Encourages appropriate risk-taking on the part of supervisees
- Supports a collaborative supervisory process
- Respects the knowledge supervisees bring to the supervisory relationship
- Appreciates individual differences among supervisees and differing opinions about theoretical viewpoints
- Is open, approachable, and supportive
- Has a keen interest in training and supervision
- Shows sensitivity to the anxieties and vulnerabilities of supervisees
- Values supervision sessions as "protected" time
- Provides honest constructive feedback

"A struggle I had from the beginning was to find a way to not get in the way of the trainees as they facilitated the group. What helped me as a supervisor was recalling what it was like when I first began. This gave me a continued appreciation for the difficulty they were experiencing as trainees. Although I wanted to be helpful, I learned the importance of not being too helpful to the extent that they are deprived of finding their own voice and direction, thus becoming dependent on me. A key issue has been to avoid taking over a group too soon. I learned to let the trainees find their own way. I wanted to let them know that my way is not the only way, nor is it the way they should be.

"It has always been a challenge for me to communicate to group supervisees in a way that I can offer direct and constructive feedback without being perceived as being judgmental and critical. Many trainees lack confidence and sometimes feel inept. I want to offer hope and specific feedback that trainees can use to increase their self-confidence and enhance their level of skills. When I first began supervising, it was essential for me to establish my own style of supervising. I found out there is no one right way of supervising, yet carving out my own identity as a supervisor took some time.

"There was some struggle in learning how to allow the trainees to accept responsibility and trust that they would learn through a process of experimenting with supervision. At times group workers did not do an adequate job in leading, yet my challenge was to find a way to make this a teaching opportunity. My goal was to assist trainees in becoming less aware of me and to focus on the group members instead. I am very aware of the performance anxieties of most trainees. I strive to gain their trust that my intention is to help them become more skilled clinicians, not to criticize them or put them down. I typically tell them that a great mistake they could make is to give into the fear of making a mistake.

"A main challenge was creating a safe and accepting group atmosphere where they could learn new skills as a group facilitator without converting the group into a therapy forum for them. Supervising experientially always presents the challenge of teaching in a personal way by dealing with personal concerns brought up by the members but maintaining appropriate boundaries where the supervision goals are not lost. For example, at times supervisees comment that they feel stuck with a particular client because that individual triggered them. They may even be willing to describe what personal problems were surfacing for them as they attempted to focus on a client. While I use this opportunity to teach the importance of handling countertransference, I do not abdicate my role as a supervisor and become a therapist in the supervision session. Instead, I encourage them to consider further exploring some of their personal issues with a therapist."

- What causes you anxiety at the prospect of becoming a supervisor? How might you deal effectively with these anxieties?
- What would be helpful to you in carving out your own identity as a supervisor? What might get in your way of developing your unique style as a supervisor?
- How do you go about creating a safe and accepting atmosphere for supervision?

Muriel Yáñez, Psy.D.   "I think the most difficult aspect of supervision has been the feeling of juggling and attending to different levels of information simultaneously. There is a sense of responsibility to monitor the supervisee's practice, the well-being of the client being served, the development and training of the supervisee, and monitoring one's own process as well. Watching for dual relationships and maintaining boundaries has been more of an issue than I had originally thought. This is illustrated by not falling into 'doing therapy' with the supervisee, or maintaining some amount of distance instead of developing friendships."

- To what degree are you concerned about maintaining boundaries with your supervisees?

Bill Safarjan, Ph.D.   "Probably the biggest initial struggle for me was overcoming the feeling of having to know everything—a holdover from my days in graduate school. At the beginning, I felt that it was important to be able to answer every question and solve every problem brought to me by the supervisee. Not only was this an impossible task, but I began to see how I was discouraging independence, which was exactly the opposite of what I was intending to do."

- As a supervisor, what can you do to challenge your belief that you must know everything in order to be an effective supervisor?

Stacy Thacker, Ph.D.   "When I first became a supervisor, I had just recently stopped being a supervisee. That being the case, one of the first struggles was actually 'seeing' myself as a supervisor and believing that I was qualified to take on such a responsibility.

"The next struggle was in determining what type of supervisor or what style of supervision would fit best with my skills as well as my personality traits. My graduate training did not provide much information about becoming a supervisor. Consequently, I have had to gain knowledge in this area by reviewing the literature, attending workshops, and speaking with colleagues. Since providing supervision is 'in addition' to my other job responsibilities, finding the time to do this research has been a challenge."

- What steps will you need to take to transition from viewing yourself as a trainee to viewing yourself as a supervisor?

Steve Arkowitz, Psy.D.   "A potentially difficult area of supervision for me involves incidents in which I believe a supervisee has made a significant clinical error. Situations that involve either trivial mistakes or blatant ethical violations will be easy for me to address. However, once again it will be the ambiguous realms of clinical judgment that I will find most difficult to tackle in supervision. This will be a struggle for me because it clearly relates to feelings of competence. Initially it will be a challenge for me to feel that my opinion is somehow more valid or 'right' than someone else's. Also, I am close enough to my own training days that I still remember what it feels like to have a supervisor lord his or her opinions and knowledge over me. These recollections may cause me to be hesitant or even reluctant to play the role of the expert with a supervisee."

- Identify the approach you would like to take to assist your supervisees when they make a clinical mistake.

Heriberto G. Sánchez, Ph.D.   "My first major assignment as a supervisor was supervising other licensed psychologists, many of whom had years of clinical experience. The most difficult challenge for me was accepting the different levels of motivation and commitment of the professionals I supervised. As a supervisor, I tried to motivate psychologists to work at their highest potential and to lead them in a direction I believed was good for our profession. I expected my supervisees to be enthusiastic about their work and committed to the advancement of our profession. I realized that my personal goals as a supervisor were not shared by all of my supervisees. I needed to take into account each individual's stage of their life, and not just their professional development. For example, one psychologist was looking forward to retirement and did not share my enthusiasm for making improvements in our department. Others were excellent clinicians but did not participate in professional activities. These types of experiences forced me to reassess my goals as a supervisor. I had to be less idealistic and more realistic. Although this was difficult to accept, eventually it made my job less frustrating and more enjoyable. I realized I had to redefine goals and measure progress in small increments. On the other side of this struggle, I also learned that our department had some highly skilled psychologists who were intrinsically motivated to do good work, had admirable work habits, and were committed to their profession. All they needed was my support and freedom to work independently."

- How do you imagine you would go about motivating your supervisees, including those that are less than enthusiastic about their work? How might it be for you if your expectations were not met?

Todd Thies, Ph.D.   "My struggles as a new supervisor were similar to my struggles when I first went from intern to psychologist. I had to find my own identity and priorities as a supervisor. I also had to struggle with periods of self-doubt. Not too long ago I was in supervision myself, and now I am providing direction and training others. I think I also struggled some with identifying comfortable boundaries between my supervisee and myself. At times, it is easy to overidentify with the supervisee, which makes it difficult to evaluate the supervisee in an objective manner."

- Identify a few specific self-doubts that you hold about becoming a supervisor. How might you help supervisees who are struggling with self-doubts?

A summary of the struggles identified by our contributor supervisors is provided in Box 11.2. This is indeed an interesting list. The struggles these supervisors experienced when they first became supervisors mirror the fears and concerns of many new supervisors. In becoming a supervisor, you can expect to experience fears, doubts, and uncertainty about your role and the goals of supervision. This seems to be a common experience when clinicians make the initial transition from supervisee to supervisor. With experience, knowledge, and learning from readings, courses, and workshops on the topic of supervision, you will be able to develop into the supervisor you would like to be when you make the transition to this new role.

OUR THOUGHTS ON BECOMING AN EFFECTIVE SUPERVISOR

In addition to specific knowledge and skills that supervisors need to possess, it is our belief that supervisors must also be therapeutic persons. This is especially important in supervisors' ability to form working relationships with supervisees. Effective supervisors are able to maintain healthy personal and professional boundaries, which they model for their supervisees. They have a

THE STRUGGLES OF BEGINNING SUPERVISORS

- Developing one's identity as a supervisor
- Setting priorities for what is important in supervision
- Conquering self-doubt
- Setting appropriate boundaries and maintaining some distance
- Learning what supervisors do instead of just giving answers
- Juggling the various goals and roles of supervision
- Providing feedback to supervisees in a constructive manner
- Feeling a need to know everything to be able to assist the supervisee in every case
- Discovering how to let supervisees come up with their own answers
- Finding one's own style and realizing there is no one right way to supervise
- Helping supervisees accept responsibility for and to have trust in the supervision process
- Creating a safe and accepting atmosphere
- Avoiding becoming the supervisee's therapist
- Making the transition from supervisee to supervisor and overidentifying with the supervisee
- Lacking self-confidence to know what to do as a supervisor
- Knowing how to handle the supervisees' serious clinical mistakes
- Hesitating to play the role of expert
- Having expectations and goals for supervision that are too high and unrealistic when supervising veteran clinicians

sincere interest in the welfare of others, and their concern is based on respect, care, and trust. They are able to experience the "now" and be present with others in the now.

Effective supervisors know who they are, what they are capable of becoming, and what they want out of life. They respect and appreciate themselves. They feel adequate with others and allow others to feel powerful with them. They can give help and live out of their own sense of self-worth and strength.

Effective supervisors exhibit a willingness and courage to leave the security of the known if they are not satisfied with what they have. They make choices that influence the direction of their lives, and they are aware of early decisions they made about themselves, others, and the world. They are not the victims of these early decisions, for they are willing to revise them if necessary. They feel alive, and their choices are life-oriented. They are committed to living fully rather than settling for mere existence. They are authentic, sincere, and honest. They do not hide behind masks, defenses, roles, and facades.

Effective supervisors have a sense of humor. They are able to put the events of life in perspective. They have not forgotten how to laugh, especially at their own foibles and contradictions. They make mistakes and are willing to admit them.

They appreciate the influence of culture. They are aware of the ways in which their own culture affects them, and they have a respect for the diversity of values espoused by other cultures. They are also sensitive to the unique differences arising out of social class, race, sexual orientation, and gender.

This description of the characteristics of effective supervisors might seem unrealistic and unattainable. These personal characteristics are not based on an all-or-nothing perspective, however; rather, they exist on a continuum. A given trait may be highly characteristic of someone at one extreme, or it may be very uncharacteristic of someone else at the other extreme. It seems to us that these traits and characteristics can be translated into specific behaviors that can be assessed in the development of a supervisor. Those supervisors who possess many of these characteristics are in a good position to develop their own style of supervision.

FINDING YOUR OWN STYLE AS A SUPERVISOR

Some trainees limit their own development by trying too hard to copy the style of a supervisor or a teacher. Chances are you will observe supervisors you respect, and you may tend to adopt their methods. It is important, however, to be aware of how easy it is imitate another person. You can get the most from your supervision by being open to learning from peers and supervisors. Try on different styles, but continually evaluate what works for you and what does not. You might ask yourself: "What fits my belief system, both personal and theoretical? Do I have any conflicts between the theory or application of my supervisor's way and my own?" If you pay too much attention to another person, you are not likely to discover your uniqueness. You need to be able to take what is good from your various supervisors and teachers, yet it is important to avoid being a clone. If you learn to listen to your own inner voice and to respect your inner promptings, you will eventually have less need to look to outside authorities.

People are not "naturally born" counselors, supervisors, or supervisees. The skills associated with each of these roles are learned, practiced, and refined. Perhaps the best way to learn how to become an effective supervisor is to reflect on lessons you are learning as a supervisee. We hope this book has given you a better idea of the kind of supervisor you are striving to become. As you consider what is involved in the overall process of becoming an effective supervisor, you may feel somewhat overwhelmed by all that needs to be done. You may be intimidated by all of the variables you are expected to pay attention to in your training. As is the case with learning any new skill or craft, it takes time and practice to become accomplished.

When you began your training program, you may have made the mistake of being so focused on anything your clients said and did that you forgot to pay attention to your reactions. By trying too hard to catch every gesture and to understand every sentence, you can easily distract yourself from being present with clients. One supervisor gave a student sound advice when she said, "If you miss something with a client, the person will no doubt bring it up again later."

In a similar manner, if you are learning how to become a supervisor, it is to be expected that feeling comfortable in this role will also take time and practice. When you eventually begin to supervise others, it is not essential that you know all the right things to say to all those whom you supervise in every situation. We see the learning of these abilities and skills as an ongoing process rather than a state that is achieved once and for all. You need not be perfect, and it is important to give yourself the latitude to learn from any mistakes you might make. Giving yourself permission to be less than perfect applies equally to becoming a counselor, a supervisee, or a supervisor.

WHERE CAN YOU GO FROM HERE?

It is clear that we believe who the supervisor is as a person is the central aspect of being able to carry out the demands of supervision. It follows, then, that whatever supervisors can do to enhance their personal development will pay dividends in their professional roles. Here are some way to enhance your development as a supervisor.

Read articles on the theory and practice of supervision in professional journals. Read selective parts of books on supervision. (The References and Suggested Readings at the end of this book is full of works that can be of value to you.) Join a professional organization that has some linkage with supervision. For example, if you join the American Counseling Association (ACA), you can also join the Association for Counselor Education and Supervision (ACES), which is the major professional organization for supervisors and counselor educators.

At various points in your career, consider taking a course or a continuing education workshop on clinical supervision. You will be able to glean ideas that you can translate into your supervision practice. Look for ways to co-supervise with colleagues. For example, if you do group supervision as part of a course in a university program, invite a colleague to join you for some sessions so that both of you can provide supervisees with feedback. In addition, you may also consider peer supervision as a learning tool.

If at all possible, ask a colleague or a professional with considerable experience to supervise your supervision. This supervision can go a long way toward giving you a sense of what your supervisees experience in their supervision. Be willing to share feelings of vulnerability, including your feelings about your limitations as a supervisor. Don't feel like you have to have it all together before you can begin to supervise. Realize that you will learn a great deal about supervision as you reflectively engage in this work.

Ask your supervisees for feedback. Just as instructors ask students for anonymous feedback by way of student evaluations of courses at the end of a term, you can provide an avenue for your supervisees to give anonymous input regarding the value of the supervision they received from you. Keep notes or a personal journal in which you record your thoughts about being a supervisor. Write about struggles you may have and how your professional work as a supervisor is affecting you personally. A journal is an excellent way of keeping track of patterns that you can build upon or change.

Over the years we have learned that becoming an effective supervisor entails the willingness to continue engaging in a process of self-reflection. Rather than reaching a final goal of competence, effective supervisors, much like skilled therapists or competent teachers, are continually rethinking what they do and how they might do things more creatively. Effective supervisors are willing to be part of a process rather than remaining in a fixed state.

SUMMARY

We hope you have a clearer picture of the characteristics of an effective supervisor as a result of having read the contributors' thoughts on this topic. As you learn more about supervision and gain experience as a supervisee and a supervisor, your picture of an effective supervisor is likely to change.

The struggles of our contributing supervisors show that we have all experienced doubts and difficulties in becoming supervisors. This is a normal part of learning a new role and the associated new skills. Make sure that you gain the knowledge necessary to become a competent supervisor and that you give yourself time to adjust to the role. Be open to your continual learning, and do not be afraid to seek additional supervision and consultation when needed.

SUGGESTED ACTIVITIES

1. In small groups, brainstorm the most important characteristics of the effective supervisor. Members might take turns role-playing how that supervisor would interact with supervisees. Each group could then share with the larger group their findings and thoughts.

2. In pairs, have each class member share with their partner whether they have been supervised by someone who closely approximates the effective supervisor, and what that experience was like. What was the most outstanding characteristic of that supervisor? How did that experience influence your idea of how you would like to work as a supervisor?

3. Interview two or three individuals who are currently supervisors. Ask them what their struggles were when they first became supervisors and how they dealt with them. Bring the results back for discussion in your class or in small groups.

4. In small groups, discuss what you think will be the major struggles you are likely to encounter in becoming a supervisor. Then discuss ways you

can deal with those struggles. Small groups could then share their major findings with the large group, and a master list of ways to deal with the struggles could be developed.

5. Access the Web site for this text at http://info.wadsworth.com/haynes, and complete the self-assessment inventory. Additional contributor perspectives and other activities specific to this chapter, are also available to your through this Web site.

REFERENCES AND
SUGGESTED READINGS

Acuff, C., Bennett, B. E., Bricklin, P. M., Canter, M. B., Knapp, S. J., Moldawsky, S., & Phelps, R. (1999). Considerations for ethical practice of managed care. *Professional Psychology: Research and Practice, 30*(6), 563–575.

Alle-Corliss, L., & Alle-Corliss, R. (1998). *Human service agencies: An orientation to fieldwork.* Pacific Grove, CA: Brooks/Cole.

American Association for Marriage and Family Therapy. (1999). *AAMFT approved supervisors: Mentors and teachers for the next generation of MFT's.* Washington, DC: Author.

American Association for Marriage and Family Therapy. (2001). *AAMFT code of ethics.* Washington, DC: Author.

American Counseling Association. (1995). *Code of ethics and standards of practice.* Alexandria, VA: Author.

American Counseling Association. (1999). *Ethical standards for internet on-line counseling.* Alexandria, VA: Author.

American Psychological Association. (1992). *Ethical principles of psychologists and code of conduct.* Washington, DC: Author.

American Psychological Association. (2001). Ethical principles of psychologists and code of conduct [Draft]. (June 24, 2001).

Anderson, R. D., & Price, G. E. (2001). Experiential groups in counselor education: Student attitudes and instructor participation. *Counselor Education and Supervision, 41*(2), 111–119.

Antonio, V. (1999, Spring). Ten ingredients for a rewarding supervision experience. *ACES Spectrum,* 3–4.

Arredondo, P., Toporek, R., Brown, S., Jones, J., Locke, D., Sanchez, J., & Stadler, H. A. (1996). Organization of multicultural counseling competencies. *Journal of Multicultural Counseling and Development, 24*(1), 42–78.

Association for Counselor Education and Supervision. (1987). *Handbook of counseling supervision.* Alexandria, VA: Author.

Association for Counselor Education and Supervision. (1990). Standards for counseling supervisors. *Journal of Counseling and Development, 69,* 30–32.

Association for Counselor Education and Supervision. (1993, Summer). Ethical guidelines for counseling supervisors. *ACES Spectrum, 53*(4), 3–8.

Association for Counselor Education and Supervision. (1995). Ethical guidelines for counseling supervisors. *Counselor Education and Supervision, 34*(3), 270–276.

Association of State and Provincial Psychology Boards. (1998). *Report of the ASPPB: Task force on supervision guidelines.* Montgomery, AL: Author.

Bemak, F., & Epp, L. R. (2001). Countertransference in the development of graduate student group counselors: Recommendations for training. *Journal for Specialists in Group Work, 26,* 305–318.

Bemak, F., Epp, L. R., & Keys, S. G. (1999). Impaired graduate students: A process model of graduate program monitoring and intervention. *International Journal for the Advancement of Counseling, 21,* 19–30.

Bernard, J. M. (1979). Supervisor training: A discrimination model. *Counselor Education and Supervision, 19,* 60–68.

Bernard, J. M., & Goodyear, R. K. (1998). *Fundamentals of clinical supervision* (2nd ed.). Needham Heights, MA: Allyn & Bacon.

Binder, J. L., & Strupp, H. H. (1997). Supervision of psychodynamic psychotherapies. In C. E. Watkins Jr. (Ed.), *Handbook of psychotherapy supervision* (pp. 44–62). New York: John Wiley & Sons.

Bongar, B. (1991). *The suicidal patient: Clinical and legal standards of care.* Washington, DC: American Psychological Association.

Bongar, B. (1992a). Guidelines for risk management in the care of the suicidal patient. In B. Bongar (Ed.), *Suicide: Guidelines for assessment, management, and treatment* (pp. 268–282). New York: Oxford University Press.

Bongar, B. (Ed.). (1992b). *Suicide: Guidelines for assessment, management, and treatment.* New York: Oxford University Press.

Bongar, B. (2002). *The suicidal patient: Clinical and legal standards of care* (2nd ed.). Washington, DC: American Psychological Association.

Bongar, B., Lomax, J. W., & Marmatz, M. (1992). Training and supervisory issues in the assessment and management of the suicidal patient. In B. Bongar (Ed.), *Suicide: Guidelines for assessment, management, and treatment* (pp. 253–267). New York: Oxford University Press.

Borders, L. D. (1991). A systematic approach to peer group supervision. *Journal of Counseling and Development, 69,* 248–252.

Borders, L. D. (1992). Learning to think like a supervisor. *Clinical Supervisor, 10*(2), 135–148.

Borders, L. D., & Leddick, G. (1987). *Handbook of counseling supervision.* Alexandria, VA: Association for Counselor Education and Supervision.

Bordin, E. S. (1983). A working alliance model of supervision. *Counseling Psychologist, 11,* 35–42.

Bradley, L. J., & Gould, L. J. (2001). Psychotherapy-based models of counselor supervision. In L. J. Bradley & N. Ladany (Eds.), *Counselor supervision: Principles, process, and practice* (3rd ed., pp. 147–180). Philadelphia: Brunner-Routledge.

Bradley, L. J., Gould, L. J., & Parr, G. D. (2001). Theoretical approaches to counselor supervision. In L. J. Bradley & N. Ladany (Eds.), *Counselor supervision: Principles, process and practice* (3rd ed., pp. 28–57). Philadelphia: Brunner-Routledge.

Bradley, L. J., & Kotter, J. A. (2001). Overview of counselor supervision. In L. J. Bradley & N. Ladany (Eds.), *Counselor supervision: Principles, process, and practice* (3rd ed., pp. 3–27). Philadelphia: Brunner-Routledge.

Bradley, L. J., & Ladany, N. (Eds.). (2001). *Counselor supervision: Principles, process, and practice* (3rd ed.). Philadelphia: Brunner-Routledge.

Brown, M. T., & Landrum-Brown, J. (1995). Counselor supervision: Cross-cultural perspectives. In J. G. Ponterotto, J. M. Casas, L. A. Suzuki, & C. M. Alexander (Eds.), *Handbook of multicultural counseling* (pp. 263–286). Thousand Oaks, CA: Sage.

Burian, B. K., & O'Conner Slimp, A. (2000). Social dual-role relationships during internship: A decision-making model. *Professional Psychology: Research and Practice, 31*(3), 332–338.

Calhoun, K. S., Moras, K., Pilkonis, P. A., & Rehm, L. P. (1998). Empirically supported treatments: Implications for training. *Journal of Consulting and Clinical Psychology, 66,* 151–162.

California Department of Consumer Affairs. (2000). *Laws and regulations relating to the practice of psychology.* Sacramento: Author.

Campbell, J. M. (2000). *Becoming an effective supervisor: A workbook for counselors and psychotherapists.* Philadelphia, PA: Accelerated Development.

Capuzzi, D., & Gross, D. R. (Eds.). (2000). *Youth at risk: A prevention resource for counselors, teachers, and parents* (3rd ed.). Alexandria, VA: American Counseling Association.

Carifio, M. S., & Hess, A. K. (1987). Who is the ideal supervisor? *Professional Psychology: Research and Practice, 18*(3), 244–250.

Carroll, M. (1996). *Counseling supervision: Theory, skills, and practice.* London: Cassell.

Carta-Falsa, J., & Anderson, L. (2001). A model of clinical/counseling supervision. *The California Therapist, 13*(2), 47–51.

Chiaferi, R., & Griffen, M. (1997). *Developing fieldwork skills: A guide for human services, counseling, and social work students.* Pacific Grove, CA: Brooks/Cole.

Christensen, T. M., & Kline, W. B. (2001). Anxiety as a condition for learning in group supervision. *Journal for Specialists in Group Work, 26*(4), 385–396.

Cobia, D. C., & Boes, S. R. (2000). Professional disclosure statements and formal plans for supervision: Two strategies for minimizing the risk of ethical conflicts in post-master's supervision. *Journal of Counseling and Development, 78*(3), 293–296.

Constantine, M. G., & Ladany, N. (2000, April). Self-report multicultural counseling competence scales: Their relation to social desirability attitudes and multicultural case conceptualization ability. *Journal of Counseling Psychology, 47*(2), 155–164.

Cook, D. A. (1994). Racial identity in supervision. *Counselor Education and Supervision, 34*(2), 132–141.

Cooper, C. C., & Gottlieb, M. C. (2000). Ethical issues with managed care: Challenges facing counseling psychology. *The Counseling Psychologist, 28*(2), 179–236.

Corey, G. (2001a). *The art of integrative counseling.* Pacific Grove, CA: Brooks/Cole.

Corey, G. (2001b). *Student manual for theory and practice of counseling and psychotherapy* (6th ed.). Pacific Grove, CA: Brooks/Cole.

Corey, G. (2001c). *Theory and practice of counseling and psychotherapy* (6th ed.). Pacific Grove, CA: Brooks/Cole.

Corey, G., Corey, M. S., & Callanan, P. (2003). *Issues and ethics in the helping professions* (6th ed.). Pacific Grove, CA: Brooks/Cole.

Corey, M. S., & Corey, G. (2002). *Groups: Process and practice* (6th ed.). Pacific Grove, Ca: Brooks/Cole.

Corey, M. S., & Corey, G. (2003). *Becoming a helper* (4th ed.). Pacific Grove, CA: Brooks/Cole.

Costa, L., & Altekruse, M. (1994). Duty-to-warn guidelines for mental health counselors. *Journal of Counseling and Development, 72*(4), 346–350.

Crespi, T. D., Fischetti, B. A., & Butler, S. K. (2001, January). Clinical supervision in the schools. *Counseling Today,* pp. 7, 28, & 34.

D'Andrea, M., Daniels, J., & Heck, R. (1991). Evaluating the impact of multicultural counseling training. *Journal of Counseling and Development, 70,* 143–150.

Davenport, D. S. (1992, June). Ethical and legal problems with client-centered supervision. *Counselor Education and Supervision, 31,* 227–231.

Davis, S. R., & Meier, S. T. (2001). *The elements of managed care: A guide for helping professionals.* Pacific Grove, CA: Brooks/Cole.

DeAngelis, T. (2001). Surviving a patient's suicide. *Monitor on Psychology, 33*(10), 70–73.

DeLucia-Waack, J. L. (Ed.). (1996). *Multicultural counseling competencies: Implications for training and practice.* Alexandria, VA: Association for Counselor Education and Supervision.

DeShazer, S. (1991). *Putting difference to work.* New York: Norton.

Disney, M. J., & Stephens, A. J. (1994). Legal issues in clinical supervision. In T. P. Remley Jr. (Ed.), *The ACA legal series: Vol. 10.* Alexandria, VA: American Counseling Association.

Dougherty, A. M. (2000). *Psychological consultation and collaboration in school and community settings* (3rd ed.). Pacific Grove, CA: Brooks/Cole.

Ekstein, R. (1964). Supervision of psychotherapy: Is it teaching? Is it administration? Or is it therapy? *Psychotherapy, Research, and Practice, I*, 137–138.

Ekstein, R., & Wallerstein, R. S. (1972). *The teaching and learning of psychotherapy* (2nd ed.). New York: International University Press.

Faiver, C., Eisengart, S., & Colonna, R. (2000). *The counselor intern's handbook* (2nd ed.). Pacific Grove, CA: Brooks/Cole.

Falvey, J. E. (2002). *Managing clinical supervision: Ethical practice and legal risk management*. Pacific Grove, CA: Brooks/Cole.

Falvey, J. E., Caldwell, C. F., & Cohen, C. R. (2002). *Documentation in supervision: The focused risk management system (FoRMSS)*. Pacific Grove, CA: Brooks/Cole.

Feist, S. C. (1999). Practice and theory of professional supervision for mental health counselors. *Directions in Mental Health Counseling, 9*(9), 105–120.

Forrest, L., Elman, N., Gizara, S., & Vacha-Haase, T. (1999). Trainee impairment: A review of identification, remediation, dismissal, and legal issues. *The Counseling Psychologist, 27*(5), 627–686.

Foster, V. A., & McAdams, C. R. (1999, September). The impact of client suicide in counselor training: Implications for counselor education and supervision. *Counselor Education and Supervision, 39*(1), 22–33.

Frame, M. W., & Stevens-Smith, P. (1995) Out of harm's way: Enhancing monitoring and dismissal processes in counselor education programs. *Counselor Education and Supervision, 35*, 118–129.

Frawley-O'Dea, M. G., & Sarnat, J. E. (2001). *The supervisory relationship: A contemporary psychodynamic approach*. New York: Guilford Press.

Fukuyama, M. A. (1994). Critical incidents in multicultural counseling: A phenomenological approach to supervision research. *Counselor Education and Supervision, 34*(2), 142.

Gardner, G. T., Bobele, M., & Biever, J. L. (1997). Postmodern models of family therapy supervision. In T. C. Todd & C. L. Storm (Eds.), *The complete systemic supervisor: Context, philosophy and pragmatics* (pp. 217–228). Needham Heights, MA: Allyn & Bacon.

Garner, B. A. (Eds.). (1999). *Black's law dictionary* (7th ed.). Eagan, MN: The West Group.

Getz, H. G. (1999, Fall). Assessment of clinical supervisor competencies. *Journal of Counseling & Development, 77*(4), 491–497.

Getz, J. G., & Protinsky, H. O. (1994). Training marriage and family counselors: A family-of-origin approach. *Counselor Education and Supervision, 33*(3), 183–200.

Giordano, M. A., Altekruse, M. K., & Kern, C. W. (2000). *Supervisee's Bill of Rights*. Unpublished manuscript.

Goodyear, R. K., & Nelson, M. L. (1997). The major formats of psychotherapy supervision. In C. E. Watkins Jr. (Ed.), *Handbook of psychotherapy supervision* (pp. 328–344). New York: John Wiley & Sons.

Gould, L. J., Bradley, L. J. (2001). Evaluation in supervision. In L. J. Bradley & N. Ladany (Eds.), *Counselor supervision: Principles, process and practice* (3rd ed., pp. 271–303). Philadelphia: Brunner-Routledge.

Granello, D. H., Beamish, P. M., & Davis, T. E. (1997, June). Supervisee empowerment: Does gender make a difference? *Counselor Education and Supervision, 36*(4), 305–317.

Greenwald, M., & Young, J. (1998). Schema-focused therapy: An integrative approach to psychotherapy supervision. *Journal of Cognitive Psychotherapy: An International Quarterly, 12*(2), 109–126.

Grieco, E. M., & Cassidy, R. C. (2001). *Overview of race and Hispanic origin: Census 2000 brief* (Publication No. C2KBR/01-1). Washington, DC: U.S. Government Printing Office.

Grote, C. L., Robiner, W. R., & Haut, A. (2001). Disclosure of negative information in letters of recommendation: Writers' intentions and readers' experiences. *Professional Psychology: Research and Practice, 32*(6), 655–661.

Guest, C. L. Jr., & Dooley, K. (1999, June). Supervisor malpractice: Liability to the supervisee in clinical supervision. *Counselor Education and Supervision, 38*(4), 269–279.

Guy, J. D. (2000). Holding the holding environment together: Self-psychology and psychotherapist care. *Professional Psychology: Research and Practice, 31*(3), 351–352.

Hamilton, J. C., & Spruill, J. (1999). Identifying and reducing risk factors related to trainee-client sexual misconduct. *Professional Psychology: Research and Practice, 30*(3), 318–327.

Henderson, C. E., Cawyer, C. S., & Watkins, C. E. Jr. (1999). A comparison of student and supervisor perceptions of effective practicum supervision. *Clinical Supervisor, 18*(1), 47–74.

Herlihy, B., & Corey, J. (1997). *Boundary issues in counseling: Multiple roles and responsibilities.* Alexandria, VA: American Counseling Association.

Hermann, M. A., & Remley, T. P. (2000). Guns, violence, and schools: The results of school violence—litigation against educators and students shedding more constitutional rights at the schoolhouse gate. *Loyola Law Review, 46*(2), 389–439.

Hess, A. K. (1980). Training models and the nature of psychotherapy supervision. In A. K. Hess (Ed.). *Psychotherapy supervision: Theory, research, and practice* (pp. 15–28). New York: John Wiley & Sons.

Hollander, P. (1996, Winter). Legal issues relevant to due process at APPIC internships. *The Association of Psychology Postdoctoral Internship Centers (APPIC) Newsletter,* pp. 1, 34–36.

Holloway, E. L. (1992). Supervision: A way of teaching and learning. In S. D. Brown & R. W. Lent (Eds.), *Handbook of Counseling Psychology* (pp. 177–214). New York: John Wiley & Sons.

Holloway, E. L. (1995). *Clinical supervision: A systems approach.* Thousand Oaks, CA: Sage.

Holloway, E. L. (1997). Structures for the analysis and teaching of supervision. In C. E. Watkins Jr. (Ed.), *Handbook of psychotherapy supervision* (pp. 249–276). New York: John Wiley & Sons.

Holloway, E. L. (1999). A framework for supervision training. In E. Holloway & M. Carroll (Eds.), *Training counseling supervisors* (pp. 8–43). London: Sage.

Holloway, E., & Carroll, M. (Eds.). (1999). *Training counseling supervisors*. London: Sage.

Housman, L. M., & Stake, J. E. (1999). The current state of sexual ethics training in clinical psychology: Issues of quantity, quality, and effectiveness. *Professional Psychology: Research and Practice, 30*(3), 302–311.

Janoff, D., & Schoenholtz-Read, J. (1999, April). Group supervision meets technology: A model for computer-assisted group training at a distance. *International Journal of Group Psychotherapy, 49*(2), 255–272.

Kadushin, A. (1992). *Supervision in social work* (3rd ed.). New York: Columbia University Press.

Kagan, N., Krathwohl, D. R., & Miller, R. (1963). Stimulated recall in therapy using videotape—a case study. *Journal of Counseling Psychology, 10*, 237–243.

Kaiser, T. L. (1997). *Supervisory relationships: Exploring the human element*. Pacific Grove, CA: Brooks/Cole

Kanz, J. E. (2001). Clinical-supervision.com: Issues in provision of online supervision. *Professional Psychology: Research and Practice, 32*(4), 415–420.

Kiser, P. M. (2000). *Getting the most from your human service internship: Learning from experience*. Pacific Grove, CA: Brooks/Cole.

Kitchener, K. S. (1984). Intuition, critical evaluation and ethical principles: The foundation for ethical decisions in counseling psychology. *The Counseling Psychologist, 12*(3), 43–55.

Kleespies, P. M., Smith, M. R., & Becker, B. R. (1990). Psychology interns as patient suicide survivors: Incidence, impact, and recovery. *Professional Psychology: Research and Practice, 21*(4), 257–263.

Kurpius, D. J., & Morran, D. K. (1988). Cognitive-behavioral techniques and interventions for application in counselor supervision. *Counselor Education and Supervision, 27*, 368–376.

Ladany, N., Lehrman-Waterman, D., Molinaro, M., & Wolgast, B. (1999). Psychotherapy supervisor ethical practices: Adherence to guidelines, the supervisory working alliance, and supervisee satisfaction. *The Counseling Psychologist, 27*(3), 443–475.

Ladany, N., & Melincoff, D. S. (1999, March). The nature of counselor supervisor nondisclosure. *Counselor Education and Supervision, 38*(3), 191–204.

Ladany, N., Walker, J. A., & Melincoff, D. S. (2001). Supervisory style: Its relation to the supervisory working alliance and supervisor self-disclosure. *Counselor Education and Supervision, 40*(4), 263–275.

LaFromboise, T. D., Coleman, H. L. K., & Hernandez, A. (1991). Development and factor structure of the Cross-Cultural Counseling Inventory–Revised. *Professional Psychology: Research and Practice, 22*, 380–388.

Lambers, E. (2000). Supervision in person-centered therapy: Facilitating congruence. In E. Mearns & B. Thorne (Eds.), *Person-centered therapy today: New frontiers in theory and practice* (pp. 196–211). London: Sage.

Larson, L. M., Clark, M. P., Wesley, L. H., Koraleski, S. F., Daniels, J. A., & Smith, P. L. (1999, June). Videos versus role plays to increase counseling self-efficacy in prepractica trainees. *Counselor Education and Supervision, 38*(4), 237–248.

Laske, O. E. (1999, Summer). An integrated model of developmental coaching. *Counseling Psychology Journal: Practice and Research, 51*(3), 139–159.

Lee, R. E. (1999). Getting started. In R. E. Lee & S. Emerson (Eds.), *The eclectic trainer* (pp. 33–44). Galena, IL: Geist & Russell.

Liddle, H. A., Becker, D., & Diamond, G. M. (1997). Family therapy supervision. In C. E. Watkins Jr. (Ed.), *Handbook of psychotherapy supervision* (pp. 400–418). New York: John Wiley & Sons.

Liese, B. S., & Beck, J. S. (1997). Cognitive therapy supervision. In C. E. Watkins Jr. (Ed.), *Handbook of psychotherapy supervision* (pp. 114–133). New York: John Wiley & Sons.

Locke, D. C. (1998). *Increasing multicultural understanding: A comprehensive model,* (2nd ed.). Thousand Oaks, CA: Sage.

Loganbill, C., Hardy, E., & Delworth, U. (1982). Supervision: A conceptual model. *Counseling Psychologist, 10,* 3–42.

Lopez, S. R. (1997). Cultural competence in psychotherapy: A guide for clinicians and their supervisors. In C. E. Watkins Jr. (Ed.), *Handbook of psychotherapy supervision* (pp. 570–588). New York: John Wiley & Sons.

Lower, R. B. (1972). Countertransference resistances in the supervisory relationship. *American Journal of Psychiatry, 129,* 156–160.

Lowry, J. L. (2001, August). Successful supervision: Supervisor and supervisee characteristics. In J. Barnett (Chair), *The Secrets of Successful Supervision.* Symposium conducted at the meeting of the American Psychological Association, San Francisco, CA.

Lumadue, C. A., & Duffey, T. H. (1999). The role of graduate programs as gatekeepers: A model for evaluating student counselor competence. *Counselor Education and Supervision, 39*(2), 101–109.

Madanes, C. (1984). *Behind the one-way mirror.* San Francisco: Jossey-Bass.

Magnuson, S., Norem, K., & Wilcoxon, S. A. (2000). Clinical supervision of pre-licensed counselors: Recommendations for consideration and practice. *Journal of Mental Health Counseling, 22*(2), 126–186.

Magnuson, S., Wilcoxon, S. A., & Norem, K. (1999, March). A profile of lousy supervision: Experienced counselors' perspectives. *Counselor Education and Supervision, 39*(3), 189–202.

Martinez, L. J., Davis, K. C., & Dahl, B. (1999). Feminist ethical challenges in supervision: A trainee perspective. *Women and Therapy, 22*(4), 35–54.

Martino, C. (2001). *Secrets of successful supervision: Graduate student's preferences and experiences with effective and ineffective supervision.* Symposium conducted at the meeting of the American Psychological Association, San Francisco, CA.

McCarthy, P., Sugden, S., Koker, M., Lamendola, F., Maurer, S., & Renninger, S. (1995). A practical guide to informed consent in clinical supervision. *Counselor Education and Supervision, 35*(2), 130–138.

McGoldrick, M., & Giordano, J. (1996). Overview: Ethnicity and family therapy. In M. McGoldrick, J. Giordano, & J. K. Pearce (Eds.), *Ethnicity and family therapy* (pp. 1–27). New York: Guilford Press.

McNeil, B. W., & Worthen, V. (1989). The parallel process in psychotherapy supervision. *Professional Psychology: Research and Practice, 20,* 320–333.

Miars, R. (2000). *The evolution of ethical responsibility and legal liability in clinical instruction and supervision.* Paper presented at the Western Association for Counselor Education and Supervision meeting, Los Gatos, California, November 10, 2000.

Microsoft Encarta College Dictionary. (2001). New York: St. Martin's Press.

Miller, G. M., & Larrabee, M. J. (1995). Sexual intimacy in counselor education and supervision: A national survey. *Counselor Education and Supervision, 34*(4), 332–343.

Miller, R. K., & Van Rybroek, G. J. (1988, February). Internship letters of recommendation: Where are the other 90%? *Professional Psychology: Research & Practice 19*(1), 115–117.

Mitchell, J. T., & Everly, G. S. Jr. (1993). *Critical incident stress debriefing (CISD): An operations manual for the prevention of traumatic stress among emergency services and disaster workers.* Ellicott City, MD: Chevron Publishing Corporation.

Mitchell, J. T., & Everly, G. S. Jr. (1994). *Human elements training for emergency services, public safety and disaster personnel: An instructional guide to teaching debriefing, crisis intervention and stress management programs.* Ellicott City, MD: Chevron Publishing Corporation.

Moline, M. E., Williams, G., & Austin, K. M. (1998). *Documenting psychotherapy: Essentials for mental health practitioners.* Thousand Oaks, CA: Sage.

Monahan, J., & Steadman, H. (Eds.). (1994). *Violence and mental disorder: Developments in risk assessment.* Chicago: University of Chicago Press.

Montalvo, B. (1973). Aspects of live supervision. *Family Process, 12,* 343–359.

Morey, R., Burton, D., & Roske, A. (1998). *Clinical supervision in a forensic setting.* Unpublished manuscript.

Mothersole, G. (1999). Parallel process: A review. *Clinical Supervisor, 18*(2), 107–121.

Mulvey, E. P., & Cauffman, E. (2001, October). The inherent limits of predicting school violence. *American Psychologist, 56*(10), 797–802.

Munson, C. E. (1993). *Clinical social work supervision* (2nd ed.). New York: Haworth Press.

Muratori, M. C. (2001, September). Examining supervisor impairment from the counselor trainee's perspective. *Counselor Education and Supervision, 41*(1), 41–56.

National Association of Social Workers. (1994). *Guidelines for clinical social work supervision.* Washington, DC: Author.

National Association of Social Workers. (1999). *Code of ethics.* Washington, DC: Author.

National Board for Certified Counselors. (1999a). *Code of ethics.* Greensboro, NC: Author.

National Board for Certified Counselors. (1999b). *Standards for the ethical practice of clinical supervision.* Washington, DC: Author.

Nelson, M. D., & Johnson, P. (1999, December). School counselors as supervisors: An integrated approach for supervising school counseling interns. *Counselor Education and Supervision, 39*(2), 89–100.

Neufeldt, S. A. (1999). *Supervision strategies for the first practicum* (2nd ed.). Alexandria, VA: American Counseling Association.

Norcross, J. C., & Halgin, R. P. (1997). Integrative approaches to psychotherapy supervision. In C. E. Watkins Jr. (Ed.), *Handbook of psychotherapy supervision* (pp. 203–222). New York: John Wiley & Sons.

Norcross, J. C., & Newman, C. F. (1992). Psychotherapy integration: Setting the context. In J. C. Norcross & M. R. Goldfried (Eds.), *Handbook of psychotherapy integration* (pp. 3–45). New York: Basic Books.

O'Hanlon, B. (1999). *Do one thing different.* New York: Harper Collins (Quill).

O'Hanlon, B., & Beadle, S. (1999). *Guide to possibility land: Fifty-one methods for doing brief, respectful therapy.* New York: Norton.

O'Hanlon, B., & Weiner-Davis, M. (1989). *In search of solutions: A new direction in psychotherapy.* New York: Norton.

Patterson, C. H. (1997). Client-centered supervision. In C. E. Watkins Jr. (Ed.), *Handbook of psychotherapy supervision* (pp. 134–146). New York: John Wiley & Sons.

Pedersen, P. (1991). Multiculturalism as a generic approach to counseling. *Journal of Counseling and Development, 70*(1), 6–12.

Pedersen, P. B. (2000) *A handbook for developing multicultural awareness* (3rd ed.). Alexandria, VA: American Counseling Association.

Pedersen, P. B., Draguns, J. G., Lonner, W. J., & Trimble, J. E. (Eds.). (2001). *Counseling across cultures* (5th ed.). Thousand Oaks, CA: Sage.

Peruzzi, N., & Bongar, B. (1999). Assessing risk for completed suicide in patients with major depression: Psychologists' views of critical factors. *Professional Psychology: Research and Practice, 30*(6), 576–580.

Polanski, P. (2000). Training supervisors at the masters level: Developmental consideration. *ACES Spectrum Newsletter, 61*(2), 3–5.

Ponterotto, J. G., & Casas, M. (1991). *Handbook of racial/ethnic minority counseling research.* Springfield, IL: Charles C Thomas.

Ponterotto, J. G., Casas, J. M., Suzuki, L. A., & Alexander, C. M. (Eds.). (2001). *Handbook of multicultural counseling* (2nd ed.). Thousand Oaks, CA: Sage.

Ponterotto, J. G., Potere, J. C., & Johansen, A. (2002). The Quick Discrimination Index (QDI): Normative data and user guidelines for counseling researchers. *Journal of Multicultural Counseling and Development, 30*(3).

Ponterotto, J. G., Rieger, B. P., Barrett, A., Sparks, R., Sanchez, C. M., & Magids, D. (1996). Development and initial validation of the Multicultural Counseling Awareness Scale. In G. R. Sodowsky & J. C. Impara (Eds.), *Multicultural assessment in counseling and clinical psychology* (pp. 247–282). Lincoln, NE: Buros Institute of Mental Measurements.

Ponterotto, J. G., Rieger, B. P., Gretchen, D., Utsey, S. O., & Austin, R. (1999). *A construct validity study of the Multicultural Counseling Awareness Scale (MCAS) with suggested revisions.* Unpublished manuscript.

Pope, K. S., Sonne, J. L., & Holroyd, J. (1993). *Sexual feelings in psychotherapy: Explorations for therapists and therapists-in-training.* Washington, DC: American Psychological Association.

Pope, K. S., & Vasquez, M. J. T. (1998). *Ethics in psychotherapy and counseling: A practical guide for psychologists* (2nd ed.). San Francisco: Jossey-Bass.

Porter, N., & Vasquez, M. (1997). Covision: Feminist supervision, process, and collaboration. In J. Worell & N. G. Johnson (Eds.), *Shaping the future of feminist psychology: Education, research, and practice* (pp. 155–171). Washington, DC: American Psychological Association.

Priest, R. (1994). Minority supervisor and majority supervisee: Another perspective of clinical reality. *Counselor Education and Supervision, 34*(2), 152–158.

Protinsky, H. (1997). Dismounting the tiger: Using tape in supervision. In C. L. Storm & T. C. Todd (Eds.), *The reasonably complete systemic supervisor resource guide* (pp. 298–308). Needham Heights, MA: Allyn & Bacon.

Prouty, A. M., Thomas, V., Johnson, S., & Long, J. K. (2001). Methods of feminist family therapy supervision. *Journal of Marriage and Family Therapy, 27*(1), 85–97.

Ramos-Sánchez, L., Esnil, G., Goodwin, A., Riggs, S., Touster, L. O., Wright, L. K., Ratanasiripong, P., & Rodolfa, E. (2002). Negative supervisory events: Effects on supervision satisfaction and supervisory alliance. *Professional Psychology: Research and Practice, 33*(2), 197–202.

Ray, D., & Altekruse, M. (2000). Effectiveness of group supervision versus combined group and individual supervision. *Counselor Education and Supervision, 40*(1), 19–30.

Remley, T. P., & Herlihy, B. (2001). *Ethical, legal and professional issues in counseling.* Upper Saddle River, NJ: Prentice-Hall.

Richards, P. S., & Bergin, A. E. (1997). *A spiritual strategy for counseling and psychotherapy.* Washington, DC: American Psychological Association.

Riemersma, M. (2001, September/October). Myths and realities of supervision. *The California Therapist,* 14–23.

Robiner, W. N. (1998a, July). The development of quality assessment systems in psychology internship training. *The Association of Psychology Postdoctoral Internship Centers (APPIC) Newsletter* (pp. 10, 22).

Robiner, W. N. (1998b). *Quality assessment and improvement systems*™. Minneapolis, MN: University of Minnesota.

Robiner, W. N., Fuhrman, M. J., & Ristvedt, S. (1993). Evaluation difficulties in supervising psychology interns. *Clinical Psychologist, 46,* 3–13.

Robiner, W. N., Fuhrman, M., Ristvedt, S., Bobbitt, B., & Schirvar, J. (1994, Winter). The Minnesota Supervisory Inventory (MSI): Development, psychometric characteristics, and supervisory evaluation issues. *The Clinical Psychologist, 47*(4), 4–17.

Robiner, W. N., Saltzman, S. R., Hoberman, H. M., Semrud-Clikeman, M., & Schirvar, J. A. (1997). Psychology supervisors' bias in evaluations and letters of recommendation. *The Clinical Supervisor, 16*(2), 49–72.

Saccuzzo, D. (1997). Law and psychology. *California Law Review, 34*(115), 1–37.

Sánchez, H. G. (2001). Risk factor model for suicide assessment and intervention. *Professional Psychology: Research and Practice, 32*(4), 351–358.

Sandhu, D. S., & Aspy, C. B. (Eds.). (2000). *Violence in American schools: A practical guide for counselors.* Alexandria, VA: American Counseling Association.

Scherl, C. R., & Haley, J. (2000, July-September). Computer monitor supervision: A clinical note. *American Journal of Family Therapy, 28*(3), 275–282.

Skovholt, T. M., & Ronnestad, M. H. (1992). *The evolving professional self: Stages and themes in therapist and counselor development.* Chichester, England: Wiley.

Smith, R., Mead, D., & Kinsella, J. (1998). Direct supervision: Adding computer-assisted feedback and data capture to live supervision. *Journal of Marital and Family Therapy, 24*(1), 113–125.

Sodowsky, G. R., Taffe, R. C., Gutkin, T. B., & Wise, S. L. (1994). Development of the Multicultural Counseling Inventory: A self-report measure of multicultural competencies. *Journal of Counseling Psychology, 41,* 137–148.

Starling, P. V., & Baker, S. B. (2000, March). Structured group practicum supervision: Supervisees' perceptions of supervision theory. *Counselor Education and Supervision, 39*(3), 162–176.

Stoltenberg, C. D., & Delworth, U. (1987). *Supervising counselors and therapists: A developmental approach.* San Francisco: Jossey-Bass.

Stoltenberg, C. D., & McNeill, B. W. (1997). Clinical supervision from a developmental perspective: Research and practice. In C. E. Watkins, Jr. (Ed.), *Handbook of psychotherapy supervision* (pp. 184–202). New York: John Wiley & Sons.

Stoltenberg, C. D., McNeill, B., & Delworth, U. (1998). *IDM supervision, An integrated developmental model for supervising counselors and therapists.* San Francisco: Jossey-Bass.

Storm, C. L., & Todd, T. C. (1997). *The reasonably complete systemic supervisor resource guide.* Needham Heights, MA: Allyn & Bacon.

Sue, D. W., Arredondo, P., & McDavis, R. J. (1992). Multicultural counseling competencies and standards: A call to the profession. *Journal of Counseling and Development, 70,* 477–486.

Sue, D. W., Bernier, J. E., Durran, A., Feinberg, L., Pedersen, P., Smith, E. J., & Nuttall, E. V. (1982). Position paper: Cross-cultural counseling competencies. *The Counseling Psychologist, 10*(2), 45–52.

Sue, D. W., Carter, R. T., and colleagues. (1998). *Multicultural counseling competencies: Individual and organizational development.* Thousand Oaks, CA: Sage.

Sue, D. W., & Sue, S. (2003). *Counseling the culturally diverse: Theory and practice* (4th ed.). New York: John Wiley & Sons.

Sumerel, M. B., & Borders, L. D. (1996). Addressing personal issues in supervision: Impact on counselors' experience level on various aspects of the supervisory relationship. *Counselor Education and Supervision, 35*(4), 268–286.

Sweitzer, H. F., & King, M. A. (1999). *The successful internship: Transformation and empowerment.* Pacific Grove, CA: Brooks/Cole.

Thomas, F. N. (1994). Solution-oriented supervision: The coaxing of expertise. *The Family Journal: Counseling and Therapy for Couples and Families, 2*(1), 11–18.

Todd, T. C. (1997). Self supervision as a universal supervisory goal. In T. C. Todd & C. L. Storm (Eds.), *The complete systemic supervisor: Context, philosophy and pragmatics* (pp. 17–26). Needham Heights, MA: Allyn & Bacon.

Todd, T. C., & Storm, C. L. (Eds.). (1997). *The complete systemic supervisor: Context, philosophy and pragmatics*. Needham Heights, MA: Allyn & Bacon.

Vontress, C. E. (1979). Cross-cultural counseling: An existential approach. *Personnel and Guidance Journal, 58*, 117–121.

Vontress, C. E., Johnson, J. A., & Epp, L. R. (1999). *Cross-cultural counseling: A casebook*. Alexandria, VA: American Counseling Association.

Ward, C. C., & House, R. M. (1998). Counseling supervision: A reflective model. *Counselor Education and Supervision, 38*(1), 23–33.

Watkins, C. E. Jr. (Ed.). (1997). *Handbook of psychotherapy supervision*. New York: John Wiley & Sons.

Weaver, J. D. (1995). Disasters: Mental health interventions. In F. M. Dattilio, & A. Freeman (Eds.), *Crisis management series*. Sarasota, FL: Professional Resources Press.

Welfel, E. R. (2002). *Ethics in counseling and psychotherapy: Standards, research, and emerging issues* (2nd ed.). Pacific Grove, CA: Brooks/Cole.

Wetchler, J. L., Piercy, F. P., & Sprenkle, D. H. (1989). Supervisors' and supervisees' perceptions of the effectiveness of family therapy supervisory techniques. *American Journal of Family Therapy, 17*(1), 35–47.

Wiederman, M. W., & Sansone, R. A. (1999). Sexuality training for professional psychologists: A national survey of training directors of doctoral programs and predoctoral internships. *Professional Psychology: Research and Practice, 30*(3), 312–317.

Williams, A. (1995). *Visual and active supervision: Roles, focus, technique*. New York: W. W. Norton.

Witherspoon, R., & White, R. P. (1996, Spring). Executive coaching: A continuum of roles. *Consulting Psychology Journal: Practice and Research, 48*(2), 124–133.

Woods, P. J., & Ellis, A. (1997). Supervision in rational emotive behavior therapy. In C. E. Watkins Jr. (Ed.), *Handbook of psychotherapy supervision* (pp. 101–113). New York: John Wiley & Sons.

Yarhouse, M. A., & VanOrman, B. T. (1999). When psychologists work with religious clients: Applications of the general principles of ethical conduct. *Professional Psychology: Research and Practice, 30*(6), 557–562.

Yontef, G. (1997). Supervision from a Gestalt perspective. In E. Watkins, (Ed.), *Handbook of psychotherapy supervision* (pp. 147–163). New York: John Wiley & Sons.

York, C. D. (1997). Selecting and constructing supervision structures: Individuals, dyads, co-therapists, groups, and teams. In T. C. Todd & C. L. Storm (Eds.), *The complete systemic supervisor: Context, philosophy and pragmatics* (pp. 320–333). Needham Heights, MA: Allyn & Bacon.

Zinnbauer, B. J., & Pargament, K. I. (2000). Working with the sacred: Four approaches to religious and spiritual issues in counseling. *Journal of Counseling and Development, 78*(2), 162–171.

NAME INDEX

Acuff, C., 38
Alexander, C. M., 146
Alle-Corliss, L., 30, 31
Alle-Corliss, R., 30, 31
Altekruse, M., 85, 87, 235
Altekruse, M. K., 36, 43
Anderson, L., 122, 123
Arredondo, P., 134, 135, 146
Aspy, C. B., 236
Austin, K. M., 202
Austin, R., 148

Baker, S. B., 86
Barrett, A., 146
Bearnish, P. M., 62
Beck, J. S., 120, 121
Becker, B. R., 228
Becker, D., 121, 122
Bemak, F., 73, 162
Bergin, A. E., 74

Bernard, J. M., 5, 7, 21, 22, 28, 32, 56, 96, 111, 112, 126, 155, 192
Bernier, J. E., 146
Biever, J. L., 122
Binder, J. L., 118
Bobbit, B., 245
Bobele, M., 122
Boes, S. R., 159, 205, 206
Bongar, B., 228, 230, 232
Borders, L. D, 106, 178
Bordin, E. S., 31
Bradley, L. J., 3, 5, 85, 111, 112, 117, 123, 183
Brown, M. T., 140
Brown, S., 146
Burian, B. K., 165
Butler, S. K., 88

Caldwell, C. F., 265
Calhoun, K. S., 87

309

SUBJECT INDEX

TO THE OWNER OF THIS BOOK:

We hope that you have found *Clinical Supervision in the Helping Professions* useful. So that this book can be improved in a future edition, would you take the time to complete this sheet and return it? Thank you.

School and address: _____

Department: _____

Instructor's name: _____

1. What I like most about this book is: _____

_____

_____

2. What I like least about this book is: _____

_____

_____

3. My general reaction to this book is: _____

_____

4. The name of the course in which I used this book is: _____

_____

5. Were all of the chapters of the book assigned for you to read? _____

   If not, which ones weren't? _____

6. In the space below, or on a separate sheet of paper, please write specific suggestions for improving this book and anything else you'd care to share about your experience in using the book.

_____

_____

_____

_____

_____

Optional:

Your name: _____ Date: _____

May Brooks/Cole quote you, either in promotion for *Clinical Supervision in the Helping Professions* or in future publishing ventures?

Yes: _____ No: _____

Sincerely,

Robert Haynes
Gerald Corey
Patrice Moulton

- -

FOLD HERE

FOLD HERE

Attention Professors:

Brooks/Cole is dedicated to publishing quality publications for education in the social work, counseling, and human services fields. If you are interested in learning more about our publications, please fill in your name and address and request our latest catalogue, using this prepaid mailer. Please choose one of the following:

☐ social work   ☐ counseling   ☐ human services

Name: _____

Street Address: _____

City, State, and Zip: _____

FOLD HERE

NO POSTAGE
NECESSARY
IF MAILED
IN THE
UNITED STATES

BUSINESS REPLY MAIL

FIRST CLASS   PERMIT NO. 358   PACIFIC GROVE, CA

POSTAGE WILL BE PAID BY ADDRESSEE

ATT: *Marketing* _____

The Wadsworth Group
10 Davis Drive
Belmont, CA 94002

FOLD HERE

IN-BOOK SURVEY

At Brooks/Cole, we are excited about creating new types of learning materials that are interactive, three-dimensional, and fun to use. To guide us in our publishing/development process, we hope that you ll take just a few moments to fill out the survey below. Your answers can help us make decisions that will allow us to produce a wide variety of videos, CD-ROMs, and Internet-based learning systems to complement standard textbooks. If you're interested in working with us as a student Beta-tester, be sure to fill in your name, telephone number, and address. We look forward to hearing from you!

In addition to books, which of the following learning tools do you currently use in your counseling/human services/social work courses?

_____ **Video** _____ in class _____ school library _____ own VCR

_____ **CD-ROM** _____ in class _____ in lab _____ own computer

_____ **Macintosh disks** _____ in class _____ in lab _____ own computer

_____ **Windows disks** _____ in class _____ in lab _____ own computer

_____ **Internet** _____ in class _____ in lab _____ own computer

How often do you access the Internet? _____

My own home computer is a:

_____

The computer I use in class for counseling/human services/social work courses is a:

_____

If you are NOT currently using multimedia materials in your counseling/human services/social work courses, but can see ways that video, CD-ROM, Internet, or other technologies could enhance your learning, please comment below:

_____

_____

_____

Other comments (optional): _____

_____

Name _____Telephone _____

Address _____

School _____

Professor/Course_____

You can fax this form to us at (650) 592-9081 or detach, fold, secure, and mail.

NO POSTAGE
NECESSARY
IF MAILED
IN THE
UNITED STATES

BUSINESS REPLY MAIL

FIRST CLASS   PERMIT NO. 358   PACIFIC GROVE, CA

POSTAGE WILL BE PAID BY ADDRESSEE

ATT: *Marketing*

The Wadsworth Group
10 Davis Drive
Belmont, CA 94002